WESTERN
KENTUCKY
UNIVERSITY

WESTERN
KENTUCKY
UNIVERSITY

LOWELL H. HARRISON

THE UNIVERSITY PRESS OF KENTUCKY

Copyright © 1987 by The University Press of Kentucky
Scholarly publisher for the Commonwealth,
serving Bellarmine College, Berea College, Centre
College of Kentucky, Eastern Kentucky University,
The Filson Club, Georgetown College, Kentucky
Historical Society, Kentucky State University,
Morehead State University, Murray State University,
Northern Kentucky University, Transylvania University,
University of Kentucky, University of Louisville,
and Western Kentucky University.

Editorial and Sales Offices: Lexington, Kentucky 40506-0024

Library of Congress Cataloging-in-Publication Data

Harrison, Lowell Hayes, 1922-
  Western Kentucky University.

  Bibliography: p.
  Includes index.
  1. Western Kentucky University—History. I. Title.
LD5941.W5H37 1987   378.769'74   86-32456
ISBN 0-8131-1620-1

Contents

Illustrations follow pages
62, 126, and 222

Tables

Chart

MOST individuals and most institutions believe they are unique in some way, and Western Kentucky University is no different. Western takes pride in a lovely campus, the friendly spirit that pervades it, and the fierce loyalty of its alumni. Its history is an almost perfect case study of how scores, perhaps hundreds, of American schools have developed: private school, state normal school, normal school and teachers college, teachers college, general college, university.

In 1938 Dr. James P. Cornette of the Department of English published a carefully researched and amply documented history of the college to the close of President Henry Hardin Cherry's administration in 1937. Cornette's account is particularly valuable because he knew many of the early faculty members and students. At the sacrifice of considerable statistical data, I have tried to present a general picture of the institution that is both as comprehensive as space will allow and as readable as I can make it. Because of the wealth of available material, I have had to be highly selective in deciding what to include. Space did not allow the inclusion of histories of departments and other administrative units, and many of the faculty, staff, and students who contributed to the development of the institution have not been named. Western probably has as many able, interesting, and eccentric personalities now as it ever did, but they are obscured by the size of the university. Gone are the days when one faculty member could teach a sizable portion of the student body and when the daily chapels brought together practically the entire population of the Hill. No adequate substitute has been found for the chapel periods in which Henry Hardin Cherry inspired countless students and faculty.

Despite the belief of some of my colleagues, I did not greet President Cherry when he led the students and faculty up College Street to the Hill in 1911. My campus stay, however, did extend from kindergarten in the Training School through a bachelor's degree, and after an absence of over twenty years I joined the faculty in 1967. While I have a strong affection for the school, the Western of today is a much changed institution from the one I knew as an undergraduate, and I believe I have retained some degree of objectivity in my study of it. Because I have confined the story to verifiable data, readers may note the omission of some traditional gossip, legends, and myths. Interpretation of data varies with the interpreter, and the same information may produce varied results when studied from different perspectives.

There is no completely satisfactory way to write institutional history. My study is centered around presidential administrations because Western's governance during most of its history came largely from strong, paternalistic presidents. The chapter divisions are designed to allow quick access to topical themes. My intent was to close the account with the status of Western in the summer of 1985, but the resignation of President Donald Zacharias and the search for his successor made necessary an extension of time through February 1986.

So many people have aided me in this study that it is impossible to list their names here. Many of them have been cited in footnotes; all of them have my sincere thanks. I am especially grateful to the many Westerners who donated materials and recollections for my use. The Board of Regents appointed me University Historian in 1979, and the Faculty Research Fund has provided welcome assistance. Load reductions have helped with what at times seemed an endless task. Mrs. Helen Knight and Mrs. Ann Williams have been indefatigable in locating materials in the University Archives, and Dr. James D. Bennett's collection of interviews in the Department of History's Oral History Project has been invaluable. Graduate assistants Mary Jude Hagan, Virginia Davis, and Mary Jane Lowe assisted on locating and checking data. Marsha Bailey and Kim Cash have borne the major burden of typing from my script.

Drs. John D. Minton and Paul B. Cook have read the manuscript and have given me the benefit of their unique knowledge of Western, based upon long tenures as historians and administrators. My wife, Penny Harrison, an archivist-historian, also gave a careful reading to the manuscript. I must make the usual disclaimer that any remaining errors are my own, but I will try to find someone to blame for them.

1906-22	Western Kentucky State Normal School
1922-30	Western Kentucky State Normal School and Teachers College
1930-48	Western Kentucky State Teachers College
1948-66	Western Kentucky State College
1966-	Western Kentucky University

Presidents

1906-37	Henry Hardin Cherry
1937-55	Paul L. Garrett
1955-69	Kelly Thompson
1969-79	Dero G. Downing
1979	John D. Minton
1979-85	Donald W. Zacharias
1985-86	Paul B. Cook (interim)
1986-	Kern Alexander

One

In the Beginning
(to 1906)

THE ORIGINS of Western Kentucky University include the development of normal schools for the training of teachers, the deplorable state of public education in Kentucky, and the presence of an exceptional Kentuckian who devoted his life to the cause of education. These factors converged in southcentral Kentucky in the late nineteenth century.

The idea of special schools for training teachers did not originate with Horace Mann, but he did more than any other American to create normal schools. The 1838 act of the Massachusetts legislature that provided for the establishment of three such institutions was a true landmark in education, and some of Mann's principles helped shape teacher training in the United States well into the next century. He insisted that the normal schools should be separate institutions, not appendages of existing institutions that had other functions. A normal school should devote itself exclusively to the preparation of better teachers who had a comprehensive knowledge of the common school subjects and knew how to teach them. The teacher did not need a command of subject matter much in advance of the level at which he taught.[1]

The number of normal schools in the United States increased rapidly during the late nineteenth century, but little was done in Kentucky. A state-supported institution was authorized at Transylvania in 1856, but the legislature repealed the act two years later. In 1880 the General Assembly established a Normal School Department in the Lexington Agricultural and Mechanical College, but it received little support from the college. Six years later a "State Normal School for Colored Persons" was created; it was later located in Frankfort. In 1878 the State Superintendent of Public Instruction was given permission to conduct a ten-week normal school in each of the next two summers. But the General Assembly did not fund the program, and the permission was not extended in 1880. Starting in 1869 teachers' institutes attempted to provide some assistance to poorly qualified teachers, but few of them lasted longer than a week and they were inadequate.[2] Since the state did not provide the needed training, some private institutions tried to meet the need.

In 1874 a tall, energetic nineteen-year-old youth named A.W. Mell completed work at the National Normal University in Lebanon, Ohio, and accepted the principalship of the Urania Common School in Glasgow, Kentucky. When the term opened in late summer, he had a staff of two assistants; a third teacher was added during the term. Mell decided to open a private normal school to follow the short public term. He was well aware of the need for such institutions, and he was confident he could meet it. A longtime friend and colleague described him as "the most enthusiastic and optimistic man I ever knew. He believed in himself and in his mission and had the rare gift of inspiring faith and the spirit of optimism in his pupils."[3]

In 1876 Mell secured a state charter for the coeducational Glasgow Normal School.[4] A number of business courses were offered in addition to the "common school courses." The common school was a part of the Normal until 1881-82 when the latter's growth allowed Mell to drop the public school. The business department was growing so rapidly that in 1882 J. Tom Williams, an 1877 graduate of Glasgow Normal, became head of that division and a partner in the enterprise.[5] By the fall of 1883, over three hundred students were enrolled in the expanding institution.

But growth also brought problems, the most urgent being housing and feeding the students. When the Glasgow citizens failed to provide the needed support, Mell and Williams moved to Bowling Green. Although the Normal School had been started and operated as a private enterprise, concerned Glasgow citizens suddenly decided that the school remained fixed; the only change was that Professors Mell and Williams were leaving.[6] The ensuing controversy involved both towns and allowed newspaper editors to use their most scathing denunciations. Most of the students sided with their professors, and when the move to Bowling Green was made in the late summer, Glasgow was left with only some buildings and a charter. Several efforts were made to continue the school, but by the early 1890s it had died.

In order to secure the services of Mell and Williams, Bowling Green subscribers had paid three thousand dollars in cash for tuition vouchers that would be accepted at the new "Southern Normal School and Business College." Some benefactors gave the vouchers to students; others sold them, often at a discount. The proprietors purchased for twelve thousand dollars a large building located on College Street between Eleventh and Twelfth streets that had housed the defunct Bowling Green Female College. The facilities were not entirely adequate, and each morning Professor Mell led the students and faculty to the Opera House on the town square for chapel exercises. Some of the business classes were apparently held in Getty's Hall on the north side of the square. As soon as possible,

Mell and Williams built eating and housing accommodations for the students. Bowling Green sophisticates often called the mess hall "the soup-house," a term resented by many of the students. When a charter was granted by the General Assembly in 1886, the school's name was shortened to "Southern Normal School."[7]

Many students attended for only part of the year, so that out of the nearly seven hundred listed in the 1884-85 school year, perhaps no more than four hundred were enrolled at any time. This number meant that Mell and Williams had to employ ten teachers in addition to the four who taught in the adjunct department of music. The school's catalog showed eight departments, but that was done largely for publicity purposes. A more realistic division would have been the normal school, the literary department, and the commercial department. Nearly two-thirds of the students in 1884-85 were enrolled in the commercial department headed by J. Tom Williams, who also served as business manager. Mell supervised the remainder of the work and was listed on the faculty of seven of the eight departments, music being the only area he avoided.

Only two of the courses of study, the scientific and the classic, led to the granting of bachelor's degrees. The degree requirements tell a great deal about the Southern Normal's level of work.

That candidates be past sixteen years of age; that they shall have studied here or elsewhere, all the subjects embraced in the respective courses; that they faithfully attend upon the proper classes with us for at least six consecutive months; that they attend upon the training classes here for at least one term; that they attend upon all examinations and carefully submit the answers in writing; that they prepare a thesis upon a subject assigned by the Faculty, and deliver the same before an invited audience; that they pay all dues at least thirty days before Commencement.[8]

As weak as these requirements were (the "thesis" was the equivalent of a short term paper), they represented a definite effort to upgrade the qualifications for teachers.

Mell and Williams attempted to attract students with low costs. In 1884-85 the total expenses for forty weeks in the Normal School were listed at only $110.50. In order to reduce costs, textbooks could be rented at 15 percent of the purchase price.[9] Tennessean Cordell Hull, a future Secretary of State, and his brother enrolled in 1886 because they had heard that the school was both good and cheap. By doing housekeeping they held their total costs for ten months to $175—and that included everything, even the tickets for the first train Cordell had ever seen.[10] Enrollment doubled over what it had been in Glasgow, and in a burst of enthusiasm the National School of Telegraphy, Civil Service, Railroading, and Express was added in 1888. Then the Columbian School of Oratory and Elocution enhanced the imposing title.[11]

But within a few years, enrollment began to decrease and income fell. When Professor Mell married in the late 1880s, he discovered that two could not live as cheaply as one, and Professor Williams lost interest in the floundering institution after marrying a wealthy woman whose capital allowed him to think in terms of more profitable investments. In the summer of 1890, both men quit the school and turned control over to H.A. Evans and W.J. Davis, two recent graduates. They lasted only until the end of the fall term when J.R. Alexander and H. McD. Fletcher assumed control. Alexander, an 1885 graduate of the Southern Normal, had taught there until 1888 when he accepted a teaching position in Texas where he became acquainted with Fletcher, a scholarly Ulster Irishman. They came to Kentucky in 1890, conducted the Glasgow Normal for one term, then moved to the Southern Normal in Bowling Green. But the ship was sinking, and Fletcher departed in 1891. Alexander remained another year, then accepted the principalship of Calhoun Institute in Mississippi.[12] Little was left of the institution, and it seemed destined to join scores of dead schools that littered Kentucky's academic landscape.

As the nineteenth century gave way to the twentieth, Kentucky's public school system was in deplorable condition. The 1838 General Assembly had made a legislative start, and measurable progress occurred between 1847 and 1853 under the direction of a stern divine, the Reverend Robert Jefferson Breckinridge, the best superintendent of public instruction in the prewar era. But the ravages of the Civil War eroded much of the modest beginnings, and the freeing of the slaves added another dimension to the postwar problems. Governors frequently advocated educational reforms, but parsimonious legislators were hesitant in providing adequate funds, and most of the control of the educational system rested with local school boards whose members were usually reluctant to seek more support from their constituents.[13]

Superintendent H.V. McChesney reported some improvements in 1900-1901, but most of his statistics were encouraging only when measured against the even more dismal past. Louisville had four high schools, but many of the cities and most of the counties had none. Lexington offered two years of high school work, but Bowling Green's public schools stopped at the eighth grade. Bowling Green had "three institutions for higher education," Superintendent Edward Taylor explained, and they "meet the demand for a high school to some degree." Few of the common schools went beyond a five-month term, and many of them lacked such essentials as books and classroom supplies. The typical school building was the one- or two-room "little white schoolhouse." In 1900-1901 there were 6,752 frame structures, but log buildings outnumbered brick ones by 1,238 to 150. According to census figures, only 46 percent of white children attended school; the "colored" figure was even lower, 41 percent. The total annual cost of teaching each child was $6.49

for whites, $7.44 for blacks. The state treasury contributed only $1,483,240.70 toward the 1900-1901 educational expenditures. School district libraries did little to supplement the inadequate school holdings, for the 593 district libraries had an average holding of just 43 volumes.[14] It was not surprising that in 1900 16.5 percent of all Kentuckians over ten years of age admitted illiteracy. Had tests been required, the number would have been higher.[15]

Exceptional teachers and receptive students did exist, and when they met the results often exceeded all reasonable expectations. But many concerned critics saw inadequately trained teachers as the major barrier to substantial improvements in public education. In 1900 certified teachers numbered 11,010, although only 9,057 were teaching in the common schools. First Class Certificate holders numbered 6,346; Second Class, 3,622; and Third Class, 1,041, but the qualifications were so low that the state superintendent urged the legislature to abolish the lowest rank. The average common school teacher had approximately a seventh-grade education. In 1900-1901 only 416 white and 83 black teachers had graduated from a normal training school. A major cause for such poor preparation was the low salaries. Most school districts were more concerned with cheap instruction than with its quality, and in too many instances the trustees got what they paid for. "A No. 1 teacher can not afford to teach in our common schools for any great while," wrote Warren County Superintendent T.T. Gardner, "the remuneration is too small." The average monthly wage for white teachers in 1900-1901 was $34.10; for black teachers it was $29.95.[16] And most of the teachers taught only five months a year.

A few years later, State Superintendent James H. Fuqua told the General Assembly, "The crying need of our rural schools is better teachers." Hundreds of schools were being conducted by unqualified persons who "are not teachers in any sense of the word, but only lesson hearers."[17] By any objective measurement and by any realistic subjective judgment, public education was one of Kentucky's most neglected undertakings and most shameful failures. But slowly a growing number of Kentuckians became convinced that something had to be done.

Obviously, not all that needed to be done could be accomplished at once; priorities had to be established. Among the reformers who stressed the need for better trained teachers was Henry Hardin Cherry, the head of the private Southern Normal School and Bowling Green Business College. The man, the school, and the effort to prepare better teachers were all essential ingredients in the establishment of the State Normal School that became Western Kentucky University.

George Washington Cherry and Frances Martha Stahl Cherry made a difficult living on a farm in the sandhills of Warren County, about ten miles west of Bowling Green. Life was hard and labor was exacting, and

G.W. Cherry considered his sons bound to work for him until they became twenty-one. His nine sons gave him a sizable work force. Because of the farm's constant demands, the boys received only limited schooling, when they could be spared from farm work; yet several of them developed a desire for more education and the determination to obtain it. Thomas Crittenden, born April 24, 1862, was the sixth of the boys. He entered Glasgow Normal in the fall of 1883 and, like so many teachers of that period, alternated between studying and teaching common schools. After graduating from the Southern Normal in 1889, T.C. went to Arcadia College in Louisiana as head of its commercial department. In January 1890 he became president, a position he held until 1892 when a younger brother enticed him into returning to Kentucky.[18]

Henry Hardin Cherry, born on November 16, 1864, was over two years younger than T.C. Perhaps influenced by his brother, Henry also decided to get an education. G.W. allowed his sons to retain what money they could earn during the last six months before they reached their majority; and in 1885 Henry Hardin cut hickory trees for axe handles and sold them in Bowling Green for $2.50 a load. After six months of intense effort, he had accumulated $72.00. Armed with it and a firm determination to secure an education, he left the farm to enter Southern Normal. Cherry liked to tell his story as an example of what could be done by anyone with ambition. "On the seventeenth day of January, 1886, when the snow was more than fourteen inches deep, I packed all of my earthly belongings into a twenty-five cent pasteboard valise and walked to Bowling Green to enter school. I rented a room at fifty cents per week and did self-boarding, which cost me on an average of $4.72 per month."[19] His cooking consisted largely of rice; it was cheap and he could cook enough at one time to last a week. His diet was supplemented by supplies brought from the farm. The snow tended to grow deeper with the telling, despite T.C.'s declaration that there was no snow on the ground when Henry first made the trip.

Henry Hardin's scanty schooling left him with a great deal of catching up to do, and his money ran out long before his studies were completed. He had done well in penmanship—his signature became a work of art—and when he had to drop out of school he taught penmanship in Warren and nearby counties. The young teacher guaranteed satisfaction, but he warned that there would be "positively no spectators after the first lesson." Cherry's ability and determination impressed the owners of the Bowling Green school, and he was employed to teach penmanship there for room, board, and six dollars per month. Classes in shorthand and bookkeeping were soon added, and in 1891 President Alexander allowed Cherry to teach "Civics," one of his favorite subjects. Records of the Southern Normal were later destroyed by fire, but it is doubtful that Henry Hardin Cherry ever did enough academic work to graduate from the school.[20]

When President Alexander fled southward in 1892, Henry Hardin was one of the few people who saw any hope of keeping the institution alive. Its prestige had declined sharply with decreased enrollment and growing debts, and local support had almost vanished. But Henry Hardin saw possibilities in the situation, and he persuaded his brother T.C. to return to Kentucky and invest his abilities and savings of sixteen hundred dollars in the enterprise. In the fall of 1892, they opened the "Bowling Green Business College and Literary Institute," but they always thought of it as the direct successor of the Mell and Williams school.

By then enrollment had declined to only twenty-eight students, and only four rooms were in use. Equipment was scarce and in poor condition, liabilities were heavy, morale and prestige low. The situation challenged Henry Hardin Cherry's abilities to the utmost as he plunged into the restoration of the school. A natural promoter, he concentrated upon that phase of the operation while T.C. supervised the academic program.

Henry Hardin was a great believer in advertising, and, as one of his successors wrote, "He covered the South with advertising 'like the dew.' " In future years the school drew heavily from Louisiana and other southern states. The *Southern Educator*, Cherry's major publication, was filled with photographs of crowded classes and exhortations to join the student body. By 1905 its circulation had reached forty thousand. Some of the publicity would not have stood close scrutiny. There were eight typewriters, recalled a student from that era. "Mr. Cherry assembled his eight machines in one corner of a room with eight typists at work, and then shifted the machines with another eight operators to the opposite corner and put under the picture, 'The Typewriting Department in the Northeast Corner' and 'The Typewriting Department in the Northwest Corner.' " Both Cherry brothers worked diligently in the field to recruit students, and their buggies went into most communities in southcentral Kentucky. In every possible way, they built up an extensive mailing list. Henry Hardin also made use of another technique. He would send an advertisement to a newspaper but enclose a check for only a portion of the customary amount; if you can't print it for this, please return the check. Few checks were returned to him.[21]

Such promotional techniques could and did have an effect on enrollment, but they did not alone explain the phenomenal growth of the next few years. During the 1897-98 school year, 683 students were enrolled, and the number continued to increase. Much of the credit belonged to Henry Hardin Cherry and the spirit of pride and fierce loyalty that he inspired in the student body. Throughout his career Cherry was an academic preacher, and chapel was his favorite pulpit. Chapel "was a builder of both morals and morale," recalled a student of the 1890s. "So fresh and vigorous were the programs that the students seldom absented themselves from them."[22] Cherry brought in outstanding speakers and programs to lift the intellectual horizons of his largely provincial student body, but it was he who formulated the principles and preached the homilies that influenced students for nearly half a century. When the school opened in 1892, he published a *Declaration of Principles and Policies* that expressed his educational philosophy and goals.

To be a live school and to impart to its students a burning zeal to do and be something.
To be progressive, to use modern methods and equipment, but reject all worthless educational fads.
To let the reputation of the school be sustained by real merit.
To seek recognition of the public to the extent the school deserves it.
To fight against ignorance, and for higher education and the liberation of the human soul.
To cooperate with all educational institutions that do honest work and to bid them Godspeed in their efforts.
To teach that self-control is an imperative duty and the first great obligation that every person must fulfill, if he would succeed.
To instill in the minds of the students the great truth that every person is created to do something, to be a producer.
To teach students the power of earnestness and to warn them against all show and pretense.
To make the school self-governing and to create a high moral sentiment among the pupils.
To refuse to organize or permit the organization of any club or society that would foster caste and destroy cooperation, but rather to teach that the good of one is the good of all.
To recognize no aristocracy except that of work and character.
To lead the student to understand that a broad and liberal education is essential to the highest degree of success in any endeavor of life and that unless he has a purpose in life and is willing to pursue it closely and courageously, he will fail.
To lead the student to see that success depends mainly upon his own efforts, and that he must discover the man in himself before he can become a being of power and influence.[23]

Changes were made occasionally, but this statement stood as the creed of the school long after Cherry's death. As he exhorted the students in his chapel addresses, Cherry developed a store of favorite stories that he used time and again to drive home the points he wanted to make. Long after most of their detailed knowledge had been lost, countless students could recall the morals taught by "Paint your fenceposts red," "It's what's above the rim that counts," "Life, more life," and "The spirit makes the master."[24]

Both Henry Hardin and T.C. were concerned about the poor preparation of teachers, and in 1894 they added a Southern Normal School that they soon described as "The Leading Normal School in the South (Established 1875)." Enrollment increased in the Southern Normal School and Bowling Green Business College, but the Normal School drained profits from the commercial branch. Tuition for the normal students was usually one dollar per week, with discounts for stays beyond ten weeks. This did not meet expenses, but many of the teachers who enrolled were not able to pay more. As the major administrator, Henry Hardin must have sometimes considered dropping the normal school; T.C. seems to have been instrumental in keeping it alive.[25]

The Cherry brothers had to put most of their income back into the enterprise, so there was little left for their salaries. The financial pinch worsened after Henry Hardin married Bessie Fayne of Crab Orchard on April 3, 1896, and T.C. married Bessie M. Swartz on June 21, 1898. Miss Fayne had enrolled as a student in 1895; Miss Swartz, a graduate of the noted Boston School of Oratory, had joined the faculty in 1896. Mrs. Henry Hardin Cherry soon joined the staff on a part-time basis as "Director of Social Features of the Institution." Dissatisfied with his own education, T.C. sold his interest in the school to Henry Hardin in 1899 for $1,250, which he used to study at the State Normal School at Westchester, Pennsylvania, and at Harvard University. He returned to Bowling Green in 1902 and taught in the Southern Normal until 1905 when he became superintendent of the city's public schools. He retired from that position in 1937, the year of Henry Hardin's death.[26]

The growth of the school forced expansion in several directions. By 1898 the faculty that had numbered four in 1892 had increased to eighteen, including the Cherry brothers and Mrs. H.H. Cherry. Two young men who taught commercial subjects, W.S. Ashby and J. Lewie Harman, were in the trio that purchased the Bowling Green Business University in 1906 after the state normal school was created. The third member was J.S. Dickey, an 1881 graduate of Glasgow Normal, who replaced T.C. Cherry in 1899. J.R. Alexander had returned from Mississippi in 1894 to rejoin the faculty. A beloved mathematics teacher, he remained with H.H. Cherry until his retirement in 1930. Salaries were low and loads were heavy, and there was considerable faculty turnover, but several of the faculty members stayed to become the nucleus of the state normal school's faculty in 1907. They included Miss Mattye Reid in English, R.P. Green in geography, Colonel John M. Guilliams in English, and Frederick W. Roman in history. Another notable late addition to the staff was Miss Mattie McLean, who became H.H. Cherry's secretary in 1903, a position she held until his death. Faculty members might be assigned to a particular subject, but they were expected to be versatile and to teach wherever the demand was greatest.[27]

Increased enrollment also necessitated physical expansion. In January 1898 the Cherry brothers rented the top floor of the Neale Building on the Bowling Green square and moved the Business College classes to that location. But facilities were still inadequate, and during the summer Henry Hardin Cherry worked to enlist local assistance. On July 14, 1899, the Southern Educational Building Company was incorporated with forty thousand dollars in capital stock and a debt limitation of five thousand dollars. J. Whit Potter, Alex Duvall, L. Greer, Max B. Nahm, E.G. McCormack, L.R. Porter, A.H. Taylor, D.M. Lawson, and C.U. McElroy were the original members; T.J. Smith and H.H. Cherry were later added. Their purpose was to "promote and advance" education by providing essential buildings, including dormitories. It was understood that Cherry would continue to manage the school.

The public was slow to subscribe, but on November 1, 1899, the company purchased from J. Tom Williams the 256 foot lot, running through from College Street to Center Street, on which the normal school building stood. Even before that date Cherry showed a picture of a new building in the *Southern Educator* and announced that it would be occupied by January 1900.

Then on the night of November 16—Henry Hardin's birthday—a fire consumed most of the main structure and its contents. Practically all of the school records were lost, most of the equipment was ruined, and the interior of the building was gutted. Cherry escaped with little more than his nightshirt. It was one of the most discouraging moments in his life, but resiliency was one of his great attributes, and by morning he faced the future with revived confidence. "Between the hours of three and six in the morning a decision was made to continue the institution," Cherry said. "I have often wondered since that time if I were not insane when the decision was made." Classes opened on time in hastily rented rooms in the business district, and Cherry boasted that only two students left school because of the disaster.

The insurance had lapsed, and, as Cherry later admitted, both he and the school were bankrupt. A western railroad made him a substantial offer to manage its advertising office, and several Kentucky towns indicated an interest in obtaining the school if it moved. That danger and the obvious needs of the normal school generated community support. The debt limit for the Southern Educational Building Company was increased to ten thousand dollars, and with the support of the local newspapers additional subscriptions began to come in. Work on the new building, which included the standing walls of the burned structure, was completed in 1901. The castle-like structure that became a Bowling Green landmark was named Van Meter Hall in honor of Captain C.J. Vanmeter, one of the most liberal contributors towards its construction. Enrollments continued to grow, with the annual total after 1901 usually in excess of one thousand.

Henry Hardin Cherry made a substantial financial contribution to the new facility in addition to his energy and vision. Although he could ill afford it, he took $1,250 of stock and then paid $2,250 in final bills when the company's funds were exhausted. However, he and his family did occupy "handsome rooms on the first floor of the new building."[28]

As the enrollment increased, the boarding houses within walking distance of the school became inadequate for housing and feeding the students, and the school had to step into the breach. A large frame building on the Center Street side of the lot was converted into a dormitory known as "Bailey Hall" after its managers, Dr. and Mrs. W.M. Bailey. Another building on Center and Twelfth streets, used as a dormitory by Mell and Williams, was also renovated. Then in 1903 H.H. Cherry, Max B. Nahm, J.E. Potter, W.S. Ashby, C.J. Vanmeter, and J.S. Jenkins incorporated the "Students' Home Company" to erect buildings that would furnish "nice, inexpensive, comfortable rooms" and board with preference given to the Southern Normal School and Bowling Green Business College students. A three-story brick building with such welcome conveniences as indoor plumbing was built on the Center Street side of the property for forty thousand dollars. Named Frisbie Hall for Cherry's three-year-old daughter, Josephine Frisbie, it opened in the spring of 1904. Used by young women, Frisbie Hall had "hot and cold baths, steam heat, electric lights, elegant parlors, cultured and refined atmosphere and home-like environments." Rooms rented for $3.00 to $4.50 per month, well below the price charged by private families. In 1908, after the state school was created, a small Science Building was also erected on the crowded lot.[29]

One other organizational change occurred before the state normal school was created in 1906. In 1904 C.J. Vanmeter, M.O. Hughes, J.E. Potter, H.H. Cherry, J. Whit Potter, Max B. Nahm, and J.S. Dickey formed a corporation called the Southern Normal School and Bowling Green Business University. The organization had no capital stock, and "no private pecuniary profit is to be derived." The corporation did not actually operate the school, and when the Business University was sold Cherry did so as if it were his private property. Although the new title did not indicate it, a law school had been added in 1899 with several local attorneys teaching classes. The legal course could be completed in just under a year for forty dollars in tuition. A School of Telegraphy was advertised, but its enrollment was apparently very small.[30]

By the early 1900s, Henry Hardin Cherry had overcome many obstacles and had built one of the largest private normal schools in the nation. Despite his lack of formal education, his relentless determination, his ceaseless energy, and his optimistic vision had made him one of Kentucky's best known educators. A major key to his success was his uncanny ability to inspire those associated with him, to impart to them some of his zeal and enthusiasm and vision of the future. Without his charismatic leadership, many faculty members would have fled the low salaries and intolerable loads that he gave them. Countless students since the 1890s have testified to the effect that Cherry had on them and their lives.

The students enrolled in the Southern Normal School had a degree of unity that later vanished. All of them were preparing to teach, and most of them would teach the first six or eight grades in a one-teacher school. Indeed, most of them were already teachers when they enrolled in the Southern Normal, although many of them had not completed the equivalent of an eighth grade education. The normal school afforded many students their first opportunity to do high school level work; few of them in the early years were ready to take even junior college courses. On the whole, they were older than the typical college freshman of a later generation. They were, of course, much older than the junior high and high school students of later years. The median age in one class of over 100 students around 1904 was twenty-three years.[31]

Most of the students came from the predominantly rural area of western and southcentral Kentucky, but Cherry's persistent advertising attracted a surprising number of out-of-state students, especially from Louisiana where T.C. Cherry had taught. The out-of-staters, however, were more likely to take business courses than the normal school work. Since the public school terms were very irregular, students appeared almost anytime. The Southern Normal calendar was divided into four terms of ten weeks each, plus a summer term of eight weeks. But a notice that classes would be organized on January 17, 1899, carried a reassurance for any late comers: "However a student can enter at any time and get perfect classification."[32] Departures were as erratic as arrivals, and the registrar worked with fractional course credits for many students. There was no governmental aid, and when money ran out, students left school to earn more.

Most of the students came from relatively poor families, and, since many of them were teachers, their financial resources were limited. Cherry kept tuition low, in part by drawing money away from the Business University to make up deficits in the Southern Normal's operation. During most of the Normal's history, the basic tuition charge was $1.00 per week with discounts for paying in advance or for registering for more than one term. Thus forty weeks' tuition could be discharged with $35.00 instead of $40.00, and special courses such as music, art, and elocution could be taken for half-price. In theory, tuition had to be paid at the start of a term; in practice, many paid small sums as they could, others promised to pay later, and some discharged their obligations by working for the school. It is doubtful if Cherry ever refused admittance to a student solely on the basis of lack of money.[33] Of course, such irregularities helped explain the low faculty salaries and the uncertainty of their payments. The salaries of 1904-5 ranged from $3,500 for President Cherry to $650 for the lowest paid full-time faculty members. Incomplete records indicate that promised salaries were ultimately paid, but during some periods of fiscal exigency faculty members drew upon the school's reserves only for essential household needs.[34]

All schools with which Henry Hardin Cherry was associated were coeducational, but, as would have been expected for that era, blacks were excluded. After the passage of the Day Law in 1904, integration was illegal in Kentucky until mid-century.

Since most of the Southern Normal students were seriously interested in making as much educational progress as possible during their limited stays at the school, and since many of them lived on very restricted budgets, few participated in the more expensive entertainments available in the city. Walking was a popular pastime, and many romances progressed through strolls to such favorite spots as Vinegar Hill and the Covington Woods or, for the more athletically inclined, Lost River Cave. Sometime around the turn of the century a steamboat trip became an annual spring event. On a May day in 1901, students and faculty boarded the streetcars in the downtown area and rode for half-fare to the boat landing. Then with "Banners Flying and Cheers Ringing," some five hundred enjoyed the boat trip to Woodbury where they went ashore for a picnic lunch. A social convention declared that in a dating couple, the man bought the tickets and the woman supplied the lunch. In some years when the crowd was especially large, two steamboats had to be chartered. One would make a short trip for those who had to return early; the other would venture onto Green River before finally unloading its tired but happy passengers at Bowling Green around nine or ten o'clock in the evening.[35] The Mammoth Cave excursion also became a spring feature, but it was usually confined to those students who were taking geography. It was a field trip lasting several days rather than a picnic ramble. Some energetic young men walked the entire distance, but for the less hardy, transportation was available.

Noticeably missing from the student activities were intercollegiate athletics. Henry Hardin Cherry saw little inherent value in them, and they would require expensive equipment and trips. Football had no place in a college, he told a commencement audience in 1900. The school "has and it will continue to advise against the organization of football teams and recommends instead frequent nature excursions into the hills, woods, and on the rivers, that the soul may commune with God through nature." But Cherry was competitive, and around 1905 he became concerned that some rival institutions with teams might outdistance the Southern Normal. So he hired Dan McGugin, the famed Vanderbilt coach, to build a team. McGugin caught an early morning train to Bowling Green two or three times a week, worked with the squad, then caught the noon train back to Nashville. Six games were reported played that year, but then the experiment was discontinued. In addition to costs, players entered and left school at such irregular intervals that developing team play was almost impossible. For years to come, athletics would be intramural with intense rivalries sometimes developing among the classes and literary societies.[36]

Cherry was even more adamantly opposed to "any club, sect or party that would divide the students into separate grades of society." He was convinced that any Greek letter society was both undemocratic and un-Christian and therefore unsuitable for his school. This ban extended even to honor societies, and for many years after Cherry's death this heritage lingered on. Instead of honor groups, the school had departmental clubs, usually named after one of the early department heads. In 1931 Cherry wrote in response to an inquiry about establishing a chapter of Phi Sigma Phi: "We have never had a fraternity of any type in our institution. We are really hoping to escape having one in the future."[37]

Realizing that most of his students had had limited cultural experiences, Cherry brought outstanding programs to the school, where they were often the featured chapel program. He did not make chapel compulsory but most of the students found the programs so interesting and inspirational that they seldom missed the daily session. Some of the programs were also attractive to the community, and occasionally a charge was made for ones with particular appeal. Confederate General John B. Gordon, for example, spoke on the evening of June 6, 1901, and "for two hours he held the vast audience in the most riveted attention" as he described "The Last Days of the Confederacy." The admission charge was fifty cents.[38] Among other noted speakers were William Jennings Bryan, Henry Watterson, Russell H. Conwell, and any number of ex-governors of Kentucky and other states.

Debates and oratorical contests were also an important part of the entertainment fare, as well as being an educational feature that Cherry encouraged. Banners were made, organized cheering encouraged the participants, emotions sometimes led to confrontations as partisans urged on their champions. A highlight of the year was the annual session of a mock House of Representatives, presided over by Cherry himself. Such experience may have been of considerable value to him in future years when he lobbied in Frankfort for funding for the State Normal School. Cherry's interest in government and his conviction that it should be taught in the public schools led to the publication of his 341-page textbook *Our Civic Image and Our Governments*, published in 1904.[39]

Most of the students attended local churches, and their social functions increased the recreational opportunities open to the students. These contacts perhaps decreased the possibilities for town-and-gown conflicts. During much of the history of the Southern Normal, Bowling Green boasted of two other colleges, Ogden College for men and Potter College for Young Ladies, and many local citizens believed that the Normal School and Business College lacked the prestige and sophistication of the other two. Detractors took the nickname of "Soup" that the Normalites applied to themselves and made it into a jeering, derogatory epithet that led to angry clashes. According to a Bowling Green youth, Mr. Cherry filed charges against one offender after a city ordinance was passed making it illegal to use the term. A small fine was assessed, and, the informant added, "Thereafter, although we made fun of the student body privately by the old name, we did not affront them publicly." Indeed, he concluded later, "we but deepened the enthusiasm and loyalty of its personnel."[40]

The Southern Normal did have an unusual degree of unity. A student who first enrolled in 1893 recalled that the school "reached its highest marks in creating inspiration. The loyalty of the teachers and the students never ran low. They thought of the institution as their own. It was their first love. They gloried in its growth." Many students underwent drastic changes in "character and custom," but the changes were made "by suggestion and not by edict." It was a democracy, this alumnus said, where "the will of the many was the rule of the school." Another alumnus put it simply: "We may have been underpriviledged in those days but fortunately we never realized it."[41]

Even as the Southern Normal School increased its enrollment, it neared the end as a private institution. Cherry had constant financial problems, and despite its growth the Normal had not reached enough teachers to bring about substantial improvement in the qualifications of the state's public school teachers. The Kentucky Educational Association (KEA), founded in 1857, and associated local and regional groups helped educate the public to the need for state-supported teacher training institutions. Support also came from various Superintendents of Public Instruction who recommended state support. Cherry was a strong backer of that approach, although its implementation could well have destructive effects upon his school. In June 1904 when the KEA met in Maysville, a committee of three was appointed to formulate plans for a federation of teachers and to report to the KEA at its Mammoth Cave meeting in June 1905. The growing demand for change led to a well-attended April 1905 conference in Frankfort that met at the invitation of State Superintendent James H. Fuqua. A six-man committee was selected to meet with the KEA's three-man group in June. Among the six members of the committee were Superintendent Fuqua, President James K. Patterson of the Kentucky State College, and H.H. Cherry.

The Mammoth Cave meeting resulted in the formation of the Kentucky Educational Improvement Commission. Three of its thirty-three members came from each of the eleven Congressional districts. The KEA elected an Executive Committee of five for three-year terms, as well as a president, secretary, and treasurer of the commission. The commission's major purpose was to arouse public sentiment in support of education. The Executive Committee was authorized to spend available funds for such promotion and to represent the cause of education to the General

Assembly. Fuqua; the superintendents of schools at Louisville, Frankfort, and Richmond; and H.H. Cherry formed the Executive Committee. They decided to focus on the establishment of state schools for training teachers as their first priority. During the next few months, voluntary collections at the short-term institutes raised nearly fifteen hundred dollars to further the crusade.[42] They were aided by the interest of Governor J.C.W. Beckham, who as lieutenant governor had succeeded William Goebel upon the latter's assassination in early 1900. Victor in a special election held in November 1900, Beckham won a full term in 1903. Although he could not be called a reformer, Beckham did support educational reforms.[43]

The Executive Committee directed a massive educational campaign designed to bring pressure upon the General Assembly that would convene in January 1906. Weekly articles went out to the newspapers, pamphlets and brochures explained the state's needs, dozens of speakers carried the appeal to every part of the state. The campaign was successful, and by January legislators were disposed to heed the clamor for reform. The Executive Committee avoided the shotgun approach of requesting everything and placed its major emphasis on the creation of a state normal school. Such a bill was introduced in the House on January 9, 1906.[44]

H.H. Cherry played a prominent part in the crusade. By his own account, he spent seventy-one days in Frankfort in 1906 lobbying for the normal school measure at his own expense. (Years later Cherry continued to believe that the citizens of Bowling Green should have shared the one thousand dollar cost of his efforts.) The first bill called for three state normal schools, but when objections were raised as to cost, the number was reduced to one. Of course, Cherry saw Bowling Green as the desirable site. He was dismayed when Richmond put in a vigorous claim for the new school, but a conference between the rival delegations resulted in an agreement upon two schools, one in Richmond, the other in Bowling Green. Beckham warned that specifying the two towns might create opposition elsewhere, so the bill finally called for one school in the eastern district and one in the western with a site selection committee to be appointed by the governor. This bill passed the House on March 2 and the Senate on March 8. Because of an emergency clause, it became law on March 21 when the governor signed it.[45]

The governor then appointed a seven-member Locating Commission to select the sites for the two schools. Although other cities indicated some interest, the two most determined bidders were Richmond and Bowling Green. Bowling Green offered the established Southern Normal School, including the buildings with all debts paid, the good will of the school, and a student body of several hundred students. The property was valued at upwards of $100,000, and the students had been enthusiastic in their support of the change. Meeting in Louisville on May 7, the commissioners selected Bowling Green and Richmond as the locations. The act provided for a line to be drawn that would divide the state into two districts containing equal populations; each school was restricted to activities in its assigned area.[46]

Two days after the sites were selected, Governor Beckham appointed the regents for the two schools. State Superintendent Fuqua was *ex officio* chairman of both boards. H.K. Cole, E.H. Mark, H.C. Miller, and J.W. Potter were the first members of the Western Board of Regents. They met in Fuqua's office on June 2, 1906, and elected Henry Hardin Cherry president of the Bowling Green school at a salary of three thousand dollars. Cherry always insisted that he had never applied for the position, but the assumption that he would be the state normal's president undoubtedly reconciled many people to the change. He had been generous in helping pay off the Southern Normal debts before its transfer to the state, and with the transfer he surrendered his equity in the school. He was directed to select faculty, subject to the Board's approval, and to make other preparations necessary to open the state normal school in September.[47]

This time schedule could not be met, in large part because of a challenge to the constitutionality of the act that created the normal schools. It had appropriated $5,000 to each school for equipping its buildings and improving its grounds, in addition to an annual $20,000 appropriation for current expenses. But when Fuqua applied for the $5,000 that had been authorized, a small property holder in Bell County filed for an injunction to block the transfer. R.A. Marsee contended that the act violated Section 184 of the state constitution which said in part, "No sum shall be raised or collected for education other than in common schools until the question of taxation is submitted to the legal voters, and the majority of votes cast at said election shall be in favor of said taxation…." The injunction request was denied in the Franklin Circuit Court on July 30, 1906, and on September 27 the court rendered a decision in favor of the state. On December 18, 1906, that decision was appealed to the Court of Appeals which upheld the ruling on April 24, 1907. The delay prevented a fall opening, and another joint meeting of the regents on July 25 decided to open the normal schools "sometime during the month of January, 1907." Model schools could begin sooner if arrangements could be completed.[48]

The hundreds of students enrolled in the Southern Normal in the fall of 1906 continued work as usual while President Cherry prepared for the January opening. It was assumed that most of the faculty would continue teaching in the state school, but Cherry added a dean who was invaluable in directing the school's academic programs, an area in which Cherry himself had little background. Dr. A.J. Kinnaman resigned as president of Central Normal in Indiana to accept Cherry's offer. A graduate of Indiana

University, he received a doctorate in psychology from Clark University in 1902. Pale, bespectacled, with stooped shoulders, he was almost a caricature of a college professor. Cheerful and good humored, he bore a heavy burden during the school's transitional period. Kinnaman, a masterful teacher who stimulated his students, more than any other person gave the school academic credibility during its early days.[49]

To provide a model school for the training of teachers, Cherry and the Regents arranged with the Bowling Green City Schools to transfer some students and teachers to rooms in the Southern Normal building. The costs were shared, an arrangement that was used until 1920 when Western established its own training school. New forms were designed and printed, minor repairs put the buildings in good condition, and Cherry used his own funds to let prospective students in the western half of the state know about the impending change.[50]

The opening of the state normal school necessitated a separation of the main components of the Southern Normal School and Bowling Green Business University. J.S. Dickey, W.S. Ashby, and J. Lewie Harman purchased the commercial portion of the institution for $15,000, a sum, Cherry complained, that represented only a third of its true value. Since all of the buildings belonging to the Cherry school had been donated to the state, the Business University moved to the McCormack Building at State and Tenth streets.[51] No students were lost by either school as a result of this amiable educational divorce.

Adjustments were made, difficulties were overcome or ignored, and on January 17, 1907, the Western Kentucky State Normal School opened for classes.

Two

The Normal Years
1906-1922

HERMAN LEE DONOVAN of Maysville was the first student enrolled in the State Normal School. A nineteen-year-old youth who had already taught several schools, he had saved enough money by 1906 to continue his education. Without even writing for information, he arrived at the Bowling Green railroad station at 4:30 A.M. on a September morning in 1906. When Donovan entered the Southern Normal building a few hours later, "Mr. Cherry greeted me cordially and made me feel at home." Professor Frederick W. Roman enrolled him, and by that afternoon Donovan was in class. His classmates "were ambitious to succeed and most of them had a clear idea of their objective," and the young man was stimulated and challenged by their example. Donovan's future took him to several institutions of higher education, including the presidencies of Eastern Kentucky State Teachers College and the University of Kentucky, but, he testified from the vantage point of retirement, "I have never seen in any school such a passion for learning as I found on the campus of Western and teachers so anxious to serve students." President Cherry and "a faculty of devoted, consecrated teachers" called out the best in students.

On a January morning in 1907, Dean Kinnaman was experimenting with the new registration cards when he saw Donovan outside the door. He called Donovan in, registered him as a test case, then noted across the face of the card that H.L. Donovan was the first student enrolled in the Normal School.[1]

Donovan and over seven hundred other students who enrolled that spring were taught by a faculty of twelve members, headed by President Cherry. The others were: A.J. Kinnaman, Ph.D., dean; Fred Mutchler, Ph.D., science; Frederick W. Roman, A.M., history and literature; J.M. Guilliams, A.M., English and mathematics; J.R. Alexander, A.B., mathematics and physics; R.P. Green, A.B., geography and ancient classics; Sarah E. Scott, primary supervisor; W.L. Gebhart, public school music; C.W. Fulton, drawing and penmanship; Irene Russell, instrumental music; and Annie Marie Egenhoff, expression. Some of the faculty, including President Cherry, did not hold a bachelor's degree. The faculty also included the four public school teachers who taught in the Model School: Susan Irving, first grade; Anna Barkley, second grade; Jennie West, third grade; and Lydia Flenniken, fourth grade. Miss Mattie McLean was secretary, H.H. Eggner was registrar and bookkeeper, Josephine Fayne was hostess of the Students' Home, and Parathenia Weller had custody of the small library. Captain C.J. Vanmeter, an important benefactor of the school, was elected to the honorary post of chancellor.[2]

An interesting pattern developed with enrollment and the size of the faculty. Since many of the students taught in the public schools, the enrollment was smallest during the fall months. It increased after Christmas as the schools completed their terms. The Normal's enrollment was largest during the late spring and early summer; it began to decline in July and August as the common schools resumed sessions. A nucleus of full-time people taught throughout the year, but a bewildering number of others came and went. This flexibility allowed Cherry to hold down costs, and it also allowed him to win friends for the school. Many county superintendents were proud to be asked to teach during a summer session, even if the pay was poor, and many of them became devoted friends of Cherry and his school.

Several members of the original faculty left within the next few years. The resignation of Dr. Mutchler in 1913 was damaging for he had done much to improve instruction in both agriculture and biology, and the Normal could ill afford the loss of a doctorate. Roman left in 1908, earned a doctorate at the University of Berlin, and began a distinguished career in education and economics at Syracuse and New York universities. Nearly two-thirds of the original faculty was gone by the fall of 1909, and Guilliams resigned in 1911 to seek a better climate in Florida. His departure received mixed reviews. His gruff, brusque manner intimidated many people, but he quietly helped a number of needy students attend college. Guilliams was a martinet in class, and students learned "to memorize his pet definitions, to parrot off his exact phrases." But he insisted on clarity and exactness, and he loved grammar, which to him was "as exact a science as mathematics."[3]

Of the remaining members of the original faculty, Green taught until 1920, Alexander until 1930, and Kinnaman's health forced him to retire in 1926. These stalwarts who gave continuity to the faculty were joined by a number of other long-time members within the first few years of the State Normal. On a January day in 1908, two new faculty members got off the same train in Bowling Green and met for the first time. W.J. Craig, later known to generations of Westerners as "Uncle Billy," had been a farm boy in Daviess County. After teaching several years in the common schools in Kentucky and Colorado, he earned a B.S. degree in science. Dean Kinnaman returned from a school meeting and told Cherry that in a two-block walk with Craig, nineteen mothers had stopped Craig to talk about their children. Cherry immediately offered Craig a position at the Normal where he taught chemistry and physics for many years. In the 1920s he organized the Alumni Association and became its secretary, and then he became the head of the placement service. An avid hunter and basketball fan, Uncle Billy retired in 1953 after forty-five years of service.[4]

A.M. Stickles, who met W.J. Craig on the railroad platform, was born in a log cabin in Indiana. He had earned a master's degree from Indiana University and was teaching as a department head at Evansville high school when Dr. Mutchler recommended him to Cherry. Well-dressed, handsome, and one of the school's first published scholars, Stickles attracted attention wherever he went. One student recalled that when they staged a mock chapel, "We chose the handsomest student we could find to represent Mr. Stickles." His chapel talks on national and world affairs became a Western tradition. An inspiring teacher, when Stickles retired in 1954 he had been head of the history department for forty-six and one-half years.[5]

Four other longtime members joined the faculty in 1908. John H. Clagett was a gentle man, courteous, enthusiastic, inspiring. His loves included Dante, Milton, Shakespeare, nature, fishing, and hunting quail. His class in Shakespeare became one of the most famous courses on the campus, in part because as the years passed he became an easy grader, in part because many who enrolled for easy grades became infected by his love for what he taught. He taught himself Italian after he was sixty so he could read Dante in the original. Impatient of useless forms, he once returned to the dean an unfilled questionnaire for the U.S. Bureau of Education. "Most of it impresses me as platitudinous twaddle," he wrote. "Do you think the sun will fail to rise tomorrow if my name is left off that questionnaire?" Near the end of his life he remarked to a friend: "I have had a happy life, for no man ever loved poetry so much, and had so much opportunity to study it; no man ever loved teaching so much, and had such delightful pupils; and no man ever loved the out-of-doors and hunting and fishing so much, and had so much time to devote to it." He had taught several years in both Ogden and Potter colleges in Bowling Green, as well as in public schools, before joining the Normal faculty. Shortly before his death in March 1937 Clagett said to his wife, "When I am no longer able to teach on the Hill, then I no longer desire to live."[6] Such dedication helps explain why H.H. Cherry was able to keep a strong faculty.

A native of Arkansas, Macon Anderson Leiper was another 1908 recruit who lent strength to the school. He arrived with an M.A. from Columbia and a year of classical studies at Princeton. After Western became a four-year college in 1922, he went to George Peabody College for a doctorate. Leiper taught Latin for several years, then became head of the English department. A "tireless, prodigious worker," he was considered one of the most demanding and one of the best teachers on the faculty. He told students, "You may think what you please about me if you will only learn to think." One of his best students credited Leiper with introducing the bibliography to the campus; "Before that, scholarship stood upon the two legs of the teacher, and asked for no other props." Unlike Guilliams, Leiper detested memorized definitions, and he promoted and provoked class discussions. Neat, well-groomed, always perfectly organized, he was one of the early faculty supporters of organized athletics and the author of several texts on grammar. A student who had classes with him for ten consecutive terms wrote that "a scholar and a gentleman" fitted Leiper better than anyone he had ever known. Seldom well, Leiper was forced by illness into premature retirement in 1928.[7]

Miss Florence Ragland joined the faculty in 1908 as librarian. She and Clagett had conducted a private school in Bowling Green for several years. Although her library domain was small, she transmitted her love for books to many of the students. She wanted the books used, and, a student recalled, "It was our notion that Miss Ragland knew every book in the library, knew whether it was out and who had it, and when he was to bring it back. Furthermore, it was our reinforced notion that promptness in such matters was a great preserver of peace and amity." She knew the students so well that she recommended books to fit individual needs. When she left the library in 1923, Miss Ragland taught in the English department until 1930. Her hobby was gardening, and she was active even in retirement in beautifying the campus.[8]

Miss Mattye Reid was a 1901 graduate of the Southern Normal who then became a member of its faculty. She was not listed as being on the 1907 faculty of the new state school, but she began teaching English in 1908. Summers were spent doing additional work at the University of Chicago. Known as "a tireless worker and excellent teacher," she taught until 1918 when marriage ended her association with Western.[9]

This nucleus continued to grow during the years before World War I as a dozen other longtime members joined the faculty. Franz Strahm, born in Freiburg, Germany, was the nineteenth boy in a family of twenty-four children. A student of music from childhood, his teachers included Franz Liszt. He answered an advertisement and journeyed to Nashville in 1891 to join a theater orchestra. He taught at the Nashville Conservatory of Music, then went to Bowling Green in 1910, an exotic on the Normal scene. He loved food, beer, cigars, dancing, and classical music, and his fractured English broke up classes as he tried to call the roll or explain what he wanted done. At an operetta rehearsal he exploded: "You Altos, Vy don't you zing? Open your mouths and throw yourselves in!" Practice resumed five minutes later. He became famous for his stories, in most of which he deprecated himself. Strahm brought good music to the school, and soon he inaugurated a series of special programs and events that attracted widespread attention. Despite his considerable girth he loved to dance to jazz, but his own compositions were in a classical style. His "Normal March" became the traditional ending to any program on which he appeared. Strahm was a perfectionist; he retired in 1940 when he could no longer play difficult passages to his standards.[10]

Two ladies who came to Western in 1911 left a lasting imprint upon the Normal School. Iva Scott established home economics as a subject and provided a role model for the girls on the campus. "Charming in appearance and manner, stylish and immaculate in dress," she was a campus favorite until her untimely death in 1921, just months before her intended marriage. One piece of practical advice she gave her girls was not to marry "unless he promises to get you a roll of heavy brown paper, mounted in your kitchen." Miss Scott never understood jokes, and less serious-minded colleagues were delighted by her serious approach to outrageous assertions.[11] Miss Elizabeth Woods spent much of her childhood in Glasgow and Bowling Green, but she had lived in Europe for ten years before accepting President Cherry's offer of a position in 1911. She taught French and German and, when necessary, Spanish. After her retirement from the classroom in 1935, she devoted much of her time to the landscaping of the campus with particular attention to the Kentucky Building grounds. Miss Woods died in October 1967 at age 102.[12] Her right-hand man in the campus work was R.C. Woodward, who began work at Western in 1910 as a carpenter and later became the official superintendent of grounds.[13]

In 1911 Cherry was trying to persuade the Mayfield superintendent of schools to join the faculty. One of A.C. Burton's replies told something of his sense of humor and Cherry's method of negotiating. You've asked me to do something impossible, Burton commented; "That's to tell you whether I would accept an offer that is not made—and keep the matter in strictest confidence."[14] They reached an agreement, and Burton came to Western in 1912 where he taught education until his death in 1933. An acknowledged authority on rural education, "Daddy" Burton was also noted for his deadpan humor and his ability to catch flies with his hand without interrupting his lecture. His most famous performance consisted of reciting, complete with gestures, Caroline E. Norton's famous poem "Bingen on the Rhine" as done by a young man with a homemade wooden arm that had to be moved into appropriate positions. Audiences demanded that performance again and again, and Cherry sometimes told program chairmen at educational meetings to ask Burton to do some readings after his speech.[15] More than any other person, Daddy Burton brought a sense of humor to the campus.

Gordon Wilson arrived in Bowling Green on the old 10:18 P.M. train on January 18, 1908. The son of a country doctor at New Concord, near Murray, Wilson had already taught several common schools, and he continued to do so while completing his work at the Normal. In 1912 he began to teach at Western, first Latin and then English. He was apparently the first permanent Western faculty member who was a product of the school, but several others joined that category within the next few years. They raised the question of inbreeding, a topic that has often been considered since. When Gordon Wilson retired in 1959 after thirty-two years as head of the English department, he had taught over thirty-six thousand students. A noted ornithologist and folklorist, he probably gave more high school commencement addresses than anyone in Kentucky. "When I try to separate my life from that of the college," he said in 1970 shortly before his death, "I have great difficulty, for both of them have run along together so long that they seem to be one instead of two."[16]

Marion Conner Ford and Finley C. Grise joined the faculty in 1913 for long tenures. Ford, then twenty-one years old, enrolled at Western in 1909 with $60.00 in savings. Active in school affairs and an excellent student, Ford impressed both students and faculty with his unlimited energy. He taught science and agriculture, became head of the Department of Agriculture and Natural Sciences, earned a doctorate at the University of Wisconsin, and became one of Cherry's key supporters before he died in an automobile accident in 1940.[17] Finley C. Grise, who came to the Normal from Logan County as a student, taught languages. Later he became head of the foreign languages department, went to George Peabody for a doctorate, and was appointed dean in 1927. He held that position until his retirement in 1959. Grise was a superb teacher, and some of his colleagues thought that it was "a tragedy" when he became an administrator.[18]

Miss Ella Jeffries was first assigned to the Training School staff, but in 1920 she became head of the Department of Geography, a position she retained until her retirement in 1942.[19]

Four other important members of the faculty arrived before the end of 1917. Gabrielle Robertson enrolled as a student in 1912 and became a history faculty member two years later. Although Miss Gabie later did work at Indiana and Chicago universities and the University of London, she never completed the doctorate. Many of her students would have explained that she was too busy seeing that they got a sound training in history. Miss Gabie was notorious for keeping her classes overtime while insisting that they arrive on time. The one always-accepted excuse for being late for a class anywhere on campus was, "I'm sorry, but my last period class was with Miss Robertson." A former student said she "had only one fault as a teacher; she expected a beginning freshman to be interested enough in history to start graduate work at once and was disappointed when most students were not so well equipped."[20] Henry M. Yarbrough became a member of the mathematics department in 1915. He received his doctorate from Indiana University and served as head of the department from 1930 until his retirement in 1958.[21] Alfred Leland Crabb, a native of Gerkin, Kentucky, first enrolled in the Southern Normal in 1904, then returned in 1910 to get a life certificate. Active in student affairs, he had a successful career in public school administration before Cherry brought him back to Western in 1916 as a teacher of education. Crabb attended Chicago and Columbia universities and earned his doctorate at George Peabody. He became dean in 1925 but resigned two years later to go to George Peabody, where he had a long and distinguished career. Crabb was a prolific author, and he left a great deal of information about the early history of Western and her people.[22] George Page was another Western student who became a faculty member. He began teaching science (chiefly physics) in 1917 and became head of the department in 1920, a position he retained until his retirement in 1960.[23]

The faculty would have additions and would suffer losses, but by the time of the United States' entry into World War I, President Cherry had put together a cadre that would have amazing stability. His success in this area has often been overlooked because of his accomplishments in building the physical plant. But much of Western's reputation was based firmly upon a strong faculty. Cherry did not lure them with money, which was always in short supply and with many urgent demands upon it. When Cherry was asked in 1917 to list the ten top salaries in the school, they dropped off sharply after his $4,000. The dean received $2,700; the ones at the bottom of the ten highest were about $1,700. And those figures included summer-school teaching. President Cherry was sometimes disarmingly frank in his approach. "I am writing to ascertain what would be the least amount it would take to secure your services as a regular teacher in the Training School," he wrote in 1922. "I hope ... you will be as liberal in the matter of finances as you can afford to be." Franz Strahm was only one teacher who accepted a cut in salary when he came to Western. Many of the teachers received flattering offers to go elsewhere; A.M. Stickles explained why so many of them rejected such inducements. "Had it not been [for] Mr. Cherry's powers of persuasion and inspiration I would not have remained here. I may say I had many chances to leave but finally decided I might as well wear out here as elsewhere."[24]

Working conditions were also less than ideal. The state was niggardly in supporting its creation, and Cherry always had urgent needs for money. Once when Cherry was proudly showing a longtime friend around the growing campus, the visitor pointed to a new building and asked, "Whose salary built that one?" The usual teaching load in the Normal era was twenty-five to thirty hours a week, and, one faculty member recalled, class sizes "were limited only by the chairs a room could possibly contain, plus and including the number of windowsills available as seats."[25] Guilliams left in 1911 to seek a better climate for a persistent sore throat; he said that in his first semester in 1907 he taught eight classes a day with an average enrollment of 125.[26] As late as 1922 when Gordon Wilson was teaching only four classes in the winter term he had a load of 420 students. That year seven faculty members had no vacant period in the day, and Yarbrough's six math classes averaged sixty-six students. In June 1916 Cherry wrote Guilliams, "The intense strain under which the teachers have worked, however, has about broke all of them down. They are the most worn-out bunch you ever saw."[27] President Cherry was aware of what he was doing, and he recognized that the English teachers were "literally overwhelmed with the work of grading papers" in their free hours. But, as he told the Regents in 1909, "I make no concealment of the fact that out of a desire to economize and use as much of the annual appropriation as possible for equipping the school and for providing a fund to supplement the general appropriations to be used in the purchase of grounds and the erection of buildings, we have overworked the teaching force of the institution and we have failed to provide for a few needed teachers and have frequently permitted some of the classes to be over-crowded."[28]

There were no salary scale, no written contracts, and no system of faculty ranks. President Cherry did what he could within the limits he had imposed to reward those who did outstanding work, and he sometimes did so with a fine disregard for any state personnel regulations. He never abandoned the paternalistic attitude he had when he was head of the private school. Thus he wrote to Miss Gabie Robertson who was studying in London in 1925: "I believe you were entitled to pay for ten days when you left here but I have asked Miss Schneider to deposit a month's salary instead of for the ten days." Charles L. Taylor of the Agriculture Department was surprised the same year while in school at the University of Wisconsin to receive a check for $216.66. Cherry had recalled that Taylor had worked during what should have been his vacation. On the other hand, in 1930 a prospective music teacher accepted an offer of $2,400 but made the mistake of inquiring about faculty rank and future possibilities of promotion and salary increments. Cherry immediately withdrew the offer. "I do not care to pursue negotiations further.... Your rank would have been all that an industrious young man could have desired."[29]

Physical conditions left much to be desired in addition to the crowded classrooms. Faculty offices were few and cramped, and as the school grew they often had to be used for the occasional small class. Books and equipment were in short supply, and teachers often bought what was essential from their own scant funds. The late spring and summer terms were especially uncomfortable as students and teachers perspired in the heat of Kentucky summers. Their discomfort was compounded by their formal dress. "I would not have dared to come to class without collar and tie and coat, even though the temperature reached 100," Gordon Wilson recalled. The "stiff, laundered collars had a way of melting and running down my neck." The students were equally stiff and formal and uncomfortable.[30]

Despite such handicaps, improvements were made, and most of the faculty who remained found satisfaction in their work. Franz Strahm grew homesick for the Hill during the summer of 1911 when he was teaching in a summer assembly in Monteagle, Tennessee. "I never dreamed that I could get so attached to teaching," he wrote his president. "I love it.... The students seem to be like they are my children, even if some of them are nearly my age."[31] Many of his colleagues would have endorsed his sentiments.

At the beginning of the State Normal years, the students were as poorly prepared as they had been at the Southern Normal. Only four of the more than seven hundred students enrolled in the spring of 1907 had high school diplomas; most of them had done no high school level work. The "Educational Legislature of 1908" required a high school to be established in each county, and in time better prepared students came to the Normal School. But as late as 1922, when Western became a degree-granting institution, fewer than a third of the students were high school graduates. The proportion was higher among the younger students, many of whom had never taught. The average age of the student body was considerably higher in the late spring and summer when the common school teachers flocked back to the campus.

Thanks to the line of demarcation ordained by the legislature, most of the students came from the Western District, whose fifty-one counties contained approximately half of the state's population. A student living in one district who wanted to attend the normal school in the other district had to secure permission from both presidents. This territorial suzerainty was officially ended in the 1920s after the creation of other state institutions at Morehead and Murray, but the concept died slowly. Of 3,097 students enrolled between September 1911 and September 1913, 96 percent came from the Western District, 3 percent were fugitives from the Eastern District, and 1 percent came from other states. Warren, Daviess, and Graves counties usually supplied the largest number of Western students in the early years.[32]

The purpose of the Normal School was to train teachers, and most of the students entered that profession. Those who did so found Western to be very inexpensive. Starting in 1908 each county superintendent could make an appointment (scholarship) to the Normal School for each five hundred white children listed in the last school census. Each appointment was for four years or completion of the regular course of study. Recipients had to be sixteen years of age and of good moral character. Seldom were all appointments made, and "There is plenty of free tuition in the Western Normal District for all eligible persons desiring tuition" appeared on many of the publications Cherry sent out. For those who did pay tuition, such as out-of-state students, the tuition in the early years was only $10.00 for each ten-week term and $8.00 for the summer session. And those fees were reduced for advance payments. In 1907-8 when a number of Southern Normal students from out-of-state were completing their work, Western received a welcome $7,896.93 in tuition fees. Then the total fell drastically, and tuition ceased to be an important source of revenue during the rest of the Normal era. Students who received an educational appointment were supposed to teach in Kentucky, but little effort was made to collect tuition from those who did not carry out their pledges. Taking one of the regular courses of study was apparently enough to satisfy the requirement. In 1908-9, 1,074 students enrolled from the Western District, and all but 75 qualified for free tuition. It is almost certain that some of the remaining 999 did not use their training for the purpose of teaching.[33]

There must have been some poor students and some who preferred fun to study, but with few exceptions the students of the early twentieth century are described as earnest, dedicated, and eager to get an education. Herman L. Donovan's first term courses were mathematics, English literature, Latin, English history, and physics. He usually studied until ten or eleven o'clock and stayed in the top 10-15 percent of his class. He found his classmates "friendly and serious about their work; ambitious to succeed and most of them had a clear idea of their objective." Looking back from the perspective of close association with half a dozen schools, Donovan declared that "Western was for me at that time better than Harvard or Princeton would have been."[34] Gordon Wilson, another exceptional student in the early days, admitted, "In many ways we were a sort of odd-looking group." Many students were poorly prepared, but "Our enthusiasm triumphed over obstacles that seem now too big to have overcome."[35]

One obstacle, of course, was the academic work, and if much of it in the beginning was on the sub-high school level, so were many of the students. Educational requirements were changed from time to time, but for several years there were five main courses of study. The Review Course attempted to prepare students for the county teaching examinations; it stopped with the eighth grade level of work. The County Superintendent Course was much like the certificate courses except that it added a sort of weekly seminar that stressed school law, principles of school administration, and other issues with which a superintendent would have to deal. Most of the regular students enrolled in one of the three certificate courses. The Elementary Certificate Course, which qualified a student to teach anywhere in the state for two years, listed twenty-seven subjects that were to be mastered. Twenty-eight weeks in residence were required, but most students needed a full academic year to complete the work. However, in all of the courses, a student who was well prepared could get credit by passing an examination.

The Intermediate Certificate also required twenty-eight weeks of residence work and twenty-six classes beyond those in the Elementary requirements. Four of the classes were electives; the Elementary Course had none. The Intermediate Certificate was good for four years. The Advanced Certificate Course led to the coveted Standard or Life Certificate, which was the closest thing Western had to a degree during the Normal era. Twenty-two additional courses were required, including one elective and a "thesis." The residence requirement was reduced to forty weeks from the original requirement of forty-eight. The 1908 legislature made the certificate valid for three years. It became a "Life" certificate after the holder completed three years of satisfactory teaching.[36]

A striking feature of the requirements was the small number of professional education courses; the assumption was that a knowledge of the many subjects a common school teacher must teach was more important. Professors who knew that most of their students were working for a certificate undoubtedly tried to impart pedagogical skills along with subject matter, but the Elementary and Intermediate Course requirements each listed just one course in "Pedagogy." Only in the Life Certificate Course was there a heavy concentration: two courses in Method, two in Practice, and one in History of Education. Many students of the modern era would have turned to some other occupation when confronted with the Life Certificate requirement of five courses in Latin.

A High School Course was added in 1915 as the growing number of high schools increased the demand for teachers on that level. Applications for admission had to be made to the Committee on the Second Elective Course. Successful applicants were required to take a core of thirty-nine courses, including eleven in English and grammar and six in each of Latin, mathematics, and science, regardless of the major and minor. The major required a minimum of twelve terms of work, but the catalog added ominously that a student "may take and may be required to take, all of the work offered in the department." Eight term courses were required for the minor. In addition to the required work in pedagogy, observation, and practice teaching, at least sixty-four term credits had to be earned in not less than forty weeks of residence study.[37]

Toward the end of the Normal era, the work in the Elementary and Intermediate courses had become nearly the equivalent of high school work while the Life Certificate course was approaching the junior college level. Since students entered with widely different backgrounds, evaluation of records was a difficult, individual matter that must have caused many problems for the dean. The guideline most commonly used was a liberal interpretation favorable to the student. In April 1908 Miss Flora Stallard received the first Life Certificate awarded by the Western Normal School. Her previous work was done in elementary schools: two years in the Lebanon, Kentucky, high school; one year at the Bardstown Institute; and seventeen months at the Southern Normal School. In view of that extensive training, she received the Life Certificate after completing the following courses:[38]

Name of Course	Grade	Credit
Observation	96	1 semester hour
Practice Teaching	96	2½ semester hours
Psychology I	95	2½ semester hours
Logic	92	2½ semester hours
Music I	100	no credit
Tacitus	86	2 semester hours
Methods I	95	2½ semester hours
Pedagogy I	—	credit granted
Ethics	90	2½ semester hours
Music II	90	1 semester hour
Supervision	95	2½ semester hours
Practice Teaching	96	2½ semester hours
Political Economy	85	2½ semester hours
Criticism	96	2½ semester hours
Music III	95	1½ semester hours
Physics II	87	2½ semester hours

H.L. Donovan's previous training had been less extensive than Miss Stallard's: common schools, a year at Maysville High School, a year at Minerva College, twenty weeks at Southern Normal in its last terms. His record, therefore, is more typical of the Life Certificate Requirements in 1908. Numeral I indicates high school level courses; Numeral II identifies courses called college level.[39]

Numeral	Name of Course	Grade	Credit Received
I	Caesar	90	½ high school unit
I	Algebra II	83	½ high school unit
II	Milton	85	2½ semester hours
II	Music	90	standing, no credit
II	Chemistry	95	2½ semester hours
I	Caesar	78	½ high school unit
II	Physics	94	2½ semester hours
I	Grammar II	90	½ high school unit
I	Music I	84	⅙ high school unit
I	Civics	95	½ high school unit

Numeral	Name of Course	Grade	Credit Received
II	Cicero	89	2 semester hours
II	Observation I	80	1 semester hour
II	Physics II	90	2½ semester hours
II	Drawing I	99	1 semester hour
II	Methods	85	2½ semester hours
II	Algebra IV	88	2 semester hours
	Forensics	95	no credit
I	Geometry I	90	½ high school unit
II	Observation II	86	1 semester hour
II	Botany I	90	2½ semester hours
	Forensics	95	
II	Drawing II	98	1 semester hour
I	Geometry II	91	½ high school unit
II	Algebra V	90	2 semester hours
II	Pedagogy I	95	2½ semester hours
II	Methods II	87	2½ semester hours
II	Sociology	85	2½ semester hours
II	Virgil	78	2 semester hours
II	Practice Teaching	83	2½ semester hours
II	Practice Teaching II	86	2½ semester hours
II	Trigonometry	89	2½ semester hours
II	Medieval History	92	2½ semester hours
II	Dynamic Geology	88	2½ semester hours
II	Nature Study	90	2 semester hours
II	History of Education	92	2½ semester hours
II	Surveying	87	2½ semester hours
II	Greek History	94	2½ semester hours
II	Music	90	1 semester hour

President Cherry ran the school with a firm, paternalistic hand, and the faculty seemed content with that arrangement. (Those who were not did not remain long on the faculty.) The first faculty meeting was held in the president's office on the evening of January 11, 1907, and for years they were a weekly event. But most of the discussions centered around the classifying of students, their absences from class, and efforts "to stop them from throwing paper on the floor" and to warn them "of the evil effect of tobacco on the young student."[40] The faculty was small, and there was little need for an elaborate organization. Academic departments were recognized, perhaps largely for convenience in listing courses, and someone was more or less in charge of them. But the catalog often made no mention of a department head, and teachers often taught in more than one field. A number of courses were interdisciplinary. The thirteen courses enumerated under "Agriculture" included two in physics, one in chemistry, and two in geography that were listed in other departments.

The departmental and faculty listings in the 1915 catalog were typical of the Normal School years.[41]

Agriculture	O.L. Cunningham, M.C. Ford
Athletics and Physical Culture	J.L. Arthur
Domestic Economy	Iva Scott, Betsy Madison
Drawing and Penmanship	Alice E. Van Houten
Education	A.J. Kinnaman, A.C. Burton, Mattie Hatcher, Belle Caffee, T.J. Coates
English	J.H. Clagett, Mattye Reid
Geography	R.P. Green
English Grammar	M.A. Leiper, A. Gordon Wilson
History, Government, and Economics	A.M. Stickles, Margaret Acker, Gabie Robertson
Latin	M.A. Leiper, A. Gordon Wilson
Library Economy	Florence Ragland
Mathematics	J.R. Alexander, H.M. Yarbrough
Public School Music	Franz J. Strahm, Sally Rodes
Modern Languages	Elizabeth Woods
Natural Science	O.L. Cunningham, M.C. Ford
Physical Science	W.J. Craig
Reading	A.C. Burton, Belle Caffee
The Training School	Mattie Louise Hatcher, Principal
The Library	Florence Ragland
School of Music	Franz J. Strahm, Director Sally Rodes, Nell Travelstead

Progress was often slow and not always sure, but gradually the State Normal School came closer to the status necessary for a degree-granting institution. When that permission was granted in 1922, the school was both larger and better than it had been in 1907.

Enrollment increased from a total of 1,024 students during the 1907-8 academic year to 2,616 in 1921-22. The only decline of any consequence during those years resulted from the First World War. The 1917-18 head count was 1,241, the smallest number since 1908-9, and the prewar peak of 1,821 in 1915-16 was not exceeded until 1920-21. Cherry's active recruitment in the Southern Normal days carried over into his State Normal tenure. The more trained teachers he could produce, the more success his educational crusade would have. And the more students enrolled, the better were his arguments for increased state aid. He continued wide dissemination of promotional materials, except that it was now confined largely to the western district. Each student who left the school was expected to be a recruiting agent, and many of them worked diligently to keep the classrooms filled. At the conclusion of a short summer institute in Owensboro, J.D. Burton called a meeting to order in the grand jury room of the courthouse. As he reported to Cherry, "I had a true bill returned against the persons not having attended Our School, caused them to plead guilty and passed sentence of confinement upon them for such a space of time necessary to complete such a course as you saw fit after entering W.K.S.N.S." Arthur Lott wrote from Beaver Dam in November 1907 that Ohio County would send thirty or thirty-five students to the Normal instead of the seven who had been there. "Count on me for anything I can do, and be assured of my presence there in January," Lott concluded.[42] Such expressions were repeated countless times, for many students left Western fired by Cherry's missionary zeal.

The *Western Normal Letter* of August 1915 urged every former student to send one or more students to Western for the fall semester. Then Cherry extended a promise of concern for the individual student that became a Western trademark. "If you will write us a day or two before you leave home, telling us when to expect you, our representative will be glad to meet you at the train, go with you and aid you in selecting the kind of boarding plan you desire, and see that you are properly classified and started off in your work." Such promises assuaged the fears of many hesitant parents and helped many uncertain students fit more easily into a strange environment. When Gordon Wilson and four girls from Calloway County got off the 10:18 P.M. train they were met by L.L. Hudson, whom Wilson knew. Hudson introduced Wilson to Corbett McKenney, who became his roommate and best friend during their Western days.[43] Meeting the trains also provided enough income for some students to enable them to remain in school.

Cherry also made extensive use of county clubs that formed a recruiting base, provided mutual aid for their members, and enhanced the students' social life. One or more teachers met with each club, and the faculty members were expected to do field work, often in connection with the short-term summer institutes in which many of them participated. M.A. Leiper worked a five-county area in Tennessee during the summer of 1911 in an unusual out-of-state venture. He interviewed at least once every teacher in the five counties; some he saw as many as three times. He predicted an enrollment increase of 15-20 percent from three of the counties; he had not done as well in the other two, but even they would send more students to Western.[44]

The success of such efforts forced an early change in the school's location. The space left by the exodus of the Business University in 1907 was soon filled, and Cherry's vision for the future greatly exceeded the limits of the College Street site. Unfortunately, the funds that had been appropriated were totally inadequate for the needed expansion. President

Cherry, the faculty and students, and as many regional supporters as he could enlist, worked actively in the "Whirlwind Campaign" that resulted in the "Educational Legislature" of 1908. Cherry spent most of the legislative session in Frankfort lobbying for a more adequate appropriation, and students wrote letters and signed petitions of support. The act that emerged appropriated $150,000 to Western for capital construction—dormitories for men and women, a Science Hall with equipment, suitable classrooms, a library and laboratory building, needed repairs and equipment—and raised by $30,000 the appropriation for operating expenses. Governor Augustus E. Willson hesitated, held the bill for his full ten days, then signed it.

When a telegram informed the school of the victory, a major celebration erupted. Dean Kinnaman tried to postpone it until President Cherry got back, but the students could not be restrained. They rang the courthouse bell continuously until the following morning, and an impromptu parade clogged traffic around the town square. When the students learned that Cherry would arrive on the midnight train, some three hundred of them met him at the station. As Cherry descended from the last car onto the dimly lit platform, he saw a mob rushing toward him. The Night Rider era had left many Kentuckians apprehensive, so Cherry dropped his bag and used his umbrella to fight off his attackers. Some of the boys had to overpower him until they could explain their intent. When Cherry calmed down, he apologized for his response to their welcome.[45]

If the legislators thought $150,000 would take care of Western's expansion for the foreseeable future, they had not consulted Henry Hardin Cherry's vision of the future of the school. The money meant that he could move quickly to find a more adequate site for the developments he had in mind. As Cherry and the regents considered various possibilities, strong differences of opinion split the town. Some citizens hoped to resurrect Potter College for Young Ladies, which was closing. Cherry declared that a hundred prominent citizens appeared at a Board meeting to protest the decision to acquire a site on Vinegar Hill. "I personally stayed off the streets of Bowling Green for three or four months," Cherry said, "in order to avoid embarrassing experiences."[46] The regents ignored such efforts, and in 1909 they purchased some 162 acres of land for $102,031.76, a sum that seriously depleted the $150,000. Starting near the crest of Vinegar Hill, 232 feet above the level of Barren River, the tract stretched southward between the Nashville and Russellville roads. Several small private holdings within the area were not included in the purchase. Most of the hill was covered with cedar thickets, dense underbrush, vines, and rocks; an abandoned rock quarry and a lime kiln told of previous commercial usage. It took a visionary to see the hill's possibilities, but Cherry had that vision. He may well have been attracted by the symbolic possibilities of building a college upon a commanding hilltop.

Another attraction was the presence of two buildings that could be used for educational purposes. In the late 1880s the Reverend B.F. Cabell, head of the Cedar Bluff Female College in Warren County, decided to move to Bowling Green and establish a college there. Pleasant J. Potter was the major subscriber to the stock of new enterprise, and when it opened on September 9, 1889, the Potter College for Young Ladies carried his name. The college was located in a Vinegar Hill clearing of about seven acres that looked toward downtown Bowling Green. Included near the back of the site was one of the Civil War forts built by the Confederates in late 1861 and later occupied by Federal troops. Cabell built a large two-story house of local white stone west of the large three-story brick structure that contained both academic and living facilities for the students. Potter College opened with eleven faculty members and two hundred students who came from thirteen states. The curricula ran heavily to genteel subjects suitable for young ladies—music received considerable emphasis—but there were a few commercial classes. For several years Potter College enjoyed a fine reputation that attracted students from as many as thirty states. Then the growth of public colleges cut into its enrollment, and a prolonged illness left President Cabell unable to provide the guidance he had given during the college's first years. The school closed in 1909, and the property was sold to the State Normal School.[47]

The Potter College facilities were inadequate for the growing Normal population, and Cherry and the regents decided not to move until a new administration-classroom building was added. The basic construction contract was for $116,100; the total cost was approximately $125,000. In either case the cost was more than double the amount remaining from the $150,000 appropriation. Although their request for an additional appropriation for capital construction failed in the 1910 legislature, Cherry and the regents continued with the project. Two years later Cherry conducted one of his most intense lobbying efforts; it was "one of the hardest and most disagreeable experiences" of his life. He was attacked by hostile legislators "and even on one occasion was hissed and insulted as I passed down the isle [sic] on the invitation of the House of Representatives for the purpose of explaining the situation." The General Assembly finally authorized the Board of Regents to borrow money for the new building by placing a mortgage on the school's property. The state agreed to pay interest on the bonds but not to redeem them. The $100,000 issue was to be paid for at the rate of $5,000 on June 1 of each year from 1913 through 1922 with the remaining $50,000 redeemed in 1932. The legislature made it a criminal offense for any official of the state schools to spend more money than had been appropriated, and Cherry claimed in later years that the House passed a resolution requesting him to leave Frankfort. The president had to dig into his scanty operating funds to pay the first four bonds, a considerable burden since in 1912 Western was existing on about $6,250 a month. After more intensive lobbying, the state agreed in 1916 to take over the indebtedness. In 1922, after another intensive Cherry campaign, the state refunded the $20,000 that Western had paid.[48]

In the meantime the new Van Meter was built and occupied. A student who first saw the campus in 1913 thought that Van Meter "was the biggest building in the world." In early 1909 the Regents employed Captain Brinton B. Davis of Louisville as the architect, thus starting a long and generally harmonious association that lasted for three decades and left his imprint upon a dozen campus buildings.[49] Henry Wright, a noted landscape architect from St. Louis, was also employed to help plan the development of the hill. Wright, who was described as having "an almost sensuous feeling for land and contour," worked closely with Davis and Cherry to develop Cherry's vision of what Western could become.[50] Few campuses of that era had that degree of professional planning.

An inexperienced contractor could not meet the building schedule, and Cherry fumed in the old buildings near downtown until February 4, 1911. Much detail work remained to be done, but he could wait no longer. The last chapel held in the old building ran late as a number of speakers said goodbye to that location. Alexander's tribute to "dear associations" was especially touching, for his was the longest tenure with the school. Then at one o'clock students and faculty assembled at the old building and moved up the hill to the new campus, carrying with them some of the lighter pieces of furniture and equipment. Gordon Wilson was ill, but, he recalled, "I got up out of bed and helped move the library books, a two horse load of them, from down in the valley to the top of the Hill. It was necessary to come around by State Street because of the steepness of College and the nonexistence of any street from the Russellville Road to the three buildings on the hill. For a long time Fifteenth, between College and Center, was a gullied path, where even a cow would have had unsure footing."[51]

The Cabell residence, converted into Cabell Hall, was assigned to the departments of music and home economics. The latter was placed on the second floor lest the aroma rising from the cooking classes distract the musicians. Professor Strahm was noted for his love of food, and he was always willing to keep an eye on the upstairs cooking if the home economics people had to be away.[52] The main Potter College building, now called Recitation Hall, was crowded from the day classes opened. In addition to most of the classrooms and faculty offices, it contained the library, the training school, and offices for the State Board of Health and State Bureau of Vital Statistics. Several classrooms were used in Van Meter, but most of that new building was devoted to the auditorium and offices.[53] The auditorium was used for the first time on Monday, February 6, 1911, when a welcoming ceremony was hastily put together. It featured prayers, music, several short speeches, and President Cherry's exhortation, "Life, More Life." Professor Strahm provided a stirring rendition of "The Normal March," and the first of many Van Meter chapels closed with nine "Rahs!" for President Cherry. Then the students and faculty started looking for their new classrooms.[54]

After Western moved to the hilltop, the Bowling Green Business University shifted back into the castle-like structure it had once shared with the Southern Normal. For several years Western continued to use Frisbie and Bailey halls for dormitories, but their distance from the new campus made them inconvenient for Western students. Frisbie Hall, which housed women, was still reasonably modern and in good condition, but Bailey Hall and Cherry Hall, which was rented from J. Tom Williams, provided more primitive quarters for men. Cherry Hall had only an outdoor toilet; water for drinking and bathing had to be carried from a backyard hydrant, and waste water was carried in buckets to the outdoor toilet to be emptied. Coal for the stoves was available in the basement of Frisbie Hall. Cherry's long-range development plan included on-campus housing, and, obviously, something needed to be done.

Little building could be done, however, during the remainder of the Normal years. Cherry's main concern had to be with the debt he had incurred in making the move to the Hill. Some temporary barracks were erected as a result of the First World War and the regents' official decision "That the institution cooperate in every possible way with the War Department in the winning of the war." Many of the male students had already entered military service, but in 1918 Western was able to form a unit of 150 men by including some Ogden College students. Members of the Students' Army Training Corps (SATC) received some military training but continued civilian courses until called into active duty. Two two-story barracks, a mess hall, and offices were hastily constructed at the corner of Fifteenth and State streets, facing Fifteenth Street. President Cherry was asked to send three faculty members and ten students to the army camp at Plattsburg, New York, for instruction that would qualify them to assist with the training of the Western unit. The program had little chance to prove its value, for the war ended in November 1918, and a few days later the War Department ordered Western to terminate the SATC program as quickly as possible. According to one report, full uniforms were received the day before the demobilization order arrived. When financial accounts were balanced, Western was due $1,775.89. The War Department discharged this obligation by giving Western title to all the structures.[55]

The barracks were soon put to use, for a serious housing shortage hit

Bowling Green soon after the war when southcentral Kentucky enjoyed an oil boom. Hotel rooms were filled, and boarding house prices rose beyond the means of some students. The barracks were quickly converted into forty-four rooms to house two students to a room at a cost of eighty cents per week—one dollar if the school supplied linens. As an added inducement, Cherry announced, "All students will have the opportunity of hot or cold water shower baths, a magnificent arrangement has been developed along this line." The buildings also accommodated some of the overflow classes from the top of the Hill. One instructor had such a large class that twenty students had to sit in the hall. The students rotated seats so that everyone got inside part of the time. The flimsy structures were removed in 1924 to make room for the Training School building.[56]

The master plan called for dormitories, the need was urgent, and by the end of the war Cherry had reestablished some credit with the state government. The 1918 General Assembly changed the support of the normal schools from a fixed appropriation to a flexible millage arrangement that in 1918-19 gave Western $97,727.03 for operating expenses, over $12,700 more than it had ever received before. Then the 1920 legislature provided $150,000 for capital outlays, considerably less than the $500,000 Cherry had requested and well under what was needed to construct even one dormitory. By selling lots along the east side of the school property, by anticipating revenue from oil leases and the sale of the old Southern Normal building to the Bowling Green Business University for $35,000, and by holding the faculty and their salaries to minimal figures, Cherry was able to scrape together enough to build and equip a $233,407.08 building that was named J. Whit Potter Hall. One wing was never built, and in an effort to cope with the housing shortage three girls were assigned to a room. In some of his more desperate financial moments, Cherry even calculated what the income would be if four students occupied each room. Western's literature soon boasted of the Murphy beds that folded into the walls, the modern laundry in the basement, the large parlor for gracious entertaining, the modern kitchen and dining room in the basement that could feed eight hundred table boarders for $4.50 per week, and a view that "is not surpassed in America."[57] Occupation of Potter Hall in 1921 prompted a faculty discussion "relative to the spiritual side" of dormitory life. "This included conduct at the table, decoration, method of sitting at the dining table, returning thanks, etc." The faculty decided that a senior should be the head of each table for at least two weeks—presumably long enough for correct principles of etiquette to be instilled.[58]

Although it could not match the grandeur and gentility of Potter Hall, Cherryton was Western's most unusual housing effort of the period. Dormitories, present and hoped for, would not meet the needs of married students with families. President Cherry found at least a partial solution to that problem when he "invented Cherryton." Using some student labor, Western constructed as cheaply and quickly as possible several dozen cottages on the south slope of the hill. Cherry was not too inaccurate when he called the site "a jungle," but the vines, trees, and underbrush also imparted an idyllic charm. The seventy-six furnished cottages ranged in size from one room to four, and there were two communal bath houses and, later, a small commissary. A water hydrant was provided for each four houses. Cherry worked out a "purchase" arrangement by which the student in effect leased the structure for several years. The total construction cost was just under forty-two thousand dollars, and by using the new Manual Training Department and its students, Cherry held maintenance costs to a minimum. Sizable families often rented a large cottage, or leasers rented out rooms to other students to reduce their costs. Living in Cherryton produced a sense of unity that in time led to the election of a mayor and council for the community.

Within a few years the housing situation eased, and as campus construction increased parts of Cherryton had to be razed. By the late 1930s only a dozen cottages remained, and then the inhabitants were athletes. The remnants of Cherryton (also known as The Village) sometimes housed faculty members. In later years a few of the structures were moved southward to a site on Regents' Avenue, next to the Russellville Road. They fell victim to the need for a parking lot in 1976, and Cherryton finally expired. President Cherry's imaginative approach to housing attracted national attention in the 1920s when it helped alleviate a critical problem.[59]

Two other unusual buildings were constructed near the end of the Normal years. In 1920 the General Assembly made a course in physical education compulsory after July 1, 1921, for anyone receiving a teacher's certificate.[60] Western was then in the process of reviving the athletic program that had been a wartime casualty. Dependence on the overtaxed YMCA facilities was no longer feasible; something would have to be erected on campus. As usual, money was lacking. Cherry's solution was to build a temporary wooden gymnasium back of the Recitation Hall in 1920. Using mostly student labor, lumber "that does not have to be of the very best," and the student incidental fee fund, the rough structure was hastily erected.[61] Always optimistic, President Cherry told the regents that it "will be a success except in very cold weather." Despite the installation of two large stoves, he feared that wallboard would have to be added. Baths were too costly to be installed, but he had purchased for only four hundred dollars the gymnasium equipment of the Madisonville YMCA when it closed. The "Old Red Barn" was obviously temporary, but in those cramped quarters a young coach named E.A. Diddle began to develop basketball teams. The housing shortage was so acute in 1920 that forty young ladies were temporarily housed in the gym. They erected a sign, "No Man's Inn." In his efforts to cope with the acute housing crisis, Cherry even erected tents in the old fort area during some summer months.[62]

When Cherry wrote a Mississippi friend in 1922 that six hundred students were living on the Hill, he did not exaggerate when he described it as "a tremendous achievement."[63] Confronted by a critical housing situation and plagued by the usual shortage of funds, Cherry had displayed ingenuity, determination, and resourcefulness in finding solutions that eased, if they did not completely solve, the problem. The only housing facility that fitted into the development plan was Potter Hall. The rest were temporary expedients.

The campus buildings were so crowded that students had no place where they could relax between classes, visit with friends, or hold meetings. In the spring of 1920, the Senior Class proposed to build a student community house from the dead cedars that had been killed by unusually harsh weather and unusually numerous bagworms. Cherry promised his support (the dead trees had to be removed somehow), and during the summer of 1920 Professors Craig, Page, and Yarbrough led the student volunteers who cut down the trees and trimmed the logs. The Murphy Brothers firm in Louisville donated plans, and Cherry provided some funds from various student and alumni funds. The faculty signed a joint note for six thousand dollars to keep the construction going, and student projects such as a comic opera production helped retire the debt. The Senior House—more often called the Cedar House—quickly became a popular gathering place. It was also used frequently for school social events. A landmark innovation came during the 1928-29 academic year when a "handsome radio" was installed.[64]

Thanks to Cherry's building program, the students—at least the female ones—had a chance to live in improved housing after the early 1920s. During the Normal years, however, most of the students lived in the private boarding houses that made up one of Bowling Green's main industries, for only a minority of the growing student body could be housed in Bailey, Frisbie, and Cherry halls. One of the best known private boarding places was run by Ma and Pa Reynolds. A tall, large, grey-haired lady, Ma dominated both the boarders and her short, heavy-set husband, who was "bald as a peeled onion." In the early days of the State Normal, she charged $2.50 per week for family style meals. One day when the menu featured hot biscuits, butter, and sorghum molasses the students conspired to "eat her out of house and home." When they cleaned the table, they claimed they were still hungry. The cook was gone, so Ma went to the kitchen and baked another batch of biscuits. When those biscuits disappeared, the stuffed students insisted they were still not filled. Ma came into the dining room, hands on hips, and shouted: "Get out of here!"[65]

The inevitable bull sessions in the halls and boarding houses may well have been one of the most educational aspects of the school. In the manner of college students of any period, topics ranged widely. Corbett McKenney, one of the Cherry Hall boarders, called the bull sessions there "The Cherry Hall School of Philosophy."[66]

Talking, and listening to others talk, was one of the most prominent aspects of the students' social life. Literary societies were an important part of both the social and academic life of the institution. Their origins went back into the Southern Normal years, but in the fall of 1911 the students organized four societies: the Seniors' Society, the Juniors' Society, the Kit-Kat Club, and the Loyal Society. In time their membership tended to correspond with academic standing. Students were likely to start with the Loyals, move on to the Kit-Kats, then the Junior and Senior societies, in that order. These groups competed fiercely in debates and oratorical contests as well as in athletic events, and the cheers usually associated with the latter also encouraged their representatives in other events. The debates covered a wide range of topics: millionaires are a benefit to our country; corporal punishment should be abolished; modern civilization owes more to Greece than to Rome; ministers should participate in political affairs; Napoleon was a greater general than Caesar. New students were told in 1911 to "join one of the societies and become a part of those organizations which help to make the life and spirit of a school." In 1922 the faculty "agreed that attendance at the Literary Societies should be compulsory."[67]

The Moot Congress that had been a feature of the Southern Normal flourished for years in the state school, perhaps because President Cherry enjoyed presiding. The partisanship of the literary societies spilled over into the mock legislature, and Cherry sometimes had to intervene to restore order. He had a great deal of practical legislative experience dealing with the Kentucky General Assembly, and he obviously believed that the mock session performed a valuable role in educating students to the realities of government.[68]

Despite Cherry's efforts to channel all available funds into campus construction, he was willing to spend some money to bring outstanding speakers and performers to campus. He recognized the provincialism of most of the students, and he wanted to expose them to a glimpse of a larger world. Of course he tried to get programs as cheaply as possible. Some of the appearances were special performances at which admission was charged, but most often the performers appeared in chapel.

"In its final analysis, chapel is the place where Western is daily born," Cherry asserted, and many students and faculty agreed with him. Chapel had been a prominent feature of the Southern Normal, and it continued that role in the state school. Chapel usually met in Van Meter at 9:30 each morning. Scheduled for half an hour, it often ran longer. Although it was nondenominational, there was a distinct Protestant religious flavor. An opening prayer and a benediction were common, as were brief scripture readings, and many programs were delivered by ministers. Cherry never made chapel compulsory, but it was well attended. The faculty was aware that he considered a teacher who did not attend regularly unfit for the Western faculty, and since the faculty usually sat on the stage, habitually in the same seats, an absence was readily noticeable. Cherry had an uncanny ability to discern which students did not attend regularly, and they were often sought out and reminded of chapel's value. One faculty member recalled that on a nice day the President might direct him and some of his colleagues, "Go out here and see if you can't round up the students that are in the spoonholders." Sometimes he would personally herd the unwary into Van Meter.[69]

When a nephew missed chapel, Cherry "spoke to him about it" and also wrote the youth's father to explain the stress he placed upon attendance. He had discovered, Cherry added, that practically all successful students were those "who never miss chapel." Such friendly persuasion was unnecessary in most cases; the majority of chapel goers went because they found it interesting, informative, and often entertaining. Chapel was one of the fondest memories that many students carried from the Hill, and their most vivid recollections were often of Cherry's own inspirational talks. "Never will I forget the great resolves I made to go on and up in life while listening to your chapel speeches," wrote one former student, and many others echoed the sentiment. H.L. Donovan, speaking from a lifetime spent in colleges and with educators, wrote, "I have left his meeting many a day feeling that I just had to run to a class, to the library, or to my room to study. He possessed the greatest power I have ever known to kindle the flame of the torch of learning. Each person felt that President Cherry was talking directly to him." Students sometimes joked about Cherry's frequent discourses on the same themes, but, as one student testified, "I found out later in life what he was saying."[70]

William Howard Taft, William Jennings Bryan, Robert M. LaFollette, Eugene V. Debs, Robert Hutchins, Helen Traubel, Jacob Riis, Alexander Meiklejohn, Lorado Taft, Madame Schumann-Heink—these were a few of the personalities who came to Western or to Southern Normal. To them should be added numerous governors, noted ministers, state officials, county superintendents. Cherry was a master of public relations, and it was a rare visitor who received an enthusiastic Western welcome who was not thereafter favorably inclined toward the Hill. Cherry made a particular effort to impress members of the legislature whenever he was able to lure a number of them to board the train for a trip to Bowling Green. Such lobbying frequently paid off in favorable budget decisions.

Most of the chapel programs were locally produced, and they took many forms. Faculty members were called on frequently, often with little warning. At the faculty meeting of December 2, 1918, assignments were made for the following week: Burton, Clagett, Mattie Hatcher, city ministers, and Strahm. Cherry saw faculty presentations as a means of informing the students about areas in which they might not be taking courses. Miss Dietz was to speak twice in one week during the summer session of 1918, Cherry ordered, to "give her a chance to deliver her message. I have been a little worried that she has not been recognized at chapel before now." Faculty appearances often featured Strahm at the piano or Daddy Burton doing a comic sketch, but they also included Mr. Clagett comparing Nietzsche's philosophy with that of the Beatitudes and reading from *Thus Spake Zarathustra*. Faculty members also presented programs that featured their students. Musicians and musical groups performed frequently, and orators were given a chance to orate before their peers. On a February morning in 1913, four members of a history class gave a "clear and concise" discussion of the Hay-Pauncefote Treaty.[71]

The students sometimes contributed more levity to the proceedings than did the discussion of the treaty. A recurring program was one in which students impersonated members of the faculty. The program on December 19, 1910, was so well done that several of the faculty "have promised to reform at once." Gordon Wilson participated in such impersonations as a student; then in 1912 he suddenly found himself as a young faculty member being mocked by others. When nothing else was prepared, President Cherry, sometimes with advance warning, liked to call upon members of the audience for their favorite literary quotations. One chapel legend tells of the day when a melancholic man rose and intoned soulfully, "It is better to have loved and lost than never to have loved at all."[72]

Perhaps the most dramatic moment in the history of Western's chapel came the day after the United States declared war against Germany in 1917. Professor Franz Strahm arose from his usual seat near the stage piano and asked Cherry's permission to make a statement. As long as the United States was neutral, he had favored the German cause, he explained in his fractured English, because he had many relatives and friends in his homeland. But now that war had come, his regret was that he was too old to fight for his adopted country. Then with tears flowing down his cheeks, he choked, "I got a boy. He go." Tears also flowed in the audience as prolonged applause rocked Van Meter. Victor Strahm became an American air ace.[73]

Chapel was also one of the school's major modes of communication. Since most of the students and practically all of the faculty were present, an announcement reached almost everyone on campus. Dean Kinnaman usually had a handful of announcements to make in addition to those the president chose to emphasize. Not all announcements dealt directly with school events. A "storm of applause broke forth" in 1912 when the audience was told that popular Professor Craig was engaged to Miss Ethel

Grant of Danville.[74] The faculty mailboxes were located outside the president's office, and most of the faculty paused there on their way to the stage. When Western outgrew chapel, one of the main bonds of unity was lost.

The library played an important role in the lives of many of the students, for recreation as well as study. Inadequate by later standards, it awed some students who had never seen such a large collection in their home communities. Cherry placed more emphasis on the library after the State Normal was created. Senator Albert Beveridge sent a full set of *Congressional Records*, two bags of government documents were received from Washington, and small sums were used to purchase books and journals. Professional development began in 1908 when Miss Florence Ragland joined the staff. A student of Simmons Library College in Boston, she loved books "with missionary zeal." Locked cases were replaced by open shelves, more works were ordered, the Dewey classification system was installed. As she became acquainted with students and faculty, she directed their reading on an individual basis. When Western moved to the Hill, the old dining room in Potter Hall became the library, and the growth of the collection accelerated. By May 1911 there were five thousand volumes and subscriptions to seventy-two periodicals. Despite the disruption caused by the move up the Hill, the circulation for February and March 1911 was an astonishing 12,471. The 1910-11 library budget was $2,500; the annual circulation was 41,650. In 1921-22, the last year of the Normal School, the periodical list was 101 (after reaching a peak of 115 in 1914-15), the books totaled 10,638, circulation was 55,638, and the budget had risen to $5,448.79. Total enrollment had increased from 1,362 in 1910-11 to 2,616 in 1921-22, so the per capita circulation had fallen. Indeed, for some unknown reason the 70,285 circulation in 1915-16 was the peak for this era.[75]

Space became a critical problem, and shifting some departments to other less crowded areas and annexing part of a wide hall provided only temporary relief. In January 1923 the library moved to the also inadequate Senior House where the wooden structure presented a constant fire hazard. It remained there five years until funds finally became available to erect a more adequate modern building.[76]

When students were not talking or listening to others or reading they seemed to be walking, the only mode of transportation available to most of them. The automobile began to appear in Bowling Green soon after the creation of the state Normal, and by 1910 progressive concerns such as W.O. Toy and Son, Livery, were advertising "Auto For Hire," but such luxury was far beyond the means of most students. Upon a rare occasion a young man might rent a buggy to carry his girl to the chestnut hunt or for a day's ride in the country, but the early century rate of three dollars per day was so high that spending that amount was almost tantamount to an announcement of an engagement.[77] Walks were a way of getting exercise in the absence of extensive athletic facilities, a way of gaining some degree of privacy, a social event when a group went together. For those who were committed to serious ornithological study, a daily hike was an opportunity to count more species. Walks were especially favored on weekends during good weather. A typical Sunday for many Westerners included Sunday School and church, Sunday dinner, an afternoon hike, and evening services.

Walking could also be a way of gaining recognition. At the end of the 1912 summer session, five students from the Jackson Purchase region decided to walk home. They agreed (1) that the entire distances must be walked with no exceptions, (2) that they would sleep in no inhabited building, and (3) that they would believe everything told about the venture. They left Bowling Green at 4:00 A.M. on July 24, and five days later the last one reached home on blistered feet.[78] Most students who lived at a distance took the trains. Connections were often poor, but an amazing number of Kentucky towns were accessible by rail. Some students, of course, used the passenger facilities of the Barren-Green River steamboats.

Pictures of students and faculty from the Normal era show a formality in dress that would appall their descendants in the last third of this century. That formality belied an official statement: "Neat, simple clothes are worn, and nothing showy or expensive is encouraged. Very little, if any, more expense need be attached to this item than there would be if the student remained at home."[79] Many of the students had few clothes, but most of them would not display their poverty by dressing beneath the dignity of a scholar.

Student discipline was handled on a paternalistic basis; it is doubtful if anyone, including student offenders, ever thought of student rights. "Student responsibilities" was a more meaningful term, but there was a genuine concern for student welfare. The Normal School had no dean of student life or even dean of men or dean of women. The faculty knew most of the students, and the faculty meetings devoted much time to dealing with student problems. At the February 3, 1913, meeting, the group concluded, "Mr. Bushart is discouraged. It will be a good idea for someone to talk with him and put new life into him." Later in the month there was an informational item about another student: "Mr. Vinson has withdrawn in order to return home and 'make a crop' so that he will have sufficient funds to return and remain in school next year." At the same meeting, the faculty noted "Misses Bess and Katherine Combest are recently talking too much, loitering in the halls, etc." (Two years later Bess Combest sent a fruit basket to a faculty meeting.)[80]

Infractions were sometimes reported by townspeople. Even before fraternity days, there was some friction where town and gown lived closely together. Mrs. J.A. Harding reported to Mrs. R.P. Green that one of the young ladies at Frisbie Hall "sat on my side porch last night until 4:00

o'clock with a young man." Professor Green handled the ensuing correspondence with the young lady's family, and she ultimately left school.[81]
The Western faculty and administration made every effort to keep students in school, but for those who could not adjust, separation was the
solution. As Cherry wrote the father of one young lady, "Unless a student
is satisfied in school, it is useless for him to remain.... We have done
everything we could."

If Henry Hardin Cherry ever thought it necessary to defend Western
against charges of excessive paternalism he would have responded that
many, probably most, parents expected it. An anxious father wrote in
November 1907 that he and his wife were concerned that their daughter
("She is only a bit of a child yet") was keeping company with boys, and
running around, and doing things they had never permitted. Would
President Cherry and Mrs. Green look after Alma and have her write? "I
do not object to her going out with your consent or Mrs. Green's."[82]
Cherry and the school would have received heavy criticism if students
had been told to go their own way, to do their own thing.

Despite his handling of the more serious disciplinary cases, Cherry
insisted, with some justification, that most of the discipline come from the
students themselves. "We do not sustain a reform school and want no
students who are already spoiled before coming," he wrote in one of the
school's major publications. "We shall harbor none of that class. We want
all young men and women who come for work, and such are pleased to
find their way to the Normal. You may feel assured, then, of good, clean,
aspiring associates." A nephew, one of Cherry's disappointments, told
his father that his classmates were ostracizing him. "Perfectly ridiculous,"
Cherry retorted. "The student body has but little, if any use, for a boy
who will shirk school responsibility, who is not at his post on the night of
the Literary Society. John failed to make a record in his literary society,
and I think his Society went after him.... They did for him what they
would have done for any other student."[83] Most of the students were
mature individuals who were in school for a serious purpose; they did, in
large measure, discipline themselves and their classmates.

Of course the situation was not as idyllic as President Cherry pictured
it. Gordon Wilson recalled that Bowling Green had fourteen saloons in
1908, "and some of them get some of our faculty and students as custom-
ers." Gambling attracted some students, and a few of the boys boasted of
patronizing a "bawdy house" down by the depot. But, he added, "even
the poverty of most of our students helped the moral atmosphere for it
takes money to play a big part in being bad."[84] The lack of money kept
many of the students close to campus, threw them largely upon their own
resources for entertainment, and kept them from the more expensive
brands of wickedness.

Any coeducational institution is conducive to romantic imbroglios,
and a number of students met their future spouses at Western. Such

involvements were a matter of concern to the administration, and a campus policeman was called before a faculty meeting to give information about the situation. "Mr. Pillow," Dean A.L. Crabb inquired, "Dr. Cherry and I want to know what goes on out on the campus in the evenings, nice sunshine summer days." Mr. Pillow thought for a moment. "Well, Dr. Crabb, I'll tell you. If you want to stop the boys and girls from sitting under the bushes and hugging one another, you're gonna have to raise an armless generation."[85] That problem continued.

A number of the outings that had originated during the Southern Normal days continued as a part of the Western tradition. The chestnut hunt at the old Cherry farm continued to be a favorite event. In 1911 the students and faculty left Bowling Green about 7:30 on a lovely autumn morning. In that modern era the vehicles included one automobile and a truck, but they were outnumbered by the buggies, haywagons, and wagonettes. Since the distance was only ten miles, most of the students walked. They hunted for chestnuts and persimmons before lunch, then afterwards played a variety of games that involved everyone. They ate supper at President Cherry's summer home on the Barren River and got back to town well into the evening, tired, but pleased with the day.[86]

The steamboat trip usually took place in May. The excursion was so large in 1909 that both the *Evansville* and *Chaperon* were needed to carry the seven hundred passengers. The trip down the narrow Barren River was leisurely with an occasional stop, but they reached the mouth of Gasper River about noon. They ate dinner at Sallie's Rock, then the *Chaperon* returned to Bowling Green with those who had to be back early. The *Evansville* halted a couple of hours for shore leave at Greencastle and made another stop for supper. Night had fallen before the boat was halfway back to Bowling Green, but the powerful headlights pierced the darkness, and the passengers cheered and sang their way back to the boatlanding. They disembarked around nine o'clock, rode the streetcars to town, and ended an enjoyable day.[87]

The "clean-up days" could also be considered recreational in nature, for they brought students and faculty together in an informal atmosphere, they included a picnic meal, and they often converted into a social affair once the work was over. But as was the case with many of Henry Hardin Cherry's projects, there was also another purpose. The clean-up days helped beautify the campus while enabling him to hold down the cost of maintenance. The first clean-up day was March 24, 1911, when "a great host of Normalites" assembled at 7:30 A.M. to begin work. The students were divided into companies with faculty members commanding each group. By four o'clock when they quit, dead trees had been removed, trash raked up, stones carted off, trees and shrubs pruned.[88] The venture was such a success that for years it was an annual or semiannual event.

The campus provided numerous other opportunities for recreation.

The four literary societies usually held their weekly meetings late Friday afternoon or evening. Programs took many forms, but debates were most common. Many of the topics dealt with important contemporary issues, and the discussions enlivened the society meetings and often led to challenges to other societies. The Oratorio Association, organized in the autumn of 1910, was only the first of several musical groups directed by Professor Strahm. The county clubs helped combat loneliness, assisted in recruiting students, and promoted sociability. The Lyceum Course brought an average of ten or twelve speakers and programs to the campus during the course of a year. The programs were varied, but the majority consisted of speeches, musical presentations, and plays. Admission was charged for many of them and the audiences often included townspeople.[89]

Students with literary aspirations had the *Elevator* ("Going Up?") as an outlet. Started in November 1909, it was published until July 1916, usually on a monthly basis. A hybrid between a literary magazine and a newspaper, it ran from thirty to fifty pages and sold for fifty cents a year. It contained general news (usually stale by the time it appeared), clipped items of interest, articles from graduates, and literary efforts. Most of the humor was decidedly sophomoric, and few of the literary efforts matched the aspiration of their authors. Of course few of the authors were anywhere near sophomore status, and the *Elevator* did allow an A.L. Crabb and Gordon Wilson to see their works in print for the first time. The editors were A.L. Crabb (1909-10), G.C. Morris (1910-11), Gordon Wilson (1911-12), W.L. Matthews (1912-14), J.S. Brown (1914-15), and M.E. Harelson (1915-16). The *Elevator* died when President Cherry decided to replace it with a somewhat different publication that he called *Teachers College Heights*. The new publication, started in 1917, was a straightforward promotional vehicle that eschewed literary compositions. A 160-page yearbook, the *Vista*, was published by the senior class of 1915, but the next appearance of an annual was the *Talisman* of 1924.[90]

Despite President Cherry's preference for nature excursions, he had experimented with football at Southern Normal. Organized athletics became a part of the Western campus life well before the First World War. Cherry was competitive, and if rival schools were attracting publicity and students by their sports programs, well, Western would enter the field. And once Cherry made that decision, he wanted to see Western win more than a fair share of the contests. The advent of organized athletics did not end the spirited intramural games that provided entertainment and exercise for much of the student body.

The first formal move toward intercollegiate competition came at the February 21, 1910, faculty meeting, a year before Western teams could be called the Hilltoppers. Dr. Mutchler moved "That this institution give Inter-Normal School Athletics a trial." That motion passed, and the next one called for a faculty committee of four to confer with two students and develop an athletic policy. Mutchler suffered the fate common to makers of motions; he was placed on the committee, along with Leiper (chairman), Craig, and Clagett. This was the origin of the Athletic Committee.[91]

The committee moved quickly, for the first institutionally sponsored game was played just over two months later. On May 2, 1910, the Western Normal baseball team defeated the Eastern Normal squad 6-0 as Greer, the Western pitcher, threw a no-hitter. The game, played on the Ogden Park fairgrounds field, attracted six hundred students. Later that spring Professor Leiper arranged a train trip to Richmond and Berea. Eastern got revenge with a 5-0 shutout, but Western beat Berea 6-4.[92]

Baseball set the athletic pace for the next few years, including the introduction of the cliches that are an inseparable part of athletics. The 1911 team won five of ten games, "despite the difficulties through which we have had to pass," but prospects were great for the next season when "A new plan will be introduced and it will bring out the enthusiasm and interest of every student." One problem was to determine the best level of competition. Since most of Western's students, despite their ages, were not taking college work, the Athletic Committee decided in 1912 not to play college teams. This rule was later relaxed, but most early games were played with high school and normal teams. In March 1912 the Normal Athletic Association was established to give direction to the program. Professor Leiper was the general manager, Professor G.H. Reams was manager and coach, and students H.W. Nichols and B.F. Stillwell were, respectively, president and secretary-treasurer.[93]

The 1913 baseball team compiled a gaudy 13-2 record and outscored its opponents 106-22. It was, wrote an enthusiastic scribe, "a percentage sufficient to turn Connie Mack green with envy." The team's success impelled Fred Mutchler to ask President H.S. Barker if a game could be arranged between Western Normal and the State University. "I believe it would have a healthy influence in bringing the institutions closer together," Mutchler wrote, "and in developing that splendid spirit of unity and cooperation which should exist and which does exist at this time." Dr. Mutchler was too sanguine in both his analysis of the existing relations and his expectations of scheduling a game. Existing records do not indicate that the baseball teams met during this era.

The baseball squad could not maintain the pace that Connie Mack might have envied, but it compiled a respectable record until the country's entry into the First World War and the subsequent decline in enrollment caused the athletic program to be suspended. President Cherry's aid was invoked in helping solve at least one minor crisis. "I am writing to ask you to kindly return the baseball suit which you used on last year," he told a former player. "We need the suit at the earliest possible date."[94]

Baseball's success encouraged those who wanted a broader athletic program, and a football squad began practicing in the autumn of 1912 for the 1913 season. The first game was apparently played in December 1913 when the Hilltoppers defeated Elizabethtown High School 20-0. By the following season, Western had its first real coach, J.L. Arthur, who came to Western in September 1914 after coaching stints at several schools. Arthur coached all sports, aided by the team captains and an occasional faculty volunteer.[95] Football did not enjoy as much success as baseball, and the prewar record was 7 won, 7 lost, and 2 tied. One of the most memorable and controversial games was a 1915 Thanksgiving Day engagement at Richmond that Western lost 6-0. The *Elevator* charged that "unsportsmanlike tactics" marred the "laudable spirit of rivalry that should exist between the two institutions, whose work and whose aims are so closely related as these."[96] These charges were not the last exchanged in the intense rivalry that developed between the sister institutions.

A school publication indicated that basketball teams for both men and women were organized in November 1913, and that games were played at Central City and Greenville no later than January 1914. Athletic records for the prewar years are incomplete and sometimes contradictory, and the 1914-15 season is usually cited as the first season of intercollegiate basketball for the "Pedagogues." Bethel College, which lost 38-21, may have been Western's first victim.[97] Arthur's two year record (1914-16) was 7-3 with several results not reported. Intercollegiate basketball was then suspended until 1921-22 when L.T. Smith, who had joined the faculty in 1920 as head of the new Manual Training Department, became both athletic director and coach. The incomplete records indicate that Smith's team had a 3-1 record, but other games were apparently played.[98] By the end of the Normal School era in 1922, Western's basketball teams had given little indication of the eminence they later achieved.

A track and field squad was casually organized in May 1915. Thirteen events were listed, and any male student who wanted to enter was welcomed. The top finishers then became the squad that competed in a twelve-event dual meet with Eastern. One indication of the proficiency level of these amateurs is that the hotly contested pole vault ended with two contestants tied at nine feet. A tennis court was built in 1912, but competition on it was only intramural.[99]

Intercollegiate athletics for women began at Western on March 1, 1915, when the Normalites outscored the Amazons of Logan College, Russellville, 12-8. This "varsity team" consisted of ten players selected from the intramural teams that had just completed their season. Mary Brown was the captain, and Josephine Cherry, the president's daughter, was one of the forwards. The players were handicapped by bloomers that reached below the knee and contained two yards of material in each leg. Stockings covered the rest of the lower limbs, but even so males were not allowed to watch the women's games in the early days of intramural competition. In December 1916 the faculty agreed to let the women have two intercollegiate games, one at home and one away. The women's intercollegiate basketball also fell victim to the war.[100]

The future of intercollegiate athletics at Western was in jeopardy toward the end of the Normal era. The cost troubled Cherry. To compete successfully—and Henry Hardin Cherry could never have tolerated any other status—would necessitate expenses for equipment, coaches, and travel that would siphon funds away from his building program. Intramural competition cost little and involved a much larger number of students than did varsity teams. By 1917 the athletic committee had been discontinued. As late as March 1920, President Cherry saw no reason to return to intercollegiate competition, but that policy was altered in the next few months. The Red Barn had 250 seats for spectators, something that was lacking in Room 108 of Recitation Hall, and Cherry could not allow rivals to gain publicity advantages over Western because of their athletic teams.[101]

By early November 1920, the decision had been made to resume a limited outside schedule, whenever possible with other normal schools and junior colleges. Josephine Cherry was employed to teach physical education for women; L.T. Smith did so for men, and they doubled as coaches. Progress was so rapid that in December 1921 the faculty accepted the recommendations of a committee on the awarding of varsity letters to athletes.[102] After the early 1920s, intercollegiate athletics became an important part of the Western scene. Some critics claimed that their role was overemphasized to the detriment of other aspects of the institution.

The new State Normal School had some exceptional faculty members and students who contributed greatly to its success, but Henry Hardin Cherry was clearly its dominant force. When Western became a state school, Cherry exchanged some problems for others. He had to become a lobbyist with the legislature, and he was subject to state laws and regulations that had been less important for his private school. Despite such limitations, he ran the school very much as he had in its private years. After the untimely death of Ruric N. Roark, president of the Eastern Normal School, in 1909, Cherry was probably the most influential educational leader in the state.[103]

Cherry left most of the routine academic decisions up to the faculty and dean, but any significant decisions came to him for an answer. "We put no emphasis whatever upon a mechanical organization," he declared in 1913, and he could have said much the same two decades later. Western was "a growing, living organism that has a vision," and the school "is ruled largely by a spiritual spontaneity" that formulated policies and standards. The faculty's respect for his judgment was demonstrated vividly in 1925 when he asked for faculty opinion of the proposal by Murray and Morehead to start offering four years of work: "The faculty ... authorized him to use his judgment in the matter ... and that whatever he did would be the sense of the faculty." President Cherry was usually prompt in making decisions, unless they involved spending money, but catching him long enough to present a problem was sometimes difficult. Dean Kinnaman explained to the Franklin Superintendent of Schools why he had not taken action on an issue. "I wanted to talk the matter over a little while with Mr. Cherry, but when I broached the subject I got a glimpse of his coat-tail as he shot from the office, for he too is too busy to say scat."[104]

Cherry worked at a killing pace, especially during the first two decades of the life of the state school. An early riser, he often ate at a local restaurant, then walked over the campus before going to his office for a day's work. Life was especially hectic during legislative sessions. On February 25, 1918, for example, he arose at 3:00 A.M., ate at the L and N depot, and was in his office at 4:00 o'clock. Then at 3:00 P.M. he caught a train to Frankfort to push for the passage of bills that were vital to Western. He exaggerated little when he declared, "I am in a sense a slave, absolutely bound hand and foot to this institution and its demands." One of his regrets was that he did not have time to read on issues about which he should be knowledgeable.[105]

Cherry's proximity to the campus facilitated his early morning inspections. His homes were in the thirteen- and fourteen-hundred blocks of College Street until 1919 when he built a new home at 410 East Fifteenth Street, across the street from the future Training School. The Cherrys camped out in the army barracks while waiting for doors and windows to arrive from St. Louis. A president's home was not provided by the school until 1931 when one was constructed on the campus above the Russellville Road.[106] His children, Josephine (1900), Elizabeth (1911), and Hardin (1916), almost grew up on the campus.

The pace and intensity with which Cherry worked worried his friends. He had been frail and sickly during his youth, and during his years at the Southern Normal he appeared destined for a short life. An inner fire sometimes appeared to be consuming him. He wore his dark hair long from his receding forehead, his gray eyes "burned with a sort of holy fire," and his strong, jutting jaw testified to his determination. Poor teeth led to many painful dental sessions. His health improved after dentures were fitted, but thereafter he always appeared uncertain that they would stay in. When he laughed he put his hand in front of his mouth, as if to catch the dentures if they fell out. He had extensive dental operations in 1919, and his tonsils were removed in 1922. His weight, which had been about 145 pounds until 1910, increased nearly 40 pounds, and he sometimes worried about it.[107] Cherry was proud of his resiliency, but by 1913, under prodding by some of the Regents, he agreed that an occasional vacation would be in order. Florida, where he spent a month in 1914, became one of his favorite havens, but he also visited such noted watering places as Dawson Springs. But the haven that meant most to him was the simple cottage that he built around 1910 on the bank of the Barren River, just a few miles from Bowling Green. He could get there quickly, it was quiet and restful, and he could indulge in his favorite sport, swimming, in which he excelled.[108]

In the early days of Western, Cherry carried much of the administrative load, but as the school grew he finally began to delegate some of the work. Academic details were not his forte, and, blessed with a series of able deans, he relinquished detailed supervision of that area sooner than he did any of the others. Much of the delegation of authority came after 1920 when he reached his mid-50s. Then L.T. Smith began to assume some of the burden of directing athletics and campus construction; Kelly Thompson a few years later became active in field work and public relations; and M.C. Ford, a superb speaker, after the late 1920s did much of the lobbying with the legislature and state administration.[109] Cherry also developed some administrative shortcuts. He prided himself upon answering most letters the day they were received, and for years he dictated each answer. But many were routine, and so were his answers. "Many earnest thanks for ... " and "Your esteemed favor is received" were his favorite openings and "Fraternally yours" was his often used complimentary close. By the 1920s he had developed seventeen stock letters that answered most of his extensive correspondence, and by then more answers were going out from the dean's and registrar's offices.[110] Still, most of the secretarial help on the campus was in the president's office, and a faculty member who wanted a letter typed had it done in the president's outer office.

Despite his administrative burdens, Cherry was active in several off-campus activities, most of which he saw as being helpful in promoting Western. In 1912, with the financial backing of John B. McFerran of Louisville, he started a "Rural Chautauqua" program that attracted national attention. The usual pattern was to hold meetings in a large tent in four rural sections of Warren County, followed by a county mass meeting. The programs were inspiring, informative, and entertaining, and Cherry was delighted with the results. He wrote every property-holder in the county, and the response amazed him. The tent could seat up to one thousand crowded spectators, and it was often filled to overflowing. Several committees started local social centers as a consequence of this work.[111] In later years Cherry frequently booked the Redpath Chautauquas for a week-long campus appearance. Their tent was usually pitched on the field near the future site of Central Hall, and their performances attracted visitors from a wide region.[112] Cherry was concerned about the improvement of rural life, and the Rural Chautauqua was supplemented by a Rural Life Conference that first met on campus on February 17-23, 1917. Regular classwork was suspended, but students received a week's credit for attending the conference. The annual convocation of county superintendents met at the same time, and the Van Meter auditorium was often filled with hundreds of people standing outside and straining to hear what was said. The *Normal Heights* was guilty of hyperbole when it asserted, "The Conference should mean to Western Kentucky what the Continental Congress meant to the colonies in 1775," but it did touch thousands of rural Kentuckians. In the 1930s it became an annual summer meeting and fish fry for public school administrators with a much smaller attendance.[113] In an effort to encourage young farmers, President Cherry sponsored for several years a "Boy's Corn Show" with prizes for the best crops produced on one-acre plots. The 1912 winner was fifteen-year-old Lester Bryant of Rockfield whose yield was 148 bushels. His trip to Washington ended in tragedy when he blew out the gas light in his hotel room and died of asphyxiation.[114]

During the First World War, Cherry served on the Kentucky Council of Defense and was chairman of its Committee on Publicity and Speaker's Bureau. Some 3,217 meetings were held under his auspices, and he delivered a large number of speeches himself, usually speaking without notes. Cherry was a forceful speaker, especially when discussing topics such as education and democracy about which he felt deeply, and his deep resonant voice carried to all parts of even large halls. He used certain stories and illustrations time and again, but countless listeners testified to the way he inspired and uplifted them. Cherry was always optimistic, and his "factual" statements were occasionally suspect.[115]

Two personality quirks of the president sometimes caused problems for his associates. "His sense of humor," said a longtime friend, "was as odd as were his habits of work." Subtle humor left him perplexed and wondering why others laughed, but some ridiculous or outrageous joke would leave him convulsed with laughter.[116] And he was notoriously absent-minded. Among Miss Mattie McLean's primary functions were to steer him to his next appointment, tell him whether or not he had lunched, and remind him of promises made. (And in her gentle, efficient manner she smoothed many feathers ruffled by Cherry's sometimes brusque manner.) Cherry seldom traveled without leaving something in a hotel room or on a train—keys, hats, hair brush, nightshirts, coats, architects' drawings, spectacles—he abandoned them wherever he went. In his preoccupation with whatever absorbed him at the moment, he left hotels and restaurants without paying bills. Upon one occasion in Bowling Green he was so absorbed in a talk he was giving at the Helm Hotel that he forgot where he had parked his car. He reported it stolen, but three days later discovered it in front of the post office where he had left it. Upon another occasion Cherry climbed into another man's car in downtown Bowling Green and drove off. When Mr. H.P. Endsley recovered his vehicle four days later, he was understanding about the oversight: "I know you have been busy, I know you are still busy. No serious damage has been done. No hard feeling has been incurred." But he did think that Cherry should pay $12.85 for his calls to sheriffs in surrounding counties, the rental fee for another car, and the ten gallons of gas Cherry had used. On yet another occasion two travelers who spent the night at a Bowling Green hotel were surprised to find a bundle of Western mail in their car when they reached Louisville. Cherry, who liked to pick up the school's mail himself, had again mistaken his car. He summed up this failing when he told a genealogist, "I frequently forget the date of my own birth."[117]

During the Normal years, Henry Hardin Cherry succumbed twice to political temptation. He was an active Democrat, but he was careful to keep Western from taking a partisan stand. Getting state money for the Normal was essentially a political undertaking, and Cherry became adept at that phase of politics. Admirers suggested that he run for governor so that he could be of even greater benefit to the state. Cherry was wary, yet intrigued by the idea, and at least as early as 1914 he sounded out possible support in various parts of the state. Given his usual sanguine outlook, it is not surprising that by April 1914 he was confident that "I would have no trouble in winning the nomination."[118] Cherry vacillated in reaching a decision, but on January 12, 1915, he submitted his resignation to the Board of Regents. As governor, he explained, he could "render a larger service to my state than if I should remain in my present position." The editor of the *Elevator* bemoaned the loss of "the Father of the Institution," but declared "it would indeed be selfish and most unpatriotic for us to stand in his way." Cherry opened his campaign in the crowded court room in Maysville and spoke for two and a half hours on the need for Kentucky to reach out boldly to attain needed objectives. On the sensitive liquor question, he called for the county unit approach.[119]

The regents, perhaps anticipating Cherry's return to the Hill, appointed an eight-man faculty executive committee to run the school. Dean Kinnaman was chairman; Alexander, Burton, Clagett, Craig, Green, Leiper, and Stickles were the other members. The decision was a wise one, for Cherry's candidacy was brief. He failed to get the endorsement of the J.C.W. Beckham faction that decided to push for state prohibition rather than the county unit rule. Cherry had little money or organization, and he soon realized his cause was hopeless, although he later insisted that he could have won had he remained in the race. Many voters who revered Cherry as an educator did not see him in the same light as a political candidate, and he was not well known in the eastern half of the state. On April 29 Cherry issued a card of thanks to the voters and withdrew from the race. At their May 19 meeting, the regents received a recommendation from the Executive Committee that Cherry be reappointed as soon as possible. The regents elected him at the June 1 meeting and set his salary at $4,200, an increase of $200 over his precandidate income. Cherry did not endorse anyone, but he was elected permanent chairman of the August 1915 State Democratic Convention that the A.O. Stanley faction controlled.[120]

President Cherry was convinced that his statesmanlike approach had earned him increased respect and visibility. "I have more influence than ever before," he wrote a friend that autumn. Friends continued to urge him to seek the governorship, and in December 1918 Cherry again announced his candidacy. This time, he wrote a friend, "There will be no looking back." His platform included improvements in agriculture and education, women's suffrage, a nonpartisan judiciary, and acceptance of state-wide prohibition. Cherry did not resign as president, which was well, for his candidacy was again short-lived. His strength in southcentral Kentucky was diluted when H.H. Denhardt of Bowling Green and Tom Rhea of Russellville entered the race. Cherry did not receive the enthusiastic support of the Stanley faction, it was rumored, because he had refused to commit himself to making certain political appointments if elected. His health was poor, and on April 7, 1919, the day he was to have opened his campaign in Benton, Cherry withdrew from the race. He remained active in Democratic politics, but he did not again seek office. The exposure he received in these two abortive efforts probably helped him in his lobbying on behalf of Western.[121]

Political astuteness and diplomatic cunning were important presidential qualifications in dealing with the other state schools. The relationship with the Eastern Normal School and the state university can be described as wary cooperation. It was unfortunate that the autocratic James K. Patterson was president of the Lexington school when Western and Eastern were created. Ruric N. Roark, Eastern's first president, had resigned from the State College faculty in 1905 after stormy battles with Patterson and the Board of Trustees, and Patterson had opposed the creation of the state normals. However, their common needs were so urgent that the other presidents and governing boards accepted Cherry's suggestion that they confer upon a common legislative program for 1908. They agreed upon the creation of a state university that would drop its subfreshman and normal work and would substitute a Department of Education for its Normal School. The General Assembly approved these changes and was generous (by Kentucky standards) in providing additional funds. Patterson had apparently not realized that the changes would reduce his enrollment, and when that occurred he blamed it upon "the sinister influence" and "the persistent jealousy and hostility of the Normal Schools." Cherry wrote a brother, "President Patterson has never failed during my whole educational experience in putting a dagger into me whenever he had the opportunity." Cherry blamed Patterson for opposing the creation of the normals in 1906. He believed Patterson had had the act contested in the courts, and he accused Patterson of trying to block the 1908 appropriations for the normal schools. In Cherry's heated opinion, Patterson, "about the most stupid public official that I have ever met," had "done more to block the progress of universal education than any other man who has ever lived in the Commonwealth."[122]

Relations improved when Judge Henry Stites Barker succeeded Patterson in January 1911. When Cherry assured him of his support, Barker replied that he had no doubt of "the loyalty of the Western Normal School to the University. I regard you as one of my staunchest supporters and I assure you that I am always ready and willing to uphold the course of the Normal Schools.... If we have internal jealousies and bickerings, we are sure to fail of reaching the high usefulness which should be our aim." The University of Kentucky conferred an honorary LL.D. degree upon President Cherry in 1911. When Patterson launched a savage attack upon his successor that reached into the General Assembly in 1912, Cherry took an un-Christian delight in supporting Barker and helping block a proposed investigation of the university. Cherry and Barker roomed together during their sojourn in Frankfort, where they cemented a friendship.[123]

When funding was again a major problem after World War I representatives of the three schools worked closely together to make plans for the 1920 legislative session. Such cooperation continued spasmodically, its degree depending upon specific circumstances and the personalities involved, and with a note of suspicion always present. The state schools competed for limited funds, and the University of Kentucky tended to view the other schools as unwanted siblings who should never have been conceived and who should certainly be satisfied with a distinctly inferior role. Many Westerners (and those associated with the other state schools) saw the university as a selfish big sister who refused to share common belongings upon an equitable basis except upon humiliating terms or when forced to do so by higher authority. The animosities that developed in the early days of the state normal schools have fluctuated in intensity, but they have never disappeared.

A mixture of hostility, suspicion, and cooperation also marked Western's relationships with Eastern. They often closed ranks in common efforts against such threats as the University of Kentucky and some of the state's private schools, but they also competed fiercely with each other. For most of their early history, Western was the larger and better known of the two, and Western often felt discriminated against because governors and legislatures treated them as if they were the same. Relations improved in 1928 when H.L. Donovan became Eastern's president, but, despite his love for Western and his respect for Cherry, Donovan's primary concern was naturally for his school. Western and Eastern officials watched carefully to see that the rival institution did not gain an unfair advantage by lowering fees and certificate requirements. The line of demarcation was guarded jealously, and a student who wanted to attend the school in the other district might receive reluctant permission after intensive negotiations. John Grant Crabbe was particularly suspicious of Cherry's actions, and Cherry was pleased when T.J. Coates, one of his Southern Normal graduates, became Eastern's president in 1916. "We will put our heads and hearts together," Cherry wrote in his congratulatory letter, "we will pool our patriotism and we will make the Normal schools stand out in Kentucky as they have never done before." The Normal Executive Council was the formal agency through which the schools worked, but many of their problems were handled by direct presidential contact.[124]

The dividing line was abolished in the 1920s after the creation of additional state schools at Morehead and Murray, but the concept lingered on in the Eastern mind. In 1936 Cherry spent considerable time investigating charges that Coach E.A. Diddle had been "very active and sometimes unethical" in recruiting athletes and other students in the eastern part of the state. Diddle replied that "it is perfectly legitimate" to visit someone who invites you to do so. And one boy had told him that Mr. McDonough of Eastern had warned, "Whatever you do, don't go to Western." Dr. Ford and Mr. W.J. Craig were also accused of tampering because they had spoken to Western alumni groups in Ashland and Covington. Ford replied, "It would be a sorry state indeed if professional jealousies were to reach such a state where any educator could not visit any section of Kentucky and appear before groups of the profession without his motives being brought into question."[125] It is doubtful that Cherry was ever seriously concerned over the charges.

By 1922 the State Normal School at Bowling Green was firmly established. Considerable building had been accomplished, the 1921-22 enrollment was 255 percent larger than that of 1907-8, the nucleus of a strong faculty was in place, "the spirit of the Hill" was evident. Despite such progress, Henry Hardin Cherry was not satisfied, for his vision reached far beyond the present and the existing resources. Professor Alexander once said, "Cherry could never have played football because the goal posts were too near each other. He would have set one pair in New York and the other in San Francisco." Another friend commented, "He discussed his plans and purposes as if they were the plans and purposes of all humanity." As the institution moved into its post-Normal phase, important changes occurred, and the institutional character began to change. "It is hard to explain Western State Normal School if you have never been there," one of its students wrote many years later. "There was an atmosphere different from any college I have ever known. In my day there was a dedication both on the part of the students and teachers to learning."

Cherry wasted little time with nostalgic memories of the past. "The next term is always the best in the life of the institution," he told a parent, and he believed what he said.[126]

Three

...And Teachers College
1922-1930

WHEN THE General Assembly added "Teachers College" to the titles of Western and Eastern in 1922, the change indicated the growth both of the two schools and of the public school system. Progress had been slower than educators wished, but the number of public high schools had increased rapidly after passage of the 1908 act that required at least one in each county. The state had 106 in 1910, 400 in 1920. As more students entered college with a high school diploma, the normal division work decreased while the junior college level work increased. The state normals had been recognized as junior colleges in 1917, and more work was actually done on that level. As usual, Kentucky followed a national trend rather than leading it. More and more, teachers were expected to have a college degree as one of the requirements for a teaching certificate. In the first two decades of the century, scores of normal schools became teachers colleges with a four-year curriculum leading to a bachelor's degree and with professional education courses offered in a department or school within the institution.[1]

The change in title did not occur spontaneously. The time seemed ripe by 1921, and the presidents and regents of Eastern and Western met on November 19, 1921 to plot strategy. George Colvin, superintendent of public instruction, and Presidents Cherry and T. J. Coates were instructed to draft a bill for introduction in the 1922 General Assembly. Cherry was already busy soliciting support for the change, for, as he wrote Judge J.P. Haswell, "I am fully convinced that the time to enact legislation is before they meet at Frankfort." Cherry's efforts extended beyond the state when he involved the aid of a former student, H.E. White, who lived in Galesburg, Illinois. "Do you know of a senator or representative in Kentucky who will be in the next General Assembly of the state? If so, sit down and write him a letter now. Urge upon him the importance of making the Western Kentucky State Normal School a Teacher's College." He had "never turned down an earnest request of a former student,"

Cherry asserted; now he was asking for their help.[2] Numerous letters seeking such aid went out from his office.

Cherry did not believe that Eastern was as ready for advanced work as Western, but as usual there was no way in which Western could be separated from her sister institution. He often felt like a child who is told that he cannot go somewhere unless he takes his little brother. But there were obvious political advantages to including both schools in the bill. Cherry maintained that Eastern played a passive role until the legislature met; it was Western that "stirred the woods and set the leaves on fire." The preliminary lobbying was so effective that the bill encountered no open opposition. Covert opponents presented the danger of a veto, but further lobbying avoided that fate. The General Assembly also created two additional schools at Morehead and Murray because, the act said, "the two present ones cannot reach or train all the elementary teachers needed for the common schools." Cherry was less than enthusiastic about the additions. Western had drawn many students, including some of its very best, from the Murray area, and Cherry believed that he could handle any number of students if the state provided adequate funds. After 1922 he had to contend with three siblings instead of just one, and the possibility of establishing an independent identity became more remote.[3]

On April 17, 1922, "the faculty of the Western Kentucky State Normal School and Teachers College met in regular session ... with full attendance." The change "will give us a great opportunity in the future," Cherry exalted, but as always the basic problem was the lack of adequate funding. Enrollment soared to over one thousand in the fall of 1922, and the educational level of the students was much better than it had ever been. A few students could have graduated in 1923, but the faculty decided to move slowly. The first Westerners to receive bachelor's degrees graduated in 1924.[4] The new status led to numerous changes over the next several years.

Elevation to college rank meant that the role of the dean became increasingly important as numerous adjustments had to be made. Dean Kinnaman had worked without complaint and had carried the additional burden of being registrar during much of his tenure. He enmeshed himself in minor details, and by 1922 his health had broken under the intolerable strain. He resigned as dean in November 1922 and became head of the Department of Psychology. He never taught again after a stroke in 1925, but in respect for Kinnaman's devoted service Cherry held his position open until his death in 1928.[5] His successor was Dr. Guy C. Gamble who, in his brief tenure, 1922-25, did much to move the institution into its new college status. A Columbia University doctorate, he had several years of experience on both the public school and college level. "He is an academic engineer who is able to make blueprints and write specifications," Cherry boasted after persuading Gamble to come to Western. In three years he made great improvements in the college organization and in academic standards. When he resigned in 1925 to join Griffenhagen and Associates in Chicago, the regents thanked him for his "mastery of those larger problems of the institution and of the state requiring vision and grasp of affairs ... you held students and faculty to standards that could and should be maintained." Cherry and Gamble remained good friends, and in 1933 Cherry again thanked the former dean for his pioneering services. "It was necessary for somebody like you to come into our organization and do exactly what you did."[6]

President Cherry's account of Gamble's departure tells much about Cherry's view of the ideal relationship between president and faculty. If for some rare good reason a faculty member left Western, this was the way to go. "His leaving was in every way a beautiful one. Nothing finer has ever happened on the Hill. I made a statement prior to his leaving and one I think he appreciated. He was so overcome he could not speak. He sent a Special Delivery letter from Louisville to the faculty, students and myself which was read at chapel. The letter expresses in every way the character of a man who is highly professional. Dean Gamble reached the highest eminence of his career during the last few months he was with us, and even after he knew that he would not be with us next year. I really think a great deal of him and will go to the last inch in helping him in his future."[7]

Gamble's successor was A.L. Crabb, who had attended the Southern Normal, received a life certificate from the State Normal in 1910, and earned degrees at Columbia University and George Peabody College. Although he had often been on leave for his graduate work, Crabb had joined the Western faculty in 1916. Cherry was fond of the "first and most original editor of *The Elevator*," and he worked hard to get Crabb back on the Hill after he completed graduate work. Crabb returned in 1925, was appointed chairman of the faculty, which was equivalent to dean, and resigned in 1927 to go to George Peabody, where he had obtained his doctorate.[8] He was succeeded by Finley C. Grise who was first designated as director of instruction but who was in reality dean of the college from 1927 until his retirement in 1959. A Logan County native, Grise received the life certificate at Western in 1914 and later earned three degrees from George Peabody College. He started teaching on the Hill in 1913, and retained the headship of the language department for many years. He tried to teach a class each semester until his administrative burden became too heavy. When he lost his temper, Grise commanded one of the finest cussing vocabularies on the campus. A student who once saw the Dean about changing a class decided that he would have a much greater need before repeating the visit. The student who preceded him upset Grise, who "was very graphic in his descriptions."[9]

By the end of the decade, several other names had been added to the list of officers of administration and instruction. Ernest H. Canon, another of the capable Calloway countians, earned a Life Certificate at Western in 1916 and A.B. and M.A. degrees at the University of Kentucky before accepting President Cherry's invitation to become Western's registrar in 1925. A quiet, modest man, Canon "carried the catalog in his head, and it was he who produced it." For many years prior to his 1959 retirement, Mr. Canon, perched on a high stool, inspected every registration card to make sure that it was in order.[10] Miss Florence Schneider graduated from the Bowling Green Business University and started work at Western as a stenographer (1910-17). She was promoted to bookkeeper (1917-20) and registrar (1920-24) before becoming the college's bursar in 1924, a position she held until 1956. When she retired in 1958, Miss Schneider had served Western faithfully for forty-eight years, the longest tenure in the school's history. Blessed with a phenomenal memory, she answered most detailed questions without having to delve into the clutter on her desk.[11]

Other administrators and offices were added as the school grew and became more complex, but by the end of the 1920s, Grise, Canon, and Schneider carried much of the responsibility for the school's operation. Cherry gradually relinquished some direct supervision, but he maintained close touch with all phases of Western's activities. The president liked "to talk things out," and decisions were usually presented verbally; internal memoranda were rare during the Cherry years. Cherry's colleagues were free to present their recommendations and to exercise initiative, and they were usually consulted before a presidential decision was made. But the ultimate authority for determining policy rested with President Cherry and the Board of Regents. He worked with governors to get appointed the regents whom he wanted, and his recommendations to the board were usually accepted without serious questioning.

Increased enrollment forced Cherry to add faculty and staff, although he continued to keep the total as low as possible while meeting the standards of the accrediting associations to which Western belonged: American Association of Teachers Colleges, 1924; Kentucky Association of Colleges and Secondary Schools, 1925; and the Southern Association of Colleges and Secondary Schools, 1926. The total staff increased from 57 in 1921-22 to 148 in 1931-32; the instructional faculty grew from 41 to 101 during the decade. By the spring of 1924 faculty meetings could no longer fit into Cherry's office; by 1928 they were being held in the Little Theatre in the new library building. The teaching faculty maintained a close balance between male and female members: 20 men and 21 women in 1921-22; 52 men and 49 women in 1931-32. The faculty's academic qualifications improved substantially during the decade. Twenty of the 41 faculty members of 1921-22 did not have a bachelor's degree, and there was only one doctorate in the group. There were 12 doctorates in 1931-32, and only 4 of the 101 members did not have the bachelor's degree.[12]

Henry Hardin Cherry,
president
1906-1937.

Chapel, shown below
in Van Meter Hall,
1911, was the pulpit
from which President
Cherry exhorted the
students.

Above, students and faculty pose in front of the old Southern Normal School on College Street in 1908. Shown below is Cherry's ambitious 1909 plan for the future hilltop site of Western, which came near to being realized. Compare this with the 1928 view shown on the last page of this section.

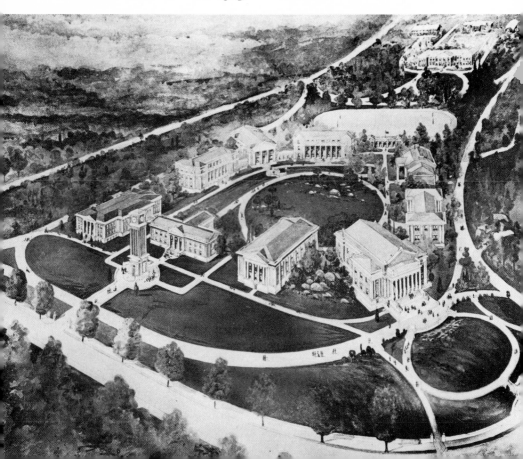

On February 4, 1911, after an emotional farewell chapel, students and faculty posed for the photographer on their way up College Street to become Hilltoppers.

This was Western in 1912. Left to right, Recitation Hall, Cabell Hall, and Van Meter Hall.

Steamboat excursions on the Barren and Green rivers (above) became an annual spring event during Normal School days. Below, students and faculty gather in front of Recitation Hall at the start of Cleanup Day, a tradition begun on March 24, 1911, that held down maintenance costs and helped unify the campus community.

Dormitory room decor has generally reflected the tastes of the era. The scene above is probably in Frisbie Hall, 1911. Below, the Old Red Barn, hastily constructed in 1920 as a gym, housed forty young ladies during a room shortage.

This hard-bitten 1922 football squad had a 9-1 record under its newly hired coach, E.A. Diddle.

Were the costumes worn by the 1926 girls' basketball squad too revealing for mixed audiences?

Professor Strahm (back row, third from left) and his 1924-25 orchestra are seen in front of Potter Hall.

The Student Army Training Corps pose in front of their 15th Street barracks in 1918. Several trainees still wear civilian dress.

President Cherry loved to stage elaborate pageants on the football field. This 1928 event depicted Kentucky's colorful history.

An aerial view of the campus in 1928. Ogden College (bottom) merged with Western that year.

Several members of the original faculty were gone by the time Western became a college, but a solid core remained to give continuity to the institution. During the 1920s Cherry added a number of teachers who would also remain at Western for long periods of service. Among them were Margie Helm (library, 1920-65), Ivan Wilson (art, 1920-58), L.T. Smith (industrial arts, 1920-65), C.A. Loudermilk (agriculture, 1920-56), and William M. Pearce (extension work, 1920-59). Others soon joined them: G.G. Craig (penmanship, 1922-66), E.A. Diddle (athletics, 1922-64), L.Y. Lancaster (biology, 1923-60), Bert R. Smith (education, 1923-56), and Charles Taylor (agriculture, 1923-58). The number continued to grow as Western's faculty acquired its second major generation of teachers: M.L. Billings (psychology, 1926-50), Marie Adams (home economics, 1925-69), Mrs. T.C. Cherry (English, 1923-50), Lotta Day (home economics, 1924-56), Ercell Egbert (history, 1924-66), Will B. Hill (field work and publicity, 1928- 57), C.P. McNally (chemistry, 1926-68), Mary Marks (geography, 1927-29, 1933-56), Frances Richards (English, 1925-64), N.O. Taff (economics, 1924- 51), and Warner Willey (education, 1925-67). Of course there were teachers who made contributions to Western who did not linger long on the Hill, but President Cherry continued to demonstrate his ability to attract and hold capable people despite the low salaries and lack of fringe benefits. In 1921 he told the state examiner and inspector that Western must have more funds. "A school can have no greater asset than the steadfast loyalty of its faculty. This cannot be bought directly with money," Cherry declared. "Not a member of the faculty is extravagant. Everyone is wearing clothes beneath his ideals. Not one is saving money. Only six have their houses paid for." Half of those with college degrees had received better offers during the past year but had stayed despite average monthly salaries of $207.14—less than the wages of the plasterers who were working on the new dormitory. The average salary for the entire faculty was under $160 per month, and many recent graduates earned more than the faculty who taught them.[13] In many instances Cherry inspired faculty as he did students with his love for the school. He was not infallible in his judgment of prospective faculty members, but those who did not meet his expectations seldom remained long.

Although the Normal School had offered some work in other areas, its main function had been the training of common school teachers. Well before the four-year status was achieved, Cherry was planning for an expanded mission. His goal was "to make College Heights an outstanding West Point, a great plant for the training of teachers." In order to accomplish that, considerable upgrading of curricula would be necessary as well as additions to the physical plant.[14]

A comparison of the departments and course offerings in the 1920-30 period illustrates some of the academic changes that occurred. In that decade the number of departments grew from fifteen to nineteen. The

1920-21 departments were agriculture, chemistry, education, English, geography, history and government, home economics, Latin, mathematics, modern languages, military science, public school music, physics, physiology and biology, and the Conservatory of Music. Ten years later agriculture and biology had been combined into the Ogden Department of Science, public school music and the conservatory had become the Department of Music, and geology had been added to geography. The new departments were art, economics and sociology, library science, manual arts, penmanship, and physical education.

Most departments added new courses to their offerings, many of them on the upper division level. Education increased the number of its courses in the catalog listing from 19 to 36, English from 21 to 30, and history-government from 17 to 26. Mathematics was one of the few departments with a decline in the number of courses, from 18 to 13, but this decrease was due to the upgrading of its work. In the earlier year, two courses were on the elementary level and five classes were offered in algebra. In the latter year, the elementary classes had been deleted and algebra had become one college course. An explanatory note in the 1920-21 catalog explained that an H after the course number indicated high school work, a C meant college level work, and nonmarked courses were for elementary school work. Such indicators were gone ten years later, and the catalog explained that the Normal Department had been integrated into the Training School and no longer existed as a separate department.

The three deans who followed Kinnaman bore the burden of bringing the academic requirements into conformity with the regulations of accrediting agencies. No longer could students enroll at any time during a term and take practically any course they wanted or could pass. Many students and some faculty had difficulty in adjusting to the new system, but progress was gradually made, and registration deadlines and course prerequisites became a part of the academic requirements. The problems eased as more and more of the entering freshmen were high school graduates.

Western would have made some changes regardless of external factors, but new state certification requirements accelerated the rate of change. When the supply of teachers under a certification requirement became adequate, the school authorities, including the teachers college-normal schools, would request the General Assembly to raise the standards. Then the Normal Executive Council would establish basic requirements for each level of certification. Each college would then put these requirements into effect, supplemented by any additional local requirements that its Board of Regents approved. Such differences tended to be slight, for no college wanted to put itself at a competitive disadvantage in recruiting students, especially after the abolition of the old dividing line.[15]

The 1924 General Assembly made sweeping changes in the certification requirements, and other changes were added from time to time.[16] In 1930 Western offered four basic certificates. The College Elementary Certificate, valid for two years in any elementary school, required at least 16 hours of college work done in residence. It was renewable each two years upon completion of at least 16 additional hours of college work. The Standard Certificate, valid for three years in any public school, required completion of 64 hours of college work, at least 48 of them done in residence. It could be renewed for life after three years of successful teaching; up to two years of additional college work could be substituted for the teaching experience. It could also be renewed upon presentation of 16 additional semester hours, at least 12 of which were done in the college granting the certificate. The College Certificate, valid for five years in any Kentucky public school, required completion of 128 semester hours, 96 of which were done in residence. It was renewable for life after three years of successful teaching; one additional year of college work could be substituted for one year of experience. Renewal was also possible upon the completion of 16 hours of additional work. A Standard or College Certificate, valid only for teaching special subjects, could be issued when the Standard or College certificate requirements were met and the student had completed at least 12 hours of residence work in the special field in which certification was desired.

The general degree requirements in 1930-31 included a minimum of 128 semester hours, 36 weeks minimum of resident credit, and a C average. One-third of the total hours had to be on the upper division level; at least one-half of the hours required for a major and the first minor were required to be upper division. The A.B. degree was conferred upon students who majored in education (early elementary, later elementary, rural school, administration and supervision), English, economics and sociology, French, history and government, Latin, mathematics, and music. The B.S. degree was conferred upon majors in agriculture, biology, chemistry, geography, industrial arts, home economics, and physics. Only minors were available in art, penmanship, and physical education. The general requirements for curricula leading to a degree and the College Certificate were: agriculture 100, 2 hours; education, 18 hours; English, 12 hours; health and physical science or military science, 1½-2 hours; language (Latin, French, or German), 12 hours; mathematics, 7 hours; social sciences, 12 hours; science, 12 hours; major, 24 hours; first minor, 18 hours; second minor, 12 hours.[17]

The 1930-31 students who read the catalog were told, "The curricula... have been planned to prepare teachers for the various types of public school service, and also to give students who are preparing for the teaching profession opportunity for acquiring a general higher education." They were advised to study the curricula carefully and select the one that seemed most suitable. Once the choice had been made, the catalog provided a semester-by-semester list of the courses that should be taken. Nine curricula were available for selection.

1. General Curriculum. 4 years, leading to degree and the College Certificate. For administrators and high school teachers.

2. Special Smith-Hughes Agriculture Curriculum. 4 years, leading to degree and the College Certificate. (Western had been approved for Smith-Hughes work in 1924.)

3. Special Home Economics Curriculum. 4 years, leading to degree and the College Certificate.

4. Special Public School Music Curriculum. 4 years, leading to degree and the College Certificate.

5. Early Elementary Teachers Curriculum. 2 years, leading to Standard Certificate.

6. Later Elementary Teachers Curriculum. 2 years, leading to Standard Certificate.

7. Rural School Teachers Curriculum. 2 years, leading to Standard Certificate.

8. Degree Curriculum, no certificate. 4 years, No education or agriculture required.

9. Elementary Curriculum. 16 semester hours, leading to College Elementary Certificate.

The degree curriculum without a teaching certificate marked a significant change in Western's academic programs. At least in theory, all students who entered the Normal School were preparing for the teaching profession. By the 1920s a growing number of students who had no interest in becoming a public school teacher wanted to enroll. Especially strong was the demand for premedical work, and on February 23, 1930, the Board of Regents voted to offer it. The next year the faculty agreed to award a degree to a student who had done ninety-six hours of work at Western after he completed an additional year of work in medical school. C. P. McNally of the chemistry department was instrumental in developing Western's early premed program, and by early 1931 twenty-five students were enrolled in it. L. Y. Lancaster became the premed advisor and made an enviable record in placing Western students in medical schools. A former student testified that during his days at Western, "it was widely known that a B average in Dr. Lancaster's classes would get a pre-medical student into any medical school throughout the land." Another of his outstanding products wrote, "Dr. Lancaster expected and demanded high performance with little tolerance for poorly done work, but he never demanded more of his students than he already had demanded of himself." His technique of drawing names from a goldfish bowl for class questions was an unmatched way of holding students' attention. By 1936 the premed program enrolled eighty-four men and six women.[18] Its success gave Western academic recognition, and it led the way into the development of a more diversified nonteaching curriculum.

Prelaw and pre-engineering programs were added within the next few years, and a growing number of students on the Hill were interested in obtaining a liberal arts education and not a teacher's certificate. These changes marked an important shift in the focus of the institution. As the student body became more diversified, some of the old unity was lost.

Western's growth, both in number of students and diversity of course offerings, intensified the usual financial crisis. Fortunately, more aid was available in the 1920s than in the preceding decade. Western's income came from three major sources: the state appropriation for current expenses; the occasional state appropriation for capital expenses; and other sources, the most important being student fees. From 1906-7 to 1918-19 the current expenses had been a lump sum appropriation: $20,000 per year in 1906-8; $50,000 in the 1908-12 years; $75,000 from 1912 to 1918. The 1918 General Assembly put the colleges on a millage basis instead of a flat sum, so that their income increased when state *ad valorum* revenues did. In 1921-22 Western received $136,720.20, the most income the State Normal School ever got. The act also provided that any surplus funds could be used for "the erection of buildings and the purchase of land and equipment." This finally legalized President Cherry's actions since the State Normal was founded.

During the Normal years the total appropriations for capital outlay amounted to only $385,000. Five thousand dollars had been appropriated in 1906, $150,000 in 1908, and $150,000 in 1920. In addition, the state had finally agreed in 1916 to assume the bonded debt of $80,000 contracted when the Hill was purchased and Van Meter constructed.

The income from "Other Sources" was comparatively small before 1920 as most students paid no tuition and few fees. In 1919-20 "Other Sources" produced only $45,501.95. At the beginning of the 1920s, students preparing to teach paid no tuition if they secured an appointment from their county superintendent; others paid $10.00 per term, $8.00 for the summer session. All students paid an incidental fee of $2.50 per term which provided admission to school events. Laboratory fees ranged from $.50 to $3.00 in a few departments. Income from housing increased sharply after Potter Hall was completed but so did expenses. There were also some occasional sources of income—the sale of lots along Normal Boulevard, an oil lease on the Western farm, the disposal in 1920 of the old Southern Normal building to the Business University for $35,000. The total receipts and expenses from 1906-7 through 1921-22 are shown in Table 1.

The school often lived from hand to mouth, and Cherry sometimes drew upon his own resources and those of the faculty to meet emergencies. At the faculty meeting of October 11, 1920, "The President discussed

Table 1. Total Receipts and Expenses,
1906-7 through 1921-22

Receipts	
State Appropriation for Current Expenses	$1,184,440.29
State Appropriation for Capital Outlay	385,000.00
Other Sources	701,821.03
Total	$2,271,261.32
Expenses	
Capital Outlay	$ 724,983.55
Salaries	1,001,890.48
Other Expenses	430,458.25
Total	$2,157,332.28

Source: James P. Cornette, *A History of Western Kentucky State Teachers College* (Bowling Green, 1938), 154-56.

the finances of the school and made a statement relative to the urgent need of money to provide proper equipment for the new Girls Dormitory, suggesting that the faculty sign a note that would assist in raising the funds. Every member present signed it, and also all member[s] of the office force." The basic problem, Cherry wailed in 1922, was, "The institution is larger than the appropriation."[19]

The financial improvements in the 1920s did not come easily. The elevation to Teachers College was welcome, but it created problems. More advanced courses had to be offered, some new departments were needed, a training school that included high school was urgently required for the practice teaching in the Department of Education. President Cherry was indefatigable in lobbying for more adequate appropriations. He bombarded governors, legislators, state officials, and newspaper editors with statistics demonstrating Western's needs and impassioned pleas for their support. And when the legislature was in session, Cherry probably spent more time in Frankfort than some members of the General Assembly. The sympathetic editor of the *Cynthiana Democrat* wrote in 1923 that it was folly to create two new colleges when the state did not provide adequately for the existing ones: "At every session of the Kentucky Legislature, Dr. Cherry must go to Frankfort with his hat in his hand and his mouth in the dust like a common beggar, imploring the representatives of the people to make appropriations of the people's money for the benefit of the people's children."[20] The 1922 session was disappointing. The state schools angered the governor by getting a special appropriation passed despite the adverse recommendation of the Budget Commission, and Republican Governor Edwin P. Morrow vetoed the bill too late in the session for his veto to be overridden. "I think Kentucky will be better off in the hands of the Democrats than in the hands of Republicans," Cherry concluded. The twenty thousand dollars obtained for capital outlays did little to meet the pressing needs.[21]

Western was more successful in 1924 with Governor William J. Fields and the General Assembly that met that year. Confronted with an anticipated deficit of some $60,000 by the end of the 1923-24 fiscal year and fearing that survival of the school was at stake, Cherry redoubled his efforts. Most of the legislators visited Western by special train in late February. The reception they received and their firsthand perception of the college's needs may have contributed to the welcome results. It was "the most difficult experience in my public career," Cherry wrote. When the recommendations of the governor and the Budget Commission were inadequate, Cherry and his associates carried the fight for funds to the Senate and House floors. Their supporters held up the introduction of a new tax bill for two weeks until an acceptable distribution of educational funds was written into it. The new inheritance tax that emerged earmarked one-half of its payments for the state's general fund, one-fourth for the University of Kentucky, three-sixteenths for Western, and one-sixteenth for Eastern. The income from this source fluctuated, but Cherry estimated that Western gained $75,000 to $100,000 in operating expenses. Western also received a $200,000 appropriation for capital outlays, and political pressure warded off a threatened veto. It was a wearying, sometimes humiliating experience that left Cherry in "poor standing with the present administration," but it gave him the money to embark upon a new round of building and to make some of the improvements essential for Western's development.[22] If anyone in Frankfort believed that Cherry was satisfied, they did not know Western's president.

Two years later Cherry again spent most of the legislative session in Frankfort; "I got along beautifully in Frankfort—far better than ever before." In 1926 Western received $320,000 for capital outlays, and additional appropriations of $250,000 were made in 1928 and 1930. The total for the years 1922-30 was $1,040,000, and Cherry embarked upon his most ambitious building program. During the same years the sums designated for current expenses varied between a low of $163,591.64 in 1923-24 to a high of $525,344.44 in 1930-31. "Other Receipts" also varied considerably, from $130,282.56 in 1925-26 to $215,112.00 in 1930-31. The total income ranged from $354,266.06 in 1923-24 to $990,456.44 in 1930-31—the first time Western's income approached the million dollar mark.[23]

The "Other Receipts" were boosted in the early 1920s by a special federal program for Vocational Rehabilitation of Veterans. The first student enrolled on January 6, 1919, and by 1922 some 220 were in the program supervised by M.C. Ford and Leland Bunch, who had been employed for that purpose. Most of the students specialized in some phase of agricultural training, although their paper, the *Pioneer*, reported that 36 were training to be teachers. The students participated in all aspects of college life unless unable to do so because of disabilities. The peak enrollment of 266 came in June 1923. Nearly 500 students had participated by 1926 when the program was phased out, and the payments from Washington added welcome income to the school.[24]

The income was enhanced during the 1920s from increases in the incidental (enrollment) fee which went to six dollars in 1923 and to ten dollars in 1932, from the enlarged housing and dining facilities, from the college farm and dairy, and from gradual increases in the fees charged for particular courses. The new bookstore also gave promise of adding modest profits to the school's account. Local bookstores were generally located at an inconvenient distance from the campus, and they often failed to carry required texts and other instructional materials. In 1920 the regents approved the establishment of a campus store and authorized the president to lend it enough money for a successful start. Student L.Y. Lancaster opened it in the Recitation Hall on September 20, 1920. Two months later it had made a profit of $500, and in April 1923 it repaid the $1,740 loan from the school. At that time it was turned over to the College Heights Foundation.[25]

Early financial records were kept rather casually, but starting in 1927 it was possible to ascertain the expenditures in three broad areas. For the period 1927-37 the expenditures for administration amounted to 13 percent of the budget, instructional costs were 65 percent and plant maintenance and operations came to 22 percent.[26]

More construction was done on the Hill in the 1920s than in any decade prior to the 1950s. In 1922 only the Van Meter Administration Building and the new J. Whit Potter Hall were considered permanent structures in the master plan drafted in 1909. The Recitation Hall was in poor condition, and Cabell Hall would almost certainly fall victim to future building. The gymnasium was obviously just temporary, as were the government barracks, and the Cedar House was not intended to help meet the growth demands for offices and classrooms. A decade later ten general-use structures had been added to the physical plant, and portions of Cherryton had been removed to provide for buildings on the back slope of the hill.

First priority was given to the erection of the Training School building. Organized in the fall of 1906 as a cooperative arrangement with the city school system, by 1912 the training school consisted of eight grades crowded into an inadequate wing of Recitation Hall. The ties with the city system were severed in 1920, and, in recognition of the growing number of students who planned to teach in secondary schools, a year of high school work was added. The SATC barracks were removed and construction began on the Fifteenth Street site in the late summer of 1924. The two hundred thousand dollar structure housed all of the work from kindergarten through high school, and when classes opened in 1925 many applications had to be rejected for lack of space. Leon B. Stephan, an experienced school administrator, was the school's head from 1926 until his death in 1929. Western received favorable publicity when Teacher's College of Columbia University ranked the new school's course of study among the twenty-five best in the country in 1930. Until the late 1950s most of Western's students in education did their observing and practice teaching at the Training School.[27] Its gymnasium was so much better than the Old Red Barn that varsity basketball games were moved to the new facility.

Many of Western's students would teach in rural areas, so in March 1920 a Model Rural School was opened on the Morgantown Pike, about two miles from campus. A fourteen-passenger truck was purchased to transfer the student teachers, but this awkward arrangement was ended in 1924 with the opening of a Model Rural School off Normal Drive at the southern base of the hill. Miss Ethel Clark directed the school and guided generations of fledgling teachers from 1923 until her death in 1947. She was followed by Mrs. Mae Wilson Pedigo, who conducted the school until it was closed in 1955.[28]

A library was another critical need, especially since accrediting associations placed considerable emphasis on it. Despite shifting academic departments to other areas, the east wing location in Recitation Hall was inadequate for the growing collection. Since funds were still not available for a new building, the library was moved to the Cedar House in 1923. Cramped, inconvenient, and a fire hazard, it housed the collection until 1927. The heating system was so inadequate that the library could not be used at night during winter months.[29] When construction money became available in 1926, architect Captain Brinton B. Davis drew plans for a handsome three-story building of native limestone. And, upon President Cherry's recommendation, the regents voted a specific appropriation of two thousand dollars for the purchase of books. Prior to that time, Cherry explained, there had never been such an appropriation: "We have been forced to buy a few dollars worth occasionally when the emergency need was great, and when we could get a few dollars to pay to them."[30]

The spot selected for the new structure was between Recitation Hall and Van Meter, and Cabell Hall had to be razed during the summer of 1926. Its material was used to construct the Home Economics Building across the hilltop, back of and below the site of the Old Red Barn. The displaced departments used Training School facilities until the construction was completed. Cherry's site for the new library would have destroyed much of the old fort, but Dr. Stickles persuaded the president to move the site forward, and the trench area was preserved as one of the historic spots on the campus. When the new library was completed in 1927, the students resumed recreational use of the Cedar House. The library moves were managed by Miss Margie Helm who succeeded Miss Ragland in 1922 when the latter moved from the library to the English department.[31]

L.T. Smith was brought to the faculty in 1920 to start a manual arts department. For a time he conducted his work in the old barracks, then in the summer of 1924 he and his students constructed a building down the hill and back of the site for the Home Economics Building. His students received a great deal of practical training, for Cherry used them whenever possible to hold down construction and maintenance costs. The building was not adequate for a growing department, and when it burned on the night of January 2, 1928, the regents authorized a new and larger building, not to cost more than fifty thousand dollars. It was completed in 1928.[32]

The heating of campus buildings had depended upon an inefficient system of different facilities in each building. Work started on a central heating plan in 1926, and a familiar sight during the summer was of "Uncle Alex" (Alexander) in blue denims and a straw sombrero supervising the laying of steam lines. A spur line from the L and N Railroad allowed coal to be delivered directly to the plant. It started service on February 15, 1927, and a few weeks later was reported to be highly successful.

The stadium and the classic stone colonnade that became a campus landmark were made possible by a successful bid of $37,028. "Uncle Alex" was also busy with the construction of a football field on the site of the old quarry to the east of Potter Hall. Seats were built against the quarry wall, and hundreds of loads of dirt covered the rocky shelf to a depth of one-and-a-half to two feet.[33] When that proved to be inadequate, an additional eighteen hundred truckloads of dirt were added to the field in 1939. Spectators in the upper seats had "a magnificent outlook upon the adjacent country lying to the west and south." The stadium was formally dedicated on October 15, 1927, in a game with Transylvania University that Coach Ed Diddle's team won 27-0, but in the first game played in the new facility Western had trounced Bethel (Tenn.) 61-0.[34]

By the autumn of 1927, Cherry placed the value of the grounds and buildings at $1,443,687.69 and the school's equipment at $182,548.95. As of that date the state had provided Western with only $925,000 for capital construction.[35]

Professor Strahm and the music department were made homeless by the removal of Cabell Hall. A two-story house facing State Street just back of the Training School was purchased from Dr. Frank Thomas in 1926 for $10,136. Remodeling it and adding an annex doubled the cost but resulted in a building that could house the music department with space to spare, although the adjacent playground for the Training School children created problems for the musicians. Used as a "Little Dorm" for girls during World War II, the building became famous after the war as Diddle's Dorm for basketball players.[36]

Another dormitory was urgently needed by the mid-1920s, and Cherry decided that it should also be for women. Captain Davis drew plans for a handsome white stone building designed to house 185 girls and a small infirmary. It was called West Hall when it opened in January 1929, but generations of Westerners called it White Hall.[37] The increased success of Diddle's basketball teams and a growing physical education program also required more adequate facilities. By stretching every dollar to its limit, Cherry was able to start work in the spring of 1930 on a health and physical education building. Despite a savage fight between Republican Governor Flem D. Sampson and the Democratic-controlled General Assembly, Cherry secured another $250,000 capital outlay appropriation that made its construction possible, although a planned swimming pool had to be deleted. On February 9, 1931, Western defeated Georgetown 41-24 before an awed crowd of six thousand partisan fans.[38]

Other less spectacular improvements were also made. Van Meter's interior was redone during the summer of 1928, a rock wall was built along much of the Russellville Road, campus streets and sidewalks were constructed, and the city erected an eighty-five-foot-high water tower near the crest of the hill to solve a longtime problem with low water pressure. It was typical of President Cherry's vision that he saw the tower with "a brick or stone structure around it, thus adding to the beauty and grandeur of the Hill." Other presidents pursued the dream, but the Memorial Tower was never built. Western had not provided a home for the president, but in June 1931 the regents voted to build one at a cost not exceeding thirty thousand dollars. Completed before the end of the year, the brick and stone home stood on the western slope of the hill, facing the Russellville Road.[39]

During this spate of construction, the naming of buildings became a pressing question. The decision was to endorse the recommendations of an earlier special committee: no building should be named for a living person. In 1937 when the regents voted unanimously to call a new classroom building Henry Hardin Cherry Hall, President Cherry insisted that the rule be followed. Work continued on the "New Classroom and Laboratory Building," but the president's death a few months later resolved the issue.[40]

Improvements also continued to be made on the college farms that provided both laboratory experiences for the students in agriculture and produce for the kitchen in Potter Hall. When Western purchased the hill site, about 125 acres south of the hill were in farmland or uncultivated fields. On a March afternoon in 1910, Cherry invited all the male students and some of the faculty to help clear a six-acre field of cornstalks so strawberries could be planted. Col. Guilliams, dressed in big blue overalls, led the crew. "This moment," explained the *Elevator*, "was wholly in keeping with the democratic spirit of the institution." A truck garden was created in the area between what is now Virginia Garrett and Regents avenues; dairy and poultry operations were located toward the south end of the campus. No money was available in 1922 to start the dairy herd, so Cherry, Alexander, Ford, and Loudermilk cosigned a note for twenty-four hundred dollars to purchase seven cows. The campus farm was too small, so Western first leased and then in 1927 bought the sixty-acre Miller Farm on the Nashville Pike about two miles south of the campus. An agricultural pavilion replaced the old dairy barn on the campus farm in 1931. Additional farmland—120 acres—was obtained in 1928 when Ogden College merged with Western.[41]

The ambitious plans for the agriculture department demanded still more space, and by 1933 Western had an option to purchase the Covington farm of some 560 acres located on the Nashville Pike four miles south of town. This expansion aroused the ire of both the University of Kentucky and the Griffenhagen and Associates firm that was doing a survey of Kentucky colleges. Both believed that Western was infringing upon the agricultural mission assigned to the University of Kentucky. The Griffenhagen report said that Western demonstrated the consequences of giving a board "independent policy-determining powers and independent funds which it can spend as it pleases." Cherry endeavored to placate the objectors, but in 1934 Western purchased for $33,529.42 the Covington farm it had leased for several years.[42]

The Western-Ogden merger added not only a farm but also two classroom buildings, seven acres of campus, and a rich tradition. When he died in 1873 Robert W. Ogden, a wealthy Warren County businessman who had never attended a college, astonished the community by leaving fifty thousand dollars for the establishment of a college. His executors opened Ogden College for white males in 1877 on a campus bounded by State and Chestnut streets on the eastward slope of Vinegar Hill. An addition to the Calvert home already on the property created Ogden Hall, the main classroom building. The college offered the bachelor's degree, but during much of its history the prep school enrolled the majority of the students, and the college program was suspended from 1900 to 1904. Ogden College boasted of some distinguished faculty members and graduates, but its income was inadequate to support a broad program that would attract a significant number of students. State schools, such as the State Normal School up the hill, offered more courses at considerably less cost, and Ogden was unable to secure the accreditation that was becoming increasingly important. By 1927 the situation was so desperate that something had to be done, and on November 19, 1927, the governing boards of Ogden and Western signed a merger agreement.

The Ogden campus and buildings, including Snell Hall, which was completed in 1924, and a modest presidential home, and the 120-acre farm on which the fairgrounds were located were leased to Western without cost for a twenty-year period, starting January 1, 1928. Endowment income would be used for scholarships and for the continuation of some of the cherished Ogden contests, and the name would be perpetuated in the Ogden Department of Science at Western. The lease was extended for ten years in 1947 and again in 1956 with only minor changes. By 1960 Ogden Hall seemed to be held together only by ivy, and a new science building was planned for that spot. A new agreement provided for a ninety-nine-year lease terminating on May 31, 2059. A clarifying suit elicited the decision that Ogden's "whites only" requirement was no longer valid. Hundreds of Western students have benefited from scholarships since 1928, and, although their numbers have dwindled, the alumni of Ogden College recall its existence with fierce pride.[43]

The physical plant had almost exploded after 1920, and the Griffenhagen Report of 1933 said that everything was in reasonably good condition except for Recitation and Ogden halls. In September of 1933, Cherry wrote Regent Sterrett Cuthbertson, "There is a crying and pressing need for a classroom building on College Heights." It should occupy the site of old Recitation Hall which seemed on the verge of collapsing. What is the best way to get funds from the new federal programs, Cherry inquired?[44]

After Cherry moved into the new presidential home, he could look across the Russellville Road and see the shell of a building that represented one of his most cherished dreams. It was the Kentucky Building, which he saw as one of the truly unique features of Western. But the interior was empty after construction on it was halted in 1932. The depression that had engulfed much of the world had created greater demands elsewhere for the meager funds available.

The story of the Kentucky Building really began around 1914 when Miss Gabrielle Robertson began teaching Kentucky history. She was shocked to find just one book on Kentucky in the library, so she embarked upon a lifelong crusade to add others. Of commanding presence and indomitable will, she got books, manuscripts, and other Kentucky materials from donors who had not really intended to make the gifts. As these materials accumulated, they overflowed her office and the limited space the library could provide. Miss Gabie began to envision a building adequate to house the growing collection, and she sold the idea to President Cherry.

In his characteristic fashion, Cherry enlarged the vision to include a museum as well as library—a building that would teach Kentuckians about their state, that would acquaint them with their rich heritage. Such an enterprise required a building constructed for that purpose, one that would be unique among state campuses. It could serve as a memorial to the Kentuckians who had sacrificed "their lives for freedom." One of the announced objectives of the College Heights Foundation when it was incorporated in 1923 was to provide such memorial structures.[45]

The more immediate purpose of the College Heights Foundation was to provide for student loans. Cherry knew from personal experience the trauma that sometimes accompanied leaving school for financial reasons, and he had seen too many students leave who never returned. When he learned in 1907 from Dean Kinnaman that Herman Donovan was out of funds and going home, Cherry called the young man into his office. Borrow what you need, $50 at a time, from the Business Office, Cherry instructed him, and pay it back later. The story had a happy ending, for when Herman wrote that he would not be coming home soon, his father replied that if President Cherry had that much faith in Herman he would "be damned if some other man would finance the education of his son." He sent a check for $100, and the sum had increased to $625 before young Donovan completed his certificate course. Neither Western nor President Cherry had the money to make such offers frequently. Then around 1920 Lalla Boone, a former faculty member, gave Cherry $100 to be loaned to needy students. Two people borrowed from the small fund, graduated, and repaid their loans with interest. Cherry realized that a revolving loan fund could help endless generations of future students.[46]

The articles of incorporation, approved July 17, 1923, announced that the Foundation paid "only spiritual dividends." The purposes were to create a student loan fund, to assist in the construction of memorial buildings, and to develop an endowment whose interest would be used for scholarships and emergency needs of the school. Cherry and Alexander were the two Western members on the twelve-person board of directors. Six percent was set as the rate of interest to be charged on loans. To establish a fund as quickly as possible, Cherry turned to the faculty, all of whom pledged 2 percent of their salaries for the next five years. Then he launched a campaign that aimed at raising $300,000 within a five-year period. By early August 1923, over $75,000 had been paid or pledged. The College Bookstore was turned over to the College Heights Foundation with its profits enhancing the assets, and in early 1924 the Western regents agreed to provide office space, office equipment on loan, free advertising in school publications, and $1,200 a year toward the salary of the secretary of the foundation. A longtime Western employee, Roy Seward, was elected secretary-treasurer. Cherry wrote endless appeals for funds, he sent out hired agents to solicit donations, he appealed to students both to donate and to solicit. In the summer of 1924, some of the Cherryton children wrote and produced a play for which they charged one cent admission. They personally delivered the $1.62 proceeds to President Cherry who was so touched by their gesture that he had them stage their production in chapel.[47] But he considered a pledge to be a "sacred obligation," and he could be relentless in demanding redemption. "Your indifference and failure to be responsive to your obligations has not done you any good," Cherry chided one delinquent. Unless her attitude changed, he would be forced to withdraw his endorsement to her school superintendent. If he did not hear from him at once, he angrily warned another culprit, "I will embarrass you in a way that you will not forget for many years ... I am writing your County Superintendent today. I shall take legal actions at once unless I hear from you."[48] Such appeals usually produced results.

As soon as money came in, the foundation office, located in a small frame building that had once been a creamery for the dairy and was located between the Recitation Hall and the Training School, was flooded with loan applications. By the end of the summer of 1926, the foundation had made 1,066 student loans totaling $43,824, an average of $41 per loan. Of this number, 408 had already been repaid in full. The demand was so great that the Foundation had little left to lend. Small life insurance policies were often pledged as loan collateral. By the close of 1929-30 the foundation had made 3,326 loans with a total value of $126,213.50. The average loan for this period was $37.95. Repayments had amounted to $78,419.92. The College Heights Foundation helped numerous students remain in school.[49]

The growth of the loan fund was curtailed when President Cherry decided to push for early construction of the Kentucky Building. In 1924 he had prepared a bill to provide for its erection, but he did not have it introduced in the General Assembly because Western got a special appropriation for the Training School. Besides, such a proposal would probably prompt other state schools to make similar requests, all of which would be rejected. Instead, Cherry decided by 1926 that the Kentucky Building could be financed by public donations. The foundation's articles had mentioned the construction of buildings, and Cherry decided to make use of that provision. He and the other directors agreed that two-thirds of the money raised for the College Heights Foundation would be used for the Kentucky Building, and in 1928 a renewed effort was made to raise funds. School children, provided with tiny banks in which to stash their pennies, were asked to donate a brick or half-brick; the alumni were appealed to again; and Cherry touted his dream to a dinner meeting of five hundred Bowling Green business and professional men held in the Training School gymnasium. Agents went out into the field, newspaper editorials endorsed the scheme, and money began to accumulate.[50]

Cherry failed to get a special $50,000 appropriation through the 1930 legislature, but money was coming in, so Brinton Davis drew up plans and drafted specifications. Site excavation began on August 4. In 1931 the Western regents agreed to spend $30,000 of dormitory and extension work funds on the building. As contracts were let, Cherry discovered another source of contributions. Laib and Company of Louisville protested that payment on their bill should not be withheld because their promised contribution had been contingent upon their receiving another contract. Logan and Company, also of Louisville, had a small contract for $624; their contribution to the building fund was $100. The spokesman for a Nashville company that sought the contract for bricks explained that "The 10 percent special discount is a donation by the Company to the building fund.... In addition to the 10 percent special discount the writer will give $100.00 if this Brick is accepted by the Architect and Board." Thomas L. Barrett of Louisville promised to donate $200 "if favored with this order," and Granger and Company, Louisville, offered structural steel with a 7½ percent donation to the College Heights Foundation.[51]

The exterior walls were completed and the structure was under roof by the fall of 1931, but by then many donors were unable to redeem their pledges. Construction was suspended, but interested people, such as Miss Gabie Robertson, continued to seek materials for inclusion in the library and museum. Some landscaping of the grounds continued, and a log cabin was erected on the grounds. Despite the enforced delay, Cherry was confident that some day the building would be finished.

The "teachers college" status with its bachelor's degree required a considerable expansion in the library holdings which contributed directly to a space problem that was not solved until the new library building opened in 1927. In 1922-23 the library received 107 periodicals, contained 11,018 books, had a circulation of 70,942 volumes, and spent $5,849.63 on its collections. In 1929-30 these figures had increased to 199 periodicals, 24,464 books, 199,307 circulation, and $18,291.54 spent. The circulation per full-time student equivalent increased from 71 to 99 volumes between 1923-24 and 1929-30. President Cherry recognized the necessity of improving the library holdings, and in 1928 he told Miss Helm to purchase all of the books Miss Robertson recommended. "If the budget is exhausted," he wrote, "I will try to find some extra dollars to add to it."[52]

Many of the students were bewildered by the size of the collection, so much bigger than they had ever seen at home, and many of them were not familiar with the Dewey decimal classification system. Miss Helm, who succeeded Miss Ragland as head librarian, told of one young man who was very pleased with a reference book in history that he had used. As he left he said to the attendant at the desk, "Now, you remember this book and my face, and when I come in the next time, please give me this same book." Such encounters brightened life for the overworked staff. So did the girl who sought help in finding sources for a history project. According to her notes, the topic was "Miss Conception of the South in the North."

The move into the new building allowed more adequate services to be offered. By 1930 the periodicals room was on the first floor, along with the Little Theatre and a portion of the stacks. The main reading room, the library offices, and more stacks occupied the second floor. The third floor housed the growing Kentuckiana collection, an art gallery, and the new library science department. An information desk, started in early 1930 in the main reading room, was the origin of the reference division. By then librarians were also giving lectures to new students on the use of the library.

Space became a problem soon after the new building was occupied. Although the stacks were adequate for a growing collection for years to come, the *Herald* reported in the spring of 1930 that library science classrooms had been used to seat the overflow from the main reading room. One could seldom find a seat before nine o'clock in the evening, and the library was being kept open during the dinner hour when it once had closed for that period of time.[53]

In 1917 Miss Ragland offered a course called "The Use of the Library," which was the beginning of a library science program. By 1929 there was an increased demand for trained high school librarians, and Miss Ella Warren taught several classes during the summer. By the next year thirty hours were available, enough for a major, but by 1934 the program was reduced to eighteen hours, the number required for Kentucky certification. A close connection existed between the library and the library science department with personnel often being involved in both areas.[54]

Western's students changed gradually during the 1920s as they reflected the changes in education in the state. They became somewhat younger, the percentage of students over thirty years of age declined sharply, and the proportion of high school graduates increased steadily during the decade. Despite the termination of the line of demarcation between the eastern and western districts, over 90 percent of the students on the Hill came from the western half of the state. After the creation of the college at Murray, there was a drastic decline in the number of students from the extreme western end of the state. Calloway County, which had sent so many able students to Western, was represented by only five in the fall of 1926. The founding of Murray helped explain the slow rate of growth during the decade. The yearly average attendance (based on thirty-six weeks' attendance) dropped from 1,469 in 1923-24 to 1,305 in 1925-26. Then it increased each year and in 1929-30 stood at 2,011, an increase of 54 percent. Since the student body did not expand as rapidly as the faculty, the physical plant, and the curriculum, by the early 1930s a little of the intolerable pressure had been relieved.[55]

On some American campuses of the 1920s, flaming youth reveled in the excitement of the jazz age. The Western campus showed few signs of awareness of the phenomenon; there were even fewer signs of participation in it. Students who did not conform to the mores and rules of Western seldom remained very long on the Hill. Cherry continued to rule with a firm hand, and most parents expected him to do so. When a girl living on campus in 1922 admitted to riding in an automobile from 8:30 to 10:30 at night, her sin was serious enough for the president to write her mother. "She was guilty of a few minor indiscretions on last year, and I had a talk with her," Cherry added. "In fact, I had several talks with her." Since her attitude had been good, this infraction would not be held against her, but it must not happen again. The mother thanked him profusely: "Words cannot express my appreciation of your great kindness to my little daughter.... I tremble to think of the result had you not been so lenient and liberal." There was no mixed dancing until the close of the 1920s, and the faculty's Social Committee debated at length if card playing should be allowed. (Its decision was to put out some decks in the Cedar House without giving formal permission, which might attract unwanted attention.)[56]

Yet changes were gradually occurring. Toward the end of the 1920s automobiles had almost replaced horses. Few students owned cars, but they seemed to have abandoned many of the lengthy hikes that had been characteristic of student recreation in the bygone days. Dates probably walked to the movies downtown, but they were less likely to hike to a picnic at Lost River. With the resurgence of intercollegiate athletics, campus dates became more common. Girls who lived in the dormitories were subjected to strict rules about hours and absences from the campus. In 1929 dorm girls could attend the Homecoming dance if their parents approved and if they were properly chaperoned. They could not attend Saturday night dances downtown unless chaperoned by the dormitory matron. No student was to smoke on campus, and a girl who did so might be reported to her parents. Another crime was spending too much money. Cherry was upset because a foolish father gave a wasteful son one thousand dollars, which he squandered in ten months. "I had an interview with the boy," Cherry said, "and told him very frankly that I did not want any student in school who would spend that much money."[57]

Some of the school activities that had been featured in earlier days disappeared. The chestnut hunts and the boat trips had ceased by 1931, and the work days that had produced both fun and cheap maintenance disappeared. There were specific reasons for ending some of the traditions, such as the death of the chestnut trees and the end of passenger traffic on the Barren River, but Gordon Wilson, viewing the changes from the perspective of over half a century's association with Western, saw a more fundamental cause. Wilson doubted if Cherry was "completely at ease with the student who had had a competent income, a straight-along high school career, a place already achieved socially.... The one great tragedy in President Cherry's career, as far as some of us faithful ones could see, was that the school was outgrowing his range of thinking.... There was no sudden change, and many may not have felt it at any given time." An indication of the change was the failure of the students to respond to the work days that had been so successful in earlier years. The last one, Wilson recalled, "was as nearly a flop as any program ever sponsored by Western.... I felt very sorry for President Cherry, for I know that he had not realized how the make-up of our student body had changed." In the early years, "No other ten men of my acquaintance had powers, if put together, to equal the radiance of Mr. Cherry at his best."[58]

The literary societies were another victim of changing times and interests. They had been based upon class organizations, and the classes had become too large for close rapport among their members. They were gradually replaced by the smaller departmental clubs whose members shared closer interests. The Stickles History Club (1922) was the first one organized; eleven others had joined it by the end of 1930. The faculty and administration considered class membershp to be a student's primary organization, but by 1934 attendance at class meetings was declining. Attendance was made compulsory after "President Cherry expressed the feeling that no student has a right to ask for graduation, unless he attends regularly his class meetings." The Congress Debating Club remained a lively organization, but its membership, limited to males, constituted a minute fraction of the student body.[59]

If permitted, fraternities and sororities might have come to the campus by the late 1920s, although there would be some doubt that Western was ready to support them. But President Cherry remained adamantly opposed to any Greek letter society, honorary or social. They "violated the principles of both democracy and Christianity," and he could not be moved from that stand. "Our departmental clubs are serving much the same purpose and, in my judgment, doing it more effectively than any fraternity could," Dean Grise wrote Cherry in 1930, and the following year President Cherry asserted firmly, "We have never had a fraternity of any type in our institution. We are really hoping to escape having one in the future."[60]

Homecoming was perhaps the most successful of all school activities launched during the 1920s. There was a Homecoming Week in June 1914, but the summer date was not successful. In 1927 Cherry decided to have a shorter but more intense event that would climax in the November 5 football game with the University of Louisville. The festivities opened Friday with a great pep rally in chapel, then continued with a parade and bonfire that night. The campus held open house Saturday morning with a hundred guides showing visitors around the Hill. Over a thousand visitors created an "immense parking problem," but it was handled well by the ROTC cadets. The Capital Theatre orchestra played in Potter Hall, light refreshments were served, and those who had reservations enjoyed a delicious dinner at noon for fifty cents. The afternoon game in the new stadium featured four cheerleaders, the college band of twenty musicians, and a tremendous throng of four thousand cheering fans. The day was made a success when the Hilltoppers beat Louisville 7-6 in a thrilling game.

Happy Hilltoppers attended a reception that evening in Potter Hall where refreshments of cider, gingerbread, and hard candy were served. The format was so successful that in the fourth Homecoming game in 1930 Western again defeated the University of Louisville 7-6. In 1932 a "depression supper" was served after the game. Excluding labor, Dietician Helen Gwin prepared a "fine meal" at a cost of eight cents per person.[61]

During the Normal years the *Elevator* (1909-16) and the *Vista* (1915) were the only student publications, and none appeared for several years after their demise. Then one morning in chapel in 1925 President Cherry announced that the school was going to have a newspaper. He thrust the editorship upon Miss Frances Richards, an English and history major from Simpson County who had been recommended by Dr. Leiper and Dean Gamble. Dr. Leiper worked carefully with her on the first issue, but the commercial printer made so many errors that "I cried and he cussed," the novice editor recalled. As originally planned, the *College Heights Herald* was to come out every other Thursday and be self-supporting. It ran into difficulties on both counts. In 1926 a chapel pep rally had to be held to encourage student subscriptions, and in the fall of 1926 President Cherry announced that all students were subscribers by a contribution from their student incidental fee. The *Herald* would appear once a month under supervision of the teacher of the English department's course in journalism. At the first annual meeting of the Kentucky Collegiate Press Association in 1927, the *Herald* was judged the second best college newspaper in the state; it captured top honors for the best editorial page. In 1930 the *Herald* was voted the state's best college newspaper.[62]

The *Talisman*, a 150-page yearbook, first appeared in 1924. Sponsored by the first degree class, it was edited by T.O. Hall, a senior from Hardyville. Finances threatened the annual's existence, but the senior class held a benefit circus in 1926. President Cherry provided some assistance, as he had for the *Herald*, the staff was given a broader base and more continuity by adding some underclassmen, and the 1926 deficit of $400 became a profit of $360 in 1927. The senior class turned the surplus over to the library for books or furniture. *Talisman* advisor W.J. Craig was reported framing a dollar bill as proof for future staffs that a profit could be made on the publication.[63]

President Cherry saw publicity value in the two publications in addition to their benefits for the student body. There was little if any direct censorship, but early editors understood what type of publication was desired, and they tried to provide it. On a small campus with daily chapel, there was little hard news in the *Herald* for its readers.

A new organization that became an important campus feature during the 1920s was the Reserve Officers Training Corps. As the SATC group was being disbanded, Western applied for a junior ROTC unit. Established in January 1919 on a voluntary basis, it was nearly discontinued because the minimum enrollment of one hundred was met by including Ogden College students, although joint units were prohibited. Cherry appealed to Kentucky's legislators in Washington, Regent J. Whit Potter did personal lobbying at the War Department, and the unit was saved. Intensive recruiting then got the enrollment well above the danger point, and the army uniforms became a common sight around the campus. "Spindle legs, sunken chests and shambling walks are being transformed into strong muscles, proper carriage and manly bearing," read a 1920 boast. But "there is, here, be it understood, no suggestion of militarism, no suspicion of Teutonic autocracy. The spirit is American." The members were often called upon to help preserve order whenever the campus had to cope with large crowds, and in the 1930s the Military Ball became one of the main social events of the year. In 1935 the junior unit achieved senior status. During the late 1920s and early 1930s, the Rifle Team won national recognition for its success. In 1933, for example, the team won the Fifth Corps championship for the seventh consecutive year. Teams had won the Hearst National Championship twice and the National War Department Contest four times. No other Western team came close to matching that record.[64]

The postwar revival and expansion of intercollegiate athletics began when L.T. Smith came to the campus in 1920 to head the new Department of Manual Training. Before his retirement in 1965, he had developed the state's first industrial arts teacher education program, had been responsible for much of the campus maintenance and minor construction, and had functioned as physical plant administrator (1957-63) and coordinator of construction (1963-65). He also served almost continuously as chairman of the Athletic Committee from its establishment in 1922 until his retirement. And in 1920 he supervised the rebirth of the athletic program. Smith coached the football team in 1920 and 1921 and compiled a 2-5-1 record. He also coached basketball when it was resumed in 1921-22. His record there was 3-1 with the results of several games unknown. Smith soon realized that he could not handle the coaching in addition to his other duties, and he urged President Cherry to hire a coach.[65]

The choice fell on a young high school coach at Greenville named E.A. Diddle who had been a noted athlete at Centre College. In May 1922 Cherry offered "Dittle" the position at a salary of eighteen hundred dollars for ten months. He would teach two hours in the morning, but "the classes which we would call on you to teach you could handle without any trouble." Cherry was sorry that he could not offer more, but he pictured dazzling visions of the future. "There is a great field opening here. The opportunities are many. There is a great student-body and fine spirit and if everything works out all right, I am sure you will be properly taken care of in the future and in a satisfactory way." The prospect (who had left Centre without graduating) balked at teaching, and Cherry (who had learned to spell the name) agreed to relieve him of that responsibility. Smith also urged Diddle to accept. Fifteen of seventeen lettermen were returning to the gridiron, and Smith had written to high school athletes all over the western end of the state. And so the inimitable Diddle began his coaching career at Western.

His record during the 1920s did not predict the legendary status he later achieved. His 1922 football team had a brilliant 9-1 season, losing only to the Vanderbilt B team by a score of 6-13, and his 1928 squad lost only to Union College (Tenn.) 6-7 in compiling an 8-1 record. But in the intervening five years his teams were 21-22-2. Diddle's seven-season football record was 38-24-2, good but not spectacular. Many area high schools did not play football. Tom Ellis, one of Western's great athletes, had never seen a football game until the first one in which he played at Western. He did not know how to put on his helmet. Diddle's basketball success, the field in which he attained national fame, was even less auspicious after his initial 12-2 season in 1922-23. In the eight seasons 1922-30, Diddle's record was 73 won, 57 lost, for an average of 56.1 percent. During the next decade he established himself as one of the nation's most successful coaches.

Little recruiting was done during this era of Western athletics, and what was done was usually confined to the area from which most of Western's students came. Ted Hornback came to Western from Sonora High School in 1925; he became one of Diddle's star players, and later his longtime assistant coach. Hornback said his only contacts with Mr. Diddle before coming to the Hill were when the Western coach would referee high school games. "And he would come down in the dressing room and look at us sitting around puffing and panting and he'd say 'Wait'll I get ya down to Western.' Said, 'I'll get ya in better shape than that.' So we didn't have much idea of going anywhere but Western." There were no athletic scholarships, and players who could not pay their way were found campus jobs. Another of Diddle's boys was convinced that his genius lay in his ability to inspire players; "Coach had a great ability to take a bunch of fellows and make them play better than they knew how to play."[66]

Both rules and techniques were quite different in the 1920s from those in later years. In basketball the modern spectator would perhaps be most perplexed by the center jump after each basket and the absence of the jump shot. In football some of the most obvious differences from the modern game were the absence of platooning and the paucity of protective gear, including face masks. In 1926, for example, only twenty-five

"Pegagogues" made the trip to Louisville to play the University of Louisville. In both sports, starters were expected to play most if not all of the game, and most athletes played more than one sport. In the years before World War II, a good athlete might well earn a dozen or more freshman and varsity letters. In the 1927 football loss to Kentucky Wesleyan, Western used only one substitute, and in the great 7-6 homecoming victory over the University of Louisville in 1927 no substitution was made. Western threatened to score again in the fourth quarter, "but Reynolds fell over the embankment just as the ball tipped his hands." This disappearing act continued the excitement that began with the game ball being dropped from an airplane. Athletes of the earlier years were also considerably smaller than their later day counterparts. The twenty-six men on the 1929 football squad averaged 167 pounds with a range from 150 to 185 pounds; the forty-four returning players in 1983 averaged 203 pounds with a range from 160 to 260 pounds.[67] Of course one of the most obvious differences in personnel was the absence of black athletes prior to the 1960s.

Carl "Swede" Anderson, Diddle's assistant, took over as head football coach in 1929 and compiled a 7-3 record, aided perhaps, by a new practice field built on pasture land south of Cherryton. He was followed by James Elam from Transylvania University who had seasons of 8-1-1 and 8-4 in 1930 and 1931 before he resigned. Western's 1930 game at the University of Miami was broadcast over a radio station, probably the first time that a Hilltopper game was aired. It was apparently also the first night game for a Western football team. (The score was 19-0, Western.) For fans who could not get the broadcast, Mr. Diddle arranged for quarter scores to be called to the Western Lunch Room at the foot of the Hill. Fans could get the scores by calling 1581—a service that remained a Western Lunch Room tradition for many years.[68]

Baseball was also considered a major sport, but it never had the support given football and basketball. Mr. Diddle enjoyed coaching baseball, and many basketball players accompanied him over to the diamond. The *Herald* reported that tennis became a team sport in 1929 for the first time with Mr. Leslie Hewes of the geography department as coach. Track and field competition was resumed about 1929, although some students may have participated individually in earlier intercollegiate meets. Most of the participants were athletes whose major interest was in other sports. Some hint of track's inferior status is contined in a 1930 *Herald* story: "Reynolds, heavy favorite to win the hurdles, was handicapped by being forced to avoid a tree." Golf did not become a team sport until 1935.[69]

Women's athletics were neglected in comparison to the men's program, with basketball being the only intercollegiate sport played. The team had several successful seasons despite the playing costume of middy blouse, black bloomers, black stockings, and white shoes. Girls' basketball was discontinued in the state high schools, and Western's program was apparently dropped after the 1930 season.[70]

Western's increased interest in intercollegiate athletics was indicated by conference affiliation. In December 1924 L.T. Smith represented Western at a meeting attended by Kentucky Wesleyan, University of Louisville, and Transylvania University representatives. They drafted a constitution for a Kentucky Intercollegiate Athletic Conference (KIAC). Among the more interesting provisions was a prohibition against "Proselyting: The offering of inducements to players to enter college because of their athletic abilities, or supporting or maintaining players while in college, either by athletic organizations, by individuals, by alumni, directly or indirectly." No training table was allowed for any sport, and a "Migratory Rule" forbade the transfer of athletes from one school to another unless they were premed or predental students. Western's faculty approved the proposal, and in 1925 Western became a charter member. As other schools joined, the KIAC became the primary conference for Kentucky colleges, with the exception of the University of Kentucky. Two years later Western joined the Southern Intercollegiate Athletic Association (SIAA), a far-flung organization that by the end of 1930 had thirty-six members in states spread from Virginia to Texas. An immediate result was the organization of freshmen teams, as the SIAA did not allow freshmen to play on varsity teams.[71]

Some Westerners were concerned by the late 1920s over the increased emphasis on sports. Cherry admitted the possible dangers but asserted that there were positive benefits if the program was handled adequately. Western would emphasize physical training for the mass of students, rather than winning teams for a few athletes. Several years later Cherry was incensed over an alleged statement that Western's football team had lost twice to Murray and that a third defeat would ruin Western. "I have said that if we have athletics we should try to make the standards of athletics a credit to the institution; that there is no harm in being defeated on a football field.... I have said that real victory depended upon the sportsmanship displayed by each team and not upon carrying the ball over the goal line." A college should mold character and citizenship in its students. If athletics did not help to do this, Cherry vowed, "I would go before my Board for the purpose of eliminating the organization from our program."[72] This did not prove necessary.

By 1930 Western was firmly established with a growing and better prepared student body, a fine physical plant, and a better qualified faculty. It possessed the usual symbols of a college. Red and grey had been the school colors since 1912, and two of President Cherry's favorite expressions had been adapted as school mottos: "Life More Life," and "The Spirit Makes the Master." In 1924, when Dr. Leiper requested words for a school song, the entry of Mary Frances Bradley of Franklin was judged the best. Her father, Ben J. Bradley, composed the music, and "College Heights" was first sung in chapel on March 4, 1925. Traditions were being born and nourished.[73]

Then in 1930 Western took another academic step that illustrated the changes that had occurred. The Normal Department was discontinued, and its work became a part of the Training School. "Normal School" was dropped from the title, and Western entered the new decade as Western Kentucky State Teachers College.

Four

End of an Era
1930-1937

THE CHANGE of name in 1930 was not nearly as significant as the change in 1922 had been. Becoming a degree-granting institution had necessitated extensive changes in many aspects of the institution's life; dropping the normal school designation was easily done. The change in title merely ratified what had already been largely achieved.

Of course there were changes during the next several years. Psychology broke away from education to become a separate department, but it was the only new one. Other changes were minor: modern languages and Latin merged into foreign languages, while manual arts became industrial arts. Most of the departments expanded their course offerings, largely on the upper division level as the senior college work grew and graduate work was initiated. Between 1930-31 and 1937-38 the catalog listings for art increased from 7 to 14 courses, chemistry from 10 to 14, economics and sociology from 12 to 24, education from 35 to 56 (with the latter including the psychology courses that were cross-listed in both departments), English from 30 to 47, physics from 9 to 15. History and government increased only from 26 to 27 classes, and mathematics grew from 13 to 16, but both departments had reasonably good offerings in 1930-31.[1] Since the enrollment remained stable during this period, the increased number of classes meant that many of them were scheduled on a rotating basis; a course might be offered in alternate semesters or perhaps every other year.

The 1934 legislature, acting upon recommendations from the Kentucky Educational Commission which was created in 1922, made several drastic curricular changes that became effective in 1935. The State Board of Education was given the power to grant certificates that formerly had been lodged in each school. Three types of certificates were established: Elementary, High School, and Administration and Supervision. Each type had provisional and standard certificates. A student could obtain the Provisional Elementary Certificate after two years of college work; the

Standard Elementary required four years. The High School and Administration and Supervision certificates required four years of college work, and the latter also required two years of successful teaching experience. The Standard Certificates for High School and Administration and Supervision required a full year of graduate studies. Each certificate was valid only for the field in which it was issued.[2]

In order to qualify students for these certificates, Western made some changes in the curriculum for each program. The 1935-36 catalog listed fourteen curricula. Western was then offering graduate work, and three of the curricula reflected that work:

1. A two-year curriculum for elementary teachers, leading to the Provisional Elementary Certificate.

2. A four-year curriculum for the training of elementary teachers, leading to the Bachelor of Science degree and the Standard Elementary Certificate.

3. A general four-year curriculum for the training of high school teachers, leading to the Bachelor of Arts or Bachelor of Science degree and the Provisional High School Certificate.

4. A special four-year curriculum for the training of high school teachers of agriculture, leading to the Bachelor of Science degree and the Provisional High School Certificate.

5. A special four-year curriculum for the training of high school teachers of home economics, leading to the Bachelor of Science degree and the Provisional High School Certificate.

6. A four-year industrial arts curriculum, leading to the Bachelor of Arts degree and the Provisional High School Certificate.

7. A four-year public school music curriculum, leading to the Bachelor of Arts degree and the Provisional High School Certificate.

8. A four-year applied music curriculum, leading to the Bachelor of Arts degree and the Provisional High School Certificate.

9. A five-year curriculum for high school teachers, leading to the Standard High School Certificate and the Master of Arts degree.

10. A curriculum for administrators and supervisors, leading to the Provisional Certificate in Administration and Supervision.

11. A five-year curriculum for administrators and supervisors, leading to the Master of Arts degree and the Standard Certificate in Administration and Supervision.

12. A curriculum leading to a certificate for attendance officers.

13. A four-year arts and science curriculum leading to the Bachelor of Arts or Bachelor of Science degree, but with no privilege of certification.

14. A graduate curriculum, leading to the Master of Arts degree in certain professional and academic fields.

The termination of graduate work in 1936 meant that three of the curricula had to be discontinued. An indication of academic progress was the fact that only the curriculum for the Provisional Elementary Certificate required less than a four-year degree program. A noticeable change was the decline in the language requirement. It was not required in some programs unless the student elected to get a B.A. instead of a B.S. degree, and in some others an option was provided for language or mathematics. The arts and science curriculum, which carried no certification, required six to twelve hours of a foreign language, depending upon the amount of high school work done in that area.[3]

The most significant change in Western's academic offerings during the 1930s was the addition of graduate work. It was the next step in Cherry's plans for the school's academic growth, and he moved to implement it in 1931 despite strong protests. President Donovan of Eastern had told a meeting of registrars in 1929 that one of the greatest dangers to teachers colleges was the attempt to offer graduate work before they were really ready to do so. He believed that few teachers colleges could make adequate preparation for graduate work in less than twenty-five years, but he acceded graciously to Cherry's determination two years later. "While I would prefer, personally, to wait a while before beginning such a course—nevertheless, I have no objection if you think the time has arrived when you should undertake graduate work at Western."[4]

Predictably, the most determined opposition came from the University of Kentucky, which claimed that the other state schools were not prepared to offer valid graduate work and that their efforts to do so would harm the program at Lexington. Dean Grise had recommended in 1929 that Western offer enough graduate work to fulfill its responsibilities in the training of school administrators whose requirements were being increased. He repeated the recommendation two years later, President Cherry endorsed it, and the regents voted to initiate an M.A. program for school administrators and supervisors in the 1931 summer school and to support it with ten thousand dollars for additional books. The faculty voted unanimously for the program at its May 12 meeting, and it was approved by the Normal Executive Council. Cherry and Grise defended the program against criticism, most of which came from Lexington.[5]

The only major allowed in the new program was in school administration and supervision. At least sixteen of twenty-eight hours had to be taken in the major; the other twelve were taken in one or two minor fields. Minors were available in biology, economics and sociology, English, history and government, Latin and mathematics. The only entrance requirement was the presentation of a bachelor's degree with a major or its equivalent in education. No grade point average was specified. A thesis was required, for which four hours credit was granted, and a comprehensive examination, oral or written, was taken after the thesis was approved.

Hostility to the program might have abated had it remained limited to the one major and attracted few students. But the new program failed on both counts. Sixty-one graduate students registered in the summer of 1931; the 1931-32 enrollment was 40 for the fall semester, 38 for the spring semester, and 74 for the summer session. In 1932-33 the enrollments were 42, 56, and 82 for the same periods. The graduate program attracted 435 students during its 1931-36 lifetime; 114 of them had earned the M.A. degree before the program was terminated. The number graduating increased from 12 in 1932 to 50 in 1936. Such growth, compounded by that at the other teachers colleges, threatened to siphon off an appreciable number of students from the University of Kentucky.

And Western did not remain content with just one major for administrators. By the time the 1933-34 catalog appeared, a curriculum for high school principals' certification had been added to that of administrators and supervisors, and some high school teachers "who desire to give themselves a more thorough and extensive preparation" in their teaching area were allowed to major in those fields. In addition to education, students could major in biology, English, history and government, and mathematics. Minors were available in those fields and also in chemistry, economics, and Latin.[6]

Western's graduate program received a qualified endorsement in 1933 from the Griffenhagen and Associates' study of Kentucky's education. The report recommended dropping mathematics because of insufficient faculty qualifications and because only three minors were enrolled in the spring of 1933. With eleven registrations history should be watched carefully, and education needed more than two doctorates on the faculty. With only thirty-five thousand volumes, many of them outdated and nearly all selected for undergraduate instruction, the library was called inadequate. Western should not expand its inexpensive, limited program, but, the report concluded, "this college should serve the needs of the western portion of the state for graduate instruction." The Southern Association questioned the validity of the program and requested a special report on it by September 15, 1934. "Many of your classes are quite large," wrote the executive secretary, "your faculty training is below our standards even for strictly undergraduate work, and you have heavy loads in correspondence, extension, music and other activities. Your salaries also, on a twelve months basis, seem to fall below our requirements in several instances." In his defense Cherry cited several improvements: eight new faculty members, three with doctorates; a maximum teaching load of sixteen hours; salary increases of 12 percent for 1934-35; and the professional education nature of the work.[7]

The fate of Western's graduate program was decided when the General Assembly created the Council on Public Higher Education in 1934. The Normal Executive Council, established in 1906, had consisted of the superintendent of public instruction and the presidents of the two Normal schools; two other presidents were added after the creation of Morehead and Murray. Despite some bickering, the body had functioned reasonably well in resolving problems and coordinating efforts. In 1928 the dean of the College of Education at the University of Kentucky was invited to meet with the council as a nonvoting member, and in 1932 President McVey was asked to join the group. The teachers colleges could not ignore the University of Kentucky, but its influence was somewhat indirect. Then President McVey secured passage of an act that altered that relationship and gave the university a major role in determining the policies of higher education in Kentucky.[8]

The new Council on Public Higher Education consisted of the state superintendent of public instruction who was the chair, the presidents of the four teachers colleges, the president of the University of Kentucky, the dean of the College of Education at the University, one member of the Board of Regents from each teachers college, three trustees of the university, and two members of the State Board of Education. One function was "to coordinate the work and determine the curricular offerings" of the five white schools, in addition to determining fees and admission requirements and recommending budgets. The legislature did not provide adequate funding, and prior to 1950 the council usually ignored several of its assigned functions. The one area in which it was active was teacher training. Since the 1934 General Assembly required a five-year curriculum for permanent certificates, the council was in a position to deal with the graduate program at the teachers colleges.[9]

President Cherry viewed these developments with alarm and dismay. Initially he feared the creation of a board that would infringe upon the autonomy of the individual boards of regents. "I have felt for some time and with reason that there is a deliberate attempt being made to check the influence of the Teachers Colleges," he wrote a friend in early 1933, "building a wall and prescribing their area and the field in which they will do work in the future." He clashed with McVey and others over the issue of graduate work at a meeting of the Educational Commission in mid-January 1933. After an "intense, good-natured but sometimes militant discussion," the report was sent back to committee. Convinced more "than ever before that the University is trying to control the educational policies of the Commonwealth," Cherry lobbied intensively to gain the support of anyone who might be able to affect the decision. After the council was established by the 1934 act, Cherry worried about the danger of a too powerful executive secretary. "If we are not careful a secretary will be selected for us who will later assume a lot of prerogatives and possibly get by with it," Donovan wrote, and Cherry agreed with him.[10]

The threats became reality in 1936 when Governor Chandler made a decisive entrance into the issue. He did so, the teachers colleges were convinced, at the request of the University of Kentucky, although economy was cited as the reason. At an Executive Mansion meeting on March

16, the governor "suggested" that the colleges drop their graduate programs. After "considerable discussion" the presidents worked out an agreement which the Council on Public Education accepted at its March 24, 1936, meeting. As a sop to the colleges, the University of Kentucky agreed to discontinue its two-year teacher training programs and to offer no work in its College of Education on the freshman-sophomore level. Cherry "passed," then later asked that his vote be changed to "aye" to make it unanimous "with privilege of taking it up later." Cherry hoped to change the governor's mind, and he hoped Western would be allowed to continue graduate work even if the other three teachers colleges were not. But Regent Judge F.J. Pentecost lobbied with Chandler (who "thinks he understands it better than I do") and concluded "that he was not open for any persuasion at this time."[11] And so graduate work on the Hill was terminated in 1936.

This defeat was one of the most discouraging moments in Cherry's long academic career, but he saw it as the loss of a battle, not of a war. "I believe the graduate work will come back to Western," he told a sympathizer; "in fact, I know it will some day, if not very soon." As he told his old friend Guilliams, "Western is still going forward challenging those individuals that seem to be foes to educational advancement and it will be doing this as long as it has life." The next year Cherry cautioned Grise not to be too emphatic in suggesting that Western might confine graduate work to education alone if allowed to resume it. "I have no doubt whatever that the day will come when we shall do graduate work in a broader field than education alone."[12] Had Cherry lived, resumption of graduate work would almost certainly have been his next major battle.

The battle for graduate work was temporarily lost, but an even more serious struggle was the effort to cope with the problems caused by the Great Depression. The existence of Western may not have been in jeopardy, but every aspect of the institution was affected by the most severe depression the country had ever experienced. Although the crash of the stock market is usually cited as the start of the economic crisis, the general economy was affected more gradually. As the economy declined tax revenues fell, and state institutions found their budgets curtailed.

The fiscal crunch hit Western in the 1931-32 budget year. In 1930-31 Western had a total income of $990,456.44. The state treasury supplied $525,344.44, the capital construction appropriation was $250,000, and local receipts came to $215,112. A year later the total had plunged to $571,727.92, a decline of 42 percent. Nor did the decrease stop there. In the fiscal year 1933-34 Western's total income was $396,876.80, and by 1936-37 it had increased only to $503,787.51, still far under the 1930-31 figure. The decreases came in all three broad categories of income. The state appropriation for current operating expenses decreased to a low of

$253,433.97 in 1933-34; by 1936-37 it was still only $307,220.96. Western received no capital construction appropriation after 1930-31 until 1936-37 when $10,000 was voted. The local receipts plummeted to $143,442.83 in 1933-34, then rose to $186,566.55 in 1936-37.[13] Cherry's administrative abilities were severely tested as he tried to cope with the emergency.

One problem was that in times of fiscal exigency, the state administration seemed to view higher education as the first place for extensive cuts. When Governor Ruby Laffoon called a meeting of the presidents to tell them that their budgets were to be cut 10 percent, Eastern's Donovan asked if all agencies were to be cut by that amount, including the office of the governor? Laffoon replied that other agencies could not operate with a cut of that magnitude. Neither could the colleges, Donovan retorted in an impassioned protest. "When I sat down completely exhausted from my anger," Donovan reported, "President H.H. Cherry jumped to his feet quite as angry as I was and he took up where I left off. He said he would stump the state and denounce such an action if our budgets were cut." Other presidents then joined the protests, and the draconian cut was temporarily averted.[14]

But drastic action would have to be taken locally, and by April 1932 President Cherry had formulated a plan to supplement what had already been done. He discussed its details with the faculty at a special called meeting on Monday evening, April 11. The minutes reported, "It was heard with interest." Dr. Stickles's motion that the faculty endorse the plan and pledge full cooperation passed unanimously. Three days later the Regents also endorsed Cherry's proposals.

They were based firmly upon continuation of the school despite rumors that it would close. Summer school might be reduced in length, and it might have to be discontinued in 1933. Every possible economy would be made: purchases would be held to an emergency level; capital construction would halt; maintenance and utility costs would be reduced, although every effort would be made to prevent actual deterioration of facilities. Nonessential classes would be eliminated; more students would be enrolled in classes; teaching loads would be increased above accreditation standards; less qualified teachers might be used. Everyone would take a salary cut, and some twenty-five to thirty positions would be eliminated. Cherry hoped to cut the general operating expense of $12,000 a month to $8,000 and to reduce the 1931-32 salaries of $413,000 to $309,000. In the face of an anticipated enrollment decline of as much as 25 percent, he recommended an increase in the student fee from $6 to $10. One of his problems was the uncertainty of the state funding.

Cherry succeeded in getting an appropriation of $445,000 in the 1932-33 appropriations bill, but when the governor vetoed that section, the colleges were thrown back upon the uncertain millage percentage. The inheritance tax had almost disappeared, Cherry moaned; "It seems that all of the rich men refuse to die or else are broke." The millage percentage was changed to a biennial appropriation in 1934, which made successful lobbying with the General Assembly all the more essential.[15]

Every part of the college was hit by the enforced economy moves. Sharp reductions were made in the faculty, especially among the ones who had been employed on less than a full-time basis. Those who remained were put on a nine-month instead of an annual basis, and most of them saw their salaries slashed an average of 16 percent; the president's salary was reduced from $6,000 to $5,000. The teachers who remained taught more classes with more students in them; much of the progress that the accrediting agencies had insisted on was suddenly lost. Twenty hours was a common load. Yet faculty morale remained high as its members dug in to keep the school alive. Lotta Day was in school at Columbia University when Cherry wrote that she might have to cut one or two teachers on the home economics staff. "I have the greatest faith in your judgment and fairness," she replied. "Anything you do will be entirely satisfactory with me. Even though we have a reduced staff and less salary we will put forth greater effort and hope for better results." Stickles wrote a correspondent that there was "absolutely no question" about the school continuing. "It is going to run if we have to run it with half the faculty and if all the faculty must teach with reduced wages." Nat B. Sewell, the state inspector and examiner, was "strongly impressed with the cheerful and patriotic spirit in which the management and all employees have accepted the necessary, and what we consider under the circumstances, reasonable reductions." Cherry repeatedly praised the faculty's response and even saw a positive benefit in the fiscal tribulations. "I have never seen a finer spirit in the life of the institution than exists at this time," he wrote in 1932. "There is really a wonderful attitude. Maybe we will get something out of the depression in the way of a new spirit and a re-dedication to service." Cherry did warn the faculty against comparing salaries, for he had no salary scale and he set them on an individual basis.[16]

Despite such evidences of support, there were serious consequences in addition to the overcrowded classes and overworked faculty. Some faculty members did leave as better opportunities became available, and the Western faculty became more static than was desirable. Especially harmful was the long duration of the general freeze on salaries. In 1934 the dean received $4,800, the head of the history department $4,500, and the head of the English department $3,700. In 1943 these three key figures received exactly what they had ten years earlier. James P. Cornette, a member of the English department since 1930, was considered the sure successor to Gordon Wilson when the latter retired. But Cornette became dean at Baylor University in 1945 "simply in order to keep from starving to death." His was only one of the personnel losses that Western could ill afford.[17]

The lecture series, one of the few projects other than buildings on which Cherry lavished funds, was suspended, and several telephones were removed from the twenty-nine extensions that by 1933 had placed a phone in most campus buildings. President Cherry became noted for turning off unneeded lights, and for years after his death the conservation warnings he had printed adorned many of the campus switches. Since Western was already operating "on the smallest expense of any of the state colleges," there was little fat to trim. Cherry exaggerated little when he declared, "Even a dollar looks like a mountain." When Western entered the 1934-35 fiscal year, the "cash on hand" balance was just six cents.[18]

Depression ramifications were endless. Could teachers enroll on the Hill and pay their expenses after they got delayed pay from a county school board? The campus architect would like the sum owed him as soon as possible, for his Louisville funds were in a trust company that had closed. The failure of banks left some students without "a postage stamp to write home." Applications for jobs flooded the mail at a time when faculty and staff were being reduced. One enterprising applicant wrote as soon as he saw an obituary for a Western faculty member. Other pressures came from Frankfort—provide as much employment as possible, use Kentucky materials—and local businessmen who wanted all purchases made from their stores.[19] Cherry made every effort to meet demands. One of his most frequent sentences was, "I am sure everything will work out in a satisfactory way." And in a surprising number of instances, they did.

Despite the grimness of the times, common misery eased some of the burden. The "Depression Supper" served at the 1932 Homecoming for eight cents per meal was only one indication of the spirit with which Western met its worst financial crisis. The menu for the Social Science Club's annual banquet in April 1933 showed that humor still existed on the Hill.[20]

"New Deal" Menu
Foam Cocktail
Tennessee Valley Project
Reforestation Beans
Confident Potatoes
Sound Bank Rolls
Inflation Salad—Script Dressing
Mortgage Relief Special
Three point two coffee

President Cherry's fear that student enrollment would decline by 25 percent did not materialize. Although the depression kept some would-be students from attending, others enrolled who would not have done so had they been able to find jobs. Counted on the basis of a thirty-six weeks full-time equivalent, enrollment reached a peak in 1930-31 with 2,340 students. It declined slowly to 2,064 in 1933-34, increased, then fell to 1,960 in 1936-37 as the national economy suffered another setback and graduate work was terminated. Head counts were, of course, more impressive. During the academic year 1930-31, for example, the enrollment was 4,253. By 1933-34 Western was apparently the largest teachers college in the country. The enrollment was then 75 percent as large as that of the University of Kentucky and 64 percent larger than that of Eastern. At that time the per capita cost of educating a student for thirty-six weeks at UK was $260.02, at Eastern $168.35, and at Western $147.38. An interesting development was the increased percentage of males. By the mid-1930s nearly half the student body was male, an abnormally high figure for a teachers college.[21]

In the 1930s a few more students came from the old Eastern District, a few more came from out-of-state, an occasional student was an exotic from a foreign land. In the fall of 1934, Western had 194 students enrolled in nonteaching programs. The three largest categories were medicine (82), law (42), and engineering (40). Of the 2,748 degrees awarded from 1924 through 1937, by far the most popular major was English with 630. Other disciplines with at least 100 majors during this period were: elementary education (406), administrative education (245), history (186), home economics (162), agriculture (139), biology (131), and mathematics (118). Most of the students in the noneducation majors were preparing to teach on the high school level. The annual Senior Day in the spring developed into one of Western's main recruiting techniques. Started in 1934, it grew to 4,000 students from 160 high schools in 1939. The program featured an open house, numerous activities designed to show off Western's programs, and a picnic lunch. The attire of the "semi-nude" gymnasts, one principal charged, led both boys and girls to "blush for shame." He declared that he would not again subject his students to such an exhibition. He was, however, in a very small minority.[22]

Earning enough to remain in school was a critical problem for many students and one of the most serious issues confronting Cherry. "I left my office and went home last Friday," he wrote a former regent, "in order to escape from the many, many demands made on me from students for employment." The eating facilities in Potter Hall were the major employer of student help. Students who received only meals worked about twenty-one hours per week; the coeds who received both room and board worked thirty-five hours. One of Cherry's depression solutions was to divide a position so that two or more needy students shared the job during the course of the year. This might enable two or three students to stay in school instead of just one. But the reduced budget left too little money to employ all the students who needed help.[23]

The College Heights Foundation was available for student loans, but much of its income had gone toward the construction of the Kentucky

Building. Also, as the depression pinched, many borrowers had to post-pone repayments. The treasurer's report in 1938 showed vividly what had happened. In the three years from 1927 to 30, the foundation had made 551, 632, and 614 loans with a total value of $66,264.50, an average of $36.88 per loan. Then repayments dwindled, and in 1930-31 only 261 loans were made. Only 112 loans were negotiated in 1933-34, and al-though the average loan that year was $37.96, the total for the year was only $4,251.65. Both the number of loans and the total lent increased gradually, and in 1937-38 the 651 loans amounted to $24,072.29, both figures being new annual records for the foundation. Repayments, which were vital to the revolving fund, reached a peak of $17,117.88 in 1930-31, then declined sharply to $4,449.50 in 1932-33. Then an increase began, and in 1937-38 the loan fund received $18,928 in repayments. Overall, by July 1, 1938, the College Heights Foundation had lent $202,012.25 and had been repaid $166,699.42.[24] Hundreds of students had been able to remain in school because of these small loans.

The advent of the New Deal's alphabetical agencies brought federal aid to the campus that helped hundreds of students continue their college work. Western's only previous experience with federally sponsored pro-grams, other than Smith-Hughes work, was the veterans' training pro-gram after World War I. The regulations and reports of the 1930s were irksome, but the funds were welcome. And so was the work that students performed in every part of the campus. Professors had some clerical help for the first time without seeking such assistance in the president's office.

The Federal Emergency Relief Administration (FERA) program start-ed on the Hill in February 1934 with L.T. Smith in charge. Limited at first to 10 and then 12 percent of the student body, students who qualified on the basis of need and grades could earn as much as fifteen dollars per month at the rate of thirty cents per hour. Two weaknesses of the program were the limited number of positions—157 in the fall of 1934, far short of the demand—and the absence of any aid during the summer. Political influence was often used in an effort to place individuals, and Cherry got most of those requests. Placement might appear easy, he complained, "but it really takes an expert to make these decisions without friction and without offending individuals who have influence."[25]

In 1935 FERA was discontinued as the National Youth Administration (NYA) was established under the auspices of the Works Progress Admin-istration (WPA). The requirements, limitations, and use of the NYA pro-gram were almost identical with those of FERA. To stretch funds as far as possible, students who could get by on less than fifteen dollars a month had their employment curtailed. By the fall of 1937 Western employed 180 students in the program, and the college was able to do many things that otherwise would have been left undone. As always, there were disap-pointed applicants, and L.T. Smith refuted a charge that the program was being used to provide jobs for athletes. Of the 230 student workers in 1935-36, only 10 or 12 had been athletes. The NYA program continued on into World War II on a reduced scale; then it was converted in a shop training course for war workers.[26]

The depression imposed handicaps on many students, but as one of them put it, "I didn't know I was deprived because everyone else was deprived and it made us even." Amusements tended to be of the inexpensive sort with an occasional splurge on a downtown movie for a big date. When the Capitol, "Bowling Green's Deluxe Theatre," opened in 1939, its air conditioning may have attracted more attention than the films it showed. Cars were more numerous than during the 1920s, but most students continued to walk nearly everywhere they went. Dancing had become acceptable, and the larger affairs were held in the decorated gymnasium. Fraternities continued to be barred, but the 1930s saw the start of off-campus groups. The Barons, organized in January 1934, were the first. Their existence was a widely known secret, but it was considered somewhat daring to belong to such an undercover group. The Barons and other off-campus organizations formed the nucleus for the fraternity-sorority system of the 1960s.[27]

In the 1930s Western still had no student union except for the Cedar House, but some off-campus spots attracted students. The Goal Post, "The Hub of the Hill," had the best location, just across the street from the main classroom building. In 1936 the menu included jumbo chocolate malted milks, banana splits (three dips), homemade pie (big slices), hot cakes with syrup, and delicious chili, each for ten cents. A regular dinner cost twenty-five cents, or one could get six hamburgers for that price. Toward the end of the 1930s the Goal Post became crowded during chapel hour, and it was the place to be during the evenings. Some of its habitués even made a pretense of studying there. Jam sessions were common on Saturday nights with such local groups as the Red and Grey performing. The Western Lunch Room at the Russellville Road end of Fifteenth Street was less sophisticated, but it had the advantage of being the campus bus stop for all the lines serving the city. Tichenor's lunchroom was especially noted for its pies.[28]

Students still depended upon campus events for much of their social life. The classes were becoming less active, but in 1936 there were twenty-six campus organizations, and many students belonged to at least one or two of them. Musical programs and athletic events were numerous and usually well attended. A student who was taking a full academic load and was active in an area such as music had little time for other activities. A concerned Wisconsin mother wrote President Cherry in April 1936 about her "determined, ambitious" daughter who "drives herself to accomplish what she sets out to do." She enclosed her daughter's letter in which she outlined her daily schedule. Her Monday-Wednesday-Friday schedule was: 8:30 history; 9:30 chapel; 10:10 American literature; 11:10 methods; 12:00 lunch; 1:20 algebra; 2:20 folk dancing; 3:20 English literature; 4:20 band; 6:00 dinner; 7:00 orchestra rehearsal. On the alternate days she had: 7:30 counterpoint; 8:30 harmony survey; 9:30 chapel; 10:10 study; 1:20 music practice; 2:20 folk dancing; 3:20-5:30 orchestra rehearsal; 7:00-9:00 orchestra rehearsal. She also had rehearsals on Saturday evening and Sunday afternoon for a musical program that was to be broadcast over WHAS Louisville. "Now do you wonder why I don't weigh any more or am so tired," she inquired. "This is work, but I love it." What would her mother think of her majoring in music and math with minors in English and physical education? President Cherry talked with the girl, and they agreed that she should lighten her load by dropping algebra and folk dancing.[29]

The administrators and faculty were almost always eager to help deserving students, but control was firmly fixed in the hands of those to whom responsibility had been entrusted. Neither the president nor the dean would have understood the future cry of "student power." Students were on the Hill to study, and it was their duty to follow the prescribed rules and regulations set forth by those in authority. Dean Grise responded angrily in a memorandum to President Cherry when some teacher-students and their superintendents questioned the language requirement that imposed a considerable barrier for some of them. "Why have any requirements at all if we are going to yield to expediency every time some objector raises an issue? ... If we should listen to objections from students, every department in school would be eliminated. There is someone to object to every thing."[30]

One of the inexpensive forms of entertainment available to students was attending campus athletic events, and with the improvement of Hilltopper teams, students and faculty competed with townspeople for seats. Basketball became the most popular of the spectator sports as the Diddle legend began to develop. In the seven seasons 1930-31 through 1936-37, his teams won 141 games and lost only 34 for a winning percentage of 80.6 percent. Coach Diddle's twisted syntax and towel-waving antics on the bench attracted almost as much attention as did his winning squads. The space problem was eased temporarily with the opening of the new gymnasium during the 1930-31 season, but the relief was only temporary. The 1933-34 record was 28-8; it was the first twenty-win season for a Western basketball team. During these years Western gained recognition for tournament play. The KIAC tournament began in 1926, and the Hilltoppers won it the following year. A drought followed, but Western captured the championship again in 1932 and continued to win it throughout the rest of this period. Diddle's teams were less successful in the SIAA tournament that usually brought together eight teams from the widespread conference. Western was an entry in 1928 but did not win the tournament until 1934. Western won again in 1937. National attention was gained in 1936 when Diddle's squad met the University of Arkansas team in the National Olympic Playoffs. Unfortunately, Western lost, 36 to 43 and 30 to 38.

Most of the Western athletes continued to come from the section of Kentucky from which Western drew most of its students; a major factor in Diddle's success was his ability to recognize and develop latent ability. All Western budgets were limited during the depression years, and basketball was no exception. During the early part of the great 1933-34 season, the team made a southern trip on which it won six of seven games played in three states in eight days. The traveling squad consisted of just seven players and Coach Diddle. His teams sometimes started slowly while the football players recovered from their injuries and adjusted to the different sport. The "towering Toppers" attracted attention whenever they played in 1935-36, for the five starters averaged nearly six feet three inches in height.[31]

For the seven seasons, 1930-36, the football team was almost as successful as the basketballers. The record was 48 won, 16 lost, and 2 tied for an excellent percentage of .750 despite having had four different head coaches. James Elam had a 16-5-1 record in 1930-31, Ernie Miller was 8-1-0 in 1932, Jesse Thomas was 5-2-1 in 1933, and Carl "Swede" Anderson, who had been head coach in 1929, returned to post an 18-8-1 record in 1934-36. Western Michigan, Vanderbilt, and Centre were the teams with which Western had the most difficulty; the record was fattened against the University of Louisville, Eastern, and Middle Tennessee. Western had played Eastern as far back as 1914, Murray appeared on the schedule in 1931, but Morehead was not met until 1939.

Football spectators gazed beyond a fringe of trees to the rolling countryside south of the campus with the stately stone colonnade at their backs. It was a lovely site, and for special games as many as six thousand spectators overflowed the stands. A loudspeaker system was installed in 1935 and a press box constructed in 1937, but the field was not lighted for night games until 1946.

Senior Carroll Broderick gained national recognition in 1932 by scoring 84 points, the third best in the nation. That season's climax was a 58-0 rout of the University of Louisville in the final game. Louisville lost 45-0 the next year, then vanished from the schedule until 1946.[32]

Little attention was paid to the other sports during these years. With the partial exception of baseball, they were truly minor sports. During most of the 1930s the entire coaching staff consisted of four or five men. Most of them helped with football. Diddle had an assistant for basketball who worked chiefly with the freshmen, and they divided up the other sports. The football coach usually handled track and field; Diddle coached baseball. Tennis and golf, which was apparently started around 1935, were the true orphans of the athletic program. Membership in the W Club was restricted to men who had earned a varsity letter in football, basketball, baseball, or track. This organization, organized in the spring of 1928, became an effective supporter of the athletic program. Western had no intercollegiate sports for women during this period.[33]

The depression halted the rapid building program of the 1920s. Two projects were completed in 1931, however, as construction costs declined. The president's home was constructed on campus, and an outdoor swimming pool was built adjacent to the physical education building. It was located in a lovely spot, although the overhanging trees created a problem in keeping the pool clean. Used for both classes and recreation, the pool was reserved during the 5:30-6:30 P.M. hour for the Bowling Green public. Admission was fifteen cents with discounts ranging up to twenty swims for two dollars when payment was made in advance. "A warm soap bath," "regulation cotton suits," and rubber caps were required. "Spitting, blowing the nose, spouting water are forbidden." This pool never replaced Barren River in Cherry's aquatic affections, but he was very proud of it.[34]

The last major building completed during the Cherry administration was the large classroom building that bears his name. Recitation Hall, built in 1888 of materials "second rate at best," had been over-used and under-maintained. A 1933 report was critical of the twenty-five classrooms, including two or three in the attic, that were poorly arranged, poorly lit, and poorly ventilated. As many as six teachers shared one of the sixteen offices, and the five labs were not equipped for serious work. The only storeroom was in the attic, and the building had only two toilets. In the 1933 spring semester, 97 percent of the classrooms were used from 7:30 A.M. to 4:10 P.M., and several classes met at 4:20 P.M. The interior halls were so small that outside porches had to be used for passageways. The building was a firetrap, held together by ivy and tradition. Something had to be done, but other needs in the 1920s had been even more pressing.[35]

In 1933, since state funds were not available to replace Recitation Hall, the regents approved an application to the Public Works Administration and employed John B. Rodes and Rodes K. Myers, two of Bowling Green's best known attorneys, to deal with the legal requirements. State legislation in 1934 eliminated some of the barriers toward securing approval, but Western had difficulty in fighting through the maze of bureaucratic red tape. Cherry was furious when Western's application was passed over but some other Kentucky schools received approval. "My program is to go out and set the leaves on fire in Kentucky," he stormed. "I am not going to stand for it. I will get me an automobile, a talking automobile, one with a loud speaker, and I'll go myself." He enlisted the aid of Kentucky's members of Congress and the governor, and, although details had to be resolved, a new building was assured before the end of 1935. The federal government contributed $252,819 as a grant and agreed to purchase $309,000 in 4 percent bonds to be repaid from student fees over a thirty-year period. As it developed, Almstedt Brothers and J.J.B. Hilliard and Sons of Louisville purchased the bonds at a $5,000 premium.[36]

While problems were being overcome, Captain Davis and a faculty committee worked on plans for what would be Bowling Green's largest building. The existence of the unfinished Kentucky Building made it possible—barely—to tear down old Recitation Hall and use its commanding site for the new structure. Hasty, temporary modifications in the Kentucky Building made it usable for classes, although a teacher in the main hall might be flanked by other classes that were separated only by thin partitions, stopping well short of the ceiling, that shut out sight but not sound. Classes conducted there must have reminded some of the old-timers of the once famous blab schools. The materials salvaged from Recitation Hall were later used for other campus construction, notably the Music Building that was completed in early 1939.[37]

Work on the new building progressed rapidly with the usual quota of problems. The use of local stone, which would have helped Warren County employment, had to be abandoned when the PWA authorities determined that out-of-state stone was cheaper. Laying the cornerstone occurred late in the afternoon of October 27, 1936, with Dr. Earl Moore describing the event to the WHAS (Louisville) radio audience. It was, President Cherry said, "a day of which many of us have dreamed—a day that is conspicuous and prophetic in the life of Western as we meet to lay the cornerstone of a building, representative alike of the need of the hour and the hope of the future."[38]

Cherry Hall opened for classes on September 22, 1937. By then there was no dissent over its name, for Western's first president was dead.

Henry Hardin Cherry had become sixty-six the year "Normal School" disappeared from the school's title. The end of a school year often found him exhausted, but a few days at his Barren River cottage or a longer stay in Florida restored his vigor. An exhaustive checkup by a Louisville specialist in early 1933 revealed "nothing fundamentally wrong" with his health. He was more portly than he had once been, and his hearing was somewhat impaired, although he blamed the latter on speakers who spoke too softly. Painful neuritis sent him to Hot Springs, Arkansas, for treatment in 1936, but his stamina and energy continued to amaze much younger colleagues.[39]

In view of his advancing years, there were frequent rumors of his retirement. Intellectually, Cherry recognized the inevitability of that day, but there were always obstacles to be overcome and dreams to be fulfilled.

He admitted, "I cannot think of anything that would give me as much of a thrill as to have this experience." Indeed, he added prophetically, "I am really thinking I will die in my present position as I see no way of excavating myself at this time." A.L. Crabb was one of many who encouraged Cherry to remain in his Van Meter office. "You have no right to resign nor to die before the close of the session of 1939," Crabb admonished his longtime friend, "at which time you will have served longer than any other American college president. ... After that, you can resign or die peacefully without any remonstrance from me. Personally, I don't see you in the president emeritus capacity." Yet the years were pressing on, and Cherry gradually shed some of the burdens he had carried for so long. Grise, Canon, Schneider, and Ford relieved him of some duties, and young Kelly Thompson was proving adept at filling in wherever needed. Most major departments had heads with extensive experience who could be counted on for efficient operation of their areas. President Cherry retained control of the school in its every phase, but he said in 1936, "I have given half of my life to this work, but I am now withdrawing and sending others out."[40]

Cherry also gradually relinquished some of the activities off the Hill that had once taken up much of his time. A Methodist who had little concern for denominations, Cherry taught in the Sunday school until he gave it up in the late 1920s. His church association declined to the point that in a jocular mood he told the faculty in early 1937, "Even the preacher doesn't know I am a member, but I am going to stay in the Methodist Church if they will let me." Also a longtime member of the Bowling Green Rotary Club and once its president, Cherry resigned from that organization in 1931. The treasurer expressed the regrets of the club over losing him but requested his back dues of $55.25. As he moved into the 1930s and his late 60s, Cherry declined many of the requests for speeches that he would once have accepted as an essential part of public relations. He served as president of the Kentucky Educational Association in 1926-27 but thereafter took a less active role in the organization he had strongly supported. But he made sure all members of the Western faculty were KEA members.[41]

Changes in the faculty made Cherry aware of the passage of the years. Of the dozen faculty members who taught in that long-ago spring term of 1907, only Cherry remained after the retirement of Alexander in 1930. Craig, Stickles, Clagett, Wilson, Grise, and Ford were among the old timers who were still active, and Miss Mattie still ran the presidential office with her usual efficiency, but all of them were aging. If any one thing impressed Cherry with the inroads of time, it was the deterioration and death of his old teacher and friend, A.W. Mell, in December 1931.[42]

The aging of many faculty members convinced Cherry that a retirement program had to be provided. The state did not have a retirement system for teachers, and few faculty members had saved enough from their meagre salaries to provide for retirement needs. Some had remained in the classrooms too long for their good or that of their students. In 1934, acting upon Cherry's recommendation, the regents adopted a retirement plan that allowed the president to retire faculty members. A faculty member who was seventy years old with at least fifteen years at Western was relieved of regular duties, but would perform such duties as the president might assign. The pay would be 20 percent of the salary received at age seventy, plus an additional 1 percent for each year served at Western.[43] The benefits were small, but they provided a degree of security that the faculty had never had.

Cherry often complained of being nearly destitute, especially when approached for donations. Being president of Western "has about wrecked me financially," he complained in 1927; he had had considerable property in 1905, but he owned practically none twenty-two years later. In fact, he had invested in selected stocks over a period of years, and in Perry Snell's Florida real estate enterprise. In 1936 he decided to construct several small houses and apartment buildings on the east side of Normal Drive just below the Hill. Construction began on Colonial Court before the end of the year, and the project was well advanced before his death. This court was to be his retirement home and a main source of his retirement income.[44]

The retirement of some faculty members and the departure of others for various reasons meant that some replacements were necessary. Although department heads and the dean were usually consulted, Cherry continued to be the final judge in selecting people who would become a part of Western. And he retained his ability to sell them on Western and its future. Walter Nalbach graduated in 1933 with a major in industrial arts, taught in a Louisville junior high school in 1934-35, then accepted L.T. Smith's offer of a summer job working on cabinets for the Kentucky Building. When he declined Smith's offer of a position because of prior commitments in Louisville, Cherry sent for him. The young man entered Cherry's office with his speech of rejection prepared, but Cherry started telling him about his future at Western. Finally, Nalbach recalled, "He got up and I got up, he shook hands with me and said, 'Young man, I'll see you this fall. Your salary will be $140 a month for twelve months. Next year will be $150, I'll do better if I can. Young man, we'll be looking forward to seeing you.' " When Nalbach got home he was so visibly shaken that someone asked, "What happened?" And he replied, "We're going back to Bowling Green." Cherry's salary figure was less than what he would have received in Louisville. Walter Nalbach retired from Western in 1974.[45]

As President Cherry entered the last years of his long tenure, his resiliency, as well as his stamina, continued to amaze his associates. He simply did not accept a reverse or a defeat as final. Stopped at one point, he began to look for some alternate route to his objective. People who knew him well were convinced that he was at his best when confronted by apparently insurmountable barriers. In February 1931, he experienced one of the most embarrassing moments of his life, one that might well have ended his presidency, when he was arrested in Louisville for operating a motor vehicle while intoxicated. Police filed the charges after Cherry's car collided with another vehicle at Fourth and Walnut streets. Mayor William B. Harrison quickly arranged for "parole" and supplied his official car for transportation, and the police court judge bonded Cherry $100 for an appearance on February 28. In a public statement Cherry denied that he was intoxicated or that he had a bottle of whiskey in his pocket.

The story attracted national attention and was featured on the front pages of the state's major newspapers. Then on February 26, two days before the hearing, without notification to the arresting officers and after the regular session of the court adjourned, Cherry appeared in the almost empty courtroom, was found guilty of an amended charge of a traffic violation, and paid a fine of three dollars. This expeditious disposition of the case attracted as much attention as the original charges. It led to several editorials and numerous letters to editors, as well as a massive outpouring of supportive letters to Cherry himself. Most of his correspondents refused to believe that the charges were true, and many of them were highly critical of the newspapers for even printing the story. "I think it is a damned outrage that they will print a thing like this about a man like you," fumed a Louisville friend. "I feel that the press has been manifestly unfair to you," H.L. Donovan assured his presidential colleague. "I hope that you will have the courage to ignore it and not let it affect you in any manner whatsoever." Months after the incident, J.M. Guilliams wrote that a number of people at Berea where he was teaching had asked if Cherry would not have to resign. The doughty colonel's reply was: "Cherry drunk six days a week and sober one day a week will give Western more true inspiration and determination to do more and more for childhood in Kentucky than all the other college presidents of the state can accomplish working seven days a week." He added with obvious satisfaction, "My reply has seemed to settle the discussion in every instance."[46]

Humiliated and embarrassed by "my recent unpleasant experience" but buoyed by his widespread support, Cherry decided to treat the incident as yet another of the many challenges that he had met during his years in the presidency. Instead of succumbing to the negative aspects, Cherry wrote his brother George, "I propose to make the supreme effort of my life, and I believe I shall be able to hold things together in a splendid way and go forward without any great injury to myself of [or] the institution."[47] So he resumed his efforts to cope with the depression, to secure a graduate program, and to deal with all the problems that came to his office. And always in front of him was his ever-expanding vision of an even bigger and better Western.

In July 1937 Cherry suffered severe head and body injuries in a fall at his home. He appeared to be recovering, however, until the end of the month when he became violently ill with what was diagnosed as cerebral meningitis. He died at his campus home on Sunday, August 1. Special chapel exercises were held on Monday, and the public funeral service was conducted in the Van Meter auditorium on Tuesday morning. Following private services that afternoon, he was buried in the Fairview Cemetery.[48]

The campus community was shocked by the loss of the man who had seemed as indestructable as the rocks of the Hill. "The greatest sorrow that ever came to me outside of the deaths of my own family was the death of President H.H. Cherry," Dr. Stickles mourned, and he expressed the sentiments of many of his colleagues. Dr. Ford wrote a friend, "The experience was such a shock to us that we have done little since except to take stock of our loss. However, we are recovering ourselves, and the progress of the college is going forward nicely." No one had worked as closely with President Cherry over such an extended period as had Miss Mattie, his secretary since 1907. She, too, realized the necessity of moving on, and she told A.L. Crabb, "All of us here shall, of course, undertake to do as far as it lies within our power what President Cherry would like for us to have done." In a message of thanks to the student body, the widow expressed well the legacy that Cherry had left them: "Mr. Cherry has left in your keeping 'The Spirit of the Hill'. ... The Western of the future will be largely what you make it."[49]

As early as 1928 some of Cherry's friends had begun efforts to secure a statue of him. Led by J.R. Whitmer, they finally secured Cherry's acquiescence, the services of noted sculptor Lorado Taft and the necessary funds. Taft's last major work was finished in clay in 1934, but Cherry refused to let it be cast and erected during his lifetime. After Cherry's death the statue was cast and placed in front of Henry Hardin Cherry Hall where it was unveiled in an elaborate ceremony on a rainy November 16, 1937.[50] Eulogists praised his accomplishments and paid homage to his memory, but none was more successful in capturing the essence of Cherry's legacy than the anonymous author of an editorial in the *Owensboro Messenger:* "Henry Hardin Cherry's monument is the Hill whereon he labored for more than three decades."

Five

An Interlude
1937-1955

THE SELECTION of President Cherry's successor was a matter of great concern to everyone interested in Western's future. Whoever inherited the position would be considered one of the state's educational leaders, so the succession had more than local interest. The *Courier-Journal* called for a careful, deliberate search to find the right man; "If it takes a year to find him, Western Teachers College is well enough organized to operate under provisional management that long." There was considerable sentiment for choosing from within the organization, and the name mentioned most frequently was that of M.C. Ford. Some concerned persons believed that the time had come for Western to have a president with sound academic credentials, and Ford's University of Wisconsin doctorate was impeccable. Also, in recent years he had acquired considerable political experience as Cherry's surrogate to Frankfort. Most faculty members believed that Cherry had been grooming Ford to be his successor when he did decide to retire.[1] Such speculation was useless, for on September 1, 1937, Paul L. Garrett was elected to be Western's second president.

Kentucky's governor in 1937 was A.B. "Happy" Chandler, consummate politician who believed in rewarding friends and punishing foes. He had resented what he saw as Cherry's arrogant attitude toward governors, and he was convinced that some key people at Western were members of the Tom Rhea political faction that had so often opposed him. The governor brought Paul L. Garrett with him to Cherry's funeral, possibly with the idea of having the regents elect him that day. They did not do so, but a faculty member reported that Chandler introduced Garrett to her as Western's next president. The governor did meet with the regents that afternoon, and they decided to appoint an executive committee to run the school until a successor was named. Dean Grise, Dr. L.F. Jones, head of the Department of Education, and Mr. W.L. Matthews, director of the Training School, were the faculty members; Mrs. W.P. Drake and Mr. B.J. Borrone, the local regents, represented the board. The plan was announced to the faculty at a special meeting on August 5. Grise cried as he choked, "I miss him," and could not continue. Mrs. Drake then explained that in effect the three faculty members would replace Cherry on the executive committee that had consisted of Cherry and the two Bowling Green regents. Several leading members of the faculty pledged full support in carrying on "the work of Western." Dr. Ford declared, "It isn't the province of any employee of the college to be concerned with the successor.... We will leave these problems to our Board and express confidence in that Board to select a leader that will carry on the great work of the president. Whoever the Board selects, either in the immediate or remote future, will have the full and undivided cooperation of this faculty."[2]

The special committee had a brief tenure. When the chairman of the Board of Regents, Superintendent Harry W. Peters, was out of the state, Gordie Young, the assistant superintendent, in an unusual and possibly illegal move, called a special meeting in Frankfort on September 1. The regents met in Governor Chandler's office with Peters, Drake, Borrone, and F.J. Pentecost of Henderson present; Huston Quin of Louisville was absent. On August 31 the Lexington *Herald* stated that the purpose of the meeting was to elect Paul Garrett, and that was what transpired. The board had received an application from A.R. Holley of Marshall College, and the names of A.L. Crabb, M.C. Ford, F.C. Grise, and H.L. Donovan had also been mentioned. There had been no search, no solicitation of applications or nominations. Borrone nominated Paul L. Garrett, Mrs. Drake seconded the nomination, and Garrett was elected by a 3-1 vote. Peters, the dissenter, asked for more time for mature consideration; he refused to change his vote after the choice was made.

Predictably, the governor and the regents who had made the selection denied that any political pressure was involved, but Peters said one of the regents told him that Chandler had threatened to replace them if they balked at his decision. On August 30 Regent Pentecost sent Chandler his proxy vote since he was not sure he could attend the meeting. But, he added, his presence was not really necessary. "You told me over the telephone that Mrs. Drake and Mr. Borrone were in accord with your views as to the election of the president; that Mr. Dent who has Judge Quin's proxy, is also in accord with your views. These three votes are sufficient to elect your man." When C.S. Steed of Bowling Green urged Chandler to select someone familiar with the school, the governor replied, "There has been no secret of my endorsement of Mr. Paul Garrett for the Presidency." "That it was a political appointment nobody can doubt," reported the *Lexington Leader.* "Whatever ability and special training Mr. Garrett may have, he is Mr. Chandler's man, and was given the position for this reason. That is bad for the whole educational system of the state."[3]

Garrett's appointment came as a shock to many of the Western people. It was seen as another indication of the disfavor with which Western appeared to be burdened in Frankfort; discontinuation of graduate work had occurred the year before. There was little open dissent, however, from the faculty. They were not accustomed to any great degree of academic democracy, they were genuinely concerned about preserving the integrity of the institution, and a resignation protest was not a viable option for most of them. The governor received sharp criticism from some elements of the press and from some individuals. For example, E.R. Bradley of South Hill wrote him, "I know nothing against Mr. Garrett but his qualifications and the nature of his appointment. Your maneuvering to place him at the head of Western is a cheap political stunt, pure and simple. It is evident that the qualifications of the other applicants were not considered. Surely politics have no place in our schools. I am forced to be against any man that stoops as low politically as you have."[4] Unfortunately, politics had often played a major role in the state's educational system on all levels. The manner in which he secured his appointment was one of the handicaps facing Western's second president.

Paul Loos Garrett was born in Waddy, Shelby County, Kentucky, on November 2, 1893. After attending the local schools, he earned an A.B. degree at Georgetown (Kentucky) College in 1914 with majors in history and political science and an M.A. in 1935 with majors in psychology and education. He did more graduate work at the University of Chicago and the University of Kentucky, and in 1938 Georgetown College awarded him an honorary LL.D. Garrett's career had been in school administration except for service with the 325th Field Artillery in 1918-19. He went overseas too late to see active service, but the American Legion became one of his most important associations. After holding positions at Crittenden, Campbellsville, and New Castle high schools, he became superintendent of city schools at Versailles in 1924. There he became a close friend of A.B. Chandler, an ambitious young coach-teacher who was already on the staff. In February 1937 Garrett took a leave of absence to serve in Chandler's administration as director of the Division of Personnel Efficiency in the Department of Finance. In 1921 Garrett married Virginia Ryland Ellis of New Castle; they had three sons. Garrett was a staunch Democrat, a Baptist and a Rotarian.[5]

Garrett became president under difficult conditions. Many Westerners, both on the Hill and off it, bitterly resented the imposition of a political appointee who had no previous connection with the school. The haste with which the appointment was made seemed both unnecessary and indecent. President Cherry had been a strong, domineering, sometimes flamboyant personality; Paul Garrett had an unimpressive appearance and personality. A longtime friend described him as "somewhat of a cross in looks between Will Rogers and a fellow who had just come into town dressed up for a Saturday visit." Others who listened to his nasal twang saw him as the typical New England Yankee. He did not attract attention in a crowd, and he was not a good public speaker, particularly before a large audience. He was so blunt in his remarks that he often antagonized people upon first contact. He loved fishing and reading and students, and he spent more time with those loves than he did with the boresome details of administration. Garrett was notorious for his frugality. Even minor expenditures had to receive his approval, and he made little effort to improve faculty salaries. He read more than any president in Western's history, for he spent much of his time with books instead of distasteful administrative chores. The president was the first reader of most of the new books that came to the library. He read with little discrimination; "He read the best and he read trash," a friend recalled. A student complained in his 1947 diary, "I went to the library to study. President Garrett has my book checked out." Some of the most delightful chapel programs during Garrett's administration came on the occasional days when he talked about some of his current reading.

Garrett had an open-door policy, and as they got to know him both students and faculty would drop in without an appointment to discuss problems. When he put down his book, he was likely to elevate his feet to the desktop and half recline in his chair, a cigar stub in his hand. He also spent considerable time just roaming around the campus and chatting with anyone he met. He loved athletics, and he spent many hours watching practices. The president sometimes had trouble associating names and faces, and he occasionally confused faculty members of long standing. Garrett lost one capable young faculty member who went to tell him that he was declining a good offer from another school. Garrett growled, "I'm busy, but come in. You're president of the Senior Class, aren't you?" The young man immediately decided to accept the offer. Another faculty member recalled that if he went in with a request that Garrett did not want to hear, the president would start discussing something he had read or seen, then would look at his watch and say, "Theodore, I've got another meeting. See you later."[6]

Garrett overcame most of the initial hostility and skepticism that accompanied his appointment. At his first chapel meeting he said in effect: "I did not come here to fill Dr. Cherry's shoes. In my judgment, nobody can do that. I have come here to do the very best that I can do as president of Western, and I solicit your help with all my heart." Dr. Stickles wrote a friend a month after Garrett's selection, "The new man has made a very favorable impression, and we are hoping for the best." As Westerners got to know him, Garrett won the liking of most of the faculty. In this he was aided enormously by Mrs. Garrett, an unpretentious lady who was an authority on flowers (daffodils were her favorite) and who loved to work on beautifying the campus. But many of the faculty and alumni never considered Garrett qualified for the position, and they saw little progress during his administration. "We did not go forward under Paul Garrett," one faculty member explained. "We were sort of stagnated at that time." Yet Garrett was their president, and most of the faculty were loyal to him and the office he held even if they sometimes longed for more dynamic leadership.

Garrett was pleased by the cooperation he received. "The job has been difficult," he wrote a year after accepting the position, "but it has been made pleasant by the magnificent cooperation of members of the faculty, of the people of Bowling Green, and members of the alumni group." He had the assistance of a competent, well-trained team of administrators and great continuity in the leadership of the major departments. But he did operate under some severe handicaps. Kentucky did not emerge from the depression until World War II, and funding for higher education continued to be inadequate. The war struck Western such a devastating blow that some people feared the school would have to close. Afterwards, the postwar boom in enrollment created critical problems. The loss of a son in a 1946 accident affected Garrett more deeply than many people realized. "Frankly," he told a friend, "Pete's death left so big a hole in Virginia and me that I have left many things undone which I, under ordinary circumstances, would have attended to. The work of administration here at the college too has been much harder than in the old days."[8] During his last years Garrett was debilitated by a series of illnesses and accidents that left him in poor condition to cope with the growing responsibilities of the presidency.

The completion of Cherry Hall gave Western the best classroom facilities in its history. Except for biology, agriculture, home economics, physical education, military science, and music, all academic departments were based in Cherry Hall. It proved adequate for years to come as enrollments remained relatively stable until the war years, when they declined.

Campus construction was limited during the immediate prewar years. Because of the need for classroom space while Cherry Hall was being constructed, additional work had been done on the Kentucky Building, and it was completed in 1939. With at least partial economic recovery, some of the dormant pledges were paid, and President Garrett secured a $37,800 grant from the Public Works Administration. The state attorney-general ruled that Western could borrow $34,000 in anticipation of capital funds that would become available on July 1, 1939, and two of the local banks agreed to lend the money at 3 percent interest. On December 23, 1938, the regents accepted the bid of $79,089 from the F.G. Gorrell and Sons Company of Russellville for completion of the structure. The work went rapidly, and the building was dedicated on Founders' Day, November 16, 1939. For the first time the Kentucky Library and Museum had reasonably adequate quarters. Funds were not available to furnish all of the building at that time, but the Kentucky Building housed some of the finest collections in the state.[9]

The book collection was enhanced by the assistance provided by the Tracy W. McGregor Fund. In 1933 Mr. McGregor of Detroit established a fund to help some colleges acquire rare Americana. Western applied in 1936 and was one of fourteen colleges in the nation to receive a grant. It provided five hundred dollars for each of the next ten years, and the College Heights Foundation matched that sum. Under the capable direction of Mrs. Mary T. (Leiper) Moore, these special funds brought numerous rare materials to the collection. Miss Gabie Robertson continued her indefatigable collecting, and the library soon attracted outside scholars as well as Western students in search of primary research materials.[10]

When the museum moved into the Kentucky Building, its accession list recorded 2,258 items, not counting some 5,000 or more Indian relics. The news of the move spurred additional gifts, and over 800 items were added during the first year. The first special exhibit, a traveling collection of contemporary handwoven textiles, was shown in May 1940. With the assistance of labor provided by the Works Progress Administration, Gayle Carver was able to make a start toward building display cases and cataloging the collection. Despite a limited staff that curtailed visiting hours, an estimated thirty thousand visitors entered the Kentucky Building during its first year. Carver often called particular attention to the four columns that graced the front of the building. Approximately thirty-two feet high, each was turned from one piece of oolitic limestone from the local White Stone Quarries.[11]

The construction of a music building eased a critical space problem for that department. Using some materials salvaged from the Recitation Hall and aided by a WPA grant, it was a three-story structure located between West Hall and the swimming pool, below the football field which it faced. Despite the usual delays, the music department moved into its new home during the Christmas vacation in 1939. A recurring problem following heavy rains was the flooding of the basement.[12]

Student registration declined during the decade of the 1930s and the early 1940s. The peak headcount of 4,253, reached in 1930-31, had fallen to 2,909 by the first year of President Garrett's administration. It remained relatively stable for two more years, then dropped to 2,446 in 1940-41. The war in Europe and this nation's rearmament program were at last sparking an economic recovery, and jobs were more plentiful than they had been for many years. The United States instituted the draft in 1940, and that soon affected registration. It was affected much more drastically when the United States entered the Second World War. Spring registration that had been 1,745 in 1940 dropped to 1,561 in 1941 and to 1,109 in

1942. The total number of students enrolled in 1941-42 was 2,023, less than half the number in 1930-31. The decline reached its nadir in 1943-44 when only 938 students enrolled during the entire year. Western went to the quarter system in 1942; the 1944 winter quarter enrollment was only 403 students, 76.4 percent of whom were women.[13]

Until the war changed the composition of the student body, it was much like its predecessors of a decade earlier. In 1939-40 women made up nearly 53 percent of the student body, an unusually low percentage for a teachers college. Almost half of the students came from within a fifty-mile radius; 87 percent came from within one hundred miles. One hundred four Kentucky counties were represented; 228 students came from twenty-six other states. The 64 students from Indiana almost doubled the 34 from Tennessee, the state that supplied the second largest number. No foreign students were enrolled that year. Ninety-four percent of the fall 1939 enrollment listed a religious preference; 40 percent of them were Baptist. The Baptists (571), Methodists (365), Christians (150), Presbyterians (136), and Church of Christ (80) were 90 percent of the total. Only 71 Catholics were enrolled.

Of the 1,745 students enrolled in the 1940 spring semester, 312 declared that they were preparing for professions other than teaching. Medicine (68) was by far the first choice, with law (43), engineering (27), and journalism (17) following in that order. Accounting and business had a total of 11, government service had 2, radio had 1, and social service just 4. Of the 1,517 students enrolled in the 1940 fall semester, only 107 (7 percent) were over twenty-three years of age. Students were placed on academic probation at the end of a semester if they had not made a C average. At the close of the 1939 fall semester, 46 percent of the freshman men and 30.6 percent of the freshman women were on the probation lists. For the entire undergraduate student body, 33.3 percent of the men and 24.3 percent of the women were on probation that semester.

Most 1939-40 students could have avoided academic embarrassment by a careful selection of their major and minor departments. The college's percentage of F's was 8.59, but only a determined student could have failed education (1.52), home economics (0.81), or military science (0.37), and art (2.87), library science (3.28), music (4.41), and physical education (2.84) would have been reasonably safe. Departments to be avoided by the less than serious or less than capable student were mathematics (30.6), chemistry (23), and history (21.8). If an A or B grade was needed, the best bets were art (75.3), music (72.2), home economics (60.5) and education (60).

The 334 graduates in 1939-40 included 182 women and 162 men. Among the 109 who graduated with the A.B. degree, women outnumbered men 71 to 38; among the 225 who received the B.S. degree, men outnumbered women 124 to 101. The graduates had majors in seventeen academic disciplines. The most popular choices were elementary education (86), agriculture (49), English (39), biology (30), home economics (19), and history (18). English (107) and history (40) were the most popular first minors.

Student life changed little during the years immediately preceeding World War II. More cars provided greater mobility, but in 1949 student George Simpson praised "a good walking date." Joan Soete wrote of the early 1950s, "Most of our dates walked us up from town; to us that was a thrill." She lived in McLean Hall, and as curfew neared one could find "a couple behind each of the colonial columns and in each nook and cranny of the OUTSIDE of the dorm; many of the steps toward West Hall and those from the parking lot were filled." Trips to Nashville or Louisville remained special events, but they were becoming more common. They included few girls who lived in the dormitories, where the regulations remained essentially unchanged. Because of economic pressures, the number and caliber of campus programs had declined, and such traditional outings as the steamboat excursion and the chestnut hunt had quietly died. Class organizations continued, but they were less active than they had once been. Campus dances were more frequent and more elaborate; the Red and Grey orchestra played for most of them. The departmental clubs continued to contribute to the social as well as the academic life of the campus. Some students belonged to several of the campus organizations.

Drama, still a part of the English department, increased its productions toward the end of the 1930s after J. Reid Sterrett took charge of the program. The music department sponsored several ensembles that appeared frequently on and off the campus in public performances—band, orchestra, glee clubs for men and women, the college chorus, a girls' sextet. Such groups also appeared frequently on chapel programs.[14]

Chapel was one of the institutions in which President Garrett made changes. Soon after taking office, Garrett commented that Henry Hardin Cherry was probably the only educator in America who could manage both a daily chapel and a weekly faculty meeting. Garrett reduced chapel to three days a week in 1938; by 1942 it met only on Tuesday and Thursday. Garrett usually presided, and his extensive correspondence relating to programs indicated his personal interest. Literary figures such as Jesse Stuart became more common; orators did not appear as frequently. When Garrett spoke he was most likely to discuss his recent reading. Gone were the inspirational speeches with which Cherry had stirred so many souls. Early in the decade Dean Grise had fumed because more and more students were going to the lunchrooms "to smoke and play cards" instead of attending chapel, and by the 1940s this trend was more noticeable. The *Herald* chided students who left as soon as the announcements were made and those who talked during the programs, as well as those who did not attend. The editor added that some members of the faculty set a bad example for the students. Such reminders would not have been necessary in earlier days. Slowly, almost imperceptibly, Western was changing.

After the war started in Europe in 1939, Dr. Stickles's current affairs talks became more frequent on the chapel schedule, as well as for town groups. His problem was always time. His knowledge of European history was so encyclopedic, and the need for background information was so vital, that he never had time to finish his remarks. As time closed in on him, he would hurry with frequent desperate glances at a stage clock to his left. And upon most occasions President Garrett would gesture for him to continue into the next class period.[15]

The slow changes did not extend to any form of student government. When a George Peabody graduate class did a survey of Western as a class project in 1936, President Cherry was initially bewildered by the questions concerning student government. Asked, "Do you have student self-government?," he replied, "Yes, students govern themselves as shown by their good behavior." When the question was clarified—"Do the students have an organization and make their own rules?"—he had a ready response. "No, I don't believe in that kind of government. Theirs is intangible, the spirit. If I wanted trouble, I'd turn the government over to the students." That attitude continued to prevail. In November 1938 when the *Herald* reported, "Wild rumors have been floating about lately about student councils and student union buildings," the editor advised caution. Such issues could be "disastrous if not handled rightly." Since Western stressed self-discipline, no student government was necessary, the school's official publication added.[16]

When Griffenhagen and Associates filed a study of Western in 1947, it recommended some means "to secure organized expression of student views on matters affecting them and the college." Garrett replied that he had never opposed student government if the majority of the students requested it, but "to date, the only interest manifested in it has been of a handful of students mostly out-of-state who were not interested in genuine student government but rather into an organization by which to make requests into demands."[17] This tradition and this administrative attitude help explain some of the student problems that developed two decades later.

Attending athletic events continued to be a major form of recreation, and in the early Garrett years basketball was the main attraction. In the years 1937 to 43 Diddle's team won 151 games and lost only 24, a winning percentage of 86.3. The streak of KIAC championships that had started in the 1931-32 season was extended to nine consecutive titles before being ended by Murray, 41-32, in the spring of 1941. That loss was avenged in the SIAA finals a few days later when Western beat Murray 45-41. The Hilltoppers then won the KIAC title again in 1941-42 and 1942-43. During the same six-year span, Western was the SIAA champion for five consecutive years, 1938-1942. The SIAA tournament was not held in 1942-43. Thanks to the winning teams and the tireless publicity efforts of Kelly Thompson, the Hilltoppers acquired a national reputation. Such teams as Bradley and Vanderbilt began to appear on the schedule, and the narrow 30-29 loss to powerful Duquesne in the NCAA tournament in 1940 attracted favorable attention. William "Red" McCrocklin became Western's first All-American basketball player in 1938, and the great pivotman, Carlyle Towery, captured that honor two years later.

The basketball highlight of this era was Western's first participation in the Metropolitan Invitational Basketball Tournament of 1942 in Madison Square Garden. Then basketball's most prestigious tournament, it featured eight of the nation's top teams. Diddle carried a ten-man squad to New York, including starters "Buck" Sydnor, "Tip" Downing, Billy Day, Earl Shelton, and freshman Oran McKinney. Two other freshman from an undefeated team also made the trip, Charlie Labhart and "Duck" Ray. Other squad members were Charlie Reuter, Ray Blevins, and Dero Downing. Blevins, a transfer from Lindsay Wilson Junior College, had seen limited service during the season, but he entered the first game against City College of New York when the usual top scorers faltered. Blevins's twenty-two points in thirteen minutes carried Western to an upset 49-46 victory. Then he added sixteen points in the defeat of Creighton University, a total matched by freshman McKinney who was also the game's leading rebounder. Neither Blevins nor the team could maintain that level, and Western lost the final game to West Virginia University, 47-45 on two foul shots in the last seconds. Blevins, McKinney, and Tip Downing made the All-Tournament team. A crowd estimated at over five thousand greeted the team and coaches upon their return home. Films of the tournament drew two large crowds to Van Meter auditorium and another one to the downtown Princess Theatre, with the proceeds going to the Navy Relief Fund.[18]

The next season the team made the first of many annual eastern swings and won more attention by defeating St. Bonaventure, City College of New York, and LaSalle. It lost little prestige later in the season by losing to the great George Mikan and his DePaul teammates 44-40. The 1942-43 schedule also included such new names as Fort Knox, Berry Field, and Godman Field as the effects of the war became more pervasive. Guards Buck Sydnor and Dero Downing provided experienced leadership, but six sophomores, McKinney, Ray, Labhart, Odie Spears, Dee Gibson, Chalmers Embry, and freshman John Oldham promised a bright future. Family illness had forced MIT hero Blevins to drop out of school.

At least twice during the season, the team played two of its lesser opponents in the same evening. Eighteen consecutive wins before the DePaul game gave Western a high national ranking and led to considerable speculation about a possible game with the University of Kentucky Wildcats with the proceeds going to wartime charity. Diddle responded, "I have never asked the University for a game and do not intend to." President Garrett's comment set the official line that would be followed consistently thereafter: "Western and the University of Kentucky have two great basketball teams and two great coaches in Ed Diddle and Adolph Rupp, and neither has to beat the other to prove to followers of basketball that these two teams are among the best in the nation." The season ended on an unhappy note when Fordham upset the favored Toppers 60-58 in a first round game in the National Invitational Tournament.[19]

When Diddle opened practice in the fall of 1943, his only experienced players were two substitutes from the previous year. During the next three years his record was 45-38 (54 percent), although he and assistant Ted Hornback may have done some of their best coaching. Success for the nation's coaches depended largely upon the availability of service men who could play, and the members of the air force unit at Western were not eligible. Players came and went so rapidly that printing programs hardly seemed worthwhile. Freshman Roy Mann scored sixteen points in the opening game in 1943; he got in one more game before being inducted in the Navy. Carroll Brooks played his final game for the College High team on January 10, 1944; he played for the Western varsity the next evening. After nine games in which he scored 85 points he went into military service.[20] Basketball continued throughout the war years, but it bore little resemblance to the teams of recent years.

Football fell victim to the war when the sport was suspended for the 1943-45 seasons. Coach Swede Anderson, who had returned to Western in 1934, continued his successful record in President Garrett's first year. Western won its first five games and was unscored upon until defeated by Western Michigan 13-7. A 7-7 tie with Murray was the only other blemish on a 7-1-1 season. Before the 1938 season Anderson became an assistant to Bo McMillin at Indiana University; assistant coach W.L. "Gander" Terry became head coach. With a small staff, coaches had to be versatile, and Terry was assisted by Diddle, Hornback, E.B. Stansbury, and Arnold "Winky" Winkenhofer. Using a single-wing offense in his four seasons, Terry had records of 7-2-0, 7-1-1, 7-1-1, and 4-5-1, a 73.5 winning percentage. His nemesis was Tennessee Tech to whom he lost three of four games. One of the most satisfying games was a loss to Vanderbilt in 1938. President Garrett thanked Chancellor O.C. Carmichael for including Western on their schedule. He hoped that the relationship would continue, although "We of course cannot hope to win against Vanderbilt, but we get a great thrill out of trying." Vanderbilt eked out a 12-0 victory, and Western disappeared from the Vandy schedule.

Football did not have the appeal that basketball enjoyed although Homecoming games usually drew crowds of five to six thousand fans. Garrett dropped the football program at the Training School in 1938, and he agreed with President Donovan at Eastern, "We are already spending too much on football," without taking on the added expense of scouting opponents. An innovation occurred at the Howard College game in 1938 when Director of Public Relations Kelly Thompson took movies of a Western game for the first time.[21] A manpower pinch developed in 1941 when only twenty freshman reported for practice. The SIAA altered its rules, the squad was increased to twenty-nine players, and four freshmen backs were added to the varsity. Despite their presence the season's record was a disappointing 4-5-1, and Coach Terry soon took a leave of absence to enter the Navy. Winkenhofer, elevated to the top position, labored through a 3-4-1 season in 1942. Players and even assistant coaches had disappeared for military service, and freshmen made up the bulk of the squad. "While they are gaining valuable experience," Winky commented wryly, "we are losing ball games." When Eastern won 18-0 on October 31 it was Western's first loss to a Kentucky team since 1934. Something was salvaged in the final game when injured John Mazola passed Western to a 24-13 win over Murray.

By the late spring of 1943, twenty-one of the twenty-nine football players of the previous fall were in military service, and the other eight were scheduled to be called up on July 1. Coach Winkenhofer was with the Red Cross, and football was suspended for the duration of the war. There was some criticism when it was not resumed in 1945, but President Garrett declared, "Western won't put a football team on the field until they can put a good team into competitive play."[22] Postwar football began in 1946.

Other sports also joined the casualty list. The construction of nine new tennis courts in 1934-35 sparked a demand for a tennis team, and one was started in 1935. It began to enjoy success after Ted Hornback, who joined the staff in 1938 as assistant basketball coach, became its coach. Track had been resumed in 1930 after a lapse of fourteen years, but it had received little attention. The football coach was usually the track coach, and most of the participants were gridders who were keeping in shape during the off-season. Coach Diddle enjoyed baseball, but his record on the diamond never matched his success on the hardwood. A golf team and a schedule were put together in 1939, but it was the most neglected of the minor sports. Boxing was not an official sport, but student Frank Griffin created his own squad and won considerable recognition for the sport. A heavyweight, he fought his way to the Golden Gloves matches in Chicago in 1940 where he lost a close decision to the ultimate division winner. As athletes and coaches departed and travel restrictions made

Table 2. Receipts and Expenditures for
Sports Programs, 1940-41

	Receipts	Expenditures
Football	5,074.20	9,400.64
Basketball	4,104.45	3,974.26
Baseball	90.00	771.19
Track	——	390.69
Tennis	——	182.49
Golf	——	100.00
Misc.	——	229.99
Total	9,268.65	15,049.99

Source: Business Office Records: Athletic Records, 1909-55.

trips increasingly difficult, the minor sports were dropped. By 1944-45 basketball was the only intercollegiate sport on the Hill. Garrett defended its continuance on two grounds: first, it contributed to school morale and spirit; second, it paid for itself.

Western did not lavish large sums upon the sports program in the prewar years, but neither did it generate much revenue. The Business Office recorded the figures shown in Table 2 for 1940-41. Coaches' salaries were not included in computing the costs. Most of them taught a full load of physical education classes; Mr. Diddle was the major exception. He "is a basketball genius but not very good at the routine teaching job," Garrett explained.[23]

Athletic scholarships were still missing from the budget. Coach Winkenhofer explained the school's policy in a letter explaining why a football player had been cut: "If an individual is good enough to make our squad and be considered as a regular, works hard and passes his school work, he will be given a job that will carry him through school, furnishing room, board and tuition; and further, if this individual should be so injured in football as to be incapacitated for the rest of his term in school, the proposition still holds good." But there was no guarantee of four years. Recruiting was becoming more intensive, and in 1939 President Donovan of Eastern protested that Western coaches had violated "a gentleman's agreement" that Bardstown should be the unofficial dividing line. "Should a large number of boys from eastern Kentucky go to Western as a result of the solicitation of your coaches, it may become necessary for us to cancel athletic relations with your college and explain to the public why we have done so," Donovan warned. Garrett replied, "My staff, as far as I know, have been to see no individual on whom they had not been requested to call," but Western could not be expected to ignore requests from potential students and alumni. He hoped to avoid serious disagreements, but Garrett gave little ground. He recognized more clearly than Donovan the changing character of athletic and other institutional competition.[24]

In 1944 President W.F. O'Donnell of Eastern protested that Coach Diddle, who had more workships available than players, had reportedly offered twin cheerleaders at London High School "all expenses except personal spending money and clothes" if they would attend Western. O'Donnell had also heard that Western had a field representative in Eastern's area. His protests fell on unheeding ears, for Anna Jo and Betty Jo Cook enrolled at Western that fall. Coach Diddle provided assistance from his basketball allocation.[25]

The size of the faculty increased during the 1930s, due in part to the standards of accrediting associations, and by the end of the decade the heavy teaching loads were not as common as they had once been. The change-of-work status plan that President Cherry had installed led to a few retirements. The passage of a state retirement program in 1938 provided an alternative to the local scheme, but Garrett saw human advantages to the Cherry plan. As he explained in 1944, "I can see where some retired members might become nuisances because of that status, but even at that I think a college should suffer some in the effort to do justice to those who have served the institution faithfully over a period of years." There was great continuity among the core of the faculty; by 1938 eleven faculty and staff members had received plaques honoring them for twenty-five years of service to Western.[26]

Next to Cherry's death, the one that most affected the faculty occurred on March 19, 1940, when Dr. M.C. Ford was killed in a traffic accident on his way home from Columbia. It was typical of him that he had made the trip to try to place one of his students. Long recognized on and off the campus for his leadership qualities and his unflinching zeal, he may well have expected the presidency in 1937. But he loyally supported Garrett, and Garrett was reputed to have rejected Governor Chandler's demand that he fire Ford and one or two others of the more politically minded faculty members.

Garrett found it difficult to force retirements, and he had told Professor Strahm, who had done so much to bring good music to the Hill and the community, to continue when he reached seventy, soon after Garrett became president. Strahm was seriously ill in 1940, but he returned to work in the summer, boasting of his smaller waistline and joking that he was working on a symphonic tone poem called "Double Pneumonia." But he could no longer play difficult passages to his own standards, and in the fall he called the president to say he would like to see him. In a typical gesture of thoughtfulness, Garrett went to Strahm's studio so he would not have to climb the hill. They agreed that Strahm would retire at the end of the academic year, but he died in late June 1941.[27]

The faculty continued to work without definitely assigned ranks and such academic embellishments as tenure and salary scales. The catalogs did not carry faculty ranks, and only the necessity of reporting the number of faculty by rank to outside agencies led to a somewhat secretive ranking. In 1939 the Southern Association was told that the 110 faculty members (including the teachers at the Training School) consisted of 16 professors, 23 associate professors, 33 assistant professors, and 38 instructors. Men outnumbered women 61 to 49, with the disparity being greatest in the two upper ranks where there were 36 men and just 3 women. Salary details remained largely subject to the president's discretion. In the fall of 1940, just before the semester began, Lillian M. Johnson of the psychology department requested a leave of absence because of illness. Garrett expressed concern for her recovery, told her that the payroll had already been made up for September. "It seems to me fair that you retain half of the enclosed check and return the other half to the college," he wrote. "If this does not seem fair to you, then return to the college such amount as does make you feel that you have received fair treatment." When she returned the entire check, he sent another one for $100: "Call it sick leave or whatever you please if necessary to salve that conscience of yours."[28]

Garrett consulted the faculty on many issues, and the formal meetings gave the faculty a role in college governance that it later lost for a considerable period. When he suggested that chapel be reduced to three days a week, he stated that any change would have to have the faculty's agreement. The formal motion was to support wholeheartedly whatever decision the president made on the issue. Even then Garrett asked for expressions of dissent: "If any of you thinks this change is bad, I earnestly request that you come to my office and put your feet under the table and tell me why you think it is bad." Garrett guarded the faculty against political interference, and he refused to interfere when a question of grades was raised.[29]

A survey in 1939-40 of the religious preferences of the faculty revealed that of the 91 included, 26 were Methodist, 24 were Baptist, and 21 were Presbyterian. Thereafter the numbers trailed off sharply: Christian, 7; Episcopalian, 4; Catholic, 2; Congregationalist, 2; and Lutheran, 2. Only 3 were listed as unknown. Eleven faculty members served as church officials and 15 taught in Sunday schools. This religious atmosphere helps explain why in 1937 a courageous editor of the *Herald* urged that play be allowed on the tennis courts on Sunday afternoons when it could not "interfere with some students attending church."[30]

Drastic changes came to the faculty after the United States entered World War II. Some went into military service, some engaged in war work, some moved to other schools where enrollment did not plummet as it did at Western.

It is easier to see the inevitability of war after it has started than before hostilities begin. Certainly, any Westerner who read the papers or listened to Dr. Stickles's chapel talks was aware of the conflict that erupted in Europe in 1939 and of the Japanese involvement on the Asian mainland. But the events that were described seemed remote from the Hill, and isolationist sentiment was strong in the United States prior to Pearl Harbor. Campus life was not drastically affected until after December 7, 1941. When word of the attack on Pearl Harbor came on Sunday afternoon, it was one of those moments of history that seem etched in the memories of those who were shocked by the news. Campus radios were eagerly sought the next day when President Franklin D. Roosevelt denounced the "day of infamy" and asked Congress to declare war. The men who listened to the speech could not but wonder how it would affect their future.

James Oshiro was the Western student who was suddenly placed in a precarious position. Born in Hawaii of Japanese parents, he lived in Japan for sixteen years before returning to Hawaii. Nine years later he was persuaded by a Western alumnus to go to the Hill. The short, slight, twenty-six-year-old student enrolled in September 1940 to major in history. His financial support from a brother-in-law in Honolulu was suddenly cut off after the Pearl Harbor attack, and no one could predict the reaction of Western students and Bowling Green townspeople. "It breaks my little heart even to think of this horrible war between two nations," James wrote President Garrett in late December; he would gladly fight for the United States, "and I am sure that God will forgive me having fought against my parents' country." Garrett asked the students to understand Oshiro's peculiar circumstances, and the only incident occurred when a drunk went to the Baptist church "with the announced intention of killing a Jap." Garrett gave Oshiro a room and a job in the president's home, and in December 1943 James Oshiro became a Western graduate.[31]

President Garrett spoke to the students in chapel on December 12 about their uncertain status. Some men had already left to volunteer for service, but he warned against a "sudden hysterical exodus" from the college. "Your government will call you systematically into its service as you are needed.... At present the hard task for most of you is to continue to make ready for better service in the war and after it by patiently and calmly continuing at your work." That advice was ignored by some, and the enrollment erosion continued. Many of the men who stayed enlisted in one of the reserve units that suddenly appeared for the different branches of service. Thereafter they were subjected to psychological warfare as rumor followed rumor in rapid succession—you'll be called up next week, next month, next year, you'll remain in school until you graduate. Plagued by such uncertainties, the formal induction notice often brought a sense of relief.

The war affected almost every phase of the institution. Classes shrank in both number and size, and women became the majority sex in most of them. Gordon Wilson combined two of the most difficult advanced courses in the department, English 300, History of English Language, and English 302, English Grammar, into one awesome course. Students who took it swore that he had omitted nothing from its predecessors; some of them credited this step with winning the war. History placed more emphasis on National and International Problems, Europe since 1914, and American Foreign Relations; and there was more interest in the geography classes that dealt with the strange areas from which V-mail letters now came. The library added such journals as *Aviation,* the *Infantry Journal,* and *Far East Quarterly.* Among the favorite books were Ernie Pyle's *Brave Men* and *Here Is Your War.* Books took longer to get and some were printed on inferior paper. Orders could still be sent to England, but twice ships were sunk that had Western orders aboard.[32]

As rubber came into short supply, the traditional bonfire with its core of old tires was omitted in the 1942 Homecoming, the last one of the war years. The Thanksgiving holiday was abandoned in 1942 to cut down on travel, and as gas rationing became more severe students and faculty found the trains crowded far beyond the limits that once would have been permitted for animals on the way to slaughterhouses. Silk stockings disappeared from the stores, and one often had difficulty finding the two pairs of shoes that could be purchased annually. Social events were curtailed, and girls often danced with each other at the parties that were held—"There simply weren't enough men to go around." As late as 1944 the weather bureau was not allowed to issue weather information that might be of help to the enemy in making long-range forecasts. The college invited service men from such military installations as Fort Campbell and Fort Knox to attend basketball games and plays as guests of the college. The head of the music department wrote a desperate school superintendent in 1942 that he had no man to recommend as a band director; the men were in service or already engaged for next year. "I do, however," he suggested, "have a most capable young lady whom I wish you would consider."[33]

Those who remained behind found that a part of their reading consisted of the delayed casualty lists. And as the war increased in intensity, more Western names appeared on the lists.

As the enrollment shrank, Garrett belatedly sought help from the federal government, which had already signed contracts with many colleges for the training of personnel. Western was geared to handle fifteen hundred students, Garrett wrote Senator A.B. Chandler, and if the number fell to five hundred, as seemed possible for 1943, "it could be difficult." Both Chandler and President William H. Vaughn of Morehead had already asked Garrett why he had waited so long to seek help, but as late as November 5, 1942, he displayed no real sense of urgency. "It has entered my mind that it might become necessary for us to consider seriously helping in the government training program," he wrote Vaughn when he inquired about Morehead's Naval Training Program. Garrett and Kelly Thompson went to Washington in the late spring of 1943 to find help. It was a trying experience. "I was in Washington four days recently," Garrett wrote a friend, "and have been in lunatic asylums that were quiet places in comparison." Senator Alben Barkley opened doors to them, and after a week's search they finally found an Air Force program that would utilize a good part of Western faculty in providing preflight training for four hundred personnel.[34]

There was one slight problem. Western had to house and feed the four hundred students and the cadre of the 321st College Training Detachment, and the only two dormitories were occupied by coeds. Will Hill, whose usual functions dealt with field work, publicity, and the booking of outside groups, within a few days relocated every girl within four blocks of the campus, and the dormitories were hastily converted for military use. Some thirty to forty girls were housed in the former Music Building near the Training School. A letter of intent was signed on March 12, 1943, and the four hundred preflight students arrived on April 3, 1943. The group changed frequently, but the total remained constant until the program was terminated on June 28, 1944. The military faculty provided 280 hours of instruction for each student, plus a few hours of dual flight training; the Western faculty provided 464 hours of instruction with the heaviest concentrations being in physics (180 hours), math (80), English (60), geography (60), and history (60). The program provided positions for the equivalent of twenty-four full-time Western faculty members. The school received $2,880 per month for the use of the quarters, $7,732 for instructional costs, and $1.07 per day for feeding each man. Because of changed requirements, the contract was not renewed when it expired. When the unit closed, Western bought a considerable amount of equipment at bargain prices. Twenty-five ROTC students were assigned to Western for a time but the school was unable to secure any other program.[35]

The presence of the trainees caused some minor problems—when they left the janitors had trouble removing the marks made by their heavy shoes—and the military red tape was often annoying and baffling. But on the whole relationships were excellent. Because of his own military experience, Garrett took a personal interest in the welfare of the military students, and everyone at Western realized that the contract had carried the school through one of the most difficult years of its history. As Garrett wrote Paul V. McNutt, head of the War Manpower Commission, "The financial contribution for housing, messing and training these students has been of great assistance in balancing our budget and in enabling the college to retain for post-war use members of the faculty who have served the institution well in the past and who will be greatly needed in the future." Not the least of the benefits was the faculty's reevaluation of its methods of instruction in light of the Air Force requirements. The trainees enlivened the social life on the Hill as their presence redressed the balance of the sexes. A Western alumnus inquired wistfully from North Africa, "I wonder if they realize how lucky they are to be at Western. I knew about 5,000 Western alumni who would give almost anything to swap places with them."[36]

By the time the Air Force trainees departed, the civilian enrollment was beginning a slow recovery as a trickle of ex-GIs began to return to the campus. The 489 students enrolled in the fall quarter of 1944 represented an 18 percent increase over the low mark of 1943, and the fall 1945 enrollment was 528. By then the Japanese war was also over, and the cry "Bring the boys home" forced a demobilization pace that was too rapid for the nation's best interests but was politically unavoidable. The winter quarter 1946 enrollment was 699, and in the spring quarter it was 966. By the fall of 1946 the enrollment had soared to 1,430, the largest number since the spring of 1941. Not only were the service men and women returning, the freshman class was rapidly returning to normal proportions. The fall quarter enrollment reached its immediate postwar peak in 1947 when 2,011 enrolled; it declined slowly thereafter as the bulge of veterans graduated until a new low of 1,370 was reached in the fall of 1953. Then the enrollment began to increase again. The peak spring enrollment for this period was in 1949 when 1,793 students registered. Western abandoned the quarter system and reverted to the traditional semesters in the fall of 1948.

Some of the faculty members returned along with the students, but there were some unfortunate losses. The nation endured a period of rapid inflation in the postwar years, and the faculty salaries, which were already low, fell even further behind the national average. In 1944 Garrett told a fellow president that he had during the past year raised one salary from $3,000 to $3,200 because the teacher was doing "an extraordinary job," but a number of faculty members were receiving exactly what they had when he became president seven years earlier. "If one of my men finds a better job past my ability to pay I help him get it and give him a year's leave of absence to see if he likes it. So far as I know there is no unhappiness in the staff under this system, and my folks are so happy here that it is not easy for other institutions to entice them away." Garrett was too complaisant about the situation, for he lost a number of teachers who would have lent strength to the faculty for years to come. Dr. J.T. Skinner left the chemistry department to go to the University of Kentucky in 1942, Dr. Guy Forman of the physics department moved to Vanderbilt in 1943, Dr. Basil C. Cole went from the biology department into private industry in 1945, Dr. James

By the early 1930s, Professor Alexander, President Cherry, and Miss McLean were the only remaining faculty members from Southern Normal.

Faculty, alumni, and friends of Western gathered in the Senior House for Western's 25th anniversary banquet in 1931.

Many elementary education majors did their practice teaching in the Model Rural School, built in 1924 and razed in 1955.

The Kentucky Building, which houses the Kentucky Museum and Kentucky Library, was put under roof in 1931 but was not completed until 1937.

The statue of H.H. Cherry, the last major work of Larado Taft, was unveiled on a rainy November 16, 1937. It stands in front of Cherry Hall (below), which opened for classes the same year. The building then housed most of the academic departments and some administrative offices.

Paul L. Garrett, right, was president 1937-1955. Garrett was a frequent visitor to the library's main reading room, pictured below about 1939. By present-day standards, student dress was still quite formal.

A field hockey class of the late 1930s enjoys friendly competition. In the background is the Model Rural School.

Below, High School Senior Day attracted a full house in 1937, although the "indecent clothing" upset at least one school official.

Potter Hall was the scene of this 1939 radio party (above). The kitchen of Potter, shown below in the same year, was the main source of campus jobs for students.

Until his retirement in 1959, Registrar Ernest H. Canon, shown above perched on a stool, personally checked every student's registration card.

Below, a standing-room-only crowd enjoyed football, about 1942. The sport was suspended from 1943 through 1945 because most players were off at the war.

Vets' Village, shown here about 1949, with the farm pavilion in the foreground, was a temporary solution to the postwar enrollment boom. The remnants of Cherryton can be seen at the base of the hill.

P. Cornette of the English department became dean at Baylor University in 1945, and the head of the music department, Dr. John Vincent, moved to the University of California at Los Angeles.

Dr. Stickles, one of the most distinguished members of the faculty, had his salary increased from $4,500 to $5,000 in 1948; he had received $4,500 as far back as 1930. At age seventy-six he was too old for a move, and many of the other senior members of the faculty were permanently settled in Bowling Green. President Garrett did not view with enough concern the loss of some exceptionally well qualified young teachers when he remarked to President Vaughn of Morehead College in May 1945, "I have not made up my mind as yet to what to ask the Legislature for. I am leaning toward the idea of requesting an increase with which to raise salaries."[37] Long-suffering teachers would have placed more emphasis upon the urgent need for salary improvements than did the president. A number of those who left Western did so with sincere regret, but they did leave. And the faculty was weaker for their departure.

Everyone agreed that the WWII veterans who returned to the Hill brought a new element onto the campus. They were older than the students were in normal years, and they were less parochial than their predecessors had been. Many of them had been exposed to foreign lands and their people, and, with the military's penchant for sending troops away from home, many veterans had at least seen parts of the United States that were foreign to them. A number of them were married or soon would be, and suddenly the college was confronted with unexpected housing problems. Most of the veterans had a serious purpose in being in school, and many of them had little interest in the typical undergraduate social activities. They spent more time studying, and those who had been Western students before entering military service made substantially better grades (up between .5 to 1.0) when they returned to the Hill. Few of them had a further interest in the military life, an attitude that made it difficult to reestablish the senior ROTC unit. A Veterans' Club, organized as early as the spring of 1945, developed a more activist approach than had been customary for campus organizations. It even discussed forming a student government, but that proposal was too radical for the day.[38]

The Servicemen's Readjustment Act of June 22, 1944, better known as the GI Bill of Rights, had an enormous and somewhat unexpected impact upon the postwar colleges and the postwar nation. Often amended, the original act provided for as much as four years of schooling with fees and books provided and a subsistence allowance of $50.00 a month for single veterans, $75.00 a month for those with one dependent. An Army study had predicted that not over 18 percent of those eligible would attend college on a full-time basis, but the national figure was 28.85 percent. Unfortunately, Kentucky at 21 percent fell well below the national average, but thousands of Kentuckians went to college who would never have done so without the GI Bill. During the academic year 1946-47 veterans constituted just over half of the Western student body, although the peak number of veterans was not reached until the following year. By then the number of civilian students was increasing more rapidly than the number of veterans. The influx of veterans skewed the usual sex distribution of the student body. In the fall of 1948 the enrollment consisted of 1,305 men and only 540 women.[39]

The nation experienced shortages of many commodities for the first year or two after the war ended, and many veterans continued to wear their military clothing because nothing else was then available. An indication of the important role they played on campus was the creation of Vets Village in the area between Normal Drive and the Russellville Pike, north of Seventeenth Street. With the departure of the Air Force men, the two dormitories were reconverted into housing for women. Most of Cherryton had disappeared as buildings spread across the south slope of the hill, and when the flood tide of GIs came to the campus there was an emergency need for housing for both married students and single men. Western's administrators joined in the mad scramble for surplus housing that the federal government disposed of at little or no cost to institutions. Family trailers were obtained from Willow Run and Oak Ridge, along with toilet and laundry facilities. By mid-April 1946, the Village included thirty-three houses, nine double-trailers, and thirty standard trailers, but there was a growing waiting list. The houses rented for $25 and $30 per month, the single trailers for $18. The units were furnished, although often in a Spartan fashion. An area was set aside where for a nominal fee students could park private trailers. By the early autumn, fifty more apartments were being prepared and ten metal barracks were on the way to help house single men. Living conditions were less than ideal—too crowded, too hot or too cold, too noisy, too little privacy—but everyone was in much the same status, and there was also enjoyment in the shared discomforts.[40]

Vets Village became a small community, much as Cherryton had been earlier, and a number of services were provided to help meet special problems. A noncredit cooking class for veterans' wives received first priority; it was offered weekly at the Training School as early as the fall of 1946. Then Lester Reeves opened the Vets Village Market in the right wing of the Agricultural Pavilion in April 1947. By then the Village had its own government, consisting of a mayor, an alderman-at-large, and an alderman elected from each of four districts. Since fire was a constant hazard, each district also elected a fire marshal. A nursery was opened in early 1947 to allow the mothers an occasional opportunity to escape from their cramped quarters.[41]

The Village housing had endured hard service before coming to campus, and after several years of use little of it was worth repairing. That area of the campus was needed for permanent construction, and before the end of the 1950s many of the temporary structures were being sold or demolished. The process was slow, and the last of the Village did not disappear until 1970.[42]

The postwar boom in enrollment, the belated realization that permanent campus housing should be provided for men as well as women, and the obvious need for a more adequate student center than the Cedar House led to a spate of new construction. With the exception of Cherry Hall, most of the construction during the prewar era had been financed by state appropriations and what money Cherry could divert from other needs. In 1945 Garrett, pondering the question of how much Kentucky with her limited resources could spend on education, concluded, "I think the problem can only be solved through Federal aid." For the time being, however, he had to depend largely upon state appropriations and bond issues.

In 1946 Western purchased the Rock House, on the corner of College and Fifteenth streets, from Sam Rabold for twenty-eight thousand dollars. Since the most urgent demand was housing for men, it was converted into a dormitory for approximately thirty-five students. Three years later when the housing pressure shifted, it became a small dormitory for women.[43]

The first major postwar dormitory, and the first one constructed in twenty years, was built below White Hall and the football field, facing the Russellville Road. Financed with a state appropriation and a loan, it housed 158 women when it opened for the fall semester, 1949. Two years later it was named McLean Hall in honor of Miss Mattie who had retired in 1945 after forty-three years as the president's secretary. With its completion, Potter Hall underwent another of its many conversions and was transformed into a dormitory for men before the fall semester began in 1949. The dormitory situation was reasonably adequate for the next few years as enrollment gradually declined from its 1949-50 peak with the departure of most of the GI generation. But a sharp increase in the student body in the fall of 1954 heralded the beginning of another, more permanent increase, and the administration moved to meet the anticipated need. Plans were developed for two dorms to be located in the vicinity of the Model Rural School, one facing Normal Drive, the other facing Sixteenth Street. Planning started during President Garrett's administration, and Kelly Thompson, the assistant to the president, did much of the preliminary work. A federal loan of $980,000 provided most of the financing, and construction began in December 1955. East and South halls opened for the spring semester, 1957, with room for 428 men who paid $3.50 per week for double occupancy. And Potter Hall was then reconverted into a dormitory for women.[44]

Among the less expensive construction projects during the Garrett administration was a modern dairy barn on the college farm to house the profitable Jersey and Holstein herd of one hundred head.[45] Despite wartime restrictions on construction, materials were made available for such an essential purpose. Many other campus improvements that were urgently needed had to be postponed.

One of Garrett's frequent complaints was that Western was not receiving a fair share of the limited funds for capital construction. He compiled figures to show that since 1930 only Morehead had received less than Western; both Eastern and Murray had received more. One possible reason for this neglect was the success that Cherry had achieved in erecting buildings from sources other than the capital construction funds. Garrett also had less political clout in Frankfort after Governor Chandler resigned in 1939 to become Kentucky's junior senator in Washington, and he did not undertake the prolonged lobbying that Cherry had used so effectively to secure funds. Despite his complaints of unfairness, Garrett wrote a key state official in 1954, "Instead of asking for any new construciton it seems to be sensible to ask for improvement of what I have."[46] Western's greatest building boom would come under more dynamic leadership.

The building that aroused the most enthusiasm among the students was a student union, for the Cedar House was inadequate for a growing student body. In late 1943 President Garrett, musing over postwar plans, confessed that we "even dream in our rasher moments of a student union building." In late December 1947, he told Governor Earle Clements that his priority request in capital outlays was $450,000 to build and furnish such a building. "I know of no more practical investment," the president declared, "than a student union which holds your students in hours of recreation on the campus, free from the temptations and dangers which are likely to be connected with off-campus wanderings." The money was not immediately forthcoming, but preliminary plans were being drafted by late 1949. An early decison was to hold down costs by building a two-story structure that could have a third story added later. Bids were let and construction started in 1951, and the unofficial opening occurred on Friday, April 24, 1953, when the Talisman Ball was held in its new splendor. Facing the crest of the hill and located back of Cherry Hall toward the stadium, the student union completed the inner circle of buildings that ringed the hill. Well sited for that day, it lost its central location in the next decade as the campus expanded southward. After his death the name was changed to the Paul L. Garrett Student Center to honor the late president.[47]

The postwar resurgence of intercollegiate athletics was led by the basketball team that in the eight years 1946-47 through 1953-54 compiled a gaudy record of 202 games won and 40 lost, an 83.5 percent success ratio. Diddle waved his red towel and his players ran and rebounded and scored. The 1949-50 team was Diddle's first to average over seventy points a game; the 1952-53 squad raised that figure to 82.2. The 1946-47 and 1947-48 teams won 53 games and lost just six and averaged winning by margins of 18.0 and 18.8 points per game.

The postwar era started with the return of the sophomores who had done so well in 1942-43. Most of them had played basketball while in service, so that by their senior year in 1947-48 they were playing the equivalent of a seventh year of college level ball. The usual starting line-up in 1946-47 was Ray and Spears at forward, McKinney at center, Embry and Gibson at guard. Embry had retuned a year earlier than the others, and John Oldham replaced him in the 1947-48 starting lineup. This squad won the KIAC title in 1947 and 1948. The 1948 championship was the thir-teenth in fifteen years for Diddle teams, and for the first time in KIAC history all five starters on a team made the all-tournament team. The SIAA tournament was resumed in the spring of 1947 and Western starters also made this all-tournament team. In 1948 Diddle declared, "Some day, I'm going to win one of those national tournaments," but that goal eluded him. The great 1947-48 team beat LaSalle in the NIT but then lost to St. Louis 60-53 before defeating DePaul 61-59 in a consolation match. The Hilltoppers returned to the NIT in 1949, 1950, 1952, 1953, and 1954, but they were never able to come as close to a championship as the surprising 1941-42 squad.[48] Diddle's teams were usually ranked high in the national ratings, and their style of play pleased crowds wherever they went. A feature of the regular season play was an eastern tour that usually in-volved playing three or four games in Buffalo, New York, Philadelphia, and Washington, D.C. The basketball program gave Western more na-tional publicity than it received from any other source. Measured by the number of All-Americans, this was the golden era of Western basketball. Oran McKinney had received that coveted honor in 1943. He was fol-lowed by Dee Gibson (1948), Don Ray (1948), Odie Spears (1948), John Oldham (1949), Bob Lavoy (1950), Rip Gish (1951), Art Spoelstra (1953), and Tom Marshall (1953, 1954).

Basketball fans of a later generation would not have been impressed by the shooting accuracy of that era. The 1953-54 team compiled a 29-3 record, and its 85.3 points per game was the third highest in the nation. Its field goal percentage was 42.1, but that was the sixth highest average in the nation that year. Art Spoelstra, the towering center, hit 54.3 percent of his shots, the fourth best national mark.[49]

Western became a charter member of a new athletic conference in 1948 when the Ohio Valley Conference was formed. Most of the private schools in the KIAC could no longer compete successfully with Western and the other state schools. Athletic director Roy Stewart of Murray proposed a change to Eastern and Western in 1941, but the war postponed action. By 1948 such ancient rivals as Berea, Union, Transylvania, and Centre had almost disappeared from the Western schedules, and the organization of the new conference acknowledged a change that had already been effected. At the 1948 KIAC basketball tournament, representatives of Eastern, Morehead, Murray, Western, the University of Louisville, and Evansville College formed the new league. Marshall College and Tennessee Tech were admitted in 1949, but Louisville withdrew from the conference following an acrimonious difference of opinion over player eligibility at UL. Marshall and Evansville withdrew in 1952, but Middle Tennessee (1952), East Tennessee (1957), and Austin Peay (1962) restored the convenient eight-team format. The OVC was Western's primary conference affiliation from 1948 until 1982 when it joined the Sun Belt Conference. Official withdrawal from the SIAA came in 1953.[50]

Football was not resumed until the fall of 1946 because Garrett realized that a 1945 team could not be competitive. Head Coach W.L. Terry did not return to the Hill, and in the spring of 1946 Ed Stansbury was appointed head coach (and head of the physical education department) and Jesse Thomas was named assistant coach. When Thomas declined that appointment, Stansbury recommended that Thomas become head coach. One of Dan McGugin's star halfbacks at Vanderbilt in 1929-31, Thomas had been at Western from 1932 through 1935 when he left to enter graduate school. Afterwards, he joined the staff at Louisiana State University. His 1946 squad consisted of five lettermen and twenty-seven freshmen, and the result was a disappointing 2-6 season although Louisville was defeated at Homecoming, 20-19. The 1947 record of 3-4-2 was still disappointing, and in December Thomas returned to full-time teaching in the physical education department. Thirty-three year old assistant coach Jack Clayton was elevated to the top position.

Clayton adopted the T-formation offense that the Chicago Bears had made famous. During his nine-year tenure his record was 50-33-2, a decent but not spectacular 60.2 winning percentage. His best year was 1952 when quarterback Jimmy Feix guided the Toppers to an 8-1 regular season record and a 34-19 victory over Arkansas State in Evansville's Refrigerator Bowl. When Bowling Green's Ministerial Association protested the "growing secularization" that allowed the game to be played on a Sunday, Garrett first ignored their "expression of opinion," then accepted full responsiblity for the decision.[51] Feix rewrote most of the school's passing records and became Western's first football player to receive Little All-American honors.

Clayton was not able to duplicate the success of the 1952 season. His 1954 squad started with seven consecutive wins, then faltered and lost the last three contests. Like most coaches, Clayton was convinced that he had too few scholarships, and he asked for more. The cost of scholarships had increased football expenses, but the OVC level of expenses was still low. In 1952, for example, Western had five home games, four of them with nonconference out-of-state schools; total guarantees came to $3,800. Western's guarantees for four away games was $2,600, but travel expenses were estimated at only $1,200. Coach Clayton left Western on February 1, 1957, to become head coach and athletic director at Northwestern Louisiana State College.[52]

Tennis was the most successful of the minor sports during the Garrett years. E.B. Stansbury had an outstanding 18-3 match record in the three years (1936-38) that he coached the team. Then in 1939 Ted Hornback, Coach Diddle's new assistant, took over the tennis responsibilities. In the four years before World War II suspended competition, his teams won twenty-five matches and lost eight. Hornback's netters continued their winning ways when tennis was resumed in 1946. The team was coached by player Dee Gibson, the KIAC singles champion, in 1947 when Hornback resigned to take the head basketball position at Vanderbilt University. Gibson's team had a 7-1 record and won the KIAC title. Gibson completed his collegiate tennis career undefeated in singles play.[53] Hornback soon returned to Western, and during the years 1946-54 his teams won 58 of 72 matches and five of the first six OVC tennis championships.

Coach Diddle's baseball teams were far less successful than his basketball squads, and they played before sparse crowds. He sometimes snarled a rally with his erratic signals, but he managed to win a fair number of games on the diamond just south of Cherryton. In the six years preceeding baseball's suspension during the war (1943-45), his teams won 38 and lost 44, but he celebrated the return to play in 1946 by having his best ever record, 9-0. The shock was so great that the team fell below .500 ball for the next three seasons before resuming its winning habits. From 1946 through 1954 Diddle's teams were 69-44-2, and they won the OVC playoffs in 1951, 1952, and 1953.

J.T. Orendorf, a local businessman, coached a golf team in 1935; it lost the only match for which there is a record. The sport was then suspended until 1939 when Coach Winkenhofer assumed the duty in addition to his other responsibilities. His three-year (1939-41) record was 4-8, and golf was dropped until 1947 when Frank Griffin, then an assistant football coach, revived the game. Although the team received little support, his record from 1947 through 1954 was 46-30-5. Despite a 5-7-2 record in 1947 the team won the KIAC tournament, and Griffin's squads won OVC titles in 1950, 1952, and 1953.

The least successful of the minor sports during this period was track. During the 1937-42 years "Gander" Terry's meet record was 5-6, and his squads usually finished third or fourth in state competitions. When the sport was revived in 1947, Turner Elrod, an assistant football coach, was assigned the duty. From 1947 through 1954 his meet record was 15-24, and

Western's best showing in the OVC meet was a second place finish in 1951. Track and the other minor sports suffered from the lack of adequate support in money, scholarships, and coaches. When Western athletics was mentioned, most people thought at once of basketball, then of football. And many of them never got beyond that point.

The Griffenhagen and Associates 1946 survey of higher education in Kentucky recommended that the colleges emphasize intramurals for the benefit of all their students. Western, like the other state colleges, was overemphasizing athletics, but "There are fewer foreign names on the football players payroll than is the case for some of the other colleges, yet there are a number of names that have not had their origin in Kentucky. If this college and other colleges would search as far and as wide for qualified faculty members as for football players, Kentucky would have as excellent colleges as it has excellent football and basketball teams." The 1945-46 audit that showed athletic revenue of $7,633 and expenses of $5,106 was misleading, the report charged, for the salaries of the coaches were not included. Western had also awarded fifteen athletic scholarships in 1945-46 that cost $5,324, and the number was scheduled to increase. "Athletes are also employed for work but do no work other than practice for athletic contests.... Such employment is professionalism of athletics. Amateur athletics in this and other Kentucky state colleges is purely fictitious."[54]

Garrett's heart was with basketball, which returned a profit, and he was more willing to add scholarships there than in football, which operated at a deficit. In 1953-54 the football income was $13,099.81; expenses, excluding coaches' salaries, was $16,522.00. Garrett opposed efforts to increase the OVC limit on football scholarships. "I can't see," he wrote the Morehead president, "that it makes any difference in football whether we have 25, 35, or 45 scholarships, if we can dig up a schedule in which the other members are willing to abide by reasonable limits." He would be willing to set a definite limit on the number of players on a squad. The basketball program, on the other hand, had expenses of $25,756.18 (excluding salaries) in 1953-54 and income of $42,438.33. Since it was operating at a profit and gaining national recognition, he would be willing to increase its number of scholarships if freshmen were made ineligible for varsity play.[55]

The postwar years did witness a revival and expansion of an intramural program of sports for the student body. The early athletic activities at Western were all intramural, but the program languished with the advent of intercollegiate competition. Coach "Gander" Terry tried to reactivate the program in the mid-1930s with little success, and Ted Hornback followed him in 1941. Two years later the program became another wartime casualty. In 1946, when Frank Griffin returned to the Hill after naval service, he was put in charge of the program in addition to coaching golf and assisting in football. The administration did not provide funding until 1955 when one hundred dollars was allocated, so Griffin and his disciples raised money for the program by selling popcorn at varsity games. By 1981 intramurals had a budget of $147,830 and involved several thousand students in over two dozen sports.[56]

Few academic changes occurred during the World War II era. The twenty departments that existed in 1941 were the same twenty listed in the 1955-56 catalog. The most noticeable change was that physical education and health had added "and Recreation" to the departmental title. Some departments added courses, but several were offering in 1955 almost exactly what they had listed in 1941. Some of the additional courses were added because of the resumption of limited graduate work.

Cherry of Western and Donovan of Eastern had been the most vocal objectors to the forced discontinuation of graduate work in 1936, and after Cherry's death Donovan assumed the lead in getting it restored. The Eastern president wrote Garrett in the summer of 1940 that Governor Keen Johnson was open-minded, but he feared that its resumption would result in requests for more money. He would probably accept it if assured that the program would be largely self-supporting. In their requests the teachers colleges pointed out, "The present policy may send a few hundred extra students to the university, thereby satisfying the ambitions of an institution, while denying several thousand teachers of the state who are now prepared to study at the graduate level the opportunity to pursue their work in a college near their home, where the cost of attending school is within their ability to pay for it." They emphasized that historically the teachers colleges had educated teachers at their existing level. As the level of education of the teachers increased, the schools dropped their normal work and became four-year, degree-granting institutions. By 1940 60 percent of Kentucky's teachers were ready for graduate work; the teachers colleges must assume that responsibility.[57]

The lobbying was effective, and at its September 7, 1940, meeting the Council on Public Higher Education authorized the resumption of a year of graduate work at the teachers colleges, starting in the summer of 1941. Western's M.A. degree had an education major of at least twelve hours with minors available in fifteen departments. Twenty-four hours of course work were required, in addition to a thesis for which six hours of credit were awarded. An accreditation team in 1942 found Western's graduate program small but in good condition. Twenty-four of the thirty-two faculty members offering graduate courses held the doctorate, five others had at least sixty hours of graduate work, and the remaining three held the M.A. The teaching load was too heavy, but the library facilities were described as excellent. A special grant of eight thousand dollars had increased graduate holdings, and the Kentucky Library offered excellent research opportunities. In 1942 the Council authorized colleges to offer off-campus work for resident graduate credit, and Garrett began checking with superintendents about the possibility of scheduling such work.[58]

The sixty-eight graduate students who enrolled during fiscal 1941-42 indicated the need for the program. During the following year the total fell to forty, with only three men in the group. The three M.A. degrees awarded that year were the first ones since 1936. By 1944-45 graduate enrollment was higher than it had been in the first year of revival, and it increased sharply in the early postwar years. The peak figure for this period was 214 in 1951-52, but the largest number of graduates, sixty-two, came two years later. Although the number of women seeking graduate degrees increased, they usually constituted less than a third of the graduate students after the GIs returned.[59]

The curricula available to the students of 1955-56 were not greatly different from those of twenty years earlier. The only one that required less than a college degree was the two-year curriculum for elementary teachers, but it was used much less than it had been in the past. Special curricula had been added for high school teachers who wanted to major in the areas of foreign language, science, and social science instead of specific disciplines. The most obvious addition on the undergraduate level was the addition of a four-year curriculum for the training of teachers of high school commercial subjects. When Cherry sold the Bowling Green Business University to J.S. Dickey, J.L. Harman, and W.S. Ashby on April 10, 1907, he agreed to make substantial payments to them if the State Normal School offered bookkeeping, shorthand, or typing classes within a five-year period. Furthermore, "It is understood and agreed that each party to this contract will co-operate with the other in maintaining the present cordial relations between the institutions in which they are now engaged, and that each party will to the best of his ability advance and promote the interests of the two institutions."[60]

That promise was kept. Relations remained cordial, and Cherry resisted numerous requests that Western offer commercial courses that would have been considerably cheaper than those at the private school. He retained that stance although some of the other state schools were gaining students by adding such work. President Garrett also received such requests, and in early 1952 Dr. Karl E. Ashburn, head of the economics and sociology department, proposed the addition of four faculty members to teach an extension program in the commercial sector. The students and faculty, he wrote, "have no memory of Western before the death of the late Mr. Cherry and are interested primarily in the future and not in the past." The proposal was rejected, and Dr. Ashburn soon wrote in an undated note, "The commerce matter is dead as far as I am concerned and the sooner it is forgotten the better it will suit me. I will not do or say anymore about it and I want you to know this now."[61] It may have been purely coincidental that Ashburn remained at Western only one year.

But the growing pressures were too strong to ignore, and beginning with the fall semester 1953 Western offered a curriculum for the training of high school teachers of commercial subjects with some courses taught at the Business University. The fees were the same as those of other undergraduate curricula at Western. Twenty-one students declared it as their major field in the first semester of the program.[62]

The graduate curricula of 1955 were much more specific than those of 1941. Separate curricula, usually leading to either a Provisional or Standard Certificate, were available for superintendents, principals, supervisors, and attendance officers. All of the administrative certificates required a master's degree, an obvious boost to graduate enrollment.

In the list of curricula available, those connected with professional education far outnumbered the rest, but that proportion concealed a major trend in Western's role. More and more of the students were in nonteaching programs, and this raised a question about the school's name. Should "Teachers" be retained? A *Herald* editorial in 1940 called for continued emphasis on the programs that had given Western "a distinctive and definite purpose," but four years later a bill was introduced in the General Assembly to drop "Teachers" from the names of the four colleges. The bill was introduced so late in the session that it failed to pass, but the case for the change became stronger each year. When it was done by legislative enactment in 1948, President Garrett wrote, "It was merely a recognition of an existing situation"[63] It was a vivid indication of the changes that had occurred since the State Normal School enrolled its first students in 1907.

On August 28, 1953, the Board of Regents elected Paul L. Garrett president of Western for a new four-year term beginning September 1 at a salary of nine thousand dollars per year. Garrett was nearing his sixtieth birthday, and, although diabetic, his health was generally good. He was expected to complete at least the new term before considering retirement. Then on Friday, November 20, he suffered a paralytic stroke in his office. Confined to the hospital for four weeks, he went home before Christmas. His right arm and hand were most affected, and it was some time before he could sign his name. But he was cheerful when he got home and grateful for the many expressions of concern. "They let me come down stairs now and sit by my wood fire," he wrote a friend in January. "I am doing a good deal of reading, a little card playing, and even some work. It is almost worth being sick to find how many people love me and how many of them think I am a success. I don't need to tell you that I have felt at times that I must be the most inefficient President in the world. My many letters have not utterly changed that opinion, but they have certianly made me feel good." By early spring he was able to visit his office for short periods, and on April 23, 1954, he presided over the traditional Western breakfast at the KEA meeting in Louisville.[64]

Then on Saturday afternoon, May 1, he fell while walking on the grounds outside the president's home and fractured his right hip. He was confined to a wheelchair at home, but he soon resumed some of his office work, and the regents held some of their meetings in the president's home. He was encouraged after an x-ray examination in September: "Sometimes I think Garrett will walk again." But as the slow days passed, the anticipated recovery did not develop. In November regent John E. Richardson wrote two of his colleagues, "I do not believe Paul will be with us much longer." He hoped they agreed "that the State should see him through to the end," for his retirement income would be totally inadequate. Garrett declined slowly, and doctors found a dangerous hardening of the arteries. Western's second president died at home on Monday afternoon, February 28, 1955. It was fitting that the pallbearers at his funeral two days later were members of the student body.[65]

Paul Garrett once mused that at times he wished he had become a college teacher of literature, "which I still think offers perhaps the greatest pleasure of all pursuits." But he had liked most aspects of his more than seventeen years at Western, and he had derived great enjoyment from the library. If he did not gain the respect of the faculty for his administrative skills, he won their affection as a person.

Six

More Stately Mansions
1955-1965

DURING HIS final illness, as he continued to deal with some college business, President Garrett referred to his assistant, Kelly Thompson, as "my eyes, legs, and ears." Thompson carried much of the administrative burden that Garrett found irksome even before his illness, and from 1953 on Thompson provided much of the leadership for the institution. On March 26, 1955, the regents made him acting president until a successor to Garrett was named, and instructed him to move forward with projects to alleviate yet another housing shortage. It was typical of Thompson that plans were already far advanced for two large dormitories.[1]

Kelly Thompson was born in Lebanon, Kentucky, on January 28, 1909. He came to Western in the fall of 1928 as one of Diddle's football recruits, but before the first game a severe injury to his right shoulder ended his football career. His money gone, he sat in abject dejection on the steps of old Recitation Hall before leaving for home. Coach Diddle came by, sensed that something was wrong, and asked what the trouble was. Thompson explained that he was broke and leaving school. But Diddle drove him downtown to the Bowling Green Bank and Trust Company and said to its president, "Let this boy have $25 and I'll sign his note." Thompson remained in school, and Diddle's faith in him sealed a lifelong friendship between the two. The following year Thompson became a field representative for Western, a job for which he was ideally qualified. He had few equals in dealing with people on a one-to-one basis, and he was already an accomplished public speaker. He was prompt in answering inquiries and following up leads to prospective students. Nothing stopped him from going where Western needed to be represented. "I had to ride a horse to Albany to get to the Teachers' meeting on July 4th," he wrote Miss Mattie from Jamestown in 1929, "and then ride him back to attend the one here in Jamestown. I haven't been on a horse since I was a kid, so you can imagine how spry I feel today."[2]

Such devotion to duty won the approbation of both Miss Mattie and

President Cherry. "You have impressed all of us with your earnestness and success as well," Miss Mattie told the young agent, and Cherry wrote a schoolman in Princeton, "He is really a very wonderful young man; I regard him as unusually strong in many ways and I am personally very fond of him. I love him for his positive loyalty to College Heights, as well as for the interest he has shown in me personally." Thompson often drove Cherry on some of his trips in the 1930s, and they developed a close, almost father-son, relationship. Henry Hardin Cherry was one of the major influences in shaping Kelly Thompson's character and educational attitudes, and they shared many dreams of what Western could become. In 1931 Thompson married Sarah Pearce, daughter of William M. Pearce, the director of extension and one-time president of Ogden College. They had three children, a girl and two boys.[3]

His employment slowed Thompson's academic progress, but he received his bachelor's degree from Western in 1935 with a major in English and a well-merited reputation for oratory. The speech that won the state intercollegiate contest in 1934 was called "The Cost of Education in Kentucky," a topic that occupied a great deal of his attention when he became president. In 1935 Cherry employed Thompson as director of public relations, probably the first person to hold such a position at a Kentucky college. He took a leave of absence in 1937 to organize a public relations program for the Indianapolis baseball club in the American Association, but he returned to the Hill in January 1938. During the next several years, one of his most successful enterprises was gaining national recognition for Coach Diddle and his basketball teams. Thompson also became the general manager for the *College Heights Herald* in 1940.[4] He was diligent in performing any task assigned him, and President Garrett used him as a general troubleshooter.

Thompson was a naval lieutenant in 1944-46, and Garrett feared that he would not return to Western. When he did return in 1946, the Board of Regents created the position of Assistant to the President, and Thompson became officially what he had been unofficially during his last years on the Hill. Garrett delegated many functions and responsibilities to him. Among the activities for which Thompson won particular praise were his work in helping organize the OVC and his skillful management of its annual basketball tournament.[5]

Thompson had strong support for the presidency. Unlike Garrett, he had long and close ties with the school, and he was thoroughly conversant with its people, its operations and its traditions. No one could question his loyalty and devotion to Western. During Garrett's final illness Josephine Cherry Lowman wrote Regent Bartlett, "Although my Father never said it to me in so many words, I always felt that he was grooming Kelly for the Presidency of Western for some future date and hoped that this would happen some time." Another strong Thompson supporter was Coach Diddle who waged an active campaign with Governor Lawrence Wetherby and the members of the Board of Regents. Numerous letters and many personal contacts urged Thompson's selection.[6]

Yet there was opposition. Some people objected to Thompson's religion. There was still a general belief that a Catholic could not be elected president of the United States, and some detractors extended that prohibition to the presidency of Western as well. More opposition centered around Thompson's lack of a doctoral degree and full-time teaching experience. (Thompson received an M.A. in education from Western in 1943; Morris Harvey College awarded him an honorary Doctor of Law degree in 1957). Judge Bartlett asked for Dr. Stickles's opinion before writing his fellow regents. Without naming his source, Bartlett quoted from Stickles's letter on the desired qualifications. "The man who is to be chosen in my judgment for Western's president, should be an educator of broad training who knows the problems of the public schools, above all else a scholar, one with no less than a Ph.D.degree, a man of outstanding personality who can always cope in public estimation with such men as are the present heads of Murray and Morehead. It will take all of this to keep Western in a forward position." Careful consideration should be given to finding someone with previous experience as a college president. There was also opposition from the "Ogden Group," leaders of the old Ogden College, who wanted to go outside the local community. They had support from J.P. Masters, a Bowling Green regent.[7]

There was no organized search for presidential candidates and few formal applications for the position. A number of people were recommended, including Kelly Thompson , but he did not formally apply. "I was here," he later explained. "I was my predecessor's right arm, so to speak. The people who would make that decision knew all about me. It seemed ridiculous for me to apply." Wendell Butler, chairman of the Board of Regents as superintendent of public instruction, thought that he had a good chance. As a 1936 Western graduate and a member of the board, he had close ties with the school, but he soon sensed that Thompson was the front runner.[8]

Politics became involved in the selection during the 1955 Democratic primary when "Happy" Chandler sought a second term as governor. When Governor Lawrence W. Wetherby urged the regents to delay making a selection until after the Democratic primary, Chandler accused him of "laying the heavy hand of politics" on Western in an effort to get Carlos Oakley, KEA president and superintendent of the Union County schools, elected to the position. Then Wetherby learned that regents Clarence Bartlett, Vernon Shallcross, and John Richardson had decided to elect Dr. Roy Owsley. Consultant to the City of Louisville, Owsley was a Western graduate who had an excellent record in public administration. He was reputed to have the support of the "Ogden Group," which had agreed to supplement his state salary. Richardson and Bartlett refused to pledge that no action would be taken until after the primary, although the governor promised that he would not interfere in the process after that date. The terms for Bartlett and Shallcross had expired the preceding year, but no successors had been appointed. Now, on the eve of the board meeting, Wetherby replaced them with Sheridan Barnes of Elizabethtown and H. Bemis Lawrence of Louisville. The board met on July 2, 1955, and, as the governor insisted, took no action on the vacancy. In a public statement, Coach Diddle applauded the governor's action which "saved Western from suffering a blow from which the college might not have recovered for the next 10 or 15 years." John Richardson, citing personal reasons, resigned from the board in August, and Don Campbell of Lebanon replaced him.[9]

Barnes could not be present at a board meeting on October 3, so another session was called for Monday, October 17, in the president's office at Western. When the regents met in executive session they considered seventeen names. J.P. Masters nominated Wendell Butler and Don Campbell nominated Kelly Thompson. The vote to elect Thompson was 3 to 1, with Masters casting the negative; Butler abstained since he was among the candidates. Thompson was voted a four-year contract at nine thousand dollars, the maximum then possible, with Butler and Masters abstaining. Masters also abstained from voting on a resolution praising Thompson for his performance while he was acting president. Two days later Masters resigned from the board. "There has been too much grief," he wrote, "and I feel I have served long enough.... The operations of the board are different now from what they used to be."

"I love this college with a passion," Kelly Thompson said in accepting the position. "I have been employed here 26 years and all that I have I owe to Western. I pledge to you men that you will never have any reason to regret your action. I shall never allow myself to be a part of anything that will reflect discredit on this institution." When the new president left his office that afternoon, the rotunda was packed with students who sang "For He's A Jolly Good Fellow" and gave him a five-minute ovation. "As long as I am president of Western," he responded, "we will never be satisfied with anything but the best for the college." Another standing ovation greeted him at chapel the following morning. He promised nothing spectacular, but he declared that changes would be made "because otherwise we stand still." They would come after careful study and planning, but they would be implemented vigorously. He would soon consult with the class presidents, he said, about appointing a student advisory council.

Thompson was not "the aloof, austere scholar" image of a college president, the Courier-Journal said in wishing him well on his undertaking. "Young, vigorous and friendly, he resembles the school he has for so long represented, and during his service as acting president of the school he has shown a considerable ability as an administrator. This ability, his familiarity with the school and its state, and his popularity throughout Kentucky, will, we are confident, prove the ingredients of success for the new president of Western State College."

Recent Regent Bartlett offered his congratulations and concluded, "You have the challenge of your life-time ... it is my wish that you may gloriously succeed."[10]

Enrollments soared on the Hill during the decade following President Thompson's election, and this growth was responsible for substantial changes in almost every phase of the institution's functions. This rapid growth was not unique to Western; it was a state and national trend that drastically altered higher education. Indeed, it would have been difficult for a state school to have avoided the students who were suddenly storming the admission offices. Kentucky was committed to an open admissions policy that encouraged enrollments but created problems for the students who were not adequately prepared to do college work. Remedial work was one expensive answer to this problem; lowering standards was another answer that sometimes occurred while being denied. The basic admission statement in the 1965-66 catalog said: "Graduates of any accredited Kentucky high school may be admitted unconditionally to the freshman class if they have earned an overall average of 'C' in the nine basic units (English, mathematics, science, and social studies) required for graduation from a Kentucky high school." Those who failed to meet this standard could be admitted on a trial basis.

In 1956 the high school seniors in Kentucky numbered 22,565; 23.4 percent of them enrolled in state schools. In 1965 there were 38,900 high school seniors; 39.7 percent of them enrolled in state schools. The number of freshmen in state colleges nearly tripled between 1956 and 1965. Kentucky also believed in relatively inexpensive education for the students. In 1955-56 a Kentucky student paid an incidental fee of $35.00, a health fee of $1.25, a student activity fee of $3.50, and a college annual fee of $6.00 in the first semester only. A decade later the charges had been consolidated into a registration fee of $87.50 for in-state students and a $19.00 composite fee. Although students have always claimed that college catalogs underestimate costs, the basic costs (excluding personal expenses) in 1955-56 were estimated at $230 per semester; the official estimate for 1965-66 was $497 per semester.

By this period the largest enrollments were normally in the fall semester, and these figures are the ones usually cited. The registrar's statistics for fall head counts for 1955 through 1965 were as follows: 1955, 1,975; 1956, 2,161; 1957, 2,351; 1958, 2,546; 1959, 2,917; 1960, 3,599; 1961,

4,797; 1962, 5,130; 1963, 5,917; 1964, 6,798; 1965, 7,824. These figures did not include the Training School, which averaged some 440 students, and the Western Trade School, located on the Russellville Road below the tennis courts, whose enrollment during these years ranged between two hundred and six hundred students. The Trade School started in 1941 as an NYA project. Then in 1943-46 the building was used to train war workers. In the postwar period it offered vocational training for a regional area. It was removed from the campus and from Western's jurisdiction after the mid-1960s when the state constructed a new facility.[11]

Western's enrollment increased gradually in the mid-1950s, and in the fall of 1957, both Eastern and Murray had a larger student body, but the rate of increase at Morehead exceeded that of the other state colleges. By the fall of 1960, Western was second in size to the University of Kentucky among state schools as enrollment increased 22.8 percent over fall semester 1959. That leap was only a prelude to 1961. An emergency developed when 1,198 additional students registered, an increase of 33.3 percent in a year. The student-faculty ratio had to be increased, part-time teachers were hastily employed, school officials sought rooms in private homes for those who had no place to live, and the dean requested at least a dozen new faculty members for the spring semester. That pace could not be maintained, but growth was steady, and in the fall of 1965 registration totaled 7,824. Semester records were also being set at the spring and summer registrations. To secure maximum use of classrooms, Dean Raymond Cravens developed an innovative but confusing plan in which classes met Monday, Wednesday, and alternate Fridays, or Tuesday, Thursday, and alternate Fridays. Students and faculty had to remember if a week was "round" or "square" in the printed schedule. One student protested, "Not knowing where you are is bad enough. Not knowing when you are could only happen at Western."[12]

The students were more diverse than they had been in earlier years. Now they came from all parts of the state and from most states across the country with Kentucky's low tuition as a major attraction. As a result of this enrollment explosion, 47.9 percent of the degrees granted between 1924 and 1965 were issued during the last decade of that period.

The admission of blacks added a new dimension to the student body. The Day Law of 1904 prohibited integrated schools for nearly half a century, but racial mores of southcentral Kentucky were basically southern, and for most of that period black enrollment would have been prevented even in the absence of the legal prohibition. Yet President Cherry was concerned about black as well as white education, and he worked to improve opportunities for blacks and to forge closer relations between the KEA and the Negro Education Association. C.B. Nichols, principal of the Booker T. Washington High School in Ashland, wrote in 1926: "I appreciate everything you are doing for the advancement of my race. I am personally thanking you for your promise to appear on our state inter-racial program at Louisville November 19th and 20th."[13]

President Garrett exhibited similar sympathies for black education. As he wrote President Donovan at Eastern, "I have felt for a great many years that the Negroes of the state are due one first-class college, and I hope we may live to see them get it." He pledged his support to President R.B. Atwood at Kentucky State, and he served on a Governor's Advisory Committee that studied educational opportunities for blacks. When President Atwood sent a thank you letter to the committee members, he added a handwritten note to Garrett's copy: "Just this additional word to let you know how grateful I am for your sympathetic attitude toward our problems. I believe I express the feelings of Negro people generally. Thank you." Yet the fact remained that blacks could not enroll at Western, not even for correspondence courses. Inquiries continued to receive negative answers into the 1950s.[14]

The first breakthrough in the state occurred when Lyman T. Johnson of Louisville sued for admission to the graduate college at the University of Kentucky because Kentucky State did not offer the work he wanted. A judge ruled in his favor, the University of Kentucky did not appeal, and over two dozen blacks enrolled in the graduate college on the Lexington campus in the summer of 1949. The following year the legislature amended the Day Law to allow colleges to admit black students if the courses they sought were not available at Kentucky State and if the college chose to do so. Although the famous 1954 Supreme Court decision in Brown *v* Board of Education of Topeka did not apply directly to Western or other public colleges, it clearly indicated the probable result of integration suits on the college level. In the late spring of 1954, Garrett suggested that the state colleges agree upon an admission and use of facilities policy. Then at the November 23, 1955, meeting of the Council on Public Higher Education, Thompson called for the appointment of a committee to recommend how the state colleges would implement the mandate of the Supreme Court. It would be best, he recommended, for all of them to act at one time. After some discussion Thompson moved for the admission of black students in the summer of 1956, and the motion carried unanimously.[15]

Bowling Green was still segregated. One of Western's first black students recalled buying coffee through a special window at the Greyhound bus station; he could not enter a good restaurant. Blacks were admitted only to the balcony of the movie theatres, and a black woman could not try on a dress or hat in a store. There were still separate restrooms and drinking fountains for blacks—if any were provided at all. In 1956 when H.L. Donovan was to deliver the summer commencement address, he wrote Kelly Thompson to inquire about housing for Walter who would be driving him. "If there is a negro motel in Bowling Green, I

Table 3. Physical Growth and Expansion, 1955-1965

Building	Year	Cost
East Hall, North Hall	1955	$1,195,142
Maintenance Service Building	1958	132,000
Regents Hall	1958	701,392
South Hall	1959	653,829
West Hall	1960	794,599
Kelly Thompson Science Hall	1960	1,167,471
State Hall	1961	1,294,654
Academic-Athletic Building and E.A. Diddle Arena	1961	3,089,538
Central Hall	1962	1,449,628
W.R. McNeill City-College Cooperative School*	1962	430,135
Enlarged Maintenance Service Building	1962	134,927
Expanded Heating Plant	1963	428,498
Terrace Hall	1963	842,574
Charles L. Taylor Agriculture Center	1964	90,346
New Paul L. Garrett Student Center	1964	1,423,820
Margie Helm Library	1964	1,277,451
Commerce-Education Building	1965	1,778,000
New Residence Hall for Men #6	1965	1,491,957
New Residence Hall for Men #7	1965	1,465,140
New Residence Hall for Women #4	1965	1,418,634

*Financed cooperatively by Bowling Green City Schools and Western
Source: Kelly Thompson, *A Decade in Review, 1955-1965*, 15-18.

will send him to it. If not, possibly you will have some colored men working on the campus that could arrange for him to get a night's lodging." In view of such customs and practices, Thompson prepared carefully for the impending integration. He and other administrators held at least a dozen conferences with varied groups—students, faculty, black and white community leaders—in an effort to prevent problems from arising, and he talked individually with some people in the community who appeared most adamant against the change. The result was that Western's desegregation went smoothly, aided by the maturity and earnestness of the summer school students, black and white.[16]

Black enrollment grew slowly, however, for several years. In the fall of 1963, the ninety-six black students (still called Negro at that time) constituted only about 1.6 percent of the student body. Several outstanding black athletes were recruited in 1963, and their performances helped reconcile some of the whites who may have had lingering resentments. The Taylor County superintendent of schools wrote Thompson in 1963 when he learned that one of his students was thinking of attending Western on a basketball scholarship. What treatment could he expect off the basketball court? "We have become so fond of the young fellow here that we want assurance that he would stand better than an even chance of being just another Hilltopper on and off the floor." President Thompson replied, "To my knowledge there has never been an unfavorable incident. We are grateful for this condition and have every intention of maintaining it in the years to come."[17] In 1980 this student, Clem Haskins, became the head basketball coach at his *alma mater*.

The boom in enrollment brought on an unprecedented wave of new construction as Western struggled to keep up with the influx of students. In 1955 the twenty major buildings on the campus were valued at $10 million; a decade later the forty-one major buildings were valued at some $35 million. Table 3 lists the new buildings added during this period of extraordinary growth. In addition to this construction, most of the older buildings underwent renovation and remodeling, and nearly two-dozen tracts of land were acquired adjacent to or near the campus. A number of them included houses that were used for temporary housing or office space or held for future development.[18]

One of the most unusual developments was the acquisition of both a new library and a new basketball arena. The library increased its holdings rapidly during the postwar years, and the number of potential users far exceeded the seating capacity of the building that had once seemed so large. A herald of the future may have been the purchase of a new Recordak Microfilm Reader in 1949; its arrival was said to have created "a minor sensation," although the *New York Times* was then the only available material to use on it. Both Miss Margie Helm, who became director of library services in 1958, and Miss Sara Tyler, who succeeded her as librarian, stressed the need for more space. By early 1960 half of the Little Theatre had become an annex to the periodicals room, and it was obvious that something had to be done. The Southern Association Self-Study Report of 1962 recommended that top priority be given to a new building, accompanied by increases in the acquisition budget and the library staff with faculty status for qualified members of the staff. The Library Committee also recommended that students be encouraged to read. Circulation figures pointed up that need. The 1960-61 student circulation was 58,195, up sharply from the 30,723 total in 1956-57, but the increase resulted from the rapid growth in enrollment. On a per capita basis, the students of 1960-61 were using fewer books than their predecessors of previous collegiate generations. In 1924, with a much smaller enrollment, the circulation had been 102,000. For whatever reasons, the better educated students of the 1960s were reading less than the students of the earlier era.

The most disturbing aspect of library circulation, however, concerned the faculty. Faculty circulation actually decreased from 2,906 in 1956-57 to 1,792 in 1960-61, although the full-time faculty grew from 98 to 131 during those years.[19]

The growing student body generated more strain in the fieldhouse than in the library, and the continued success of Diddle's crowd-pleasing teams created a strong demand for seats from the off-campus public. Fire laws were violated regularly as crowds exceeded the legal capacity. The solution was to construct an Academic-Athletic Building, then convert the gymnasium into a library. At a December 1960 meeting, President Thompson presented the athletic building as Western's top priority need, and the Regents authorized him to proceed with it at an estimated cost of $2,500,000. Construction began in late 1961, and by its completion in 1963 the cost had risen to $3,089,538. The 8,500 seats nearly doubled the capacity of the old gym, and seating could be expanded to over 13,000 without structural changes being necessary. In 1963 it was one of the largest on-campus athletic buildings in the South. In addition to the athletic facilities that included a swimming pool and auxiliary gym, it housed the departments of physical education, military science, and foreign languages. The elaborate dedication on December 7, 1963, was marred by the Vanderbilt University basketball team, which defeated the Toppers 82-60 before an overflow crowd of 9,811.[20]

The librarians were not enthusiastic about the conversion plan, but the need was urgent, and Dean Cravens asserted that twice as much space would be available as could be obtained by adding to the existing library. The location was also deemed better in view of future campus expansion south of the Hill, and the new site had better possibilities for adding space when needed. The initial qualms were assuaged, and the reconstructed building was ready by September 1965. With 70,000 square feet of space, 1,000 seats, and a book capacity of over 350,000 volumes, it was a great advancement over the previous facility. Its air conditioning had a particular appeal to anyone who had used the old library during summer months. Library users were sometimes puzzled by the school emblem woven in the carpet in front of the reference desk; it marked the location of the center jump circle of the old basketball court. The new library was named after Miss Margie Helm who retired in 1965 after forty-five years on the faculty. She was succeeded as director of library services by Miss Sara Tyler.[21]

Among the other major buildings were two classroom structures that helped Western cope with the rapid growth of the student body. The science facilities, divided between Cherry Hall and the Ogden campus, were hopelessly inadequate by the 1950s. A federal planning grant was obtained in 1958, faculty-administrator committees began working on plans, and Governor Bert Combs dedicated the Kelly Thompson Science

Hall on the Ogden campus on October 10, 1961. Work began in late 1964 on a Commerce-Education Building which was located below the football field in the area once occupied by Cherryton. Before its formal dedication on a special "Day of Commemoration and Dedication" on October 14, 1967, it was named for Dr. Finley C. Grise who had joined the faculty in 1913 and had been dean from 1927 until his retirement in 1959. The Garrett Student Center soon became inadequate, and a third floor and rooms on the north end were added. Air conditioning was also installed. During the construction a temporary student center was located in the M.A. Schell house at 1536 State Street. In 1966 the renovated Schell house became the president's home.[22]

To improve the teacher education program, Western cooperated with the Bowling Green City Schools in building an elementary school, named for Dr. W.R. McNeill, longtime superintendent of the city system, at the south end of the campus. Western conveyed five acres to the city and agreed to pay approximately 14.6 percent of the operational costs from 1963 to 1990. The joint venture was hailed as one of the first such undertakings in the nation.[23]

Much of the building was for dormitory construction, but Western had difficulty keeping pace with the growth of the student body. Because funds were always limited, the administration concentrated on housing single students instead of providing married students' facilities. This may well have been the most effective use of available funds, but it created a sensitive issue that has never been allayed. The construction of dormitories south of the Hill soon raised the question of how long the student center could serve its purpose adequately in its peripheral location.

Less noticeable but essential to campus development were the improvements made in support structures and services. A maintenance service building was constructed (1954) and enlarged (1962), the heating plant was expanded (1963) to carry the additional load of the new buildings, and extensive maintenance work was done on existing structures. Utility systems were extended and enlarged; new sidewalks, driveways, and parking lots were built; and much attention was paid to general campus beautification. After President Garrett's death, Mrs. Garrett spent several years helping to make the Western campus one of the loveliest in the nation.

Western had enjoyed careful planning from its establishment as a state school, but by the early 1960s growth had caught up with the existing plans. At its October 30, 1964, meeting, the Board of Regents authorized President Thompson to proceed with the development of a master plan that would guide future growth. The following March the Ann Arbor, Michigan, firm of Johnson, Johnson, and Roy, Landscape Architects, was employed to develop the plan. Officially adopted on January 22, 1966, it provided for the utilization of approximately 163 acres of campus that could serve a student body of 16,350 students. When that number was reached, the consultants recommended that another campus be created, possibly on the college farm on the Nashville Pike.[24] The plans were periodically updated in accord with changing circumstances. When enrollment slowed and then declined, the farm continued to be used primarily for agricultural purposes.

Although state appropriations increased substantially during this decade, in part because the schools began to present their consolidated requests through the Council on Public Higher Education, only a small portion of the construction could have been financed from the capital construction allocations. Other means had to be found. Federal aid became more important as a number of new programs were created, and in the 1955-65 decade Western received $1,648,388 for construction under terms of the Higher Education Facilities Act. In addition, Western received $1,383,504 in federal grants for the instructional program, much of it being used to fund institutes for precollege teachers. Most of the institutes were in the areas of science and education. The combination of state and federal construction grants was inadequate to the need, and in 1960 a plan was developed that used Consolidated Educational Buildings Revenue Bonds to increase each institution's ability to borrow larger sums than had been possible on an individual basis. The bonding capacity for instructional buildings was based on student registration fees, and the money raised increased with both the rapid increase in enrollment and the imposition of higher fees. The 1955 "Incidental Fee" of $35 for the basic full-time undergraduate student had become a $87.50 "Registration Fee" by 1965 with a scheduled increase to $100 the following year. The first use of this program at Western was the financing of the Kelly Thompson Science Hall, later the North Wing of the Kelly Thompson Science Complex.[25]

Increased construction of housing, dining, and student union facilities was made possible by the establishment of a Housing and Dining System Revenue Bonds program. Here again, revenues were consolidated, and the total amount of bonds that could be issued was increased. The system was designed to be self-supporting, and the revenue did increase sharply with the growth of on-campus housing and the increased fees. The room rent in 1955 was $45 to $54 per semester with board estimated at $126; by 1965 the room rent ranged from $95 to $110, and meals were estimated to cost $252. In 1964 when the borrowing power limit was almost reached, the regents approved the president's recommendation that $4.75 of the students' General Activities Fee be pledged to the Housing and Dining System Fund. In future years the state government provided some assistance by appropriating money for servicing debts that the colleges had contracted. Western was more conservative in going into debt than some of her sister institutions, and the state money received for this purpose was less than that going to some other state schools.[26]

Extensive administrative reorganization also took place during President Thompson's first decade. In early 1955 the administrative staff consisted of the dean (Finley C. Grise), the registrar (Ernest H. Canon), assistant to the president (Kelly Thompson), director of public relations, alumni, and placement (Robert Cochran), bursar (Florence Schneider), and director of extension (William M. Pearce). Thompson saw the need for a more adequate administrative staff, and when he became president he began work on plans to enlarge and improve it. A major problem was the presence of a number of elderly administrators who had rendered long and devoted service to Western. A special faculty committee studied the Cherry retirement program and its relationship to the state retirement program and social security. The Cherry plan was reoffered with some changes, and retirement was made compulsory at age seventy. At the September 26, 1958, regents' meeting, Thompson requested that the board declare a state of emergency for the 1958-59 school year to aid him in implementing a reorganization plan by the end of the summer of 1959. When Thompson made his recommendations on May 7, 1959, he declared "that the success and progress of Western for perhaps the next quarter of a century will, in a large measure, be determined by the action taken here today."[27]

Five key positions were filled that day with ramifications that extended well beyond that number. Dean Grise was replaced by Raymond L. Cravens, who had joined the faculty of the history and political science department in 1958. Twice a Western graduate (A.B., 1952; M.A., 1955), he received his doctorate at the University of Kentucky in 1958. Innovative and imaginative, Cravens was entrusted with much of the academic program. Dero G. Downing, director of the Training School since 1956, succeeded Mr. Canon as registrar. James H. Carpenter, the director of the South Hall dormitory, became director of the Training School. Lee Francis Jones, head of the Department of Education since 1930, was replaced by Dr. Tate C. Page, a member of that department since 1956. Gordon Wilson, a fixture in the English department since 1912 and its head since 1928, "retired" to an active life of productive scholarship; his successor was Willson Wood who had joined the Training School staff in 1941 and moved over to the college in 1947. Dr. W.M. Pearce, one-time president of Ogden College, had crossed State Street in 1920 to become Western's director of extension; P.L. Sanderfur, a member of the physics department since 1943, took his place. Grise had continued as head of foreign languages after becoming dean; Dr. Paul G. Hatcher, who joined the faculty in 1959, assumed the headship.[28]

It was the most extensive administrative overhaul in Western's history, but other changes had already taken place. In 1954 Western requested a study by the State Budget Division that resulted in numerous recommendations for improving the college's business affairs. Two years later when Miss Florence Schneider, bursar since 1919, became executive secretary-treasurer of the College Heights Foundation, the office of business manager, which had been tried several years earlier, was revised and expanded. Billy S. Smith, a former state administrator, was appointed to the position. Within the next few years, drastic changes were made in the management of business and fiscal affairs. Several divisions were created, new machinery was installed, and clerical help was added. In 1957 Western established the position of physical plant administrator with L.T. Smith, who had served Western capably in several capacities, as its first occupant. Reorganization of the physical plant operation resulted in the development of several major divisions within the next few years. Charles A. Keown, a member of the Department of Agriculture, became Western's first dean of students in the fall of 1957.[29]

In 1961 the Kentucky Press Association gave Kelly Thompson its "Kentuckian of the Year" award. In his acceptance speech he declared, "Western will seek to so conduct its affairs, meet its challenges, and drive toward excellence that when the time comes for university status to be given to it, the College will be able to take the step as a perfectly natural transition." Across the country a number of schools had made or were making that transition, and by the early 1960s Western was nearing the point where a similar change could come to the Hill. Academic politics dictated that when the change came it would cover Eastern, Morehead, and Murray, as well as Western. A major step in that direction came in 1963 when Western assumed the operations of the Bowling Green College of Commerce.[30]

By the end of the 1950s, the private College of Commerce was in serious economic distress. Costs had risen sharply, and the BU, as most Bowling Green people still called it, no longer drew students from across the nation. Some assistance came from the cooperative program with Western, but it did not restore financial stability. Ownership was transferred to a nonprofit corporation at the end of 1960, but deficits could not be eliminated, and fund-raising drives were inadequate. After detailed negotiations Western took over the College of Commerce program on June 1, 1963. The real estate was not included, but Western was allowed to use the property on College Street, from which Western had moved in 1911, during the 1963-64 academic year. Nine members of the BU faculty were given one-year contracts at Western. The students who enrolled on the Hill found their costs approximately half what they had been in the private school. The added work was organized temporarily into two departments, business-government and economics-sociology.[31]

That arrangement was only temporary, for Thompson was ready to proceed to the step next to university designation. In July 1964 the

Graduate School was organized, with Dr. John D. Minton as its dean; and the Bowling Green College of Commerce was created, with Dr. William M. Jenkins, Jr. as its dean. Then on March 22, 1965, the regents approved the establishment of three additional colleges and a number of academic and administrative changes. When the appointments were approved on June 1, Dr. Tate Page became dean of the College of Education, Dr. Marvin Russell became dean of the Ogden College of Science and Technology, and Dr. Paul Hatcher became dean of the Potter College of Liberal Arts. A month earlier Dr. Raymond Cravens was appointed vice-president for academic affairs and dean of the faculties. Dr. William Hourigan, associate dean for undergraduate instruction, supervised the departments of military science, nursing, the area of library science, and a new testing and counseling service. Dr. Charles Clark was made director of extension and field services; Dr. John Scarborough was appointed director of summer school and the community college; Mr. Ronnie Sutton became director of admissions; and Miss Sara Tyler was promoted to director of library services. Sociology, secondary education, and elementary education were added as new departments. Over ninety new faculty members came to the Hill that fall, so returning students might well have been bewildered by the changes that had occurred. To avoid the situation that had developed with aged administrators, in 1966 the Board of Regents established the policy that all administrators would be given a change of assignment at age sixty-five, although they could be continued on a year-to-year basis.[32]

The faculty was also undergoing rapid changes during this decade. Most evident was the sheer growth in numbers. The 98 full-time faculty members in 1955-56 increased to 317 in 1965-66. The 323 percent increase did not match the 396 percent increase in student enrollment during the same period, but the use of part-time instructors helped fill the gap. After 1960 graduate assistants were used in several departments to assist with the lower division classes. Their presence raised the still unresolved question of whether their enthusiasm compensated for their lack of experience and subject matter knowledge. It was assumed, however, that they did help hold down the cost of instruction.

After the 1950s passed, there were few active faculty members who had taught during the Normal School years, and retirements during the 1960s sharply reduced the number whose tenure extended into the period before the Second World War. As college enrollments soared, faculty members enjoyed a teachers' market, and most college faculties lost some of their accustomed stability. Faculties tended to become both younger and more mobile; institutional attachments were not as strong as they had once been. For many of the new teachers, allegiance was to their academic discipline, not to the institution at which they were mo-

Administrative Organization for the Faculty, Western Kentucky State College, 1965

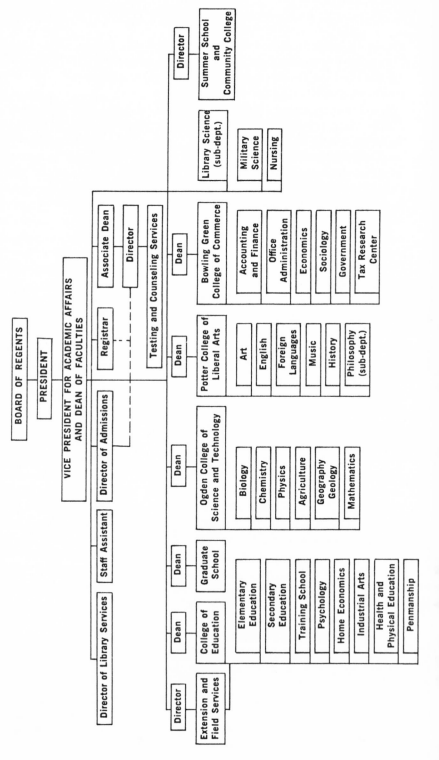

mentarily located. Western presidents who had been nurtured on the Cherry tradition of fierce loyalty to Western had difficulty in understanding some of the new breed of professors. "Western is going through a period of challenging transition," Thompson wrote A.L. Crabb in 1960. "We are making every effort possible to bring into the institution young people with the training and potential to maintain the spirit of Western in the years which lie ahead."

Despite the intense competition for well-qualified faculty members, Western was able to improve the level of academic preparation. In 1955-56 only 22 percent of the 98 full-time members of the faculty held the earned doctorate. Ten years later the 22 percent had climbed to 33 percent as 106 of 317 full time faculty had advanced degrees. The growing emphasis on graduate work increased the need for teachers with the terminal degree. Dean Cravens, assisted by the department heads, recruited actively; President Thompson reserved a veto power over selections but was not usually involved prior to that point. The main criticisms of the recruitment process centered on too much Western inbreeding and too many faculty members from southeastern universities.[33]

Despite the many changes, much of the old Western spirit remained. In 1972 a student of the early postwar era wrote that he had attended six large universities since leaving Western, and "In no one of these universities have I found quite the same finely balanced combination of professionalism, personal interest in students, and dedication to a job well done." None of them had "The Spirit of the Hill." Most vivid in his memory was the character of the Western teachers, not the courses themselves. Despite the rapid growth, there was still at times the personal touch that had been characteristic of earlier years. In the summer of 1961, a young instructor asked for an advance of salary so he could get married before the semester started. Sorry, President Thompson replied, such advances were illegal. But, Thompson added, "I have worked out another arrangement which I feel will allow you and Dan Cupid to proceed without interruption." Enclosed was a note for five hundred dollars from the College Heights Foundation that he could repay over a period of five months.

The normal teaching load was at least fifteen hours per week with little consideration paid to the number of students or preparations. The teacher was expected to be available at least twenty additional hours each week for office hours, counseling, and such special requests as might come from the president, dean, registrar, or business manager. Saturday assignments might be made if in "the best interests of the college." Regular attendance at chapel and faculty meetings was deemed an "assigned professional responsibility," and "active participation in all other college sponsored professional meetings" was assumed. Before the end of 1964 Dean Cravens reported that the fifteen-hour load was becoming a serious recruiting barrier, as well as hindering the expansion of graduate work and the encouragement of faculty research. He proposed that reductions be made, most of them in the spring semesters when enrollments declined and the departments could absorb the loss of classes. If necessary, he added, many of the younger faculty would probably like to teach an overload for extra- compensation—which would be less than half the usual cost. Several faculty resignations cited the heavy teaching load as the primary reason for leaving, and in 1965 the normal teaching load was reduced to twenty-seven hours.[34]

Through the years various accrediting associations had questioned the absence of such standard academic procedures and policies as professorial ranks, pay scale, and tenure. In the Western paternalistic system of governance, such matters had been left to the benevolent discretion of the president; many faculty members never questioned this practice. That attitude was less prevalent among the new members of the faculty, and outside organizations became more insistent that changes be made. The sheer growth of the faculty made necessary more formal policies than had been customary in the past, and a number of significant changes were made in the early 1960s.

Faculty members had usually received a letter that stated the next year's salary, but there had been no contract to be signed. In 1956 President Thompson was both provoked and bewildered when a prospective faculty member decided not to come to Western after they had shaken hands on a verbal agreement. "In all the years during which Western has operated the college has never had a written contract," Thompson wrote. By 1964 the faculty received contract forms which they signed and returned to the president. Faculty ranks had been arbitrarily assigned in order to file reports that called for such information, but the college catalogs did not carry such designations and many faculty members probably did not know what rank they presumably held. A Faculty Rank Committee, chaired by Dr. John D. Minton, drew up a list of qualifications for each rank, and the regents adopted the report on May 25, 1963. By the following spring, the faculty had 36 professors, 42 associate professors, 64 assistant professors, and 56 instructors. The 1965 catalog carried the rank designations for the first time. The usual promotion procedure was for department heads to make recommendations that were then considered by the academic deans. The results of their secret balloting went to the president who, if he approved, recommended them to the Board of Regents.[35]

The absence of a tenure policy had caused difficulty for years. As early as 1948 the American Association of Colleges for Teacher Education requested the adoption of a policy, but Western delayed taking action until the early 1960s. President Garrett insisted that Western did have a sort of *ad hoc* policy, that no one had been dismissed after three years of satisfactory service. Finally, a Faculty Committee was set to work, and a tenure statement was adopted by the Board of Regents at the same time it approved the Rank Committee's recommendations. Tenure, usually denied to instructors, was granted to the other ranks after a probationary period of not over five years. It was awarded automatically if the faculty member was employed for a sixth year. If tenure was denied, formal notice would be given no later than April 1. Although inadequate by later standards, its adoption marked an important step in the development of faculty rights.[36]

The establishment of definite ranks and the installation of more refined business office procedures led to the development of a salary scale that did away with much of the casual assignment of salaries in earlier days. A major ingredient in successful faculty recruiting was salary, and substantial progress was made during this decade as state appropriations increased. For the faculty members who were on the Hill for all that period, the average salary of $4,564 in 1955-56 had become $11,312 by 1965-66. Since inflation was relatively low during most of the decade, Western's people gained in real purchasing power. But similar gains were being made elsewhere, and Western's salaries were not fully competitive with those in much of the nation, including the benchmark institutions that were used as a standard for comparison. Improvements in the state teachers retirement system and participation in the national social security program promised more adequate retirement benefits than Western employees had ever had.[37]

Another indication of faculty change was the establishment in 1965 of a chapter of the American Association of University Professors. This national organization was viewed with suspicion in some quarters; in 1951 the founder and president of the American Flag Movement had inquired if Western had any AAUP members on its campus. Garrett assured him as far as he knew no member of the staff belonged, but the great influx of teachers toward the end of the 1950s brought several members to the campus. Although President Thompson was assured by a friend at the University of Kentucky, "It has been the most constructive organization on campus," organization was not effected until 1965. By then Western was the only state college in Kentucky that did not have a chapter. In March Dr. James N. Wise and Mr. Michael D. Patrick, both of the English department, called a meeting of interested parties in the Faculty House. As a result of that meeting, a committee of five (Elsie Dotson, Paul Hatcher, E.G. Monroe, Marvin Russell, and H.L. Stephens) discussed the matter with President Thompson and secured his endorsement. A committee consisting of Lee Brackett, Randall Capps, Ronald Kramer, Walter Nimocks, and H.E. Shadowen drafted a constitution, and temporary officers were elected. James Wise served as AAUP's first president. President Thompson later said, "The AAUP at Western started off in a dignified, cooperative manner, and as far as I'm concerned has remained that way since its inception," but not every one found it that innocuous. Gordon Wilson kept in close touch with the campus in his retirement, and he saw some of the AAUP members "as immature as any student-led organization on or off the campus. 'Let's start something' should be their motto." At least one short-time member withdrew from the chapter because of "the militant attitudes" that dominated it.[38] That criticism was hardly merited by any objective standard, but AAUP did symbolize the slowly changing character of the faculty and campus.

Another indicator of the slow change was the increased attention paid to research. So few faculty members had published during the prewar years that the appearance of an article usually resulted in a story in the *Herald*. The publication of a book was a major news event. That situation became less satisfactory as Western expanded graduate work and moved closer to university status; accrediting associations pointed out that weakness with increased frequency. Dr. R. Paul Terrill, head of the Department of Geography and Geology, warned a prospective faculty member in late 1961, "Our college makes no provision for staff research. Any writing and research would have to evolve from an exuberance of energy, and such work would be strictly an overtime activity." He should make every effort to complete his dissertation before coming to Western, Terrill added. Dean Cravens told President Thompson that autumn that obtaining federal research grants, especially in the sciences, was unlikely unless some research was already being done. In a survey done for the 1962 Institutional Self Study, 70.8 percent of the faculty reported no research publications within the past five years. Lack of time, facilities, and funds, and the absence of encouragement were the reasons most often cited for such neglect, but twenty-seven teachers confessed a lack of interest. Some determined faculty members were making significant contributions in research and other creative activities, but they had little administrative support. In the mid-1960s when Dr. Carlton Jackson was finishing his manuscript for *Presidential Vetoes*, an administrator suggested that he share royalties with Western since part of the work had been done "on college time." This attitude changed slowly.[39]

A Faculty Research Committee was appointed in 1961 and given a small fund with which to encourage research. Dr. William R. Hourigan chaired the reorganized committee appointed in 1962 "to stimulate faculty research in every way possible." The $1,000 allocated for the fall semester provided eight grants, the largest for $275, and more money was allocated for the spring semester. It was a humble beginning, but it was a start. By June 1966, the committee had approved fifty-nine requests, and ten publications had already resulted. After a visit to Texas Western College in 1965, Vice-President Cravens recommended the establishment of a special professional category "to enable us to recruit carefully selected faculty members with established reputation in their field," who would be expected to do research and publish. Within the next two years, a few such professors joined the faculty. In 1968 the Faculty Research Committee established an annual Faculty Research Bulletin, which provided an outlet for some of the products of the university's increasing emphasis on research. The first issue appeared in 1969; it is to be discontinued after 1986.[40]

Many of the faculty women were pleased in 1963 when Western was belatedly placed on the approved list of the American Association of University Women. Eastern was accredited by 1940, but President Garrett displayed little interest. By the time his attitude softened, the AAUW requirements had hardened, and Western remained outside the pale. Such faculty members as Sara Tyler and Sybil Stonecipher pushed the issue, President Thompson recognized the public relations value of membership, and in 1962 the national organization decided to accept as qualified any institution that met all requirements of its regional accrediting association. In December 1963 Thompson informed the women graduates that they were eligible for AAUW membership.[41]

Some of the faculty changes appalled some members of the community, both on and off campus, but others were dissatisfied because the changes came so slowly. There was grumbling in the Faculty House, which had been remodeled in 1959 for faculty use, but there was little overt discontent. Grievances were not likely to fester, for in most instances a dissatisfied faculty member could simply move to what was seen as a more congenial environment. Only occasionally did signs of dissatisfaction surface. When three of the four members of the physics department resigned in 1962, the reasons they cited included differences over academic standards, the absence of an effective faculty role in policy determination, and an inadequate emphasis on research. In his application for a refund from the Teacher Retirement System, one of the teachers declared under "Reasons for withdrawing" that "Kentucky colleges are more interested in basketball players than scholars. 3 + million for basketball building—nothing for library." President Thompson refused to sign the application while it carried that "barefoot lie."[42]

Another indicator of changing times appeared in the Faculty Wives Club, which had been organized by Mrs. H.H. Cherry in 1927. In theory membership was voluntary; in practice it was almost as compulsory as membership in KEA had once been for the faculty. The organization provided a number of social services for the campus, and President Thompson provided a small subsidy for its functions. A questionnaire sent to the members in the early 1960s revealed several points of dissatisfaction. A number of faculty wives wanted elected officers and an end to roll calls, compulsory attendance, and a dress code when pouring tea. A strong desire was expressed for the establishment of some worthwhile project for the school. Democratic changes were made in 1963, and a scholarship fund was established as an ongoing project. The percentage of members decreased as membership became more truly voluntary, but the organization continued as an active participant in numerous campus functions. A drastic increase in the number of working wives made it difficult if not impossible for a number of wives to join.[43]

Of course some faculty complaints were perpetual. One of the most annoying during the days of open windows was the noise made by lawn mowers that apparently were scheduled to correspond as closely as possible with class hours. Historian Walter Nimocks had been forced to dismiss a class during the last week of the 1964 summer school, he told President Thompson. "Some teaching handicaps I can overcome. Others that I knew to be inevitable I can accept with resignation. But I find it impossible either to outshout the whine of a mower or accept the implied position that custodial activities take precedence over the instructional program."[44] For such irritants there was no solution.

By 1965 the students on the Hill had a much broader range of choice among curricula and majors than any previous generation. The growth in size created problems and made impossible the degree of unity that had once prevailed, but there were more academic specialists offering more work in more areas. Five major undergraduate curricular areas were available by the fall of 1965. The Teacher Education Curricula consisted of programs in elementary and secondary education. The Arts and Science Curricula had majors and minors in thirty fields. The Special Studies Curricula, which led to the B.S. degree, was limited to majors in accounting, agriculture, business administration, and industrial arts. The Professional Curricula included work in agriculture, chemistry, engineering-physics, industrial technology, medical technology, nursing, and training leaders for Boys Clubs. The nursing program, started in 1964, and the technology programs were among the first of what would later become a large group of such programs. The Pre-Professional Curricula had eight major areas, including the long established ones in medicine and law, and foundation curricula for a number of other less popular areas. The increase in the two-year programs was reflected in the growing number of associate degrees.

The most noticeable growth in departments was in the business area. In 1965 the Bowling Green College of Commerce had departments of accounting and finance, business administration, office administration, economics, government, and sociology. The Tax Research Center created in 1965 was the first such unit on the Western campus. Among other department changes were: the creation of the elementary and secondary departments in the College of Education; the emergence of psychology as a full-fledged department; the availability of majors in speech and dramatic arts and a minor in mass media within the English department; and the addition of German and Spanish majors and a Russian minor in foreign languages. Philosophy was called an "Instructional Area" rather than a department, but it had three teachers on the staff; departmental status came a year later. Penmanship was still listed as a department although G.G. Craig constituted its faculty and only two courses were offered. Penmanship 101, once required for elementary certification, had become a recommended elective, and penmanship ceased to exist as a department when Mr. Craig retired in 1965.

Graduate studies also expanded during this decade. When graduate work was allowed to resume in 1941 the only degree that could be earned was the Master of Arts in Education. This prohibition continued until 1966, although several modifications were made before then. In 1960, acting on the recommendation of Dean Cravens and President Thompson, the Regents allowed graduate students to take as many as twenty-one hours of course work in professional fields (social science area, science area, English) other than education. Two years later Western and her three sister institutions were authorized to offer thirty hours beyond the Master's degree that would allow a teacher to achieve a Rank I certificate. The growing graduate program was handled by Dean Cravens until 1961 when Dr. John D. Minton, who had joined the Department of History in 1958, became a staff assistant in Craven's office in charge of the Graduate Division. Minton became dean of the Graduate School when it was established in 1964. In 1966 the Faculty Committee on Graduate Instruction was replaced by a Graduate Council, and a graduate faculty was appointed.[45]

Heeding a growing demand for graduate work outside the fields of Education, the Council on Public Higher Education on April 20, 1963, authorized the four state colleges to offer master's level work in the arts and sciences. Implementation was delayed by the determined efforts of the University of Kentucky to get the approval rescinded. After the UK Trustees requested the council to repeal its approval, the issue became a matter of public controversy. The editor of the Paducah *Sun-Democrat* endorsed the UK effort: "This is the proper time to call a halt to the gradual expansion of the state colleges beyond the status and function of good regional colleges." Graduate Dean A.D. Kirwan repeated the charges of the special committee: "It is an inefficient, unnecessary, wasteful effort at duplication…. No matter what they do they can't duplicate us. They'll be turning out students with master's degrees of inferior quality…. And we're not anywhere near the point of quality we want to reach. But we're incomparably above them…. It's simply absurd for them to start master's programs in such things as history, physics, chemistry and mathematics." Western maintained a low profile during the controversy, but President Robert Martin of Eastern expressed concern over the problems at Lexington: "I'm right distressed they've had so little success with their graduate program at UK that classes are not full."[46]

The intractable attitude of the University of Kentucky helped create an atmosphere of suspicion and smoldering animosity between the state university and the state colleges that has never been completely dispelled. In 1963 the presidents were voting members of the council, and at the September meeting they were in a belligerent mood. President Thompson did not attend because of the critical illness of his son Hardin, but Robert Cochran reported, "Each college president expressed the opinion that if the University created a fight the state colleges will certainly not back away." The council did not rescind its approval for graduate work in fields other than education, and in 1966 Western's Board of Regents approved the M.A. degree for English and history. The number of departments offering graduate programs increased rapidly during the next few years.[47]

Its growth was the most striking aspect of the student body in the 1960s. Despite sharp increases in out-of-state tuition, Kentucky's state schools represented a bargain when compared to most states. By the mid-1960s demands were growing that a limit be placed on out-of-state enrollment— 15 percent of the student body was the standard often cited. Western's out-of-state enrollment had inched up toward that level but had not reached it, but the other five state institutions ran well above that figure.[48] Yet for anyone who was well acquainted with Western and its traditions, the most surprising change in the area of student life was the introduction of social fraternities and sororities.

Cherry's ban on Greek organizations continued through the Garrett administration and the first several years of Thompson's tenure. Such societies were considered an important part of college life on many campuses, and their absence on the Hill caused some adverse comment. In addition, the absence of recognized Greek organizations had led to the establishment of off-campus groups over which the college had little or no control. In 1955, when he submitted a list of suggestions for "needed action," Gordon Wilson included "Something in the way of a public stand on the bootleg fraternities and sororities, for they are a distinct menace, especially the Barons." By June 1960 the five off-campus organizations for men had 121 members and the five for women had 123. Dean Charles A. Keown and a committee studied the issue and recommended the establishment of national social fraternities and sororities. The regents gave approval at their August 23, 1961, meeting, and another committee was created to provide for an orderly transition. Its report the following spring encouraged the establishment of national affiliates, prohibited the owning or leasing of property without the approval of the college, and declared that membership in unrecognized student organizations must end by January 29, 1963. By the fall semester 1962, ten groups had been recognized. The first five fraternities were Delta Kappa Nu, Lamba Sigma Epsilon, Pi Lamba Alpha, Kappa Sigma Tau, and Sigma Phi Alpha; the first five sororities were Epsilon Alpha, Phi Delta Omega, Zeta Tau Omega, Beta Omega Chi, and Pi Sigma Upsilon. By the spring of 1964, eight locals had received permission to affiliate with nationals and three other locals were in the process of becoming colonies as a step toward such affiliation.[49]

The Greeks grew rapidly during the next few years, and the people who worked with student affairs found new complications in their duties as they dealt with the Inter-fraternity Council and the Panhellenic Council, as well as with individual groups. When the prohibition against housing was amended in the spring of 1965 to allow fraternities to seek housing in existing off-campus facilities, a new set of problems was opened up. Homeowners usually opposed the intrusion of Greek houses into their neighborhood, and the college was appealed to by both parties. By 1966 the black enrollment had increased to the point that a few students indicated an interest in establishing a local black fraternity.[50]

With the college moving toward the approval of social Greek organizations, it was pointless to oppose Greek honor societies. After considerable discussion the regents on May 7, 1959, approved their establishment. When they did so, they eliminated one of the frequent editorial topics for the *Herald*. The Western Players were apparently the first organization to take advantage of the concession, and the Players became the Mu Lambda chapter of Alpha Psi Omega in the fall of 1959. By 1965 seventeen honor and professional societies had campus chapters. In several instances they had an adverse effect upon the traditional departmental clubs.

As the student enrollment increased, so did the number of student organizations. In 1965 over eighty organizations were listed in the catalog with the growth areas being the Greek societies, the honor societies, and special interest groups, such as the Western Madrigal Singers, the Western Writers, and the Young Democrats and Young Republicans. The county clubs had declined to only a dozen in 1965, and the class organizations bore little resemblance to the lively bodies of earlier years.[51]

Western also acquired a start toward a student government, another considerable change in institutional attitude. Gordon Wilson, who knew both men well, once said, "President Cherry talked about democracy but didn't practice it—Garrett was a living example of it." But neither president expected students to participate in the governance of the college. Thompson formed a Student Advisory Council in January 1956 that for the first time on an organized basis solicited student advice. Its members consisted of the class presidents, the club presidents, and the editors of the *Herald* and the *Talisman* with the dean of students as its sponsor. Its executive committee consisted of the presidents of the three upper classes and four members elected from the membership of the council. The council's first president was Ronnie Sutton, the senior class president from Brodhead, Kentucky; a quarter century later he was dean of scholastic development. The council considered such matters as Western's social program, parking problems, the registration procedure, student honors and awards, a uniform method of electing club officers, cheerleader elections, and the development of a student handbook and directory.[52]

Interest in the Advisory Council soon lagged, perhaps because it had no role in areas that some students considered important. Some excitement was created in early 1965 when Robert N. Johns, a sophomore English major, addressed a mimeographed appeal to "Students" to join a Student Government Association with the goal of establishing a student government by the end of the semester. In rhetoric radical by Western standards, he asked, "Do you have your constitutionally guaranteed rights of freedom of speech, freedom of assembly, freedom of the press, and freedom from search without a warrant at Western?" Since the *Herald* did not even have a letters-to-the-editor department, "Where does the administration expect a student to express his opinion? On the restroom walls?" The movement attracted considerable press attention, unwanted by the administration. Robert Wurster of the English department, who had been suggested as a possible advisor to the group, commented that he had been asked by the administration not to discuss the matter, but he expressed concern over both student apathy and a climate of repression that caused a student to be reprimanded because he started a petition requesting a letters-to-the-editor department in the school paper. Twenty-five students attended the group's first meeting in the Warren County Courthouse on February 23; only four attended the meeting on March 4, and Johns said that the effort would cease. Before then President Thompson had announced that Western was looking for a workable plan of student government that would not endanger the Hill. He declared, "The Communist Party has schools where people are sent to become leaders in student government. Up to now they've been working on the bigger schools."[53]

Some members of Western's administration were concerned about the lack of a viable student government. On January 25, 1965, Registrar Rhea P. Lazarus, a senior class sponsor, wrote Dean Keown that the seniors called the present system "worthless" and class organizations ineffective. They recommended "an organization which would be attractive to all students and to which all could pledge their allegiance." Lazarus suggested that a new plan for student government be started by the fall. Keown urged Thompson to move in that direction and presented a plan of action to him. The Congress Debating Club did some preliminary work, then a committee drafted a constitution. Progress was deliberate, but by April 1966 President Thompson had approved the constitution for submission to a ratification vote. A *Herald* editorial called for adoption of the not perfect but good constitution. To do otherwise would delay establishment, and "Too many yesterdays have already been lost." The document was ratified in early May 1966 by a vote of 1,812 to 726 with approximately one-third of the undergraduates voting. Elections were immediately scheduled for later in the month so that the Associated Student Government would be in operation for the 1966-67 academic year.[54]

The "radicalism" displayed in the demand for a student government was also evidenced by the emergence of a short-lived off-campus newspaper in 1965. The *College Heights Herald* had such problems as uncertain and often inadequate income, publication on an every-other-week or even monthly basis, and its use as a means of maintaining touch with the alumni. Much of the news was stale before the paper appeared, and many stories that appealed to the alumni held little interest for contemporary students. Miss Frances Richards worked diligently with her journalism classes to turn out readable copy, but students interested in journalism as a profession received little practical experience. Better working conditions were obtained after Kelly Thompson became one of the sponsors in 1940. In 1942 the *Herald* received the coveted Medalist rating from the Columbia Scholastic Press Association, an honor that it won eight more times before 1965. In 1942 and 1944 the *Herald* won All-American ratings from the Associated Collegiate Press, and first place ratings in individual categories were numerous. When Thompson became president, Robert Cochran assumed the duties of general manager. When Miss Richards retired in 1964 she was succeeded by Mrs. Judy Ecker. By then the *Herald* breakfast at Homecoming, started by Miss Richards in 1951, had become a highlight of the *Herald* year.[55]

Although an occasional *Herald* story or editorial had upset some individuals or groups, the *Herald* had been a safe, conservative, house organ. President Garrett explained that as general manager Kelly Thompson "would go over the material published not by strong arm methods, but by suggestions. He was affective [sic] in keeping out of the paper at times I am sure, material which was more likely to be harmful than helpful to the college." An excellent example of this approach occurred in 1949 when a sensational Bowling Green double murder attracted national attention. Charged in the case were a faculty member and a student who said he was the teacher's "soulmate." They were alleged to have blackmailed a former faculty member by threatening to expose some photographs. The *Herald* covered the sensational case by saying primly in the October 7 issue that in the best interests of everyone and the school it was "devoting its columns to regular news of the institution" instead of "the sensational coverage of events of the past few days." During the 1965 effort to form a student government, the *Kentucky*

Kernel reported that the *Herald* was not subjected to direct censorship. "But the editor is chosen because he is safe and reliable and the administration knows he won't cause any controversy at Western."[56]

This *Herald* blandness was countered by the October 22, 1965, appearance of the *Skewer*, a mimeographed off-campus publication that was critical of the administration and many of its policies. Its second and last issue appeared on November 29. Instead of ignoring the publication, Western suspended indefinitely Frank Bonasso, Robert Johns, and Sam Lawson; George Chakos had dropped out of school a few days earlier. In justifying the decision, President Thompson told of a visit to the Berkeley campus in September 1964 where he was appalled by "unbelievable chaos and virtual anarchy which had sprung from irresponsibility. It is our conviction that there should be no 'Berkeley in Bowling Green' because of a lack of courage on the part of those who must think of all the students or failure to take positive action when the situation warrants it."

Western was a long distance from Berkeley in many respects, but times were changing and student rights were acquiring more meaning even on campuses as far removed from the radical mainstream as Western. The *Skewer* publishers obtained a temporary restraining order allowing them to continue in classes. The local AAUP chapter protested the lack of due process, and the Kentucky Civil Liberties Union and the Kentucky Conference of University Professors expressed interest in the case. In a guest editorial in the *Herald* on December 10, the *Skewer* staffers admitted that the article ("In Defense of Chastity") the administration had called "obscene, irresponsible and in bad taste" was perhaps "too hastily written and in somewhat bad taste," but they denied that its publication was sufficient grounds for suspension. And they maintained that they had been denied due process and civil rights.

A regents hearing was held on December 18 with witnesses testifying under oath and both parties represented by counsel. The regents then adjourned to January 8, 1966. Lawson, Bonasso, and Chakos withdrew their appeals before the hearing resumed, but the Johns case continued, and the regents upheld his suspension. Thompson then announced that he would recommend readmission for the spring semester for the three who were in school when suspended and for Chakos who had quit school. The Circuit Court lifted the temporary restraining order and dismissed the students' suit. Reaction to the affair was mixed. President Thompson received acclaim for the strong action from the Third District Principals Association and numerous individuals, including many faculty members. But Western was censored by the Civil Liberties Union in a lengthy report that asserted, "The heart of the problem of student academic freedom at Western seems to be in the failure of the college's administration to keep pace with the rapid growth of their own institution and its changing student body." The *Courier-Journal* was equally harsh:

"This incident is a reflection of an official attitude that cannot prevail if Western is to become a first-rate institution of higher learning."[57] The *Skewer* did not reappear, but the *Herald*, which had become a weekly in 1961, became somewhat less conservative over the next several years.

Although there was some relaxation of the regulations concerning student life on the campus, Western continued a paternalistic approach well into the 1960s. "The College demands high standards of personal conduct from its students," the 1965 catalog warned. "Although a student who becomes involved in difficulties will be given all possible help and understanding, persons whose standards and purposes are not compatible with those of the College will be put on probation or dismissed from the College." The most common cause of nonacademic separation was drinking, especially in the men's dormitories. Alcohol influenced other unacceptable behavior such as shooting fireworks (excluding those exploded on July 4) and creating other disturbances. Dean Keown maintained in 1965 that the problem at Western was less serious than at many schools. He and his associates had not seen evidence of drinking at the Homecoming dance although the cleanup crew had collected over one hundred bottles. The Dean confessed difficulty in knowing whether a student who had listened to a rock and roll band for two or three hours was under the influence of alcohol or the music. The symptoms were much the same. In those halcyon days the drug problem was relatively insignificant. As late as 1968 when three students were arrested for selling marijuana the police estimated that only 25-30 students were users.[58]

Dormitory regulations were much more detailed and strict for the women than for the men. In the mid-1960s freshmen women had to be in the dormitory by 9:30 P.M. Monday through Thursday; curfew for all other women was 10:30 P.M. Everyone could be out until midnight on Friday and Saturday and until 10:30 P.M. on Sunday. If an on-campus, college-wide function ran beyond the regular dorm hours, the hall residents were given fifteen minutes grace to reach their dorms. Any woman leaving a dorm after 7:00 P.M. had to check out and in, giving her destination and escort, if any. Except for going home, out-of-town travel required permission from both parents and the dorm director. Sunbathing was permitted only in designated areas, screened from the general public, and shoes and an outer garment were to be worn to and from the designated location. Robes and swim suits were not worn in the lobby. Even decorative liquor containers were outlawed in the rooms, and cooking was strictly prohibited. (But coeds learned that a cheese sandwich could be grilled on an iron and soup heated in a popcorn popper.) When a violator was campused for an infraction, she could not receive callers and she had to sign in hourly during the evening. She could even be restricted to her floor or to her room. Residents were warned, "Calling out of windows is not an accepted means of communication," and ladies did not smoke outside their rooms.[59]

A dress code attempted to cover both men and women, but it encountered problems with the general trend toward more casual wear. Shorts were prohibited in classrooms, laboratories, libraries, and offices. The handbook provided specific information on what was acceptable campus dress. "Classroom wear for women generally involves skirts, blouses, sweaters, socks or nylons, and flats. Formal and semi-formal wear for women means formal or dinner dresses, whereas informal wear usually indicates class or street dresses, depending upon the time and occasion. Classroom wear for men usually includes khakis, cottons, slacks, sport shirts, or shirt and tie. In cooler weather sports coats, sweaters and jackets are worn. Dark suits, dinner jackets and tuxedos are appropriate for formal and semi-formal occasions. Dress for less formal occasion [sic] includes business suits, or sports coats with tie." Valiant efforts were made to maintain these standards, with the library as a main bastion of decorum. Senior Samuel L. Edwards "was taken aback and humiliated" on an April Saturday in 1966 when he was asked to tuck in his shirt tail before entering the library. In August of that year, a professor from another school was refused admission to the library because she was wearing shorts. After some agitated discussion, the checker agreed to send for the relative whom the visitor wanted to see.

Even then changes were occurring. After the April incident the library learned to tolerate visible shirt tails, and President Thompson assured the shorts-clad visiting professor that she would find the rules changed before her next visit. The *Student Handbook* for 1967-68 did not contain the prohibition on shorts. Campus attire became much more casual, and the relaxation soon extended to some members of the faculty who had been bound by an informal but generally effective code.[60]

The more permissive rules in the 1967-68 *Student Handbook* also relaxed the hours for the women's residence halls, but the university was still not ready to abandon regulations as some students demanded. Although enforcement was probably impossible, the traditional school policy remained unchanged for off-campus students who were expected to maintain "the same high standards of conduct" required of on-campus residents. "Men and women are not allowed to visit one another in rooms or apartments. The possession of alcoholic beverages in off-campus living quarters is in violation of university policy." The general statement remained in the 1968-69 *Handbook*, but the specific prohibitions had quietly disappeared. The *Handbook* gradually became a more realistic document.

One of the most annoying restrictions prevented freshmen and many sophomores from having cars on campus. The rapid increase in student enrollment and the size of faculty and staff and a more affluent society that had greatly expanded automobile ownership created a parking crisis on most campuses by the early 1960s. Kentucky's state colleges hesitated to risk a competitive disadvantage by imposing bans unilaterally, so at its July 9, 1962, meeting the Council on Public Higher Education assumed the odium for a state-wide regulation. Beginning September 1, 1962, freshmen, with such obvious exceptions as commuters, were forbidden to possess or to operate motor vehicles on campus; a year later the ban also applied to sophomores and to any student who was on academic or disciplinary probation, regardless of classification. The measure was often praised as a step to encourage academic achievement, and it may well have provided motivation for some students. For others, it hastened their departure into the more mobile general society. Western did free sophomores with a B average from the ban. Completion of a one thousand-space parking structure in 1969 and provision of other parking spaces allowed the policy to be ended in 1972. The Regents did, however, then impose a five dollar fee for registering a vehicle for on-campus use.[61]

Information concerning student attitudes and behavior is often incomplete, as is often true of data for social history. This would seem to be the case in a 1969 questionnaire answered for the president of Kansas State College of Pittsburg. Item 2C was "Sex," and the column checked was "Available But Seldom Used." Although the sexual revolution had not swept the Western campus, circumstantial evidence indicates that the response may not have been completely accurate.[62]

At the midpoint in the decade of the 1960s, Western had experienced little of the student unrest that pervaded a number of campuses. Most of the student problems concerned individuals, and the exceptions tended to be in the traditional vein of student disturbances. Six students were arrested on breach-of-peace charges on Wednesday, March 14, 1962, after a small on-campus demonstration developed eight hours later into a mob of nearly one thousand that temporarily blocked traffic at the College Street bridge. The demonstrators demanded a holiday because the basketball team by defeating Detroit in Lexington had earned the right to meet Ohio State, the number one-ranked team in the nation, at Iowa City on Friday in the NCAA Mid-East Regional Tournament. The students did not get the holiday, and the team lost to Ohio State. A *Herald* editorial asserted that the affair showed the need for "a method wherein the students have a right and a way to express themselves in policy-making which concerns them as much as the recent event did." Two years later the city police arrested twenty-three students, female as well as male, from a group of some four hundred engaged in a less orthodox affair. The students had assembled near the dorms on Sixteenth Street about six-thirty on the evening of April 21. Instead of dispersing when Dean Keown ordered them to, they marched to Clay Street where they threw rocks through the windows of Mrs. Pauline Tabor's famous house. A mimeographed handbill declared that the group's purpose was "to stamp out a house of prostitution, which the Grand Jury of the city of Bowling Green has reportedly for years been unable to locate." Most of the students arrested paid small fines and costs in the Police Court.[63]

On the other hand, numerous outsiders to the campus testified to the high quality of the student body. A Louisville pastor, for example, wrote President Thompson in 1958 after participating in Religious Emphasis Week: "I was literally amazed at the high caliber, serious mindedness, interest in spiritual values, and high ideals of the student body in general.... The attitude of those in the cafeteria and on the campus, even the ones who did not attend the services, was remarkable." Two years later a thousand basketball fans who were returning to Bowling Green after Western beat the University of Miami team at Lexington in a first round NCAA game were stranded in the Elizabethtown area by a massive late-season snow storm. Afterwards two Bowling Green men praised the students with whom they were isolated. "During the eighteen to twenty hours that we were together not once did anyone conduct themselves in a manner that would make you ashamed to say that they were a member of Western State College.... It certainly makes us proud to be a part of the community in which Western State College is located."[64]

The new basketball arena that was named for him was a joy to Coach Diddle, but he coached in it for only one year. He had the first of a dozen heart attacks in 1952, and from then until his death in 1970 he had numerous problems with such other ailments as arthritis, kidney complications, and gout. Diddle hoped to coach through the 1964-65 season, but he did not recover fully from two severe heart attacks in April 1963, and family and friends persuaded him to retire despite his famous declaration, "I'm going to die with my feet on." He retired after forty-two years with 759 games won and 302 lost for an overall winning percentage of 71.5 percent. Included in these totals were 180 tournament games, and his teams won 72.8 percent of them. Even detractors who thought the school overemphasized basketball had to admit that Western was better known nationally for Diddle and basketball than for any other aspects of its programs. Coach Diddle became a legend in his lifetime, and few Westerners who date from the Diddle era can resist telling their favorite stories about him whenever a group assembles. "I want you to stand up and remain seated until I've introduced you all," he told the squad one day in chapel; he ordered the freshmen "to line up alphabetically by height"; and he warned a player who used one hand that "all great players have to be amphibious." His syntax was often mangled, but for over forty years he communicated successfully.

Diddle's last nine seasons, 1955-56 through 1963-64, did not match his exceptional achievements of earlier years. Starting in 1933-34, he had ten consecutive twenty-game winning seasons, and after a three-year wartime interlude he added twenty-game seasons eight of the next nine years. During his last nine years, Coach Diddle enjoyed only one twenty-game season (1959-60), and his 126-101 (55.5 percent) record was not up to his earlier standards. Recruiting competition was much more intense, and he no longer got the steady flow of exceptional players he had once enjoyed. Only six Toppers made the All OVC first team during that nine-year span; eleven had earned that distinction in the six years of the OVC prior to the 1954-55 season.

Yet there were still some important victories, and Diddle's teams won the OVC championship five of his last nine years, and they appeared twice in the NCAA tournaments. One of the most controversial wins came in February 1959 when Eastern's Paul McBrayer forfeited the game. Western was leading 38-20 with over six minutes remaining in the first half when Bobby Rascoe stole the ball and drove for a layup. Eastern's Ralph Richardson tried to block the shot, and both players crashed into Western's bench behind the end line. Diddle said that he tried to break the players' fall; McBrayer charged that Diddle had laid hostile hands on his player. The Eastern coach led his players off the court, and the OVC had its first forfeited game.

Western fans suffered with Coach Diddle during his last seasons when the 1962-63 and 1963-64 squads had identical 5-16 records. The *Herald* reported in early 1963 that Western was actively recruiting black players, and during the 1963-64 season fans focused their attention on the freshman team that Clem "The Gem" Haskins led to a 14-2 record.[65] The last game played in the old gym was a heartbreaking 80-79 loss to East Tennessee. Despite the defeats of the last year, Diddle's record in the soon-to-be library was 336 won, 37 lost.

When it became apparent that Coach Diddle might not be able to coach until mandatory retirement age, Western looked for a replacement. Ted Hornback, Diddle's longtime assistant, certainly deserved the position, but the opportunity came too late for him. He was fifty-eight in the spring of 1964 when he decided to become athletic director and continue to coach the tennis team. John Oldham was selected instead. After winning All-American honors in his senior year at Western in 1949, Oldham played two years of professional ball with the Fort Wayne Pistons before his dislike of travel (and his absolute aversion to flying) brought him back to Western as coach of the College High team. In 1955 he moved to Tennessee Tech where in nine years he compiled a 118-83 record, won or shared three OVC championships, and won half of his eighteen games against Coach Diddle. Given Diddle's and Hornback's endorsement, Oldham resigned at Tennessee Tech on March 24, 1964, and immediately accepted an offer tendered by President Thompson. Oldham soon moved to Bowling Green to serve as special administrative assistant to Thompson until Diddle's retirement. Two other Western stars, Wallace "Buck" Sydnor and Gene Rhodes, became his assistant coaches.[66]

The 1964-65 season opened with an embarrassing loss to Belmont

College in Diddle Arena, and it ended with a close 58-54 loss to Army in the NIT in Madison Square Garden. But the overall record was a good 18-9 as sophomores Clem Haskins, Dwight Smith, and Pearl Hicks contributed heavily to the turnaround. Haskins, who set an OVC record with 55 points against Middle Tennessee, was named OVC Player-of-the-Year, an honor he won for three consecutive years. Oldham used a more disciplined offense than Diddle, and he alternated between a man-to-man and a variety of zone defenses. The 1965-66 squad, bolstered by such additions as sophomores Greg Smith and Wayne Chapman, lacked little except for a dominant big man, and it won 25 of 28 games. The most bitter loss was to the University of Michigan, 80-79, in the NCAA tournament. Western led 79-78 with eleven seconds remaining when an official called a disputed foul on Greg Smith on a jump ball. All-American Cazzie Russell hit both free throws and a brilliant season ended. Oldham was the OVC Coach-of-the-Year and Haskins repeated as Player-of-the-Year.

Coach Diddle watched games from his special box at floor level. And from time to time, when he sensed that crowd support was lagging, he ambled over to the student section waving his red towel. His cheerleading techniques may have been outmoded, but the crowds went wild whenever he appeared. In really critical moments, he might climb on top a press table to work his magic. Coach Diddle was always a competitor, and if he could no longer help Western win one way, he would do what he could in another role.[67]

Football also had a coaching change. In nine years (1948-56) Jack Clayton won 50 games, lost 33, and tied 2 for a winning percentage of 60.2. When he resigned in January 1957 to become head coach and athletic director at Northwestern Louisiana State College, thirty-two coaches applied for the position. Western selected fifty-year-old Nicholas George Denes. He had coached Western's freshmen team in 1939, but he was best known for his exceptional record in high school where his teams had won state championships in football, basketball, and track. He was noted, too, for his endless supply of stories and his pixyish sense of humor. Short and sturdy with a round face and a wide grin, "the whimsical elf" was always good for a story. In 1975 when he was battling terminal illness, Denes delighted in telling friends, "They're giving me female hormones to treat the cancer. It's done two things—retarded the growth of the cancer and made my bustline the talk of the neighborhood." When Denes was selected, it was also announced that Jimmy Feix would become a student assistant football coach as soon as he was released from the Air Force. Frank Griffin and Turner Elrod continued as assistants on the staff.[68]

During his eleven years (1957-67), Denes compiled a record of 57-39-7 (58.7 percent). His most successful season was 1963 when the only blemish on the record was a 14-14 tie with the University of Tampa. That season was climaxed by a 27-0 Tangerine Bowl victory over a highly regarded U.S. Coast Guard Academy team. Five members of the team made the All-OVC first team, one of whom, Dale Lindsey, later went on to a long and successful NFL career. That level of success could not be maintained, and in 1965 Coach Denes experienced a disappointing 2-6-2 record. Then fifty-nine, he wanted to retire, but President Thompson insisted that he wait for a winning season. The 1966 record was 5-5, and in 1967, sparked by the great running of fullback Dickie Moore, the team won seven games, tied Eastern, and lost only to Middle Tennessee, 16-14. Denes resigned as coach at the end of the season, but taught in the physical education department until 1971. Then, he explained, he found that he would receive ninety dollars a month more in retirement than he did teaching. "My mother didn't raise an idiot." He urged the selection of Jimmy Feix as his successor, and that appointment was quickly made.[69]

The last game Nick Denes coached was a 42-19 victory over Murray. It was also the last game played in the stadium near the top of the hill. The site was lovely, but expansion was almost impossible, and convenient parking was nonexistent. By early 1965 plans were underway for a new stadium, located between the Russellville Road and the railroad tracks, that would seat at least fifteen thousand people. Construction started on the academic-athletic complex a year later, and the 19,250 seat facility opened on September 21, 1968, when Butler was defeated 35-0 for Feix's first victory. The stadium was named for L.T. Smith, who had contributed much to Western's athletic program during his long term on the Hill.[70]

The cost of athletics became more of a problem by the late 1950s, as only basketball paid for itself. The cost of being competitive increased, and Western was not willing to accept a mediocre program. President Thompson defended the expenses as an essential part of Western's role in training coaches, but he was also aware that the general public often evaluated a college in terms of its athletic teams.[71] The Ohio Valley Conference was under pressure to increase scholarships in order to improve its success against nonconference teams. When the OVC in 1963 decided to offer some scholarships for spring sports, the calibre of performance improved but the costs increased. OVC teams had little chance to compete in the television market, which for nationally recognized teams was beginning to be an important new source of revenue.

Tennis and golf were the most successful of the minor sports during the 1956-65 decade. Ted Hornback's netters won 109 matches, lost only 22; they won the OVC tournament five times and finished second three times. During the same ten years, Frank Griffin's golf teams almost equalled the tennis record with 84 matches won, 22 lost, and 3 tied. In the 1964 and 1965 seasons the combined record was a gaudy 25-0-1. The baseball team was less successful, although its 49-39-1 record was respectable. It had four coaches during the ten years. When Coach Diddle gave up the job after the 1957 season, Nick Denes took over the coaching for the next five years. Dan King, a baseball and basketball star in 1950-54, coached the team in 1963 and 1964, and Gene Rhodes, also one of Western's star athletes, joined the staff in 1964 as head baseball coach and assistant basketball coach. The most dismal record of any of the spring sports belonged to track. In a six-year stretch, 1956-61, the Western squads won one dual meet (Austin Peay in 1960) and lost 38. Turner Elrod, the long-suffering track coach, could have blamed the football recruiting, for most of his participants were off-season footballers.

The renaissance of track and field came with the 1962 appointment of Tom Ecker, the twenty-seven-year-old coach at Elizabethtown High School. Brash, energetic, unpredictable, and controversial, Ecker was a winner. He had already published a very successful book, *Championship Track and Field by 12 Great Coaches*, as well as a companion volume on football that he had coedited. He was reported to have announced upon his arrival in 1962, "Within three years and with 13 boys of my choosing, we will be able to win the OVC." He won the OVC championship in 1964, after taking the Kentucky Federation Championship in 1963. Ecker was the OVC track coach of the year in 1963, 1964, and 1965. When he left Western after four years to become one of Sweden's national track coaches, he left an 18-3 record in dual track meets and a 19-3 record in cross-country, which he started in 1962. Ecker's major controversy was with the track coach and athletic director at Eastern whom he accused of "extreme reluctance" in competing with Western in both track and cross-country.[72] Ecker was succeeded in both positions by Dr. Burch Oglesby who joined the faculty in 1965.

The Ohio Valley Conference began awarding an annual All-Sports Championship in 1963. Western captured that title for the first time in 1964-65, and before leaving the OVC in 1982 the Hilltoppers won it twelve of twenty years. They were close runners-up five times. This record is perhaps the best single indicator of the calibre of the athletic programs on the Hill. Other types of progress were not as easily measured.

Forming the University
1966-1969

PRESIDENT THOMPSON had often warned zealous supporters of Western against too hasty demands for university status, but by 1965 he believed that the time had come. In his ten-year report to the Board of Regents, he pointed out the advantages of the change of status and recommended "that such a change in Western's name should be considered at the earliest possible date, … Western is ready for such change." To achieve it, however, legislation was required, and here careful preparation was vital. The major stumbling block was likely to be the University of Kentucky which had consistently opposed each step in the progress of the other state schools. Dean Cravens was told at a meeting in December 1965 "that the University of Kentucky had contacted members of the Legislature in Western Kentucky attempting to get their support in opposition to university status for the State colleges." If there were such efforts, they were unsuccessful. The Commission on Higher Education employed consultants who recommended that four state colleges (excluding Kentucky State College, the predominately black college in Frankfort) be elevated to university status and allowed to develop noneducation masters programs as rapidly as possible. The new universities should also develop research and service programs appropriate for their primary areas. Other recommendations included making the University of Louisville a state school, establishing Northern Kentucky State College in the Covington area, and continuing the state-wide community college program under the aegis of the University of Kentucky. The consultants recommended that each governing board should be autonomous and that *ex officio* memberships should be terminated at the end of the terms of the incumbents.[1]

Most of the recommendations were adopted unanimously by the Commission on Higher Education. The vote on the elevation of the colleges to universities was 13 to 3 with one abstention; the opposition, as expected, came from the University of Kentucky.

The college presidents exercised their considerable influence, and by early February Thompson wrote "There is a good chance that we will get a bill through the Legislature this session without any organized opposition and with little fanfare." The bill whipped through the House of Representatives 83-0 on February 16, 1966, but a problem developed in the Senate when Senator Tom Garrett managed to add an amendment to create a four-year college at Paducah. That decision was reversed the next day by a 24-6 vote, and the bill passed 29-6. It was a compromise between the university and the four colleges. The University of Kentucky was defined as the state's main graduate and research institution, and, in a move of far-reaching importance, a new Council on Higher Education was created. Its voting members consisted of nine laymen appointed by the governor; the presidents of the state's public universities and colleges would be nonvoting members. This change removed much of the power that the college presidents had been able to wield by bloc voting on issues vital to their welfare.[2]

Governor Ned Breathitt signed the bill on February 26, 1966. The bill was permissive, not mandatory, but the Board of Regents meeting in a special session quickly accepted the offer, and Western celebrated the impending change. The celebrating had started the previous evening at the annual Talisman Ball, for the college had opened the event to all students without charge. Saturday was declared "Western Day" in Bowling Green and Warren County, and some 650 people attended a citizens' appreciation dinner in the Garrett ballroom. In an elaborate ceremony at half-time of the Murray basketball game, Governor Breathitt presented a plaque commemorating the change to President Thompson. The basketball team delighted a crowd of 12,500 by beating the Thoroughbreds 71-59, and Monday classes were dismissed. The change did not become official until June 16, 1966, but most celebrants ignored that technicality.

Vice-President Cravens was one who warned that the task was not completed. He told a group of alumni, "It is obvious that the job of building Western Kentucky University has just begun. Western is an incipient University, a University still in its formative years, and ahead is a great challenge to move from a mature multi-purpose State College to a mature multi-purpose University."[3] There would be more changes along the way.

Enrollment continued to increase at the new university during the last years of the 1960s. The September head counts showed these totals: 1965, 7,824; 1966, 8,701; 1967, 10,197; 1968, 10,570; and 1969, 11,069. A milestone occurred in 1967 when the enrollment surged nearly 1,500 students above the number in 1966 (an increase of 17.2 percent) and exceeded 10,000 for the first time. But that year was the last of the large increases in enrollment. Only 373 more students enrolled the next year, an increase of only 3.7 percent; the 1969 growth of 499 was a 4.7 percent increase. Academic optimism had sometimes ignored demographic statistics, and the sudden leveling off came as a surprise to many people. The plans for a second campus were quietly shelved.

The leveling off of enrollment did not result in an instantaneous decline in the building program. For a decade Western had been trying to catch up with the demands for more adequate classrooms, laboratories, dormitories, and recreational facilities. The lessening of pressure allowed the university to catch up with some of the demands. Four major academic buildings were completed, or neared completion, during the 1966-69 years. Another science building erected on the Ogden campus became known as the Central Wing of the Kelly Thompson Complex for Science. The Ogden College building, nearly a century old and in poor condition, had to be razed to make room for the new building. When it opened in 1967 it housed the departments of chemistry, mathematics, and physics. A planetarium built adjacent to it was named the Hardin Planetarium in memory of Hardin Thompson, a son of President and Mrs. Thompson who died in 1963 after a lengthy illness. The Academic-Athletic Building No. 2 and the L.T. Smith Stadium housed much of the physical education department with a number of classrooms and offices underneath the stands. The Academic Complex was the first academic building constructed south of Sixteenth Street in the area between Normal Boulevard and the Russellville Pike that had once been farmland and then the site of Vets Village. Home economics, nursing, dental hygiene, radio, and television moved into the new building in 1968, and the University clinic and hospital were located in the south wing. Grise Hall, opened in the fall of 1966, housed the Colleges of Commerce and Education. A modern building with windows that did not open, it soon became infamous for the frequent breakdowns of the air conditioning system. After extensive study of the future of the Training School, the plan adopted in 1967 was to discontinue the high school program in 1970 and move the grades to a new facility to be constructed near the south end of the campus. The new building, named for Lee Francis Jones and C.H. Jaggers, who had contributed many years to the cause of education in Kentucky, received the elementary grades in 1969. In 1981 Western discontinued its instructional program and leased the property to the Warren County Board of Education.[4] The old Training School building was renovated in 1972 and reborn as Science and Technology Hall.

The building along the Russellville Road, especially the construction of the two Academic-Athletic buildings, required land that did not belong to Western. In 1961 some sixty-five householders, most of them black, lived in the area between the road and the railroad track, between Dogwood Drive and the railroad underpass, known as Jonesville. This area was one of two in Bowling Green designated for urban renewal. Most of the residences were classed as substandard, and the owners were offered the opportunity of relocating elsewhere in town with some government assistance. But many of them had strong attachments to that area, and the Reverend J.H. Taylor protested: "We cannot and will not accept such a plan." One particular objection was to dealing with the Urban Renewal Commission rather than directly with the state. Western purchased some parcels, including a few on the east side of the Russellville Road, and the probability of condemnation proceedings led to the remaining sales. The area north of Diddle Arena was obtained in the late 1950s, the area south of the Arena was purchased toward the middle-1960s. Western did ease the transition for some of the dispossessed, for example, by providing a place for a church congregation to meet, and the project perhaps created as little ill will as could have been expected, although it attracted considerable attention at the time. An estimated three hundred people crowded into the Circuit Court room on the evening of March 16, 1964, when the council heard arguments, then declared the area blighted and approved Western's development plan for it. Between 1955 and 1969 Western added 57.9 acres to the campus (bringing the total to approximately 185 acres), and most of it was obtained in the Jonesville area.[5]

A number of administrative offices moved in 1967 with the opening of the Lawrence W. Wetherby Administration Building. An annex was added to Van Meter in 1957 to house the business offices, but the building was inadequate for the rapidly expanding administrative structure. Retired Dean Grise exaggerated somewhat when he commented to a former student at a university function, "They now have seventeen people doing what I used to do alone," but the administrative structure had expanded rapidly, in part because of the growth of the school, in part because of new functions. Some of the latter were caused by the increasing complexity of the institution's relations with state and federal agencies, all of which required voluminous records. President Thompson probably experienced some pangs of regret upon leaving the corner room that had been the presidential office since 1911. Cherry had often gazed from its windows across Bowling Green to the green hills from which he had come, but his vision of what Western could become had transcended that vista. Thompson had shared both the office and the vision; his departure from the office symbolized another step toward the realization of the vision.[6]

Dormitories continued to be built as rapidly as the funding system allowed. Barnes-Campbell, Bemis Lawrence, and Rodes-Harlin halls were all occupied in September 1966, and work was underway on others. Douglas Keen and Hugh Poland halls opened in 1968, and by then plans were already well advanced for still more construction. The continued demand for housing seemed so inexhaustible that Western welcomed private plans for two high-rise dormitories on the site of the Normal School before the 1911 move to the hilltop. Another proposed project at the intersection of Chestnut Street and the By-Pass did not materialize, but the Western Towers opened in 1967. Numerous problems developed, and a bankruptcy referee explained in 1970 that the enterprise was "overfinanced and under occupied." Western considered purchasing the facility, but decided that it was not feasible to do so. After several changes of ownership, the Towers became a housing project for retired people.[7] Despite frequent *Herald* editorials that made unfavorable comparisons with other state schools, Western did not construct housing for married students.

A tower on top of the Hill was another structure that did not get built despite a great deal of planning. The eighty-five foot water tower erected near the crest of the hill in 1928 to solve the problem of low water pressure was an eyesore, and before the end of 1930 President Cherry had in hand Brinton Davis's sketch of a Memorial Tower to replace the utility. But other projects were always more urgently needed, and President Garrett had no great interest in the plan. Thompson revived and enlarged the proposal, and he told the Westerners at the KEA breakfast in the spring of 1963 that work would start "in the not too distant future" on a twenty-story classroom building on the site of the old Civil War fort. Two-and-a-half times as tall as the water tower that would be removed, it would contain a hundred classrooms and offices. Detailed plans were proposed and space allocations had begun when it was finally realized that the elevators could not handle the traffic. As a consultant explained, "Elevators and students are incompatible." The architects were surprised to learn that the classes would all begin and end at the same time. The proposal was postponed in 1964 and then abandoned. By 1971 improvements in the city water system made the campus tank unnecessary, and it was removed.[8]

Another proposed building was a modern home for the president. In 1964 the regents approved a plan for the College Heights Foundation to build a house on the south end of the campus for approximately $65,000. The foundation and the Alumni Office would then use the old presidential home. When the lowest bid in 1965 was $131,450, plans were scaled down, but the bids remained so high that the project was postponed indefinitely. In 1964 Western purchased the fifteen-room M.E. Schell residence at 1536 State Street. It was used as a temporary student center and, in 1965-66, as a women's dormitory. Then in 1966 the College Heights Foundation agreed to spend $10,000 to convert the Schell House into a temporary home for the president. The Thompsons moved into it in October, and it remained the president's home through the Downing administration. In 1979 the regents purchased a house at 1700 Chestnut Street, a block from the campus, for $165,000. Renovation costs ran much higher than estimated, and the total was about $266,000. The College Heights Foundation supplied approximately $200,000, including the original $65,000 which had grown to $97,000. Western agreed to pay $1,000 per month rent to the Foundation. The original president's home became the Craig Alumni Center, and its new wing was occupied in 1969 by the College Heights Foundation.[9] Other offices moved in later.

Extensive remodeling was done in a number of buildings including Van Meter and the old library, which was named Gordon Wilson Hall. Extensive improvements were made in the utilities distribution system. Air conditioning began to appear in portions of some of the older buildings, a Centrex telephone system was installed, sidewalks and parking areas were added, and the landscaping-planting program that had long distinguished the Western campus continued.

This wave of construction was climaxed by "A Day of Commemoration and Dedication" on October 14, 1967, when nine major buildings were dedicated in an elaborate outdoor ceremony. Even then, several other major projects were already underway or were well advanced in the planning stages.

A proposal that could have led to a revolutionary expansion of the Western campus and the university's role in Kentucky's system of higher education was broached in 1968. Kentucky Southern College, a liberal arts institution in suburban Louisville, was in serious financial condition by the late summer. Efforts to secure aid from the University of Kentucky failed, and President Rollin S. Burhams called Dr. Raymond Cravens, Western's vice-president for academic affairs, on September 7. The Southern officials had been impressed by the successful merger of the Bowling Green Business University with Western in the recent past. After intensive discussions on campus and with the Kentucky Southern officials, President Thompson recommended an aid plan that Western's Board of Regents adopted on September 21. Western agreed to underwrite a $4,200,000 bond issue that would refinance Southern's debt and guarantee it for five years. At the end of that period, if the private college was not in sound financial condition Western would take over the debt and the 238-acre campus that was appraised at $7,500,000. In addition, Western would assume the remainder of a $1 million mortgage on Southern's housing complex.

The initial response was generally favorable. Governor Louie B. Nunn, for example, praised the effort to preserve a private college. "Kelly, I think you have saved them," he exclaimed at one meeting. But that first reaction soon changed. Although Western officials then and later strongly denied that the proposal was a power play designed to get Western a campus base in Louisville, many people across the state believed that was its purpose. The Lexington *Herald* denounced "a barefaced power grab." The editor wrote, "President Kelly Thompson ... is a great educational administrator, and under his leadership the Bowling Green institution had moved steadily—indeed dramatically—from strength to strength. We fear, however, that ... they have launched a venture in educational imperialism likely to inflict deep and ugly scars on the Commonwealth's program of higher education." The editor was also critical of Western's failure to notify the Council on Public Higher Education, although the agreement had been reached before the council's recent meeting.

Legality aside, another editor added, it was "a clearly illogical arrangement" that should be dropped. The *Louisville Times,* citing Thompson's statement that Western could handle the financing with two years of careful budgeting without harming its programs, asked why Western had so much surplus money just lying around. The presidents of Eastern and Morehead were reported alarmed that the availability of funds might prompt a legislative scrutiny into the finances of the state universities. Western officials received hints that President Martin of Eastern was responsible for many of the questions that were raised.[10]

Thompson declared at a regents' meeting on October 9 that Western would not be placed on the defensive by the criticisms, but the proposal was dying. After a closed session on October 7 that lasted nearly two hours and reached "intense" levels, the Council on Public Higher Education voted to ask for a ruling from the attorney general. Before the end of October, Attorney General John B. Breckinridge ruled that Western could not legally carry out the arrangement that had been proposed. Western then abandoned the plan.

Western's bold move came as a considerable shock to the University of Louisville. It may well have hastened the incorporation of UL into the state system of higher education, and it certainly contributed to the arrangement that was worked out between the University of Louisville and Kentucky Southern College.[11]

Many of the administrative changes needed for university status were completed before the legislation was passed, and other changes were made during the next few years. The governing board continued to be the Board of Regents. Although the positions carried no salary, a number of persons often vied for the appointments. Politics inevitably influenced the selections, although the statutes required equality between the two major parties. Other qualifications were meager, except that each regent had to swear that since the adoption of the present constitution, "I ... have not fought a duel with deadly weapons within the state, nor out of it, nor have I sent or accepted a challenge to fight a duel with deadly weapons, nor have I acted as a second in carrying a challenge, nor aided or assisted any person thus offending...." On February 2, 1956, four Chandler supporters from Lebanon visited Governor Chandler to urge the reappointment of Regent Don Campbell from that town. Happy replied that he approved of Thompson's appointment, although he was not sure that

Thompson was "just right in the election," but he would not appoint Campbell under any circumstances because Campbell had not supported him in the primary. In informing Thompson of the decision, Campbell urged him not to jeopardize his position by even raising the question of Campbell's reappointment; "I am sorry that the man has such a vindictive streak in him."

Thompson maintained an excellent relationship with the regents. He started by suggesting appointments and reappointments to the governors, and he was careful to keep the regents informed about, and to some degree involved in, the operations of the institution. Every care was taken to make them feel that they were indeed important personages; Miss Georgia Bates was unexcelled in taking care of the many details that made meetings go off smoothly. As Regent Bemis Lawrence said at the dedication of the Kelly Thompson Science Hall in 1961, "Because of the administrative proficiency and the expertise, generally of our President, the duties of the Board of Regents have been of a minimum nature. Consequently, our meetings are fruitful, but not controversial." The board overrode the president's objections in naming the hall after him; occasionally the regents increased his salary more than he thought it should be; and at times they told him to take more time away from the job. Thompson did not have a serious difference of opinion with the Board of Regents during his entire tenure as president.[12]

For many years the Board of Regents consisted of four members appointed by the governor with the superintendent of public instruction the *ex officio* chairman. Then the legislature enlarged the appointed membership to six, effective April 1, 1957. In 1968 the membership was increased by the addition of a nonvoting student and nonvoting faculty member. The student member was the president of the student body, provided that he or she was a permanent resident of Kentucky. If the president did not qualify, a special election was held. William E. (Winky) Menser, a senior from Dawson Springs, became the first student regent in April 1968. The following month the faculty elected biology professor Herbert E. Shadowen as the first faculty regent. In this first election, a committee in each college nominated a candidate for the three year term. Dr. Shadowen won over Dr. Eugene E. Evans, business administration, in a run-off. In 1972 the superintendent was removed from the Board and two more appointed members were added, making a total of ten. The board, required to reorganize after each change of personnel, began to elect its own chairman, vice-chairman, and secretary, and to appoint a treasurer. The last two officers are not members of the board. Until 1970 the only board committee was the executive committee, which usually consisted of the members who lived closest to the campus. Executive committee decisions had to be ratified by the entire board. In the 1972 reorganization, the student and faculty regent received voting rights, except that the faculty regent does not vote on matters dealing directly with faculty compensation.[13]

In 1969 the regents approved the creation of another college. Several areas had not fitted well into the four undergraduate colleges, and on May 21 the regents authorized the establishment of the College of Applied Arts and Health. It included home economics, military science, library science, nursing, and the Office of Health Programs. Dr. William R. Hourigan, associate dean for undergraduate instruction, was appointed dean. The Community College, organized in 1962 as a division under the direction of the dean, supervised lower division evening classes, continuing education classes (CEU), certificate curricula, and community services of an academic nature such as conferences and lectures. It gained a number of one- and two-year degree programs when Western absorbed the Bowling Green College of Commerce, and in 1969 the regents approved its reorganization as the Bowling Green Community College. It coordinated the associate degree and certificate programs that increased rapidly in number during the next several years. Dr. Carl P. Chelf, professor of government, became director of the college and then dean when the position was elevated to that level in 1969.[14]

In 1969, therefore, Western was organized in seven colleges, the largest number it has ever had: Bowling Green College of Commerce, College of Education, Potter College of Liberal Arts, Ogden College of Science and Technology, the College of Applied Arts and Health, Graduate College, and Bowling Green Community College. A confusing element was the occasional change in name in efforts (usually in vain) to describe a college's role more accurately. Thus the Bowling Green College of Commerce became the Bowling Green College of Business and Public Affairs in 1972; although not officially dropped, Bowling Green disappeared from the title for a time, then returned; and in 1979 the name became the Bowling Green College of Business Administration. Some of the other colleges also underwent similar changes in nomenclature, as did several departments.

The administrative staff grew rapidly in the three years between 1967 and 1970. In 1967 the administrative staff in the Office of the Vice-President for Academic Affairs consisted of Vice-President Cravens and Paul B. Cook, who was a staff assistant and director of the Community College. Three years later Dr. Chelf was associate dean for instruction, Dr. James L. Davis was associate dean of faculties, and Dr. Ronnie N. Sutton was associate dean for student scholastic development and director of admissions. In 1967 there were five deans of colleges and two associate deans; in 1970 there were seven academic deans and six assistant deans. Both Ogden College and the College of Education had two assistant deans. The Office of Business Affairs, which was changed to the Office of the Vice-President for Business Affairs in 1970, increased its top staff listing from nine to thirteen. Mr. Harry Largen,who had come to the business office in 1964, became Western's third vice-president. A catch-all listing, "Administrative Officers of the University," increased from thirteen to nineteen; the most common title in this category was "director." Similar growth also occurred in other areas such as the Computer Center, Office of the Dean of Student Affairs, and Office of Physical Plant Administration.[15]

Changing emphasis in some areas and a felt need to assume new functions led to the creation of several new positions and administrative units. The Division of Academic Services was created in 1967 to provide more effective support for the instructional areas. Dr. Henry N. Hardin became dean of academic services in 1969, an indication of the importance that the university administration attached to its work. The increased size and complexity of the university made the accessibility of data both more necessary and more difficult. The Office of Institutional Research, created in 1966 with Dr. O.J. Wilson as director, attempted to cope with the problem. Some data processing equipment had been acquired in 1960, and in 1965 Western placed an order for a model 1130 IBM computer, which was soon replaced by a 1401. Plans were made for a data processing center in the new administration building, and Mr. Charles Zettlemoyer became director of the Computer Center. By 1970 an improved IBM computer, Series 360 Model 40, was installed. The Office of Admissions was established in 1962, and the Office of Testing and Counseling Services began offering nonacademic counseling in 1966. For much of their history, universities had seldom needed legal advice and representation. Upon the rare exceptions when a legal issue arose, Western had consulted an attorney and, if necessary, engaged his services. By the end of the 1960s, Western was a part of a more contentious society, and an university attorney was added to the administration in 1969 when William E. Bivin accepted the position.[16] Such new services, equipment, and programs were indicative of the increased complexity of the institution.

Several changes were made in the course and degree offerings during the last years of the decade. The five undergraduate curricular areas of 1965 had changed somewhat by 1970. Arts and Sciences remained much the same, but a Middle School program had been added to the Elementary and Secondary ones in the Teacher Education Curriculum. In the Special Studies Curriculum, five new majors (dietetics, engineering physics, engineering technology, office administration, recreation) had been added, and industrial arts had become industrial education. The 1965 catalog had listed both professional and preprofessional curricular areas; the 1970 catalog listed only the preprofessional; the professional programs had been shifted to other catagories. The fifth area in 1970 had become special curricula. It included programs in folk studies and Latin American studies (in the new Center for Intercultural Studies), and legal area studies.[17]

Numerous changes occurred on the departmental level. In several instances they reflected a change of emphasis, sometimes accompanied by the addition or deletion of an area of study. By 1970, for example, the physics department had added astronomy to its title, and home economics had added family living. Health had been removed from the Department of Physical Education, Health and Recreation and placed in an instructional area called health and safety. The College of Education added departments of counselor education and school administration, as well as several new or revised programs. In the College of Commerce, work in anthropology had been attached to sociology, and office administration had become the Department of Business Education and Office Administration. Dental hygiene, which registered its first class in 1970, was another instructional area, not a department until 1971. In 1964 the English department spawned the first of four offspring when an instructional area of philosophy and religion was formed; it became a department in 1966. Then in 1968 8 faculty members and some 650 students left English to start a separate Department of Speech and Theatre. Two years later another secession movement of 7 full-time teachers and approximately 400 students led to the creation of a mass communications department that included the work in journalism, radio, television, and photography. The Center for Intercultural and Folk Studies was organized in 1972 as an interdepartmental group with most of the initial faculty members drawn from the English department.

It was a rare department that did not expand its course offerings during this period and make adjustments in its major and minor requirements. In part, this reflected the growth in the size of the faculty and the desire of many of its members to teach in their areas of specialization; in part, it reflected some fundamental changes in approach and emphasis in certain areas. Many of the departmental curricula had changed little since the pre-World War II days, and extensive modifications were sometimes needed to bring them up-to-date. The larger student body meant that more classes could be scheduled more frequently than had been the case in earlier, smaller days.

The Graduate School (which became the Graduate College in 1969) also expanded its programs at a rapid rate. In 1967 the available degrees were Master of Arts in Education, Master of Arts with a major in English and history, and Master of Science in Engineering Physics. Two years later eight additional masters degrees were available: Master of Arts in College Teaching, Master of Science, M.S. in College Teaching, Master of Agriculture, Master of Business Administration, Master of Mathematics, Master of Music, and Master of Public Service. By then most of the departments offered graduate work with a bewildering variety of options. In agriculture, for example, a student could choose from among Master of Agriculture, Master of Science, Master of Arts in Education (with an agriculture minor), and Master of Public Service (agriculture option). In

1969 the Board of Regents authorized the development of specialist degree programs in education and other appropriate fields, and several departments began to develop programs on that level. Joint doctoral programs in education were established with the University of Kentucky (1966) and George Peabody College (1967). Although they were not used extensively, they allowed a student to do considerable doctoral level work at Western. In 1972 a joint doctoral program in aquatic biology was organized with the University of Louisville.[18]

Western graduates had done well in doctoral studies. A report released in 1963 showed that in the Kentucky-Tennessee-Alabama-Mississippi region, more Western graduates had received doctorates since 1920 than the graduates from any other state college. Excluding the professional degrees in such areas as medicine and dentistry, 145 Western graduates had earned doctorates, 101 of them after 1950. For the nation as a whole, Western ranked in the top 15 percent of all colleges and universities in the number of graduates who obtained a doctoral degree. Such reports and the growth of the university led to demands for the establishment of a doctoral program on the Hill. In the spring of 1974, state representative Ed Brown told a meeting of the Warren County Bar Association that Western should move to get a doctoral program in education at the next session of the General Assembly. He charged that Thompson and Downing had refused to act to obtain a veterinary school; such an opportunity should not be allowed to pass by again. A few days later President Downing told the regents that the time was not "propitious" for such a move; when that time came, "Western would be in the forefront."[19] It is doubtful that a doctoral program could have been secured had the attempt been made. Aside from the obvious question of adequate qualifications, the state universities with doctoral programs would have strongly opposed any expansion in that area, and the other nondoctoral schools would have fought any move that seemed to give Western an advantage over them. This opposition would have blocked approval in the Council of Higher Education, and that body was moving toward a restatement of mission that would severely restrict the programs of the nondoctoral schools.

The graduate enrollment increased sharply during the late 1960s. The increased use of graduate assistants, many of whom performed instructional duties, contributed heavily to the growth of full-time graduate students. Starting with 8 in 1960, the number reached 143 in 1969-70. In 1967 the total graduate registration for the year (spring, summer, fall) was 2,380; in 1970 it was 4,055. Enrollment was consistently higher during the summer than during either of the regular sessions; and the enrollment in the Master of Arts in Education program was much larger than all of the other graduate programs combined. In June 1969, 67 students received the M.A. in Education; 10 students were awarded other master's degrees. At the August 1969 graduation, 234 students received the M.A. in Education, and 23 were awarded degrees in the other M.A. programs. Based on

Graduate Record Examination scores for the students enrolled in graduate work in 1971-72, the departments that attracted the best qualified students were educational administration, mathematics, business administration, biology, physics, chemistry, and government. However, the number enrolled in some of the programs was small—one in educational administration, three in physics. The areas with the lowest GRE scores were industrial education, recreation and parks administration, elementary education, counselor education, and physical education.

The Graduate Council developed from a faculty committee on graduate instruction that was established in 1952. Dr. Minton, appointed associate dean of graduate instruction in 1962, became dean of the graduate school when it was elevated to that rank in 1964. In 1966 a graduate faculty was established and a graduate council formed. By the early 1970s, the council consisted of the graduate dean, a representative from each of the five academic colleges, four members elected at large from and by the members of the graduate faculty, a representative of the Teacher Education Committee, and two student members elected by their peers. After Dr. Minton became vice-president for Administrative Affairs in 1970, he was succeeded in early 1971 by Dr. J.T. Sandefur, a 1950 Western graduate who was dean of the School of Education and Psychology at Kansas State Teachers College at Emporia.[20]

During the late 1960s, increased emphasis was placed on offering graduate work in extended campus classes, despite some fears that the quality of work would be lowered. Only twelve hours of extension work (or a combination of extension and transfer work) could apply toward a master's degree. Louisville regularly supplied graduate students for a number of classes, with education being in greatest demand. A more formal arrangement was developed in Owensboro with the creation of a Graduate Consortium with Kentucky Wesleyan and Brescia colleges. Its purpose was to provide graduate extension classes in the best possible environment. The detailed agreement was approved in the spring of 1969, and 82 students enrolled that summer with 74 in an August session. The fall enrollment soared to 225, the largest number in the early years of the program. Athough most of the classes were in education, work was also offered in several other areas. Dr. J. Crawford Crowe, formerly the history department head at Kentucky Wesleyan, seemed able to create a class whenever he scheduled one.[21]

Few university presidents have ever admitted to having adequate funding, and had more money been available, Western could have used it for any number of purposes during the late 1960s. Yet for the last years of the decade, Western was perhaps as well off financially as it had ever been. Financing was reasonably adequate to meet the growing demands, and this halcyon interlude contributed much to a generally calm campus.

In the fifteen years between 1955 and 1970, the fall student enroll-

Table 4. State Appropriations and General Fund Budget
1955-56 through 1969-70

	State Appropriation	Total General Fund Budget
1955-56	$ 669,950	$ 1,152,076
1960-61	1,640,850	2,194,847
1965-66	4,996,101	6,478,683
1969-70	11,703,290	15,372,097

Source: Kelly Thompson, *A Report to the Board of Regents by the President of Western Kentucky University, 1955-1969* (Bowling Green, 1969), 38-39.

ment increased 557 percent, the faculty grew 589 percent, the state appropriation increased 1,746 percent, and the general fund budget grew 1,334 percent (see Table 4). The major change in income was the increased share that came from direct state appropriation. By the 1971-72 fiscal year, that had increased to nearly 75 percent of the total budget as several governors and legislatures proved unusually receptive to the requests of higher education. But as President Thompson told a University of Louisville dean in 1955, "Being a State institution, we have no accurate yard stick for measuring the finances of the future." That statement would be proved repeatedly in the late 1970s and early 1980s. A rare budget cut came in November 1967 when Governor Breathitt informed the presidents that their state appropriations were being reduced by 8 percent to help eliminate an anticipated state deficit. Western's share of the reduction was $603,000, and the budget year that started July 1 was already well underway. But Western had ended the 1966-67 fiscal year with a general fund surplus of $481,129.32, and only $150,000 of it had been included in the 1967-68 operating budget. Several faculty and staff positions were left unfilled and departmental budgets were cut, but the reductions were made without serious effect upon programs. The management of the cut revealed the conservative fiscal philosophy of the institution.[22]

One of President Thompson's most important achievements was bringing order to the business affairs of the school. Many of the more visible accomplishments of his administration would have been impossible without the financial reforms of which few people were aware. President Cherry's financial philosophy was simple: he wheedled all he could from a parsimonious legislature, then doled it out where the pressure was greatest, with building his highest priority. There was no internal budget and no departmental budgets. President Garrett had little interest in such matters, but he was careful to retain a surplus whenever possible. Such casual approaches upset state officials who made a number of major criticisms and suggestions in the mid-1950s. The executive director of the Council on Public Higher Education warned in 1956, "Without the leadership of a Business Manager, specifically trained in the field of modern college business management, the Business Office is drifting aimlessly.... this situation can only result in eventual disaster." A business manager was employed in September 1956 and when Thompson gave the regents a financial report for 1956-57 he commented that it appeared to be the first official report of its type ever prepared by the college. After Billy Smith resigned in December 1963, Dero G.Downing, the dean of admissions, became dean of business affairs. Two experienced staff officers were added to that area: Charles L. Zettlemoyer, who had been a budget analyst with the Legislative Research Commission, and Harry K. Largen, formerly with the Budget Division of the Kentucky Department of Finance.[23]

The Council on Public Higher Education became increasingly involved in fiscal affairs as the state moved toward a more centralized system of control and the schools realized that a united request to the General Assembly was likely to be more productive than the individual efforts of the past. When this approach began in the 1950s, the formula used excluded the University of Kentucky and assumed that program offerings were identical at the five state colleges. Several items of local income were excluded, as were expenditures in such areas as intercollegiate athletics, research, and student scholarships. "With all of its faults," Executive Director James L. Miller contended, "the formula has enabled the colleges to justify large appropriation increases in a systematic, logical, well-documented way." Then in 1963 the council adopted a new formula approach that included the University of Kentucky with adjustments for such unique features as doctoral programs.[24]

Thompson did not want to entrust everything to the formula approach, although he favored it in principle. In 1966 Western refused to submit a budget to the council and took its requests directly to the governor and the General Assembly. Thompson objected that the formula, which did not take into account bonded indebtedness, an area in which Western had been more conservative than some of the other institutions, was unfavorable to Western. This drastic step caused some consternation and criticism, but it led to improvements in the formula.[25]

By the end of the 1960s, Western's fiscal affairs were described in four basic documents that went to the regents. First was the Biennial Budget Request which in normal years was drafted in accordance with the council formula and passed through that body. Then after the legislative appropriation was made came the University Operating Budget for the fiscal year. Since the appropriation was made in a lump sum, the University had considerable latitude in the local allocation of funds. The Operating Budget was the institution's financial plan for the year. At the end of the fiscal year, the Business Office compiled the Annual Financial Report, and the Annual Audit was made by outside auditors.

Contrary to commonly held student beliefs, tuition and fees, which were set by the Council on Public Higher Education, made up a relatively small percentage of the annual budget although they had increased through the years. The freshmen who entered Western in the fall of 1970 were still told that there was no tuition, but the semester registration fee was $150 for state students, $400 for out-of-state registrants. The residence hall rates were $130 or $140 per semester, based upon double occupancy. The school estimated that the basic costs for an in-state student would be $700 a semester; an out-of-stater should expect to pay $950. The 1969-70 operating budget of $15,372,097 came from these sources: state appropriation, 76.1 percent; student fees, 6.0; auxiliary enterprises, 8.5; work-study grant (US), 2.5; grants and contracts, 2.8; organized activities, 1.3; funds carried forward, 0.7; and all other income, 2.1.

Federal grants increased slowly in the 1960s. The first one, received in September 1958, was a National Science Foundation grant for $5,250; by 1969 Western had received 41 NSF grants totaling $1,191,209. The 47 grants from the Department of Health, Education, and Welfare had produced $7,175,097, and 11 National Defense Education Act grants were for $1,908,880. Much of the building program was assisted by federal grants and low interest loans. By 1969 thousands of Western students had been assisted by federal aid, and the University had employed hundreds of students whom it could not have used without such funds. From 1958 through 1969 Western received a total of 143 grants and contracts from federal, state, and private sources, and the $11,438,064 made a welcome addition to the institution's available funds.[26]

The increased financial support made possible the rapid expansion of the faculty. The growth was slow until the decade of the 1960s. The 98 full time members in the fall of 1955 increased to 131 in 1960, and the latter figure represented an increase of only three over 1959. Then as enrollments soared, Western joined the frantic search for qualified instructors. Including administrators who taught, the 131 full-time faculty in 1966 became 577 in 1969. Sixty-seven positions were added for 1964, 60 for 1966, 54 for 1967, 75 for 1968, 75 for 1969. In addition to new positions, replacements had to be found for faculty members who retired or resigned, so that in some years approximately a hundred new faculty members came to the Hill. Their services were supplemented by part-time faculty and graduate assistants. The constant search for faculty members became a major burden for heads of large departments. Dr. Willson Wood was head of the English department from 1959 to 1972. During those years he employed 103 full-time teachers and some 100 part-time teachers and graduate assistants. During the period 1907-59, the English department had employed thirty-six full-time and half a dozen part-time faculty members. The shortest tenure anyone had in the department during Woods's administration was an alcoholic who was picked up by a campus policeman on the first day of classes and who resigned by telephone without ever having met a class.

Despite the national competition for teachers, Western continued to improve the professional qualifications of its faculty. In 1967-68, 39.52 percent of the full-time teaching faculty held a doctorate; by 1969-70 that percentage had increased to 43.4 percent; and in 1971-72 it was 50.95 percent. During the same five-year period, the percentage of nondoctoral faculty members who had at least one year of work beyond the master's degree increased from 10.22 percent to 21.02 percent; the percent holding only the master's degree declined from 43.38 percent to 24.81 percent. Wide differences existed among departments and colleges in regard to the professional training of faculty. The colleges of education and science and technology had each exceeded 60 percent doctorates by 1971, but applied arts and health was only 23.4 percent. Faculty salaries increased steadily during the late 1960s, and the Western salaries were competitive with those at the other state schools that did not have doctoral programs. By the end of the decade, fringe benefits were approximately 10 percent of salary.

The standard teaching load for instructors and assistant and associate professors who did not hold the doctorate was twenty-seven hours during the academic year; the standard load for professors and others with the doctorate was twenty-four hours. Most department heads taught six hours a semester, associate and assistant deans taught three or six hours, and the academic deans seldom taught more than one class a semester. The student-faculty ratio in the fall semester was about 20 to 1, a figure considered too high by most accrediting associations. The decline in enrollments allowed reductions to be made in the next few years.

The influx of new faculty members and the retirement of a number who had joined the faculty before World War II contributed to a relatively young faculty in the late 1960s, with the majority of them in the two lower ranks. In the fall of 1968, for example, there were 68 professors, 87 associate professors, 157 assistant professors, and 103 instructors. Among the prominent members of the faculty who retired in the 1960s were a number whose tenure at Western extended back into the 1920s: Marie Adams in home economics; Carl Barnes in industrial arts; Marjorie Clagett, Ruth Perkins, and Sybil Stonecipher in foreign languages; Ercell Jane Egbert and Gabrielle Robertson in history; Frances Richards in English; Merrill E. Schell in mathematics; H.L. Stephens in biology; Bertie Louise Redd, the school nurse for thirty-eight years; and George V. Page, physics. Miss Robertson (1914) and Mr. Page (1917) were the senior members of this group.[27]

With the growth of the faculty much of the old-time closeness was lost; by the late 1960s most faculty members knew only a few colleagues in other colleges of the university. Faculty meetings had become occasional convocations, used chiefly for informational and inspirational purposes. The faculty meetings, picnics, and parties had almost disappeared, and the faculty no longer met outside the president's office to pick up mail. Chapel was gone except for freshmen, and by 1964 they were so numerous that half the class attended in alternate weeks. When Western outgrew chapel, one of the major bonds of unity and one of the chief methods of communicating vanished. No adequate replacement for it has ever been found.[28]

Although some observers believed that Western devoted more money and attention to bricks and mortar than scholarship, faculty members who were interested in research were encouraged by several steps taken in the late 1960s. A sabbatical program was started in 1969-70; Vice-President Cravens was especially active in securing it. When the program was approved by the regents on February 15, 1969, five faculty members applied for and received sabbaticals; a sixth one was granted to a department head. There were thirty applications for 1970-71 with eleven granted. A Sabbatical Advisory Committee screened the requests, which could be for a full year at half pay or a semester at full pay, and made recommendations based upon criteria for "the professional improvement of the faculty." A summer research fellowship program was implemented in the summer of 1970, and the Faculty Research Committee continued to make small grants. The first issue of the *Faculty Research Bulletin* appeared in May 1969, but it included only a fraction of the scholarly articles being produced by the faculty. By 1972 approximately one-third of the faculty had published at least one article in a scholarly journal, and 17 percent had published at least one book. The books included textbooks, readings, and workbooks; the total based on original research was less impressive. But Western's primary emphasis remained on teaching.[29]

Publication of scholarly research was also assisted by the creation of the cooperative University Press of Kentucky in which Western was an active participant from its inception. After the creation of the four state universities, the possibility arose that one or more of them would attempt to rival the well-established University of Kentucky Press. The result would be a constant struggle for existence among poorly financed, inadequately staffed presses that might well produce some shoddy work. Professor Thomas D. Clark of the University of Kentucky was primarily responsible for suggesting a cooperative press that would build upon the foundation of the University of Kentucky Press and its capable director, Bruce F. Denbo. No one else in the state could have commanded the attention that Clark's proposal received, but the traditional suspicion of UK's motives could have doomed the idea to failure. President Thompson and Dean Minton were enthusiastic supporters of the scheme, and Western's strong support helped bring about the creation of the University Press of Kentucky. Dean Minton and Professor J. Crawford Crowe represented Western in the preliminary stages of its creation, and the regents approved Western's membership on October 9, 1968. Dr. Lowell H. Harrison was appointed chair of the local press committee and Western's representative on the central Editorial Board that held its first meeting on March 15, 1969. Professor Ronald H. Nash had a volume in press at the University of Kentucky when the change was made, and his *The Light of the Mind* (1969) was the first product of the new organization. In 1968 the UPK had six public and three private members. Since then the membership has increased to include all eight of the state institutions, five private schools and, as associate members, the Filson Club and the Kentucky Historical Society. Western has had more publications than any member other than the University of Kentucky. This enterprise remains the best example of voluntary cooperation that Kentucky has witnessed in the field of higher education.[30]

In 1969 the university and the Alumni Association established two awards to honor faculty members for "Distinguished Contributions to the University." The first recipient of the award for "basic research, creative production, or scholarly investigation" went to Dr. Mary Washington Clarke, folklorist in the English department, whose most recent book was *Jesse Stuart's Kentucky* (1968). Dr. H.L. Stephens, a member of the biology department since 1928, received the first award for excellence in productive teaching. The Alumni Association provided silver bowls and cash awards.

Much of the faculty research, especially in the area of the humanities, was done individually at the researcher's expense or with the assistance of small grants from the Faculty Research Fund. Becoming increasingly important, however, was the externally funded research that was supported largely by nonuniversity funds and often involved team research, including students. The federal and state governments were the main sources of support, with grants being most readily available in the sciences and education. In 1967-68 five grants totaled $80,047; in 1971-72 fourteen grants totaled $170,052. Several of them were contracts for services rather than research grants, and they represented less than 1 percent of the university's budget. But they added an important dimension to research opportunities in some fields, and the university recognized their potential in 1972 by appointing Dr. Glenn H. Crumb as director of Grant and Contract Services.[31]

Western had no "publish or perish" philosophy as the institution entered the 1970s, but more research was being done on the Hill than at any previous period in its history. A growing proportion of the faculty believed that this was a desirable trend.

As student government developed in the 1960s, some faculty members thought it ironic that the faculty did not have an organization that would at least express opinions in the determination of policy. The faculty was represented on the Curriculum Committee, but its responsibilities were limited. On an informal basis many academic decisions had involved the teaching faculty, especially on the departmental level where considerable discretion existed, but more substantive academic issues had usually been decided on an administrative level. After considerable discussion the regents approved an Academic Council on August 4, 1966. The forty-two members included twelve ex-officio adminstrators and thirty members selected from the faculty, among whom were nine department heads and directors; the chair was the vice-president for academic affairs. The faculty members were elected to two-year terms and could not serve more than four consecutive years. The nonvoting associate members included most of the remaining administrators and the president of the Associated Student Government. Faculty members were elected in September, and the first meeting was held on October 19, 1966.

The Academic Council recommended academic policies and regulations to the university administration, it considered proposals from the college and university curriculum committees, and it studied academic issues brought to its attention. The council's recommendations had to be approved by the administration and, for important measures, by the Board of Regents. One of the standing committees was Faculty Affairs, and some teachers hoped that it would serve as a vehicle for expressing faculty concerns. Early in the council's existence, Glen Lange and Jim Wayne Miller expressed concern that the council "has apparently been unable to discard the primary functions of its predecessor organization, the Curriculum Committee." They suggested that the council should concern itself with establishing a program of recognition for excellence in teaching, recommending long-range academic goals for Western, and creating an honors program for outstanding students.Some of these goals were later realized, but through the years the council concentrated on academic minutia.

Another objection to the Academic Council was its heavy concentration of administrators. As the teaching faculty sought a more prominent role and the students began to demand representation, there were frequent changes in the membership, most of which failed to satisfy the groups demanding change. In 1969, when a proposal to give voting rights to four students was sent to the Rules Committee for study, the *Herald* called the action characteristic of Western—"putting off until tomorrow what could have been done today." Still incensed, a few months later the *Herald* saw the Academic Council "fast becoming the most oppressive agent on campus." Yet changes were gradually, somewhat reluctantly, made. By the end of 1972, the council consisted of fifty-five voting members. The *ex-officio* members were the vice-president for academic affairs, the seven academic deans, registrar, director of library services and the three associate deans for instruction, faculties, and scholastic development. The elective members (who could include departmental heads) consisted of six members from each of the four largest colleges, four from the graduate faculty and three from the Colleges of Applied Arts and Health. One department head was appointed from each college, excluding the graduate and community colleges. Each of the six colleges (excluding the Community College) elected one student member. The fifty-five voting members were supplemented by a number of nonvoting associate members: the president and vice-presidents of ASG, the other two University vice-presidents, the dean of student affairs, and all department heads and academic directors who were not already members. More adjustments would be made in future years.[32]

National trends in student attitudes and activities often came to Western later than to many of the nation's campuses. Greek organizations, for example, were finally established at Western about the time that they were coming under attack at some of the *avant-garde* schools. The student radicalism of the late 1960s and early 1970s also came later to the Hill than it did to many campuses, and it arrived in a diluted form that spared Western much of the disruption that occurred elsewhere.

Scholars will study for many years the causes and the consequences of the turbulence that swept American society during these years; it is too soon for definitive answers, if they are ever found. But several factors seem to have primary importance in leading the nation's colleges into one of the most traumatic periods in their history. One was the growing opposition to the war in Vietnam that escalated rapidly after the mid-1960s. Unlike previous American wars, it appeared in living color on the evening news, and as it dragged on inconclusively it became a major national issue. Some of the most determined opposition came from college campuses. Deferments for college students became a controversial subject with "draft dodging" of particular importance.

The Western reaction was mixed. In the fall of 1965, Joe Glowacki, a junior from Columbia, secured over two thousand campus signatures to a letter addressed to the servicemen in Vietnam. It commended them "for your efforts to preserve the freedom and the rights for which our country was founded and should defend throughout the world" and sent them "our hopes, our love and our prayers for success in your endeavors and your safe return home." A 1966 male senior who supported the draft commented, "I won't go until I'm called, but when it comes, I won't balk at it either." Another declared that Communism had to be stopped somewhere. "Now it has to be Viet Nam. If not, we will be fighting a lot closer to home." A female student said, "Our fathers have done their part. Now it is our turn to defend our beliefs. How can it be any other way?" But many Western students disagreed with such views. "I don't want to go over and fight when I don't even think it is our place to be there," a junior declared.

"We are forcing ourselves on people who haven't wanted us." When George Solley dropped out of advanced ROTC in the spring of 1968 he explained why in a public letter. "I am against the Vietnam war—politically, economically and morally.... As an officer in the U.S. Army, I would have been required, not only to do something which violates my every moral conviction, but to force others to do the same." A mother whose son lost his draft deferment because of grades wrote bitterly to President Thompson: "If he dies, you should sign his death certificate because in truth, you may have already committed him to death." As the war controversy heated, men wearing uniforms on campus sometimes found themselves ostracized, and ROTC enrollment declined by nearly 40 percent from 1967 to 1969.[33]

Racial overtones also contributed to campus discontent. By the 1960s efforts were being made to secure civil rights in many fields. The "black power" movement attracted many of the black students who were attending colleges and universities in large numbers. Many whites felt threatened by the black demands, both in the nation as a whole and on the campuses; the race riots that swept through a number of major cities in the mid-1960s shocked and terrified many whites. The assassinations of Martin Luther King on April 4, 1968, and Robert Kennedy on June 6, 1968, seemed to symbolize the growing violence in the nation. As the number and percentage of black students at Western increased, members of both races had difficulty in adjusting to a situation that was strange to many of them. Whites sometimes felt rebuffed by blacks who seemed to prefer voluntary segregation on campus, and blacks were often suspicious of their full acceptance. Blacks might not understand why whites were puzzled by objections to the playing of "Dixie"; whites might not understand why some blacks refused to stand for the "Star Spangled Banner." Differences were legion, and adjustments were slow. The campus was better integrated than the local community, and black students and faculty members encountered problems with off-campus housing. Western authorities were reluctant to get involved in such off-campus social problems but they stood firm on issues that directly involved students. In 1967 the golf team, which had no practice course, was invited to use the facilities of the Bowling Green Country Club. Then it was discovered that the team might have a black member. The Country Club was not integrated, and the invitation came under question. Dr. Minton conferred with President Thompson and reported to the Athletic Committee "that there is no question as to how this institution stands as far as signing any agreement or any commitment that would in any way infringe upon a player's rights because of his race or color. The University would in no way approve this." The golf team commuted to Mammoth Park or used the nine-hole Bowling Green municipal course for its practice site.[34]

The more radical of the nation's students joined such organizations as

Students for a Democratic Society (SDS) and became a part of the "New Left." They did much to make the antiwar movement a national issue, and they challenged university authority on such campuses as Berkeley, Columbia, and Harvard. Although only a small number of the nation's college students joined SDS, a much larger number became adherents of the counterculture. This revolt against the conventions and values of middle class America was symbolized by long hair, eccentric dress, disregard for conventional manners and mores, the free use of drugs, rock music, and a more permissive attitude toward sex. The counterculture questioned and challenged American society as it groped its way toward an unseen Utopia. Many older members of society, including some faculty members who sought to recapture lost youth, tried to imitate the younger generation. Few Western students joined the New Left mainstream, but by the end of the 1960s its influence was evident in the campus. The dress codes were collapsing, rock concerts were the big entertainment attractions, long hair and weird garb had become commonplace, the use of drugs had increased. Veterans of the Free Speech Movement at Berkeley or the seizure of the president's office at Columbia might have laughed at the changes at Western, but they were drastic by the standards of the Hill. There was an obvious lack of understanding on both sides. "The American public at large does not understand us. They fear us because they do not understand us," an *Herald* editorial declared in 1968.[35] Such changes did not affect many of Western's students other than in superficial ways. Yet changes were taking place, and there was an unusual sense of tension on the Hill.

Most students continued their academic and social activities with little regard for the increase of tension. Since few students have much knowledge of institutional change, they were hardly aware of the changes that had occurred before their first registration on the Hill. Thus administrators were frequently frustrated by student denunciations of a current situation without any consideration being given to changes that had already taken place. By the end of the 1960s, students lived in a much less restrictive environment than those of only a decade earlier. Class attendance was one example of relaxed rules. As recently as 1966, a student was reported after three absences from a class and dropped from it after six cuts unless there were extenuating circumstances. An editorial praised the policy because it "shows that administrators are interested in students as individuals." Three years later a revised policy merely stated that a student who missed a number of classes and was doing poor work should be sent to the admissions office for counseling. If the cuts and the poor work continued, the teacher could then request that the student be dropped. This time the *Herald* condemned the "half-step which cannot possibly be the final answer." Western must "remove attendance entirely from the realm of evaluation of a student's academic performance." The same issue of the school paper reported a relaxation of dormitory rules for women and the beginning of twice weekly publication of the Herald.[36]

The growth of the university, the increased diversity of its programs, and the greater mobility of the students all contributed to changes in the students' social activities. The day was passing when most of the students and many of the faculty attended schoolwide events. Indeed, only Diddle Arena and the L.T. Smith stadium could have accommodated such a mass meeting. The disappearance of chapel eliminated one of the major agencies of providing entertainment and information for the entire academic community, and class activities had dwindled to little more than elections that attracted few voters. As the sense of institutional identity faded students turned more to special interest groups and organizations for most of their social activities. Such groups proliferated, and a student could attend a bewildering number and variety of programs. But in many instances a student complained that there was nothing to do on the campus or in Bowling Green and drove home for the weekend to a small community where the major recreation was cruising the Dairy Queen lot. More sophisticated students might head for the attractions in Nashville or Louisville.

The opening of the Arena did allow the booking of major attractions. Count Basie and his orchestra initiated such appearances on December 12, 1963, with advanced tickets selling for $1.00 and those purchased at the door for $1.50. But there were wide differences of opinion as to what should be presented, and the major concerts could not be supported by the university community alone. Any choice dissatisfied some students, and the selections brought about vociferous complaint. Nationally known groups were expensive, and a break-even season was never assured. In 1967-68 the ASG sponsored five concerts at these guarantees: The Lettermen, $3,000; Four Tops, $7,500; Wilson Puckett, $5,500; Glen Yarbough, $2,500; and Paul Revere, $7,500. Only the Lettermen and Paul Revere showed a profit, and net profit for the year was less than $900.

Some of the programs that once might have appeared in chapel were sponsored after 1961 by the Rodes-Helm Lecture Series. Mr. and Mrs. Harold Helm endowed the series with a gift of twenty-five thousand dollars and named it in honor of Judge John B. Rodes, Mrs. Helm's father, and Miss Margie Helm, Mr. Helm's sister. The first speaker in the series, on April 19, 1962, was General Carlos P. Romulo, the distinguished statesman from the Philippines. The University Lecture Series brought to the Hill other nationally known figures. Unfortunately, attendance was often poor. The availability of such personalities on television may have diminished the desire to see and hear them in person; regardless of the reason, some of the audiences in Van Meter auditorium were embarrassingly small. Such indicators of apathy extended even to campus appearances that should have been of interest to many students. In the spring of 1969, when four of the university's top administrators spent two hours in the Student Center answering questions, only sixty students attended. "The administration has long been accused of being unwilling to listen," chemistry professor William Lloyd chided. "It is ironic that when they are finally willing the majority of students have nothing to say."[37]

During the 1960s efforts were made to help both the student who was handicapped by inadequate preparation and the student with exceptional ability. With few exceptions, any Kentucky high school graduate who had a C average was admitted. Some students were not prepared to do college level work, and departments such as English had to offer remedial work. At the other end of the academic spectrum, the Honors Programs sought to stimulate and encourage the most capable students. An Honors Colloquium for twenty-five outstanding freshmen was started in 1963 under the direction of Dr. Hourigan "to afford the gifted student an academic climate in which he can put his talents to work." Unfortunately, apathy affected even this select group. In 1972 of the eight hundred students eligible for the honors colloquium, just ten enrolled. This poor response discouraged departments from offering special honors classes.[38]

Some of the dormitory residents seemed to spend much of their time moving as buildings were converted and reconverted to meet changing needs and to group all of the men's dorms at the south end of the campus. Jimmy Lowe, a South Hall sophomore, registered a public complaint in late 1968. "Last year I lived in Central Hall. I had to move this year because Central was transformed into a girls' dorm. So I moved to South Hall. Now I have to move elsewhere because, once again, girls are taking over. I wish Adam had kept his rib."[39]

Students attended some athletic events in greater numbers than they did cultural events, especially if there was a winning team, but even here they were selective. Basketball and football attracted the largest crowds, but the other sports existed in relative obscurity. The largest crowd in the history of Smith Stadium was the 20,428 that crowded in on October 26, 1968. Jimmy Feix's first Topper team went into that Homecoming game against Eastern with a 5-0 record and a point spread over their five victims of 179 to 0. The bubble burst when Eastern won 16-7. The seating capacity of Diddle Arena was increased to 12,500 in 1965 and to 13,508 in 1970. The largest crowd before 1970 was on December 1, 1966, when 13,720 saw the Big Red lose its season opener against Vanderbilt, 76-70. The per game basketball attendance exceeded 10,000 for the first time in 1966-67 when it reached 10,172 and the team compiled a 23-3 record. The average attendance per game for football was 11,024 in 1968, the first season in the new stadium.

After the heartbreaking loss to the University of Michigan in the spring of 1966, Hilltopper basketball fans anticipated the 1966-67 season when most of the squad would return. After the opening loss to Vanderbilt the team won twenty-one consecutive games. But on February 6 in the Murray game, Clem Haskins broke his right wrist and missed several games. He was named to the Associated Press All-American first team, but when he resumed play with a heavily bandaged wrist, he was unable to perform at the level that had won him such distinction. NCAA hopes died when Dayton won 69-67 on a last second shot in overtime as Haskins scored only eight points.

Oldham's record slipped to 18-7 in 1967-68 and 16-10 in 1968-69, but 1967 was probably the best basketball recruiting year in Western's history. In addition to such outstanding high school players as Jerome Perry and Jim Rose, Oldham signed Clarence Glover (6'8") and Jim McDaniels (6'11"), who inevitably became a media seven footer. They provided the size that had been lacking on the great teams of the 1964-67 era. The heralded sophomores had only a 16-10 record in 1968-69 when McDaniels led the OVC scoring with a 24.8 average, but their potential was so great that Western fans began dreaming of the next two years.[40]

Coach Feix started his head football coaching career with a 7-2-1 record in 1968 and a 6-3-1 mark in 1969. Lawrence Brame, who made all-OVC for three consecutive years, led the defensive line; John Vance provided both points and excitement from his quarterback spot where he broke many of Feix's records. (Including, Feix declared years later, the number of interceptions.) The 1968 backfield featured two explosive runners from Owensboro, senior Dickie Moore and freshman Ike Brown. Both were troubled by injuries, and Brown left school before the 1969 season to play professional football in a minor league. Faced with strong outside competition, the OVC went from 40 to 45 football scholarships in 1967 and to 50 in 1968, an increase that did not help the deficit. The highlight of the 1969 season was a 27-26 win over Eastern, Western's main rival; Western had not defeated Eastern since 1964.[41]

Jim Pickens became the head baseball coach in 1966. During the next four seasons his teams won 52 games, lost 51, and tied 2. The best season was 1969 when the record was 17-11. During 1966-69 Dr. Oglesby coached the track squad to a 12-6 record in dual meets and four more OVC championships. Henry Jackson won consistently in the long jump, the triple jump, and the high jump for four years, established a monopoly on the Trackman of the Year Award and was Western's first All-American in track. In the 1969 OVC meet Jackson won 22 ½ points. He took first place in the high jump, the long jump, and the triple jump; he anchored the 440 relay team; and he was third in the 100 yard dash. He duplicated that performance in 1970 except that he placed second in the 100 yards. Hector Ortiz, who ran everything from 1,500 to 10,000 meters, entered Western in 1968 and won All-American honors for himself and national recognition for the squad. The golf team continued its winning ways under Frank Griffin's coaching. In the four seasons 1966-69, the team's record in dual meets was 32-3, and it won the OVC championship in both 1968 and 1969 despite the lack of a adequate practice course. Ted Hornback's 1966-69 tennis teams were 66-9 in dual matches; in the last two years the record was 36-2. They won the OVC championship in 1968 and were the runner-up the other three years. As the decade closed Western added another intercollegiate sport. Swimming was not an OVC sport, but Eastern and Morehead had teams, and in 1969 William A. Powell, a successful high school coach in Michigan, was employed to start a program on the Hill. The construction of the arena with its pool had made the move possible.[42]

Occasional omens in the late 1960s indicated that intercollegiate competition for women would soon be a part of the athletic program. More women were coming to college with high school experience in competitive sports, more women were engaging in intramural sports; and federal laws, regulations, and court decisions were indicating that women must have equal opportunities if federal funds were available to the institution. The established procedure for attaining varsity team status was to organize as a club, establish a strong position on that level, then petition for varsity approval. Several women's groups were moving in that direction by the late 1960s. On April 7, 1968, a five-woman tennis club team, coached by Betty Langley of the physical education department, won all seven of its matches at Eastern; this was apparently the first organized intercollegiate competition for Western women since basketball had been discontinued nearly forty years earlier. Senior Kathy Kulp, who won both a singles and doubles match, had attracted attention as a freshman by temporarily integrating the men's varsity tennis squad. A top-ranked junior player in Delaware, she went by the courts to see Western play Austin Peay on May 6, 1963. Coach Hornback was out of town, and student Leroy Osborn was handling the team. Before the afternoon ended Kathy teamed with Bill Ward to win the number three doubles match, 6-2, 6-2. The experiment did not survive Mr. Hornback's return.[43]

Western's comprehensive athletic program continued to dominate OVC competition. Starting in 1966-67 Western won the All-Sports title for six consecutive years, missed by one point in 1972-73, then won it for the next three years. Such success required extensive recruiting of athletes and more coaches. By the fall of 1968 the athletic grants had increased to 107; football, 45; basketball, 20; track and cross-country, 14; baseball, 12; golf, 8; and tennis, 8. President Thompson saw athletics as "the glue which had held together a number of great traditions in this institution ... at a relatively small cost." Athletics were as essential for training coaches as laboratories were for training science teachers. They were also essential for public relations, he maintained. Abandon athletics, and many people forsake you—people who can influence many facets of the university, including legislative appropriations. Finding the proper emphasis, he concluded, was "one of those problems that's not going to go away."[44]

A committee composed largely of senior administrators concluded in 1969 "that the past four years have been the most significant years in Western's existence. Growth and improvement in all phases of the University's operation in these four years have far exceeded anything else that has ever happened in Western's history."

The developments had not occurred through accident, for Thompson believed in careful preparation as the essential step in coping with any problem. "A growing institution will always have many needs," he once told a reporter. "The idea is to be prepared, then take advantage of any opportunity that comes down the road." On the one hand, he had a broad vision of what Western could become; on the other, he knew the importance of not neglecting details. Thus he suggested that the young lady who sang the national anthem at the basketball games should be shifted eight feet to a better location. Thompson had the ability to mesh many factors into an interlocking whole, and he said that every step taken during the ten years before Western became a university was a part of a long-range plan. As he decribed his approach, "All possible evidence is analyzed in the light of all possible perspectives of the problem." He wanted issues studied carefully before they were presented to him; carefully prepared memoranda and studies were important tools in his decision making. A common pattern was for a paper to be sent to him with a conference to follow after he had studied it. Other administrators were consulted as needed, and *ad hoc* committees were used frequently to make special studies.

As the institution grew both larger and more complex, Thompson depended more upon the administrators who reported to him. By 1969 this group included Raymond Cravens (vice-president for academic affairs), Dero Downing (vice-president for administrative affairs), Harry Largen (business manager), Owen Lawson (physical plant administrator), Robert Cochran (dean of public affairs and public relations) and Charles Keown (dean of student affairs). Several other administrators (probably too many), including the academic deans, were frequently consulted. These were, in the main, men whom President Thompson had selected for those positions; there were no women in the top positions. Miss Georgia Bates, assistant to the president, and Miss Sara Tyler, director of library services, were the ranking female members of the university administration. Thompson was determined that a future president would not be confronted with the plethora of older administrators that had faced Paul Garrett. He brought in a number of other administrators who were expected to advance to higher positions, and he added a number of people to give strength to the academic area. "The people I brought to Western will prove to be one of my most important accomplishments," he asserted. "I knew better than anyone else," he wrote in 1969, "that such progress could not have been made had it not been for the hard work and cooperative efforts of many groups and individuals."[45]

Thompson's success at Western attracted attention, and he could have gone elsewhere upon a number of occasions. President Donovan tried to lure him to the University of Kentucky as early as 1946, and in 1962 and again in 1968 he had his name removed from any consideration of the UK presidency. His declaration, "I would under no circumstances leave this endeavor at Western for any other position in the United States, regardless of what it might be," left little doubt about his sincerity. When he rejected an offer in 1961 to join the board of an insurance company he explained, "I will devote all of my energies to Western." He saw the years ahead as critical to higher education in the state.[46]

The pace at which Thompson worked concerned his friends and associates, and the regents occasionally took official notice of his health. At the April 13, 1967, meeting when he was elected to another four-year term at a salary of thirty thousand dollars, he was "requested and directed to spend more time away from the campus for the purpose of relaxation and recreation." In the 1960s Thompson had difficulty several times with low blood pressure, and at the advice of his physician he cut back somewhat on speaking engagements. He had an emergency appendectomy in February 1968 from which he quickly recovered. He reached his sixtieth birthday in January 1969, and he seemed likely to continue in office for at least several more years.[47]

Then on May 21, 1969, the regents held a morning meeting. Around ten o'clock the faculty and staff were informed that a called meeting would be held in the Garrett Center Ballroom at 12:10. Before a hushed, almost incredulous assembly, Thompson read the resignation statement he had presented to the regents. Dissatisfied with his health, which made it impossible for him to function as he wished, he had decided during the fall that he would retire in 1969 or 1970. "It is my conviction," he declared, "that for its future best interest, Western should have at the helm a younger man who, with all the other necessary attributes, has the physical reserve to provide the vigorous and dynamic leadership which the presidency requires and which Western deserves." He offered to continue on a part-time basis with the College Heights Foundation, which needed attention, and to complete the long-range planning project that was underway. During the following weeks he received many messages of congratulations and thanks and was feted by numerous groups. The regents voted a year's sabbatical, asked him to continue as president of the College Heights Foundation at a salary equal to half his presidential salary, and authorized use of a university house.[48]

In his retirement Gordon Wilson maintained close observation of

Western, and he congratulated his friend the day after the resignation request was made; "You are bowing out at the very peak of your popularity and at a very opportune movement in the development of the school."[49]

As the faculty and staff left the ballroom on May 21, speculation was already underway about Thompson's successor.

Eight

Leveling Off
1969-1979

ALTHOUGH MANY names were mentioned as a possible successor to Thompson, five received the most attention. Vice-President for Academic Affairs and Dean of the Faculties Raymond Cravens and Vice-President for Administrative Affairs Dero G. Downing were generally considered the top candidates, but Deans William Jenkins of the Bowling Green College of Commerce and Marvin Russell of The Ogden College of Science and Technology also had support for the position. The off-campus person most often mentioned was Wendell P. Butler who had been a candidate in 1955 when Thompson was selected. A Western graduate, as were all except Jenkins, Butler was again superintendent of public instruction; as such, he chaired the Board of Regents at each of the state's new universities.

The search was perfunctory by later affirmative action standards. The regents named a three-man committee (Douglas Keen, a Scottsville attorney, and two Bowling Green physicians, William R. McCormack and J.T. Gilbert) to direct the search and to make a recommendation to the Board. Alumni, faculty, and student advisory committees made a number of suggestions, but their participation in the selection process was minimal. Approximately fifty people were recommended or applied for the position, and each member of the search committee talked with some of the applicants. But the committee, as a body, interviewed no one. Vice-President Downing had strong support from the start, both on and off the board, and at least in retrospect there was little doubt about his selection although he never applied for the position. Sounded out about the post, he indicated that if elected he would serve. When the board met on August 22, 1969, Mr. Keen nominated Downing, and he was elected unanimously to a four-year term at a salary of $33,500. Downing, Keen told his colleagues, has "an appreciation for the ever-demanding need for Western's academic advancement, a deep understanding of the problems associated with the over-all development of the university, and is excellently prepared in both knowledge and experience in fiscal management." And, Keen added, "He had, over a long period of time, demonstrated dedication to Western, and his integrity is beyond question."

The only note of dissent at the regents' meeting came from Faculty Regent Herb Shadowen. A faculty survey had shown that 73.5 percent of the respondents favored an extensive search and considered an earned doctorate to be essential. Shadowen did not object to Downing's selection, but he believed that a rigorous search would have placed the choice in a stronger position. Keen replied, "Many interviews that you perhaps do not know about took place.... we think that we exhausted our resources in this undertaking." Dr. Gilbert added, "We didn't want to call anybody in and embarrass them if we didn't think they had a very good chance." And Dr. McCormack asked, "Why go away from here two or three thousand miles when we had a very great man right here?" Unfortunately for the new president, the selection process was a handicap from the beginning of his administration in the opinion of many members of the faculty.[1]

Born at Fountain Run in Monroe County in 1921, Downing moved to Horse Cave with his family about the time he entered school. When he graduated from high school, he wanted to come to Western where brother Alec was on the basketball team, but he received little encouragement. Then he tried out (legal in those days) at the University of Tennessee and was offered a basketball scholarship. But one afternoon as he milked the family cow, Coach Diddle entered the barn, sat down on a bale of hay, and inquired about his plans. "Hell's flitters," he declared, "they can't do anything for you at the University of Tennessee; you're gonna go to Western." Downing enrolled at Western in the fall of 1939 and became known for his tenacious defense and adept ball handling that set up the scorers. He was on the first Western squad to appear in the NIT in 1942, and he was also one of Hornback's dependable tennis players. Downing was president of his senior class, and he made an excellent academic record with a major in mathematics. He and Harriet Yarnell, a student from Arkansas, married during the fall of 1943. Two weeks after he graduated in June 1943, Downing reported to midshipman's school at Columbia University. As an ensign he commanded a landing craft on D-Day. The war in the Pacific ended while his ship was being outfitted for duty there, and he got back to Bowling Green in January 1946.

College High Principal C.H. Jaggers recommended Downing to President Garrett for basketball coach and math teacher. Diddle and Hornback, who had coached the College High team during the war, were eager to give up that responsibility. From 1946 until 1951 Downing coached basketball, baseball, track, tennis, and golf, taught physical education and health, and supervised the lunch hour. He began teaching math in 1953, and three years later he was made director of the Training School when Dr.

Jaggers became head of Western's psychology department. Downing earned a masters' degree at Western (1947) and a specialist degree in education from George Peabody College (1958). Kentucky Wesleyan College conferred an honorary Doctor of Humanities degree in 1970; Murray State University conferred a Doctor of Laws degree in 1972.

Downing's hard work and administrative skills attracted attention, and in 1959 President Thompson made him college registrar to succeed Mr. Canon. There he worked closely with Raymond Cravens, the new dean, to improve registration procedures and install equipment that would enable the college to keep up with growing enrollment. His work continued to impress Thompson, and in 1963 he became dean of admissions and an unofficial assistant to the president. Two years later Thompson asked him to supervise the business office temporarily until a business manager could be found. Downing accepted, but warned that he had little knowledge of that area. Thompson replied, "Well, you've had enough math training and you know enough about figures that at least you can add and subtract." This temporary assignment became the position of dean of business affairs in 1964. The following year, as Western moved toward university status, Downing became the first vice-president for administrative affairs.[2]

When he became Western's fourth president on September 12, 1969, Downing was forty-eight years old and in good physical condition despite a recent operation for varicose veins. His bone-crushing grip was something knowledgeable people tried to avoid. Those who knew him were aware of his capacity for endless work and his meticulous attention to details. No one could question his devotion to Western and his desire to make it into an even better institution. He admitted to being conservative, and he did not like to make an important decision until all facts had been studied carefully and all options had been debated. Although he made up his own mind, Downing sought advice from those he knew and trusted. In many instances these were the people who, like Downing himself, were Western products with extended tenure on the Hill. Critics often accused President Downing of being too much influenced by "good old boys," of not listening enough to the people who had less close ties with the institution. Downing was a more emotional man than his calm demeanor indicated, but he lacked the charisma and flair for showmanship that had characterized both Cherry and Thompson. His speeches were carefully organized and well written, but they did not often arouse an audience to emotional heights; that was not his approach. Some people thought him aloof and difficult to know, but he had legions of devoted friends.

Downing was perhaps unduly sensitive about his lack of an earned doctorate, but to some faculty members that was an ineradicable blot on his qualifications. Yet he was an intelligent man who was better read in a number of fields than some of his detractors. A more valid criticism was that he had difficulty in understanding the faculty viewpoint on many issues. A collegial system of university governance was alien to his experience, and he wondered why faculty members would want to become involved in such areas. What was the need for a chapter of AAUP or a faculty senate? Why should the student and faculty regents want a vote on the board? Downing had not been a college classroom teacher, and he often failed to understand that peculiar mentality. Given his own devotion to the Puritan work ethic, he could hardly comprehend why faculty members wanted both more pay and less work. As he wrote Thompson in 1968, "It seems unreasonable to me for the average professor to teach less than 15 semester hours," although he recognized the national trend toward lighter loads. He hoped that most professors who received load reductions would then do more work in other areas, but "My observations would indicate that this is not the result in most cases." He also had some difficulty in adjusting to the growing demands of students for more freedom in their lives. He must have longed for the days when a dirty, unkept, insolent student could be summarily dismissed. As he once told an interviewer," I'm a strong believer in the fact that if we do not maintain certain standards and certain values that we're going to lose something that's awfully important in the life of this university."

One of Downing's close administrative assistants said, "He lives, breathes and is consumed with the welfare of Western." That concern manifested itself in many ways. One was his obsession with having an immaculate campus; he could not bear seeing it in an untidy state. He contributed to that neatness by picking up trash wherever he walked, and he often arrived at his office carrying rubbish he had gathered while walking across campus. Faculty and staff members who were with him when he sighted a bit of offensive debris never knew what was correct protocol; did one contest the president for the prize as he swooped down upon it, or did one ignore his diversion and continue the conversation? One of his daughters was asked what her father did by someone who did not know he was Western's president. "He's the janitor," she answered. "He cleans up the campus." Owen Lawson said that when Downing retired he had to add two groundskeepers to the yard crew.

Kelly Thompson later said that 1968-69 "was one of the most pleasant of all the years that I've been here."[3] But conditions were changing rapidly, and events in the next few years subjected Downing to pressures not experienced by his predecessors. During periods of rapid growth, imperfections may be ignored that become visible when expansion slows. Federal and state regulations created a quite different environment in which the academic community had to work, and many of the results were alien to President Downing's philosophy. He would have been better attuned to the campus of twenty years earlier than he was to the one that developed in the 1970s.

The enrollment boom of the 1960s demanded frantic construction of living facilities and classrooms, it necessitated the rapid expansion of the faculty and administration, it brought an end to Western's traditional chapel. It created an expansion philosophy that obscured potential problems as those in areas of responsibility tried to cope with their annual crises. That unprecedented pace of growth began to slacken in Downing's administration.

As late as April 1968, Western's estimates of projected enrollment were based upon strong continued growth. Although Vice-President Downing warned that projections beyond two or three years were "practically impossible," the estimate was for 17,400 full-time and 3,600 part-time students in 1978. But the head count for the fall semester of 1972 was smaller than it had been the previous year, and expectations became more realistic. The 1971-73 Institutional Self-Study report predicted an enrollment peak of 13,500-14,000 within the next decade. The peak head count of 13,533 was reached in 1979; based on full-time equivalents, the peak of 10,917 came three years earlier, in 1976. Fall head-count enrollment for 1970 through 1979 were as follows: 1970, 10,737; 1971, 11,345; 1972, 11,272; 1973, 11,723; 1974, 12,266; 1975, 13,040; 1976, 13,386; 1977, 13,490; 1978, 13,305; 1979, 13,533.[4]

The dwindling crop of high school seniors was a major cause of the decline in enrollment, but another important factor was the 1970 admission of the University of Louisville into the state system. Edward F. Prichard, Jr., a member of the Council on Public Higher Education, warned in January 1970 that the change "will have important and far-reaching repercussions on the future of all higher education in the Commonwealth." Careful study should be made "of the future needs and resources for higher education" in Kentucky before the decision was made. Downing also protested against the adverse fiscal impact that the admission would have upon Western and the other state institutions, but the change was made with little regard for future considerations. Many Jefferson County students had attended Western, and their number declined after the admission of the University of Louisville into the state system and the creation of Jefferson Community College.[5]

Despite intensified efforts to recruit students and to retain a higher percentage of those who enrolled, the University of Louisville replaced Western in the fall of 1973 as the second largest university in the state. Eastern relegated Western to the fourth position in 1974, although there was some question over the counting of off-campus students. Although Western's enrollments continued to increase for several years, with one downward blip, administrators and faculty began to realize that the institution was entering a new era. "The days of unlimited growth in any established department are past," Downing warned in 1975. "We have arrived at a point where the existing resources (faculty and others) may have to determine the enrollment level in a given department such as psychology, philosophy and religion, mass communications (photography), and perhaps some others—rather than letting the potential enrollment determine the issue." He was also concerned about the rapid expansion of the extended campus: "We cannot continue the luxury of offering a wide range of courses to unlimited numbers in a broad range of locations."[6] Yet well-established patterns and practices were difficult to change.

Like many other schools during the years of academic permissiveness, Western had relaxed the general education requirements. Campus politics forced the inclusion of something from practically every department, and students had wide latitude in selecting from an extensive variety of courses, some of which bore no discernable relationship to a core of basic knowledge that all students should possess. An entering freshman in 1975 was required to take a minimum of 53-54 hours in general education, but English 101-102 were the only courses specifically required. In meeting the 9-12 hours standard in Category B—Humanities, the student was expected to select from among 43 courses offered in 14 academic areas. The choices in other categories were equally bewildering, and advisors were often as puzzled as the students. Too often the result was equivalent to turning a child loose in a cafeteria and hoping that he would select a well-balanced meal.

In all too many instances the results were predictable. Standards were relaxed, grades were inflated, and new "relevant" courses proliferated as academic areas competed to capture a larger proportion of a relatively stable pool of students. Much of the growth in prosperous areas came at the expense of depressed units. During the early 1970s nearly half of the departments saw their enrollments shrink. There was a national trend toward more emphasis on vocational training, and technical programs, especially those on the associate degree level, grew rapidly, while most of the humanities declined. Such departments as English, foreign languages, and history endured falling enrollments. Among the growth areas at Western were philosophy and religion, home economics and family living, and mass communications. Students also flocked into the computer science division of the math department as the computer revolution promised unusual opportunities for the good life. Few new departments were created in the 1970s, although there were frequent changes in title and emphasis. When areas were formed, they usually had their origin in an existing department. Thus journalism emerged in 1976 from mass communications which had been created in 1970 and which in 1976 became the Department of Communication and Theatre. A number of departments created majors and program options that under other circumstances might have become departments.

Enrollments also fell in education, the area of instruction most closely associated with Western throughout its history. The teaching profession had become less attractive to many students, women had a growing number of other career possibilities, and the boom era in public school enrollment had ended. Secondary education enrollments at Western fell from 1,288 to 564 between 1971 and 1975, and that decline led to drastic decreases in the number of majors in such traditionally teacher-oriented areas as English and history. Many public school teachers had earned graduate degrees and completed Rank I requirements, and fewer new teachers were entering the field; before the close of the decade Western's graduate enrollment would reach its peak and begin to decline. In 1978-79 the total graduate head count (fall, spring, summer) was 9,340; in 1981-82 it was 5,808.[7]

Plans that had been based upon the anticipation of substantial growth had to be scrapped or modified, but even the scaled-down forecasts were often too optimistic. In 1977 Dean of Scholastic Development Ronnie Sutton predicted enrollment would reach fourteen thousand by the fall of 1979 and remain stable until 1982. Even that more realistic goal was not attained, and long-range predictions were decidedly pessimistic. A Faculty Senate report on enrollment projections in 1979 warned that by 1990 Kentucky might have a 25 percent decrease in the number of students of college age. The problem was compounded by the low percentage of Kentucky's high school graduates who entered college—36 percent, compared with 65 percent in Indiana and Ohio. Dr. Carl Kreisler pointed out that many high school graduates "are questioning the economic, social and traditional benefits of a college education."[8]

President Downing's concern about the growth of the extended campus was buttressed by a report Harry Largen made in early 1973. His survey showed that the 131 classes already offered in 1972-73 had enrolled 3,175 students, produced $202,872 in registration fees, and cost the university $486,042. Efforts were made to reduce the number of classes taught as faculty overloads and to cut travel costs. In 1981, for example, the extra service stipend for participating faculty was cut by 50 percent. Yet there was a strong demand for classes from numerous communities, and after the energy crises developed in the 1970s, it was difficult to argue that it was better for twenty-five students to commute to campus than for a teacher to drive to that community. By the mid-1970s some 20-25 percent of Western's total enrollment was in off-campus classes. The graduate program in education depended heavily upon the numerous classes it offered in Jefferson County. There was legitimate concern about the calibre of work done without recourse to such campus facilities as the university library. Assurances that no decline of standards occurred raised doubts about the calibre of the on-campus work. Until the summer of 1973, graduate students were required to complete 18 hours of on-campus residence work for an M.A. degree, 15 hours for Rank I, and 24 hours for the specialist degree. Those distinctions were then ended in

accordance with the relaxed policy of the regional accreditation association. In the future students could acquire graduate degrees from Western
without ever being on the campus. Starting in 1977 the Council on Public
Higher Education began approving off-campus instructional programs.[9]

One of Western's most interesting experiments in off-campus work
was the university's participation in the Eagle University Consortium at
Fort Campbell. Designed to offer work from the pre-high school to the
graduate level for military personnel, their dependents and civilian employees, the army saw the program as a valuable recruiting tool at a time
when it was having difficulty filling its ranks. Western's regents approved
the agreement on July 17, 1972, and classes soon began. Eight other
institutions were involved in the original agreement, and bickering
among them was a problem. Conflicts between class work and military
training were inevitable, and the way in which they were resolved depended largely upon the value that each commanding officer placed on
the educational program. Enrollments varied considerably, but Western
usually offered more classes and enrolled more students than any member of the consortium. In the winter quarter, 1976 the eighteen undergraduate classes enrolled 362 students, and 172 graduate students were in
the nine graduate classes. By 1977 the Army decided to terminate the
consortium agreement and replace it with contractual arrangements with
individual schools, and Eagle University ceased to exist in 1978. Western
continued a graduate program in public service, but insufficient enrollment led to its discontinuance in 1979.[10]

Another consortium of greater importance to Western was in Owensboro. That Ohio River city was the largest urban center in Kentucky
without a state institution of higher education, a fact that rankled many of
its citizens. Tuition at Brescia and Kentucky Wesleyan colleges was considerably higher than at state schools, and Western had long enjoyed substantial enrollments from Owensboro and the surrounding area. Neither
of the private colleges offered graduate work, and in 1969, with Vice-
President Cravens doing much of the planning, Western, Brescia, and
Kentucky Wesleyan agreed to establish a Graduate Extension Consortium. The private colleges made their facilities available, and qualified
members of their faculties could become members of Western's graduate
faculty. Led by the General Electric Corporation, several business concerns made donations to help start the program. Some classes were
offered during the summer of 1969, but the consortium became fully
operative in the fall semester when 223 students enrolled in twelve
classes. Several departments offered work, but nearly half of the classes
and more than half of the enrollment was in education. In 1970 Dr. Keith
Taylor replaced David Mefford who had served as director of the first
year.[11]

Several problems developed in this enterprise. Until 1973, when the
extended campus concept replaced extension work, graduate students

were limited in the amount of work that could be taken for extension credit. Finances posed another problem as the program grew. By early 1971 Director Taylor complained, "Participation of people from industry has been extremely meager," both in terms of students and donations. Operation of the consortium was a drain on Western's finances, and by 1971 Western and some of Owensboro's civic leaders were campaigning for direct state assistance. Mayor C. Waitman Taylor, Jr., praised Western's role in the "bold and imaginative project" as he asked Governor Wendell Ford for state funding. In 1974 the Council on Public Higher Education authorized its staff to request financial support for the consortium, and three hundred thousand dollars was made available.[12]

Despite such problems and various growing pains, 1,016 students registered in forty-five classes in 1973-74. That success attracted the attention of Dr. Constantine W. Curris, the aggressive, controversial president of Murray State University. On December 12, 1973, he formally requested Murray's admission to the Owensboro Graduate consortium as a full member. President Downing replied that he was pleased with Curris's wish to avoid duplication of effort; since Western was already offering an adequate program, there was no reason for Murray to be included. Curris persisted in his efforts and won some support, both locally in Owensboro and on the state level. Vice-President Cravens suggested that Murray should be denied full membership and restricted to a few special areas in which Western did not offer work. Paul Cook, however, believed that since other schools would inevitably be admitted it would be better politics to agree readily to their admission. That precedent might be helpful to Western elsewhere. Murray was admitted to membership in the summer 1974 with some restrictions designed to prevent duplication of efforts. Western continued to protest that Murray frequently overstepped the established limits.[13]

Both the Southern Association and two outside consultants in 1976 were critical of the consortium's efforts—Western and Murray fighting to protect individual interests, a lack of aggressive leadership, the need for more support. After studying the reports, a committee consisting of Deans Chelf and Gray and Director Taylor agreed with the finding of both reports that the consortium really existed in name only. The only viable choice, they asserted, was the development of a true consortium.[14]

Another complication was that some Owensboro residents were not satisfied with any arrangement that was not connected with the University of Kentucky. Western's future in Owensboro was called in question again in April 1979 when the Owensboro-Daviess County Chamber of Commerce proposed a state supported graduate and continuing education center run by UK. This issue occupied a great deal of presidential time for both Downing and his successor. Dean Chelf pointed out, "They say there are unmet needs, but they don't identify them specifically."

Other important extended campus centers were located at Fort Knox and Somerset. In an unique arrangement, students at the Somerset Technical School received credit from Western for some of their vocational courses as they worked toward an associate degree.[15]

During the boom period of higher education in Kentucky, funding was generally adequate with much of capital construction coming from bond issues and federal grants. Western's operating budget for fiscal 1969-70 was $15,372,097; in 1978-79 it was $43,210,990. New programs were created, faculty was added, student facilities were improved, athletic budgets were increased. However, inflation eroded much of the apparent increase in income, and, like any consumer, the university found itself paying more for almost everything it used. New federal and state regulations required expensive solutions to such environmental problems as air pollution from the heating plant. During the energy crises Western, cut off as a user of natural gas on November 1, 1976, switched to coal. The heating plant then failed its air emission tests, and oil became the fuel. But that added an unexpected $150,000-200,000 to the annual fuel bill. Filters would allow coal to be burned, but that installation cost several thousand dollars.[16]

Western had a conservative fiscal policy; surplus funds were often squirrelled away for future use. Thus a 1.1 percent mandated reduction in state appropriations was handled in 1970-71 with little difficulty. In 1973 Harry Largen reported these balances in the major funds: Consolidated Educational Buildings Reserve Fund, $2,159,697; Housing and Dining Series K Bond, $986,150; General Fund, $789,739, of which $202,739 was unencumbered. When a snag developed in the financing of a $3,444,000 Environmental Sciences and Technology Building, President Downing announced that Western would finance the project from available funds.[17] Such relative affluence caused some skepticism when Western presented its requests for more state money.

When he examined the 1973-74 budget, Harry Largen reported that it contained fewer new dollars than in any year since 1963-64. As the state appropriated a smaller share of its revenue to higher education, more reliance was placed on student fees. In the fall of 1974, the registration fee for a full-time in-state undergraduate was $210 a semester, and for a graduate student, $235. Out-of-state students paid $475 if an undergraduate, $500 if a graduate. Five years later the full-time in-state fees were $250 per semester for an undergraduate and $285 for a graduate, and the out-of-state fees had risen to $635 and $710. In terms of constant dollars, the state support per student was declining. Especially annoying was Western's treatment relative to the other state schools. Between 1976 and 1978 the budgets at the eight schools increased an average of 33 percent, headed by the 55 percent growth for the University of Louisville and the 50 percent increase for Northern Kentucky University. Lowest of the eight was Western with 17 percent growth. Downing cited these figures to prove that Western was being discriminated against. In the fall of 1977, disappointed and frustrated by the budget problems, he said that in the late 1970s Western might have to stop expanding and just try to hold on where it was.[18]

Another budget problem arose when the Board of Regents began to question presidential budget recommendations. Downing had a major battle in 1973 when McCormack and his associates on the board demanded that "escalating salaries" be capped, a proposal that bore little relationship to the realities of higher education. When the regents approved the 1975-76 budget, three members abstained from voting, citing as their reason inadequate time to study it. Copies had reached them only eight days before the meeting, but in the past, when few questions were asked, that would have been ample time. Later that year when the Board considered the budget requests for the next biennium McCormack objected to both the format and such specific items as the proposed Agricultural Exposition Center. Faculty Regent William G. Buckman was not convinced of the need for that project, and other questions were also raised. After Downing's explanations the requests were approved with only McCormack dissenting, but such questions had been rare in the past. By the mid-1970s President Downing found it expedient to consult in advance of meetings with such stalwart supporters on the Board as John L. Ramsey and Ronnie Clark, who were primed to respond favorably to the president's recommendations and to move their approval. If they did not agree, Downing wrote, "I am confident you will react in the manner you feel to be in the best interests of Western." The need for such arrangements was another indication of the changing role of the governing board.[19]

The budgets of the 1970s provided for faculty and staff salary increases that were usually over 5 percent and for several improvements in fringe benefits, but the increases did not keep pace with inflation. Between July 1974 and July 1979 the cost of living increased by 48.2 percent. The problem was compounded by a salary scale that was some 15 percent lower than those at comparable institutions in surrounding states. Downing had told the regents in 1975 that "compensation of employees deserves the University's highest priority consideration after it has met its obligations for legally fixed costs and commitments to existing educational programs," but the results were inadequate.[20]

Several years are required between the start of planning for a major building and its availability for use, and the building momentum of the late 1960s carried over into the early 1970s. The Cravens Graduate Center and Library annex opened in 1971, as did the twenty-seven-story Pearce-Ford Tower that housed more than nine hundred men. An early inhabitant of the tower was impressed by "the novelty of living at eye level with small (and reckless) aircraft." He was not favorably impressed by physics majors who on crowded elevators "calculated aloud the force needed to brake an elevator descending 26 floors." The perennial parking problems was eased by the opening of the one thousand-car parking structure in 1969, and classes began in the Ivan Wilson Center for Fine Arts in 1971. Completion of the Fine Arts Center on the old football field made it possible to evacuate the Cherry Hall inhabitants so an extensive renovation could be made of that venerable structure in 1973-74 at a cost approximately three times the building price in 1936-37. Another major renovation converted the old Training School into Science and Technology Hall in 1969. The Kentucky Building had become inadequate for its growing library and museum collections, and an addition that more than doubled its size was started in 1977. The library and museum existed in makeshift quarters around the campus until 1979 when they were moved back into the enlarged and renovated quarters. The Music Hall, deemed unsuitable for renovation, was torn down in 1975. The Industrial Education Annex that had once housed home economics was scheduled for remodeling, but funds were not forthcoming, and in 1983 it was finally demolished to make room for another parking lot. The last major construction of the decade was the Agricultural Exposition Center on the university farm. Constructed in 1979 at a cost of just under $3 million, it contained several classrooms and an arena that could seat nearly two thousand spectators. The construction of new dorms at last outpaced enrollment growth, and Schneider Hall (White Stone) was converted into a continuing education center. Potter Hall, the first dormitory on the Hill, was also closed as a dormitory. A later surge in demand for campus housing brought both old dormitories back into service for their original purpose, but by 1985 they had again ceased to house students.

The building and remodeling would have pleased Henry Hardin Cherry. But the pace had definitely slowed, and in November 1977 the Council on Public Higher Education recommended that the state not fund any university construction projects for at least two years. A victim of that decision was a physical activities and recreation building that was high on Western's priority list. Despite a tighter budget, Western was able to do a substantial amount of needed maintenance work on the campus and existing buildings. President Downing was deeply concerned over the campus' appearance, and he worked closely with Owen Lawson and the others who were responsible for that area. An unexpected expense resulted from a severe ice storm in January 1974 that damaged an estimated quarter of all the trees on campus. An unusually cold winter, such as the ones of 1977 and 1985, imposed financial burdens as the physical plant people worked long hours to keep the campus operational. Another major expense appeared near the end of the decade when estimates revealed that it would cost $2,200,000 to meet federal standards for providing access to buildings for the handicapped. As that work slowly progressed over the next several years, some disadvantages to a hilltop location became apparent.[21]

Both Presidents Thompson and Downing wanted to avoid having a sleezy commercial development adjacent to the campus. Whenever a property became available in the ill-defined "buffer zone," Western was likely to buy it. One of the acquisitions was the privately owned L and M Bookstore located at the foot of the hill where Center Street became the Russellville Road. After a change in the traffic patterns in that area hurt the bookstore's business, the owner sold the property to Western in 1975 for $163,150, despite some student protests against the monopoly of the university bookstore. The buildings were then razed and the area sowed in grass.[22]

University housing for married students continued to be an issue, as it had been for many years. By 1970 there were only twenty-seven apartments available on campus, whereas some of the other state universities provided extensive facilities. In May 1970 the regents approved the construction of 150 units as soon as financing could be arranged, and in September President Downing declared, "Married students housing has the top priority in building facilities." Plans were drawn for 152 apartment units to be constructed at Campbell Lane and Industrial Drive south of the campus, and the State Property and Buildings Commission approved a $2 million bond issue to finance the project. Western continued efforts to interest private developers, and in July 1971 Downing told the regents that Guthrie May and Company of Evansville would build 150 apartment units for married students near the Bowling Green Vocational School. Western then dropped the proposed project. This decision perhaps had some adverse effect upon enrollment, and it supplied a persistent theme for *Herald* editorials and letters to the editor.[23]

A university is a living organism, and changes take place continuously, even when the outward appearance gives little indication that alterations are underway. The curtailment of the building boom and the leveling off of enrollment gave the Western campus a placid appearance it had not had in recent years. Adjustment to this change was sometimes difficult, for the university had been geared to a boom environment; the shock was somewhat similar to what an individual may experience when he suddenly realizes that he is classified as a senior citizen. Yet in some respects Western needed a breathing space in which to assess its current condition and plan for the future. It was time to tidy up after the hectic pace of the 1960s.

Yet changes did continue, and several were in the university's administrative system. In the spring of 1965 when the regents approved the creation of two vice-presidencies, Cravens became the vice-president for academic affairs and Downing the vice-president for administrative affairs. On August 6, 1970, the regents approved Harry K. Largen as vice-president for business affairs. Dr. Minton, the graduate dean, became vice-president for administrative affairs. Dr. Cravens continued as vice-president for academic affairs. Largen and Minton still occupied their positions in 1985, but in May 1977 Cravens, who had been on sabbatical leave during the academic year, was named dean of public service and international programs in a move that surprised many of the faculty who saw him being shunted aside from the key role he had played for two decades in Western's development. Dr. James J. Davis, who had been dean of faculty programs in Cravens's office, was the interim vice-president until he was selected in 1977 to fill the vacancy.[24]

One of the major growth areas in the administrative sector occurred on the level of deans—full, associate, and assistant. The university catalog issued in the spring of 1969 listed five academic deans: Paul G. Hatcher, Potter College of Liberal Arts; William M. Jenkins, Jr., Bowling Green College of Commerce; Tate C. Page, College of Education; Marvin W. Russell, Ogden College of Science and Technology; and John D. Minton, Graduate School. William H. Hourigan was associate dean for undergraduate instruction, and Henry N. Hardin was associate dean for academic services. Robert G. Cochran was dean of public affairs and public relations, Charles A. Keown was dean of student affairs, and John W. Sagabiel was dean of men. By 1978 the number of academic deans had increased to ten: Hardin, academic services; Hourigan, College of Applied Arts and Health, which had been created in 1969; Carl P. Chelf, Bowling Green Community College and Continuing Education; Robert J. Oppitz, interim dean, Bowling Green College of Business and Public Affairs; J.T. Sandefur, College of Education; Elmer Gray, Graduate College; Russell, Ogden College of Science and Technology; Robert Mounce, Potter College of Arts and Humanities; Cravens, Public Service and International Programs; and Ronnie N. Sutton, scholastic development. The only dean listed outside academic affairs was Keown in student affairs. By 1978 Western also had a dozen assistant and associate deans and an even larger number of directors who supervised various areas. This growth led to frequent faculty charges of administrative overstaffing, an assertion that few administrators accepted.

During those years there were several key changes in personnel. When Minton became vice-president, a selection committee recommended J.T. Sandefur, a 1950 Western graduate who was dean of the school of Education and Psychology at Kansas State Teachers College, for dean of the Graduate College. Then in 1973 when Tate Page retired Sandefur became dean of the College of Education, where during the next few years he made substantial reorganization and attracted national attention with a plan for competency-based teacher education. The death of

Bob Cochran in 1971 created a void that was difficult to fill, for his long association with Western and his total dedication to the institution made him a superb handler of public relations. Elmer Gray of the Department of Agriculture had been associate graduate dean; he was elevated to the deanship when Sandefur moved to the College of Education. When Paul Hatcher returned to the classroom in 1974, Robert Mounce became dean of Potter College, and in 1977 Robert E. Nelson was selected to replace Bill Jenkins as dean of business and public affairs when he also resumed teaching. A rising figure in the administration was Paul B. Cook who had taught in the history department and held several administrative positions. Named assistant to the president in 1969, he later became assistant to the president for Resource Management and Director of the Budget.[25]

During the 1970s the library underwent numerous changes that dismayed some of the traditional lovers of books. Dr. Earl E. Wassom, who joined the faculty in 1967 as associate director of library services, directed much of the move toward the automation of library services. New book acquisitions were classified by the Library of Congress system rather than the Dewey system after May 18, 1970. "Project Reclass" for the existing volumes began in January 1971, and the bulk of the project was completed by the fall, although in 1985 some reclassification was continuing. Then in 1976 the traditional card catalog began to be replaced by a COM-CAT system (Computer Output Microfiche Catalog) that was said to be both more economical and more convenient than the old system. Frequent updates were promised, as was widespread distribution across the campus of the microfiche catalog and the required readers, but for years performance did not match the promises. The goal of a union catalog of all instructional resources on campus also progressed more slowly than was anticipated. A computer-operated on-line circulation system, installed in early 1972, expedited the circulation system except for the times when the computer was "down." Completion of the Cravens Graduate Center and Library in 1971 added space for four hundred thousand volumes and seating for 750 patrons.[26]

Not everyone was pleased with the computerization of the library. Books seemed to be less important, and for a number of users the library became a less pleasant place in which to work. Systems were sometimes not as efficient as promised nor completed when scheduled, and the inevitable snarls led to frustration and occasional anger. An irate reader expressed his sentiments in a letter to the school paper. "It appears that our library had degenerated from a well-ordered, helpful facility to a chronic source of frustration for anyone engaged in the fruitless search for the mysterious materials which were once known to reside within our library." Sharp faculty complaints included a senate resolution of censure in 1979 for a reduction in journal subscriptions and "the arbitrary manner in which that action was carried out."

Some faculty members who were critical of Downing's academic credentials may not have known the emphasis he placed on expanding the library's holdings. In October 1969 Cravens suggested to Downing that he set a goal of 500,000 volumes by the end of his first term as president in 1973 and the acquisition of an additional 250,000 volumes by 1978 or 1979. The president told the Academic Council in December that priority would be given to reaching 500,000 volumes during the next three years. Two years later A. Ferdinand Engel, the acquisitions librarian, told the faculty that they need not submit orders for any American university press book, or those of Oxford and Cambridge, since all such publications were on order. During the 1970s the percentage of the university budget spent on the libraries averaged over 5 percent, and in 1971-72 it reached 6.12 percent—the highest percentage in the history of the school. Unfortunately, that progress could not be maintained. Budget reductions and inflation had a devastating effect, and the 1979 annual library report declared the income "inadequate to maintain a growing and expanding collection." The number of books and periodicals purchased declined sharply, and the collections were left with gaps that would never be filled. Increased use of microforms was a partial answer to the problem, and by January 1986 the number of book titles (557,182) was not far ahead of the book titles in microform (473,750). Government documents then numbered 474,083 and there were 2,425 journal titles.

Western students in the 1970s did not use books as much as had those of earlier days. The total book circulation for 1979 was 177,545, while the largest enrollment during that year was the 13,533 registered in the fall semester. Ignoring faculty, staff, and off-campus borrowers, the average student that year checked out thirteen books. In 1929-30 the circulation per student had been close to 100 volumes. A similar decline may also have occurred with faculty members.[27]

As early as 1931 President Cherry instructed Dr. M.A. Leiper to collect materials relating to Western for inclusion in the Kentucky Building, for "all of these things will be vital in the future." Some materials were gathered, but little attention was paid to an institutional archives until December 1966 when Vice-President Downing appointed a committee chaired by Miss Georgia Bates and Miss Julia Neal. Their July 1967 report recommended establishment of the archives in the Kentucky Library, but nothing was done. In late 1969 Lowell Harrison, who had been doing research on Ogden College, wrote President Downing that many of those records had disappeared. "This points up the urgent need for the establishment of an university archives for Western as soon as possible—preferably about fifty years ago." Bill Weaver and Paul Cook added their recommendations, and Downing appointed a new archives committee in September 1970 with Miss Sara Tyler as the chair. In November 1971 Miss Tyler began to devote half time to developing the archives, and in the spring of 1972 she became archivist on a full-time basis. Scouring base-ments, attics, vaults, and other storage places, she uncovered an extensive array of materials that began to fill the shelves in Room 100 in the Helm Library. After Miss Tyler's retirement in 1975, Professor J. Crawford Crowe became university archivist. The position was not filled when he returned to the Department of History in 1980. The archives moved to the second floor of Gordon Wilson Hall in 1979 but was evicted in 1985 in favor of the dance program. The archives then returned to the Helm Library.[28]

The 1970s saw a number of changes in the university's use of its own mass media resources. As late as 1938 the *Herald* had neither a telephone nor a good typewriter, there were constant problems in getting the paper printed, even on an alternate week basis, and national advertising could not be carried until 1940. Under those conditions, it was surprising that so much good work was done and that so many *Herald* staffers did well in newspaper work. Weekly publication (on Wednesdays) began in 1961, and twice-weekly publication started in September 1969. By then the *Herald* and its staffers were regularly gaining awards in national as well as state competition. By 1973, for example, the paper received an unusual A + + rating from the National Newspaper Service. The second plus was added to honor "this great college newspaper." The creation of the *Alumni Magazine* in the mid-1960s allowed the *Herald* to concentrate on student news and features and gave alumni director Lee Robertson direct com-munication with his constituents. The *Herald's* professionalism increased after 1970 when David B. Whitaker, a former *Herald* editor, became direc-tor of university publications. A veteran newspaperman in Bowling Green and Louisville, he emphasized editing and writing over theory, and the *Herald* soon reflected that approach. His persistence in seeking more space, equipment, and staff sometimes antagonized those who had to listen to his demands, but he got results. Highlights of his efforts were the establishment of journalism as a separate department in 1977, ac-creditation of the news-editoral and photojournalism majors by the American Council on Education for Journalism in 1979, and a move to the Garrett Conference Center and Gordon Wilson Hall in 1984. Whitaker resigned as head of the journalism department in 1984 but continued as director of publications.[29]

In 1984 the *Herald* won the Pacemaker's Award of the Associated Collegiate Press—its highest honor—for the third time in four years. The *Talisman* also won the Pacemaker Award, only the second time in the ACP's sixty-year history that a school had won both honors in the same year. Western had also won both in 1982.[30]

The *Talisman*, a year older than the *Herald*, was also garnering awards. The 1972 edition, edited by Regina A. Catlett and Richard Morris and advised by Roger Loewen, won the highest possible rating given by the

National School Yearbook Association, the Columbia Scholastic Press Association, and the Associated Collegiate Press. Two years later when the ACP awarded Western's yearbook its third consecutive All-American rating it called the *Talisman* "one of the most exceptional publications in recent years." When the Columbia Scholastic Press Association gave its top "Trendsetter Award" in 1975 for the second time, the *Talisman* was one of only three yearbooks ever to receive it. The *Talisman* won this award for five consecutive years, while picking up numerous awards from other groups. Given this standard of excellence, the staff was so dismayed by the inferior printing of the 1980 issue that the resultant quarrel delayed distribution until November. By 1980 budget reductions caused cuts in the yearbook's budget, and students had to pay an additional fee. The result was a reduction in size, a drastic cut in the number of copies printed, and an uncertain future for a publication that had won national recognition in its field.[31]

Radio had attracted President Cherry's attention by the late 1920s, and he had advertised the college with a series of broadcasts, especially those carried by WHAS, Louisville. Garrett saw some value in broadcasts for publicity purposes, but he questioned proposals that radio be used for educational purposes despite pleas from Dr. Earl Moore that radio was essential for a modern college. In 1939 Garrett did not request time from WHAS for weekly broadcasts. Some broadcasts were resumed after World War II, and more use was made of local stations. By the mid-1960s there were demands for an on-campus station that would be used by the students who were working in the mass media area. In 1969 when the AAUP chapter urged the establishment of an FM campus station Downing replied that studies had been underway for five years, but he did not know when the budget would permit more progress.[32]

In 1974 the regents approved the establishment of a carrier-current campus radio station, and WKYU began twelve hours of daily programs in August 1975. Nearly three years later the regents approved an application for a noncommercial FM radio station expected to cost $170,000 to $200,000. Aided by a federal grant of $148,984, WKYU-FM went on the air on November 8, 1980, with an effective range of sixty-five to ninety air miles. A repeater station was later built at Somerset.[33]

President Thompson recognized the possible benefits of television, and in 1957 he told the people who were applying for a Bowling Green station that Western would like a Saturday morning educational program. Five years later Western was not using radio or television for instructional purposes, but planning was underway for a mass communications major and minor and for a statewide Kentucky Educational Television system, and Western was soon actively engaged in such work. Julian Goodman, a former Western student, a cousin of President Downing and the president of NBC, was instrumental in securing gifts of valuable equipment.

Kelly Thompson,
president 1955-1969.

In 1956 the bonfire was
still an important
feature of Homecoming
celebrations.

The R.O.T.C. unit, shown parading in downtown Bowling Green in 1965, still represents Western at many civic events.

Garrett Student Center was the scene of this 1967 student election.

In forty-two seasons (1922-1964), Coach Ed Diddle, shown above with his famous red towel, compiled a record of 759-302. At left is his longtime assistant, Ted Hornback.

Advanced registration has now eliminated most of the Diddle Arena lines that students once endured, shown below from the 1970s.

Dero G. Downing,
president 1969-1979.

The College of Education
building opened for
classes in the summer of
1970. It was only one of
several major construc-
tion projects in the
decade.

Alice Gatewood, Homecoming Queen for 1972, was the first black student accorded that honor.

President Downing, in characteristic fashion, picked up trash after the UT-Chattanooga football game in September 1978, just hours after resigning as president.

John D. Minton,
president 1979.

Donald W. Zacharias,
president 1979-1985.

A "Back Zack" student rally was held on the Administrative
Building steps on a frigid February 11, 1981. Zacharias was
protesting cuts in state appropriations and changes in the
university's mission statement.

All-American Lillie Mason led the Lady Toppers to the Final Four in both 1985 and 1986.

Below, Big Red has been a popular Hilltopper ever since his/her creation by student Ralph Carey in 1979.

Paul B. Cook, interim
president 1985-1986.

Kern Alexander,
president since 1986.

Regents Miller, Judd, and Iracane joined President Alexander at a Frankfort
rally for higher education on February 5, 1986. Also attending were Western
cheerleaders, the Spirit Dancers, Big Red, and many students and faculty.

When Storer Communications brought cable television to Bowling Green, Western was assigned Channel 4 in the spring of 1982. In 1983 the Regents approved an application for an educational television channel (UHF) to be assigned to Bowling Green, but it was not expected to be on the air for several years.[34]

President Downing was probably more interested in basketball than any of the other varsity sports, and the tribulations that beset that part of the athletic program seemed to typify many of the problems that he faced. Basketball had long been the most visible aspect of Western to many people, and the events of the 1970s reflected upon the school.

During the first two years of Downing's administration, basketball seemed to have regained its glory days. Led by Jim McDaniels and blessed with unusual bench strength, the 1969-70 Hilltoppers won twenty-two games during the regular season and lost only to Kansas and Duquesne. McDaniels led the OVC in scoring, field goal accuracy, and rebounding; he was the OVC player of the year; the eleventh top scorer (28.6 ppg) in the country; and a member of *Look's* All-American team. Perry and Rose joined him on the All OVC team, and Oldham was conference coach of the year. Artis Gilmore and his Jacksonville team mates ended Western's tournament play with a wild 109-96 win as McDaniels fouled out with over eight minutes remaining. Western fans swallowed their disappointment in anticipation of the next season when eleven of fourteen lettermen returned, and Jerry Dunn and Rex Bailey, two junior college transfers who had played on the Glasgow state championship team, were to join the squad.[35]

Injuries hurt the team from picture day in October 1970 when Gary Sundmacher, a dependable play-making guard, broke his arm. Then All-OVC Jerome Perry injured a knee and sat out the year. Another 1,008 seats were added in Diddle Arena, bringing the capacity to 13,508, and the average crowd that season was 12,173. An arena record was set on February 27, 1971, when 14,277 saw the Toppers beat the Murray Thoroughbreds. A highlight of the season came in Freedom Hall, Louisville, when Western outran and outshot Jacksonville 97-84 as McDaniels collected 46 points. When he scored 49 points against Tennessee Tech McDaniels broke Clem Haskins's three-year scoring record of 1,680. The regular season record was 20-5, and Western, ranked as high as fifth in the Associated Press weekly poll, ended in seventh place. In three seasons McDaniels broke Ralph Crostwaite's four-season scoring record (2,091 to 2,076) and set a new three-year rebounding record with 1,052. Austin Peay coach George Fisher called him "amazing, fantastic. He's got to be the best player to ever play in the OVC."[36]

The NCAA pairings matched Western against Jacksonville at South Bend, Indiana. McDaniels, in early foul trouble, sat out considerable portions of each half, but Clarence Glover, a favorite with Western fans, took up the slack with 16 points and 17 rebounds. Western trailed by as many as 17 points but came back to win 74-72 on Glover's last second shot.[37]

Western's next game was one that many Kentuckians had longed for—a matchup with the University of Kentucky Wildcats. Played at Athens, Georgia, it was no contest. Adolph Rupp had stubbornly resisted recruiting blacks, as had most of the Southeastern Conference schools, and his predominately white squad could not match Western's quickness. (Seven-foot center Tom Payne was UK's first black player.) "The quickness of their guards forced us out of everything," Assistant Coach Joe B. Hall explained as UK committed twenty-six floor errors. Western played eleven men, McDaniels sat out long stretches of the game but scored 35 points, and Western won 107-83. A record of the radio broadcast, called simply "The Game," sold briskly in Bowling Green; it did less well in Lexington. Cal Luther, Murray's coach, said, "It was remarkable, really, I found myself rooting for those gawddamn red uniforms for the first time in my life. Of course, it didn't take me long to get over that insanity, and I'm back to hating them again."[38]

Then Western beat Ohio State 81-78 in overtime to win the regional and go to the Final Four. The Toppers trailed by fourteen points at one time but forced an overtime when Bailey hit from the corner with thirteen seconds left. The NCAA finals were played in Houston, and a crowd of 31,428 saw Western lose to Villanova 92-89 in two overtimes despite three more field goals, fourteen more rebounds, and two fewer turnovers. Both McDaniels (22 points) and Dunn (25 points) fouled out in the second overtime. Western then took third place by defeating the University of Kansas 77-75. McDaniels closed his collegiate career with most career points (2,238), most career rebounds (1,118), most points in a season (878, 1970-71), and best season average (29.3, 1970-71). At the basketball Appreciation Dinner on April 5, President Downing announced that Number 44 would be retired—the first time Western had ever accorded a basketball player that honor.[39]

With exquisite timing John Oldham resigned as basketball coach in early April and became athletic director to replace Ted Hornback who was retiring from that position. In seven years Oldham's teams won 146 and lost 41 games for a winning percentage of .781, the best record ever compiled by a Western basketball coach. After a brief search, Jim Richards was appointed head coach. A successful high school coach, he had joined the Western staff in 1968 after his Glasgow team won the state championship. No recruits had been signed and Richards, his crew-cut an anachronism among the players he sought, got a late start.[40]

Richards inherited a difficult situation that soon got worse. Western fans, spoiled by the success of the McDaniels era, were unwilling to accept anything less than that gaudy record. But the losses from the NCAA squad were irreplaceable, and injuries hampered two probable starters. After twenty games with a small, patched lineup, the team was 10-10. Then it won five of its last six games, earned the OVC co-championship and finished 15-11. That late season spurt became a trade mark of Richard's teams in each of his seven years as coach. He won the OVC outright in 1975-76 when the 20-9 record was the best of his tenure. But two seasons (1972-73 and 1976-77) were 10-16, and after seven years his record was 102-84 for only 54.8 %. Although his crew-cut disappeared and his clothes became more modish, Richards and his assistants were not able to bring in enough top-notch players to sustain the program at the expected level. Richards was also beset by other problems.[41]

Rumors had circulated during the 1970-71 season that McDaniels had signed a professional contract, but he consistently denied having done so. At the end of March he signed a lucrative contract with the Carolina Cougars of the American Basketball Assocation. On February 16, 1971, Walter Byars of the NCAA sought Western's consent and cooperation to sue the ABA because of "substantial evidence" that McDaniels had in fact signed a contract. Downing replied that after an investigation Western accepted McDaniel's denial. A number of Western officials were convinced that the NCAA then embarked upon a vendetta against Western because of the University's refusal to become party to the suit. In early 1972 when McDaniels signed with Seattle in the NBA, the Carolina team sued. Evidence revealed that McDaniels had signed a professional contract in November 1970 and was thereafter ineligible for collegiate play. Western acceded to NCAA demands that the third-place NCAA win be vacated and the trophy and money returned. McDaniels admitted signing but, he asserted, "I was told a thousand times that I was not doing anything that would hurt my university." Western officials blamed the agents and club more than the player.[42]

Before the McDaniels case ended, Western underwent another investigation that the NCAA said was unrelated. Twenty charges of recruiting violations, improper testing procedures, and illegal tryouts for prospects resulted in a reprimand, probation for two years, and prohibition of participation in any postseason or NCAA televised games. Downing maintained that aside from some "unintentional technical violations" there were "no violations of a substantive nature," and in a rare outburst he rebuked a *Louisville Times* reporter for "unprofessional journalism." Then in June 1974 the story broke that an assistant coach had given a Louisville high school basketball prospect an envelope containing five hundred dollars supplied by a Bowling Green fan. Western reported the violation to the OVC and NCAA and announced that the assistant coach had been reassigned from coaching, that Richards had been censured for waiting a week to report the infraction, and that Richards had been told he would be dismissed if any other irregularity occurred. Western's probation was extended from January 1975 to August, which eliminated any postseason play, and recruiting was limited to staff members. In November 1974 the OVC presidents declared the Hilltoppers ineligible for the postseason tournament. These years marked a nadir in Western's basketball history.[43]

Despite those adversities, and despite losing starter Kent Allison because of an OVC violation in using test conversion tables, Richards put together a team without a starter over 6' 5" that went 16-8 and won 11 of 14 OVC games in 1974-75. Then in 1975-76 he enjoyed his best season with a 20-9 record, the OVC championship, and a brief NCAA appearance as probation had expired. (Marquette won 79-60 in Dayton). The 1976-77 record slipped to 10-16, and several players either left the squad or were dropped from it during the season. One notable mark was the 82-81 defeat of Murray on February 19, 1977; it was the one thousandth victory in Western's basketball history.[44] Richards was optimistic going into the 1977-78 season, but the team was playing under .500 in January 1978 when he announced that he had requested assignment to other duties at the end of the season. Coaching had ceased to be enjoyable, and he had not been able to recruit the players needed to make Western consistently competitive. "Youngsters don't react to discipline and authority the way they did when I first got into coaching," Richards explained, "I guess I'm just like an old oak tree. I've grown too straight for too long. It hurts now to try to bend too much." The team closed the season 13-13, won the OVC tournament, upset Syracuse in overtime for the first OVC win in the NCAA tournament since 1973, then lost to "Magic" Johnson and his Michigan State team mates. Jim Richards was appointed coordinator of men's athletics. Gene Keady, an assistant at the University of Arkansas, replaced Richards in 1978. After 17-11 and 21-8 seasons (66.7 percent), he resigned in 1980 to accept the head coaching position at Purdue. His promotional efforts put Western's basketball program on a sound fiscal base.[45]

The success that Jimmy Feix had with his first two football teams carried over into the 1970s. In the six seasons, 1970-75, his team won 53 games, lost 12 and tied one. They took the OVC championship in 1970, 1971, and 1973 and were co-champions in 1975. Feix recruited players who could win on the OVC level, and he recognized that the old motivational techniques had to be modified. "We have to give athletes more voice in the program," he explained. "They won't produce or cooperate if you don't give them a voice." Personal standards were relaxed in tune with changing student attitudes. "I'm not really concerned about hair," Feix said, "as long as my half-backs don't get dragged down from behind by flying locks." He opposed the costly effort needed to make the OVC into a big-time football conference as some people suggested.

The 1973 and 1975 seasons were among the best in Western's gridiron history. The 1973 team had a perfect 10-0 regular season and allowed opponents only 62 points, 27 of them to Murray. The eight points scored by Middle Tennessee may have come when Miss Heaven Lee, an exotic dancer from Nashville, rose to display her support for M.T. Little attention was paid to the game until she resumed her seat. Although quarterback Leo Peckenpaugh and three other regulars were ineligible for postseason play, Western defeated Lehigh 25-16 and Grambling 28-20 in the NCAA Division II playoffs before losing in the championship game to Louisiana Tech 34-0. It was the first shut-out of a Feix team at Western. Two years later the 1975 regular season record of 9-1 was marred only by a 13-7 loss to Eastern. The high point of the season was the 21-17 win over the University of Louisville before a crowd of over thirty-four thousand. Invited again to the NCAA playoffs, Western defeated Northern Iowa 14-12 in a mud game and New Hampshire 14-3 before losing 16-14 to Northern Michigan when an attempted field goal was ruled no good.[46]

Then came a slump. The 1976 record of 4-5-1 was the first losing season since 1965, but it was only a harbinger of worse days to come. In the fall of 1977 Western did not score a touchdown until the fourth game of the season when East Tennessee was defeated 33-13. That victory and a tie with Morehead produced a disastrous 1-8-1 season. Embarrassed by the debacle, Feix started an intensive conditioning program in which all the coaches participated. During a winter storm an assistant called to ask if they were meeting that day. "Of course," Feix replied. But people are being told to travel only in case of emergencies, the assistant suggested. "What do you call an 1-8-1 season?" Feix inquired. The work paid off, for the 1978 record was 8-2 and Western again won the OVC title, Feix was the conference coach of the year, and the turnaround from the previous season was the most impressive in the nation. But there was no NCAA postseason bid. During the year Western decided to become a member of the I-AA football classification, as did all the OVC schools.[47]

Western was having difficulty maintaining a consistently good football program, and the 1979 record dipped to 5-5 overall and 3-3 in conference play. Many reasons were advanced to explain what the sports editor of the Bowling Green newspaper called the "mediocrity" of the last four years. Injuries and inexperience played a part, but some knowledgeable watchers were convinced the key factor was the failure to find adequate replacements for such excellent assistant coaches as Art Zeleznik, Romeo Cremel, and Lee Murray who had left the staff. Feix had accustomed fans to success, and the roller coaster seasons of the late 1970 provoked grumblings and demands for change.[48]

The decade saw the close of Ted Hornback's spectacular career as tennis coach. When Hornback retired in 1971 as athletic director and teacher he continued to coach. Several of his teams featured foreign players, particularly Swedes. When Tom Ecker left Western in 1966 to become one of Sweden's national track coaches Hornback said casually,

"Tom, when you get to Sweden, find me a good tennis player." Ecker said he would, and he did, and as word spread Hornback began to hear from players in other lands. In 1975 Western's number three doubles team had once been Turkey's Davis Cup doubles team. Arvid Bergman, one of the Swedes, delighted in saying that he would return home as the only person in Sweden who had ever had a course in Kentucky history. Hornback continued his winning ways, and in his last seven seasons, 1970-76, his teams compiled a 116-20 record. His record over a third of a century was 370-76, an 82.9 winning percentage, and his teams won the OVC title 18 of 28 years. He was succeeded by Ray Rose, a member of the physical education department, who resigned in 1981 with a record of 48-59. Budget cuts had severely restricted his recruiting, and, like Jim Richards, he found it difficult "to communicate with these kinds of individuals."[49]

Baseball also saw a change in coaches and a new emphasis on the sport. In 1976 Jim Pickens, whose eleven-year record was 169-180, became assistant to the dean for student affairs. He was replaced as baseball coach by Dr. Barry Shollenberger from Middle Georgia College who in his first year set a Western record with twenty wins. He still had a losing season, but the forty-four games played was almost double the traditional Western schedule. In the next two years his teams compiled records of 26-19-1 and 31-22, and when he resigned after the 1979 season to accept the head coach position at the University of Alabama, Shollenberger left a 77-64 record and a new emphasis on baseball. Joel Murrie, a graduate assistant for the preceding two years, succeeded him.[50]

Swimming was added to the list of intercollegiate sports in 1969 when William A. Powell, a successful high school coach in Michigan, was employed to build a program. He had little time for recruitment, and in dual meets he had only a 3-4 record in 1969-70. The following year he had eight full scholarships, some excellent recruits, and an 11-4 record. In 1973 Rick Yeloushan, a junior from Tampa, Florida, was the first Western swimmer to compete in the NCAA championships. The 1977-78 season saw an 11-0 record, and the victory string was extended to twenty consecutive wins in dual meets until UK broke it on February 16, 1979. Then Western entered the Midwestern Independent Intercollegiate Championship for the first time and won it. Powell's dual meet record for his first nine years (1969-78) was 72-26, a fact of which many Western athletic fans seem unaware.[51]

The cross-country squad also won national attention in the 1970s as a contingent of English runners built on the records left by Hector Ortiz. Led by Nick Rose, who won four All-American ratings, 1972-75, Western's cross-country squad went to the national finals four consecutive years, 1973-76. The best team showing was in 1974 when the squad finished second as Rose took first place; four members won All-American honors by finishing in the top 25. An unusual incident occurred on

December 22, 1973, when Chris Ridler, Nick Rose, and Tony Staynings were run over in their motel room in Marlboro, Massachusetts, by a drunken driver. Staynings suffered a fractured pelvis and Rose required seventy stitches to repair his cuts.

Dr. Burch Oglesby coached the team until 1972 when Jerry Bean took over. He was succeeded in 1976 by Del Hessel who remained until 1980 when he was followed by Curtiss Long. The cross-country coach was also the track coach, and Western continued to do well in the track events. In 1973 Western's squad finished tenth in the NCAA nationals, the first time that a Kentucky or OVC school had ever had a top ten spot. In 1974 Western tied for ninth place, and Jesse Stuart won the shot put to become Western's first individual track-field national champion. In 1975 Western finished fifth in the NCAA's indoor meet although Stuart was injured and did not compete. The 1975 OVC championshp was Western's twelfth consecutive title in track. That streak ended in 1976, but in 1979 Western won it again.[52]

The golf team also continued to win the large majority of its matches in the early 1970s. In dual play its 1970-72 record was 43-1-1, but it faltered in OVC tournaments and finished as low as eighth in 1972. A chronic problem was the lack of adequate practice facilities. In 1978 Frank Griffin retired as golf coach after thirty-one years to devote more time to the expanding intramural program. He was succeeded by Jim Richards.

Almost unnoticed, there had been at least one change of head coaches in each sport except football during the 1970s. Feix, whose tenure had started in 1968, was the senior head coach by the end of the 1970s. Western's hold on the OVC All-Sport Championship began to slip toward the late 1970s. The skein of consecutive championships that started in 1966-67 reached six before being broken by Murray in 1972-73, but then Western took the title the next three years. But Middle Tennessee won in 1976-77, and East Tennesseee was best in 1977-78. Western was back on top in 1978-79, but Murray captured the title in 1979-80.[53]

The most significant development in athletics at Western in the 1970s was the introduction of women's intercollegiate competition for the first time in over forty years. The growth of the intramural program was a contributing factor, for many female athletes competing on that level began to insist on intercollegiate competition. Their demands were reinforced by the provisions of Title IX of the Education Amendments of 1972 to the Civil Rights Act of 1964 which went into effect in July 1975. The key provision read: "No person in the United States shall, on the basis of sex, be excluded from participation, be denied the benefits of, or be subjected to discrimination under an education program or activity receiving Federal financial assistance." Vice-President Minton and Dr. Faye Robinson, assistant dean of the graduate college, were named coordinators to oversee the compliance that the Regents promised on July 26, 1975. A formal grievance procedure set up in July 1976 made it easier for charges of noncompliance to be made. Title IX led to numerous changes on campus, including relaxation of the dormitory regulations that had been much more restrictive for women than for men, and it accelerated the development of intercollegiate athletics for women.[54]

By 1972 some of the women who were majoring in physical education were pushing hard for a change, and in the early fall Betty Langley of the physical education department wrote the Faculty Athletic Committee on their behalf. She charged that Western was the only Kentucky state university that had done nothing on the intercollegiate level, and her contention that the omission was a matter of concern to many prospective students and their parents was echoed by staff members engaged in recruiting. Athletic Director Oldham said that Langley's request was the first one he had received, but it was obvious that Western had ignored the movement until forced to consider it. Exasperated physical education major Pat Gilmer exploded: "This is getting so silly about red tape. The University doesn't listen to what people want. You have to have five million letters." The athletic committee considered the requests with all deliberate speed, but by the spring of 1973 Western had joined the Association of Intercollegiate Athletics for Women and the state body, Kentucky Intercollegiate Athletics for Women. By the fall of 1973 Western's women had club teams in gymnastics, tennis, golf, track and field, and basketball. Riflery was already coeducational. Shirley Laney of the physical education department coordinated the emerging program, and in September 1974 the athletic committee recommended that women's athletics come under its jurisdiction. President Downing accepted the recommendation and implemented it, Laney was appointed Coordinator of Women's Athletics, and two more women (making four of fifteen) were added to the athletic committee. By then the OVC was studying its relationship to womens' sports, and Western in early 1975 decided to grant scholarships for 1975-1976 in the five varsity sports then recognized for women.[55]

The first coaches were Ray Rose for gymnastics; Betty Langley for tennis; Shirley Laney for golf, and track and field; and Pam Dickson, a graduate student, for basketball. The program started with a modest appropriation of $5,800, but the coaches were given a teaching load reduction, and these arrangements compared favorably with those at other Kentucky schools. Plans were soon underway to add volleyball and to find a basketball coach. The January 1983 NCAA convention voted to require schools to offer the same minimum number of teams for women as for men by 1988-89. Division I schools were to have at least six women's teams by 1986, seven by 1987, and eight by 1988.[56]

The modern era of women's basketball began on January 19, 1974, when Coach Dickson's team lost to Bellarmine College, 43-41. The first victory came on February 1 when Kentucky State was defeated 40-31 as senior Patty Sutherland scored 31 points. The team's record during the abbreviated season was 4-7. Dr. Carol Hughes came to Western in 1974 and coached the team during the next two seasons to 3-14 and 19-6 records. The Lady Toppers won two games in the 1976 KWIC tournament before losing to Eastern 81-71 in the championship game. Julia Yeater coached the Lady Toppers to consecutive 22-9 seasons in 1976-77 and 1977-78. They lost to Morehead 70-68 in the KWIC tournament and to North Carolina State (70-52) and Memphis State (79-68) in the AIAW regional tournament in 1977. The following year they won their first two games in the KWIC, then lost to Kentucky, 61-49. Coach Yeater had a good 44-18 record, and the women's program seemed firmly established.[57]

Then in November 1978 Yeater suddenly resigned to become coach of the professional Minnesota Fillies, for whom former Western star Brenda Chapman was playing. Eileen Canty, a first-year assistant coach, took over the team on short notice. During the next four seasons her teams won 50 and lost 62 games. Coach Canty became better known for her sophisticated bench dress—long flowing skirts and modish hats—than for the success of her teams. All OVC Laurie Heltsley and Sharon Garland left the team early in the 1981-82 season, saying that they were unable to understand their roles on the team, and Coach Canty submitted her resignation in late March 1982.[58] Despite having four coaches in nine years, the women's basketball team compiled a winning record of 120-109. But in a basketball-oriented environment, the basketball team was the bellwether of women's sports, and a 52.6 winning percentage was not considered satisfactory.

Gymnastics had a short life as an intercollegiate sport at Western. When the program started, Adele Gleaves of Louisville was an experienced competitor who might have gone to the 1972 Olympics but for an injury. She won the women's national championship in April 1973 and finished fifth in 1974 despite a hand injury. Later performers were not able to match her achievements, not even when she was coach in 1977-78. In 1981 volleyball replaced gymnastics as one of the intercollegiate sports for women.[59]

In 1977 Regent chairman David Cole was concerned over a perceived decline in the athletic program. He saw a successful program as a means of attracting the support necessary to attain his goal of making Western within a decade one of the state's three major universities. Recruiting appeared to be the major problem. Cole supported the head coaches in football and basketball, but he questioned the effectiveness of some assistant coaches. Management problems in athletics, he pointed out, were the primary responsibility of the athletic director.[60]

Although several athletic problems concerned Downing, he was also confronted by a number of issues that involved other aspects of the university. Times were changing, and he had to deal with matters that had seldom troubled his predecessors.

Nine

Troubled Times
1969-1979

THE STUDENT unrest that became evident on the Hill in the late 1960s continued into the next decade. Although it was mild by national standards—Western students did not burn any buildings or "trash" any administrative offices—President Downing was determined that radicalism would not interfere with Western's continued progress. He accepted some relaxation of traditional mores and regulations, but he would maintain essential standards. Profoundly shocked by the turmoil he had seen on the Berkeley campus in 1965, Downing was determined that it not spread to the Hilltop. Potential problems should be resolved if possible before they escalated into conflict, and plans were carefully devised to prevent open clashes. A network was set up so that forty to fifty key personnel—administrators, coaches, faculty—could be called to the campus in a matter of minutes to cope with potentially dangerous situations. Charles Keown, dean of student affairs, and his staff were most closely involved in maintaining contacts with the students.[1]

The large majority of the student leaders during this era were moderate in their demands; few, if any of them, desired anarchy on the campus. Student opinions, requests, and demands could be channeled through the well-established Associated Student Government, and the student regent could present student views directly to the governing board. Yet there were more student demands than in previous years, and to some people both within and without the campus community they seemed radical. An indication of changing times came in the spring of 1971 when Linda Jones, a junior from Lexington, was elected president of the associated students and Reginald Glass, a sophomore from Louisville, was elected vice-president. She was the first woman, he was the first black student elected to an executive position in Western's student government. The administration encouraged student officers by awarding scholarships to the top five so that they would have more time to devote to student government. In November 1975 President Downing arranged for the College Heights Foundation to supplement these awards so that some of the student officers could reduce their outside work hours.[2]

Yet incidents occurred that created excitement on campus and a-larmed some members of the larger community. A.M. Causey, an elderly Bowling Green resident who contributed frequent letters to the news-papers, wrote angrily in May 1970: "If these rabble-rousing, disloyal students are not at Western to get an education, let them go elsewhere. This also applies to disloyal faculty members." The students and faculty members he denounced were probably never aware of the times Downing defended them from such outraged citizens.

The Viet Nam war led to some campus unrest in the autumn of 1969, soon after Downing moved into the presidency. The escalation of antiwar protests had forced President Lyndon B. Johnson into retiring, and put heavy pressure on President Richard M. Nixon to bring the long conflict to an end. In October the Associated Student Congress endorsed a peace rally planned by the Western Vietnam Moratorium Committee for Oc-tober 15, a day on which teachers were asked to dismiss classes or discuss the war instead of "business as usual." The university gave permission for use of the old stadium, provided a public address system, and arranged to open the Garrett ballroom in case of bad weather. An estimated twelve hundred persons attended the Peace Rally that ran for some five hours, but fewer than seventy signed a letter supporting President Nixon's Viet Nam policy that Dr. Ronald Seeger of the geography and geology depart-ment had posted. A *Herald* editorial asserted that it was "the first bona fide demonstration in memory at Western. For once the campus was stimulated to think about a real issue and to make a personal decision concerning it." But an antiwar rally in November attracted no more than a hundred participants and spectators, and the customary apathy seemed back in place.[3]

The Kent State incident in the spring of 1970 touched off protests on many campuses, including Western's. The Volunteers, an *ad hoc* commit-tee of student activists, called for a general strike on Friday, May 8, but most classes met, although often with diminished attendance. "Strike Western" T-shirts quickly appeared. Protests demonstrations were coun-tered by an antiprotest rally. Bruce Cook, a science major, said he spoke for "the silent majority" when he called the proposed strike "radical and ridiculous." President Downing met with a group of students on the steps of the administration building; a graduate student who was active in the peace movement was touched by "his sincerity and love of Western." Downing also met with the Volunteers and asked for a list of their demands. In a meeting with the Academic Council, he praised the sense of responsibility displayed by student leaders in keeping the demonstra-tions peaceful.[4]

Demonstrations and marches, seldom involving more than a few hundred students, continued over the weekend. A "sleep-in" Friday night on the lawn next to the administration building attracted about a hundred participants, including some small children and one dog. On Monday, May 11, Downing presented the Volunteers and associated student leaders with a nine-page answer to the Volunteer's five demands. The president called the meeting "very amiable, very courteous and very cordial"; student Bill Nelson called the reply "ambiguous as hell. ... We're going to have to get tough." William Cunningham believed "a group of people should get together and do something drastic," and Braxton Crenshaw suggested civil disobedience. Downing agreed to write President Nixon in protest of the invasion of Cambodia and the continuance of the Viet Nam war. Granting college credit for ROTC would be considered at the next regular meeting of the Academic Council, the body that had responsibility over such matters. He saw no need for the student and faculty regents to have the right to vote, but he would not object if the legislature decided otherwise. The school had experimented with un-armed campus police in the summer of 1969, he related, but events had shown that the policy was unwise. To resolve the issue of who could speak on campus and under what conditions, he appointed a special student-faculty-administrative committee, chaired by Lowell Harrison of the history department, and instructed it to prepare a written policy that would be in effect by the fall semester. In other actions administrators were told to lock all file cabinets if students stormed the administration building, and the *Talisman* was used to help identify students who were active participants in the protests. Student Russell Harris, hurrying to class one morning, "nearly trod heavily upon an earnest-looking crew-cut hiding behind a trash can. (Squatting there, he was photographing all the students.)" His camera clicked, Harris recalled, and "somewhere in an endless maze of government files labeled 'Student Subversives' is my hurried, harried, and chagrined face." The speakers' policy, with some slight modifications, was adopted by the regents on October 14, 1970.[5]

The climax of the unrest centered on the issue of speakers coming to the campus. Western had no formal policy until the early autumn of 1970, and the unrest attracted the attention of a number of off-campus civil rights activists, some of whom apparently received invitations from pro-testing students. One of the visitors was Carl Braden, editor of the *Southern Patriot* and a Louisville civil rights leader. Western made the old stadium available for protest speakers and meetings, but Braden and a crowd of demonstrators refused to move from the lawn beside the administration building. When it appeared that an element was determined to be disruptive, the university obtained on Tuesday, May 12, 1970, a temporary restraining order from Judge Robert Coleman of the Warren Circuit Court. Braden reportedly left while the sheriff was on his way to the campus, but the order was served on five students, Braxton Crenshaw,

Daniel O. Sellers, Bill L. Nelson, Gerald Lee Donaldson, and Fred Joseph Santorelli. Copies of the order were then sent to all students, faculty, and staff of the university. A student "Crisis Committee" was established, legal assistance was sought from civil liberties attorney Daniel Taylor III, and a flier appealed to the faculty for funds to support the struggle.

On Friday, May 15 the restraining order was modified to apply only to the five named defendants and "other persons in actual concert or participation with them." The *Herald* decided, "The entire situation has mushroomed into something neither group intended it to become, and the main reason—overreacation [sic] on the part of the administration that had been playing it so cool." Two bomb scares, one at Western Towers and the other at the administration building, increased the tension. A number of students publicly supported the school's policy. Phil Myers, president of the senior class, charged that the demonstrators "aimed at confrontation even without real provocation. ... When will these individuals realize that constructive changes can only take place when offered and supported in a responsible manner."

The defendants attempted to get the restraining order lifted, but on May 21, after a two-day hearing that featured sharp attacks by Daniel Taylor upon President Downing, the court ruled that there had been "a clear and present danger that disorder and violence could and would develop from continued indiscriminate demonstrations on the campus at this time." The court then issued a temporary injunction that limited demonstrations to designed areas and ordered demonstrators to refrain from disrupting normal operations. This order was upheld on appeal, and the end of the spring semester eliminated most of the possibilities for campus disturbance. President Downing was convinced that the legal actions helped prevent "widespread disruption or unrest on the Western campus."[6] The American withdrawal from Viet Nam defused one of the main causes of student discontent.

Another new dimension of student unrest came from among the growing number of black students. In 1969 only 3.9 percent of the student body was black; five years later that percentage had risen to 6.2 and the total was nearly eight hundred; and by the fall of 1976 the 7.3 percent black students was almost the same as the percentage of blacks in the state's population. Black grievances took several forms. One concerned off-campus housing in Bowling Green. Blacks frequently encountered discrimination in renting, and Western lost some black faculty and staff members because of such difficulties. But as Dr. Norman Holy, chemistry professor and a member of the Bowling Green Human Rights Commission, said, "The University is reluctant to get involved in social problems and I don't think they will in the future." Many blacks felt shut out from campus activities; a distinct minority, they were not likely to win many elections.[7] In a search for identity, some of them urged the addition of black-oriented courses that many white faculty members and students believed had little academic content or worth. In many instances the black response to real and perceived slights was to withdraw into a segregated existence that many whites made no effort to penetrate. Problems were complicated by mutual misunderstanding and distrust.

The lack of black cheerleaders became one focal point of discontent. Mrs. Charles E. Ford of Louisville wrote President Downing in the spring of 1971 that she was going to contact the National Association for the Advancement of Colored People because Western had no black cheerleaders although most of the starters on the basketball team were black. Downing replied that her complaints were quite similar to those he received because so many of the basketball players were black. "In either instance," he added, "such an attitude is evidence of misunderstanding and lack of information and perhaps a degree of prejudice as well." After naming several black students who occupied leadership positions on campus, he invited her to visit Western and become more knowledgeable about the school. Black student Larry Pruitt in a letter to the *Herald* chided fellow blacks for their behavior during the playing of the national anthem and their refusal to cheer during games. "With five black athletes starting, I have something to cheer about," he asserted. "If there is any prejudice within the basketball team, it certainly isn't shown within the statistics." On the morning of September 10, 1972, some 250 blacks staged a peaceful sit-in in the lobby of the administration building to demand that a second black be added to the cheerleading squad. The regents had added three cheerleaders, one of them black, to the six-woman squad the previous week. The protesting students left a path open, but Downing, who spoke to them in the lobby, declared, "This university is not going to be disrupted and what has happened here is disruption." But he met with a delegation of five in his office, consultations were held with Dean Keown and other interested parties, and a second black cheerleader was added to the squad over the protests of the elected cheerleaders. "We are willing to try to make it work," the squad captain was quoted, "but we felt it was wrong."[8] The mode of selection was later changed from popular election to try-outs before judges.

Blacks were increasingly prominent in athletics where they contributed heavily to successful basketball, football, and track teams. Black fraternities and sororities were established by the late 1960s (Alpha Kappa Alpha sorority in 1968, Kappa Alpha Psi fraternity in 1969 were the pioneers), and the United Black Students (UBS), formed in 1976, provided an organization in which some blacks felt more comfortable than in predominately white groups. Black leaders encountered many of the same problems as their white counterparts. "There is not another campus in the U.S. with as much black apathy as Western," UBS president Mark Turner complained in 1974. Black Awareness Week and a Miss Black

Western contest (Carolyn Brown won the first one in 1971) attracted attention to the black presence on campus. An interdisciplinary minor in Afro-American studies was approved by the Academic Council in 1971.[9]

Some members of the Western community were concerned by the campus *de facto* segregation. With rare exceptions, blacks and whites separated by choice—in the dorms, in the student union, at social events, in fraternities and sororities, in seating at athletic events, and sometimes in classrooms. Virgil Livers, a star football player and president of Alpha Phi Alpha, chided fellow blacks in 1974 for not supporting Napoleon Avery for the presidency of the associated students. Livers believed that Avery had been abandoned because he was said to be "an Uncle Tom, because he doesn't mingle or hang around the black people all the time." Christy Vogt objected so strongly to the pattern of segregation that in February 1977, acting as an individual and not as president of ASG, she tried to enter the Miss Black Western contest, as did Susan Wilk. Segregated programs and organizations "are clear-cut examples of discrimination," Vogt wrote the following year, which discouraged the blacks from participating in the mainstream of campus activities.[10]

Yet there were signs of progress outside the world of athletics. Alice Gatewood became Western's first black Homecoming Queen in 1972 after a controversial election. The first election was voided because there were approximately 275 more votes than voters. Black students, suspicious that the revoting was ordered because a black candidate had won, physically blocked the polls for over an hour until an agreement was reached. In 1974 Gregory L. McKinney was elected the first black student regent, and in 1982 Margaret Ragan was elected president of ASG.[11] An emerging problem toward the end of the 1970s was a decline in the proportion of blacks attending Western and most of the other state schools. This decrease posed serious problems as the schools tried to meet federal requirements for desegregation.

Even at the height of campus unrest not more than a fraction of the student body was actively involved. A student who entered in the mid-1970s found her classmates generally "apathetic, caught up in self— and focused on their own little world." A transfer student who praised Western's small classes and the friendly attitude of its teachers was also impressed by the partying that constituted much of the social life. The students who lived off-campus were little affected by the changes that were important to dormitory residents. The general on-campus trend was to abandon or at least modify many of the traditional regulations and, under pressures from federal laws and regulations, to grant women equal rights with men. Although complaints continued, the dormitories were made more attractive for living with the addition of refrigerators and kitchens. The dormitory issue that aroused the most controversy was open visitation. The extreme demand was for an open dorm policy with room doors closed at the discretion of the host. The administration, beset by some highly vocal opposition to a more permissive policy, retreated slowly, but dorm visitations were substantially liberalized. The story of the doors' status could well be titled, "The Door Closes Slowly." By 1982 there were eighteen residence halls with a double occupancy capacity of 5,212. Starting in the fall of 1974, most freshmen were required to live in dormitories for four semesters; a deficit of $322,000 the previous year necessitated the requirement. Toward the end of the decade the new radical demand was for coed housing. It was achieved in the fall of 1985 when Hugh Poland Hall became coeducational.[12]

What remained of the dress codes disappeared during the early 1970s, and blue jeans became the most common garment on campus for both males and females. Shorts and bare feet became commonplace during the summer. The informal dress affected even the faculty and staff; by 1971 pant suits had become officially acceptable for campus wear by female faculty and staff members.[13]

Drinking on campus continued to be a perennial problem. Individual cases usually involved disturbances in the dormitories or driving while intoxicated. Problems on a larger scale most often concerned fraternity parties. One of the more serious confrontations came in the fall of 1969, when, after protests by Bowling Green citizens, Dean Keown ordered a crackdown on the use of alcoholic beverages in the off-campus houses. At a mass meeting of fraternity members Steve Garrett, president of the Inter-Fraternity Council (IFC), proclaimed that "this final straw" had destroyed IFC's power to regulate its own members and called for a Greek boycott of all Homecoming activities. But the Pan-Hellenic Council withdrew its initial support, tempers calmed, and Homecoming survived.[14]

Thirsty students followed with interest the efforts of the Hub Pizzeria to secure a beer license in the 1970s. The Goal Post, once known as the Varsity Grill, had flourished on Fifteenth Street, across from Cherry and Gordon Wilson halls, for nearly half a century. Sam and Bob Rabold operated the campus hangout for many years. After its sale the Goal Post became the Hub Pizzeria, and in 1977 when the owner applied for a beer license Western protested. A key issue was the distance from the Hub to the nearest classroom building, for a state law required a minimum of two hundred feet from a school or church if the institution protested the license. When Western's effort to classify the Rock House as an instructional building failed, the distance to Cherry Hall became the focal point of controversy. Did one measure in a straight line, or was the measuring confined to streets and sidewalks? Was the distance to Cherry Hall 109 feet or 173 feet? That portion of the campus had never been as carefully measured as it was then. Some students and some faculty saw the university's stand as another example of an outdated, illiberal administration. "The university is wasting its money trying to do someone else's job," a *Herald* editorial declared. "It should stick to education."

President Downing and the regents were adamant in their opposition, and the license request was denied locally. Owner Gordon Mills then secured a permit on appeal to the state Alcoholic Beverage Control Board, a decision that Western then appealed to the Franklin Circuit Court. On June 20, 1978, the board's decision was sustained, so Western filed an appeal on August 24 with the Court of Appeals. In the meantime, after closing the business, the owner indicated a willingness to sell, and in September 1978 the regents authorized its purchase. The sale was completed in early 1979 for ninety-eight thousand dollars. The only use found for the building was for (dry) storage.[15]

Drugs constituted a more serious problem than did The Hub. The drug culture was spreading rapidly throughout the country, and few college towns and campuses were immune from the traffic. Detective Sergeant Fred Lancaster of the Bowling Green Police Department believed in January 1973 that the problem was less serious in Bowling Green than in most college towns, but he added that drugs up to and including heroin were readily available locally. Marijuana was most common; use of LSD had declined sharply during the past year.[16] Campus authorities cooperated closely with off-campus officials, and the arrest records indicated that their efforts had some degree of success.

Dr. W.R. McCormack, a Bowling Green physician who was chairman of the Board of Regents, was dissatisfied with both the efforts and the results, and in 1973 he opened a personal crusade against drug use. "We must take a stand now, not later," he asserted. Some students thought it harmless to smoke marijuana, "But as a doctor of medicine I know it can lead to other drugs." He recommended that teachers look at their students' eyes and expel drug users from class. Dr. McCormack's assertions aroused a storm of hostile responses that flooded the *Herald*'s pages until the editor refused to print any more. Most of them questioned his "absurd generalizations" and his knowledge of the effects of drugs. Dean Keown had been working with hall directors and counselors on drug problems since 1967, and the issue had been discussed at freshman convocations for several years. Campus efforts were intensified after Dr. McCormack focused attention on the issue, with emphasis on both education and control, and the problem was kept within reasonable limits.[17]

Civil rights attracted a great deal of attention in the nation after World War II, and the idea slowly pervaded campuses that students were citizens and therefore entitled to such rights. This concept clashed with the traditional relationship between student and college that had long existed at such schools as Western. Student activists challenged the university's authority in areas that would never have been questioned in even the recent past. Freedom of expression was one of the common grounds for challenging administrative policies. As a consequence, the university attorney became an increasingly important member of the administration.

Charges of censorship were hurled at the university in early 1972 when *The Fly*, a twenty-five-minute movie produced by John Lennon and Yoko Ono, was banned from campus showing. One of a package of four short films, it consisted entirely of a fly crawling over a nude female. The administration did not ordinarily screen films ordered by the Associated Students, but Dean Keown chanced to read a descriptive flier of this one. President Downing called it "pure filth ... , pornographic," and Keown decided it was inappropriate for public showing on campus where pre-college students often attended. He suggested that permission be sought to delete it from the series and that it be shown off-campus, but Reginald Glass, vice-president of ASG, replied, "We don't agree with censorship in any form," and the series was cancelled. On February 10 the ASG Congress barred a *Herald* reporter from its meeting while it decided what further action to take, and the *Herald* immediately charged ASG with censorship.[18]

Aided by the Kentucky Civil Liberties Union, ASG filed suit in federal district court in the persons of Linda Jones (president), Reginald Glass (vice-president), Patrick Long, and Albert Stith to determine the university's legal right to cancel activities booked and cosigned by ASG. The federal district court ruled in favor of the university, the Sixth Circuit Court of Appeals upheld that decision, and the Supreme Court in October 1973 refused to hear an appeal. By then much of the interest in the case had dissipated.[19]

Another example of student dissatisfaction during the 1970s was the sporadic effort to establish a "Free University" with courses that, in the minds of the founders, would be more relevant to the real world than those provided by the university. Some of the 1970 Volunteers established the short-lived "West Kentucky Free School" in June with such classes as women's liberation, Marxist social thought, anarchy, radical ecology, photography, and the revolutionary Jesus, as "a radical alternative to the existing educational structure." Denied the use of university facilities, classes were scheduled in the Newman Center. Interest soon waned, but in the spring of 1973 the ASG opened another "Free University" at the Newman Center. Most of the instructors were students with a small leavening of faculty members. But by the fall of 1973 there were only five classes, and the Free University disappeared.[20]

A number of short-lived off-campus newspapers also indicated the dissatisfaction of some students with aspects of the university. Usually the creation of an individual or a small group, without adequate financing and with less appeal than their founders dreamed of, few of them lasted beyond the initial issues. Although the *Herald* displayed a degree of independence that would have amazed its earlier editors, it was frequently denounced as a tool of the administration. In early 1970 editor Bruce Tucker and several other staffers quit the paper after a clash with advisor Jody Richards. Richards said the dispute concerned operational matters, not freedom of the press, but the departing journalists proclaimed that they could not "continue to work under conditions that included a corruptly-structured publications board, an administration sycophant for an advisor and direct interference by the president of the University ... either you believe in a free student press or you do not." A result was the appearance of the *Expatriate*, a hybrid between a newspaper and a magazine, which featured articles that explored the murky side of events and criticized most university administrators.[21] The *Expatriate*, which expired in the spring of 1971, was followed by the *Spread Eagle*, which first appeared in November 1971. Robert D. Hatfield, the executive editor, had largely separate staffs, one for the conservative half of the paper, the other for the liberal. The initial issue carried an article by freshman Jim Baskett which attracted considerable controversy with his criticism of "exorbitant black demands and white overcompensation" on the part of the University and the white students. But the *Spread Eagle* also soon joined the surprisingly long list of defunct organs of protest.[22]

These manifestations of campus unrest were so new to the Western scene that some campus officials may have been pleased with the occasional traditional type of nonidealogical disorder. Panty raids did still occur—although some advocates of women's liberation found them demeaning—but "streaking" was the new fad that came to Western with the advent of spring in 1974. Rumors circulated on March 6 of a mass disrobing that night, and a sizable crowd milling around the Downing Student Union tied up much of the Bowling Green police department for several hours. A few arrests were made despite the efforts of the mass of nonstreakers to shield the offenders. President Downing, awakened at 1:30 A.M. one morning by a crowd that demanded the release of a streaker, chatted with the group but indicated a strong preference for answering their questions at a more appropriate time. Dr. McCormack denounced the "corrupt indecent fad" at the next meeting of the regents and demanded punishment of the offenders. Campus and city officials did assess penalties on a number of students, and the fad soon died.[23]

Such incidents helped bring about the enlargement and upgrading of Western's security force. The campus had changed drastically since Aubrey Hoofnell became the campus policeman in 1925. Although he had not confronted many of the problems of the 1970s, some students who had imbibed too freely sometimes decided that a good way to conclude a Saturday evening was to beat up on Aubrey. As late as 1940 there were just two campus policemen.[24] Additional officers were added, but President Downing saw the need for a larger and more professional force. The regents approved his recommendations, and in 1974 Mark Wallace, a former FBI agent who was in the financial aid office, was named director of university safety and security. By 1977 the force had twenty-four members and a number of student patrolmen.[25] This enlarged and more professional staff worked well with local and state officials, and Wallace's calm direction of the campus force helped defuse possible confrontations with students.

One of the best indicators of a more conservative student body was the revived interest in ROTC. Denounced by the radicals of the 1960s, ROTC's future appeared to be in jeopardy. Western's voluntary program may have helped save it, for no one was forced into a program he detested. But fall enrollment did decline sharply from the late 1960s until it reached a low of 103 in the fall of 1972. Then the trend revised itself, and the unit regained strength as uniforms became acceptable again on campus. By 1975 the enrollment was 328.

A contributing factor to its renewed growth was the admission of women to the program. Four women were reported enrolled in Military Science 101 in the spring of 1972, but the program was officially opened to women in the fall of 1973. In addition to the quantitative increase, quality also improved. During the years 1962-66 over half of the Western graduates finished in the lower third of the officers' basic course and only 19 percent were in the upper one-third. Performance improved markedly in the 1970s, and by 1976 the unit had the top ranking among the seventy schools in its district. Senior Nate Huggins received the commanding general's award for leadership at the Fort Riley summer camp in 1977.[26]

The 1976 *Talisman* commented that President Downing "probably faces more pressures than any other president in the university's history." Rhea Lazarus from his vantage point of staff assistant in the president's office compared the president's position to a whipsaw. "He's getting it from both ends," Lazarus explained, "from students, the Board of Regents, faculty, athletics, finances. There's no way you can avoid making people mad in such a position. You've just got to give both ends assurances you're trying, working for the long range benefit of the University."

Earlier presidents would have been surprised, probably shocked, by the changing attitudes of the faculty in the 1970s. By the fall of 1970, 89 percent of the faculty had come to Western in 1960 or thereafter. The faculty was younger than it had been for many years, and few of its members had the emotional ties to Western that had characterized previous generations. Many of the newcomers had experienced collegial government at other institutions, and they saw no reason why it should not be installed at Western. More insistent upon formal statements of policies and procedures than had been true in the past, they were less willing to trust the paternal beneficence of the president. Some of the old timers and some of the newcomers deplored the emergence of this attitude and longed for the family relationship of an earlier era, but those days were gone. Some friction was inevitable as the institution and its people adjusted to the changing conditions. The national slow-down in enrollments meant that many faculty members were less able to resolve differences by going elsewhere than had been true in the boom days. Confronted by an issue, they were more inclined to argue it than to accept an administrative edict. As in the case of student unrest, faculty discontent at Western was mild when compared with that at many other campuses. But it was one of the striking aspects of life on the Hill in the 1970s.[27]

During the decade the faculty increased both in numbers and in academic qualifications. In 1971-72, 51 percent of the 528 faculty members held the doctorate; by 1977-78, 63 percent of the 582 faculty members had the advanced degree. By 1978-79 eight departments had at least 82 percent of their staffs holding the doctorate; the Department of Educational Leadership led with 100 percent. The number of full professors increased over 80 percent between 1971 and 1977, but the faculty as a whole grew only 10 percent. During the same span of years the number of associate professors grew by 31 percent.[28] This trend posed several problems for the future. How could able young teachers be brought to the campus when there were few openings? How could faculty members be motivated to work at their highest level when they became tenured full professors twenty years or so before the normal retirement age?

Teaching loads were reduced during the 1960s and 1970s. Five years after the standard load became twenty-seven hours in 1965, the academic deans proposed a scheme that would cut the teaching load to twenty-four hours for graduate faculty and/or full professors with a further reduction for those teaching only graduate work. Numerous protests pointed out weaknesses in the proposal, and Vice-President Cravens wondered how "the Deans can deliberate upon a matter such as the teaching load guidelines for six months or longer and then find that department heads and faculty members can very quickly point up quite valid shortcomings. ... Sometimes I am tempted to conclude that some of the Deans agree to the proposed policies on the assumptions that they really don't apply to them or their college." An additional complication came in the departments seeking accreditation in their fields. In addition to other requirements, such bodies usually required a maximum teaching load of twenty-four hours. But allowing such reductions in some departments led to immediate screams of outrage from those not so favored. After careful preparation of the case, the regents in 1979 adopted a normal teaching load of twenty-four semester hours for the academic year. By then the student-faculty ratio had declined to 17.2, a figure that would have amazed the faculty members of Western's early years.[29]

Some faculty members got reduced loads because of research activities. Western was far from a "publish or perish" policy, but more emphasis was gradually being given to research activities. Improvements in facilities, including the growth of the library holdings, made research more feasible in a number of areas. The administration made 3.6 percent of faculty time available for research, program coordination, and other special assignments, and the Faculty Research Fund continued to provide limited but helpful assistance. During the mid-1970s the committee awarded an average of over $12,000 per year. Nearly 90 percent of the requests were funded with the grants averaging between $500 and $600.[30]

For those involved in extensive research enterprises, the sabbatical program was a major help. The number increased as more adequate funding was worked into the budget. Eighty-two were approved during the five years 1973-77, an average of over sixteen per year. During the same years thirty-three requests were denied. Of the 82 granted, 31 went to members of the Ogden College faculty, 28 to Potter College researchers, and only 23 to other faculty members. That imbalance was a matter of some concern. Downing wondered if a department was over-staffed if it could absorb the absence of two or three of its members. In such a case, how could the department justify asking for additional personnel?[31] Regardless of such questions, the sabbatical program probably did more to stimulate productive research at Western than any other factor.

A number of other changes also benefitted the faculty. The Faculty House (the Cedar House) was subsidized by the university after being converted to that use in 1960, although efforts to house a Faculty Recreation Association on the university farm never succeeded. A third faculty award was added in 1976 when Mr. Willard Cockrill (geography and geology) received the first Distinguished Service Award for Public Service. Through 1984-85 the departments of chemistry and history had each seen five of its members receive these awards. Twenty-two departments had been represented on the awards list. The faculty component of the Academic Council also increased. By 1973, after several changes, the elected membership had been increased from twenty-one to thirty-one, the number of nonelected department heads had been reduced from nine to five, and six students had been added as voting members. And the rule limiting membership to tenured faculty members was changed to two years of service at Western.[32]

Toward the end of the 1970s, the position of faculty regent became more significant. The nomination of five candidates by a deans-appointed committee was abandoned in favor of unlimited nominations by the faculty, and, despite Downing's early opposition, both the faculty and student regents received voting rights in 1972. William G. Buckman (physics), elected the third faculty regent in 1974, enmeshed himself in board politics much more than had his predecessors, and he served on key committees as a formal committee structure was established. Re-elected twice, he resigned in 1983 to allow his successor, Mary Ellen Miller

(English), an opportunity to participate in that year's budget formulation.[33]

A number of university policies were studied and restudied during the Downing administration, and modifications leading toward more liberal positions usually resulted. Under prodding from accrediting associations, the first formal tenure policy was adopted by the regents in 1963. It fell short of AAUP standards, and in November 1974, upon the recommendation of Cravens, Downing appointed a Special Tenure Committee, headed by James L. Davis and Delbert Hayden, to study the issue. The report submitted to the president on July 11 defined the policy, outlined the procedure to be followed in reviewing nonreappointment recommendations and dismissal cases, and set up procedures for terminations due to such factors as financial exigency and changing program needs. A key provision was the establishment of an Advisory Committee on Faculty Continuance. When Downing presented the plan to the regents on September 20, McCormack called for further study by a regents committee. Part of the policy was adopted by the board on October 25, and the remainder was approved on December 20.[34]

Even as that policy was moving toward adoption, a tenure question arose that became one of the most controversial faculty issues of the decade. In April 1975 the regents, acting upon Downing's recommendation on personnel matters, voted to give one year terminal contracts to Dr. Raul Padilla, a member of the Department of Foreign Languages since 1971, and Dr. George Dillingham, a member of the Department of Secondary Education since 1969. Both men challenged the decision, citing among other factors professional differences with their department heads and deans. Dillingham was convinced that he had been "blackballed" by Dean J.T. Sandefur. There was then no clearly delineated due process procedure, but there was precedent for an appeal to the Board of Regents, and on May 31, 1975, the board went into executive session to discuss personnel matters. Buckman presented the cases of the two faculty members; Downing and Cravens defended the negative recommendations of the department heads and deans. Downing said that the cases would be thoroughly reviewed during the 1975-76 academic year, and he asked that no earlier decision be made.

But at the July 26 meeting, after a lengthy and heated discussion, the regents voted 5-3 with one abstention to grant both men tenure. The faculty and student regents, Buckman and Steve Henry, joined three members of the medical profession, McCormack, Gerald Edds, and Chalmer Embry, to defeat the administration. Such a vote was almost unprecedented in Western's history. Downing and Regent J. David Cole, a Bowling Green attorney, questioned the legality of the reversal on several points. Did the board, for example, have the power to grant tenure without a presidential recommendation? After the two men and their deans reiterated their stands in a closed session on September 20, an opinion was sought from the state attorney-general.

His opinion upheld the presidential position, but at the October 25 meeting of the board Downing proposed a compromise. Dillingham would receive a continuing nontenured appointment for 1976-77, he would be given an assignment elsewhere in the university, and his eligibility for tenure would be considered in accord with the tenure policy in effect at the time of his reassignment. Padilla would be able to appeal to the Advisory Committee on Faculty Continuance if it was established under the proposed new tenure policy. After another lengthy and often bitter discussion, the president's recommendation was approved 6-4 with Buckman, Embry, Henry, and McCormack dissenting. Downing promised that the new evaluations would be handled in a professional and unbiased way, but Dr. McCormack asserted that Dillingham and Padilla "have been shafted." A *Herald* editorial concluded, "It's time the board moved on to other things."[35]

Dillingham was reassigned in January 1976 to a joint appointment in history and secondary education and, with his evaluation coming from the history department, he received tenure in 1977. Padilla, protesting that he was being treated differently from Dillingham, filed complaints with the Kentucky Commission on Human Rights and the Equal Employment Opportunity Commission and threatened legal action. He dropped the complaints when the Advisory Committee on Faculty Continuance recommended that his probationary period be extended, although the committee reported that it found no evidence to indicate that the original decision not to reappoint was "arbitrary or capricious." Padilla also received tenure in 1977.[36]

Another tenure case also occupied a great deal of administrative time during the 1970s. In the spring of 1971, Dr. Flonnie Strunk, an associate professor of business education and office administration, was one of four faculty members whose contracts were not renewed. A member of Western's faculty since 1966, she claimed sex discrimination and filed charges with the federal Equal Employment Opportunity Commission. Although she told university authorities in 1971 that she had a terminal illness, she displayed amazing persistence in pursuing efforts to secure reinstatement through all available sources, state and federal, administrative agencies and courts.[37] Her unsuccessful efforts may have encouraged the administration to correct some inequities in such areas as salaries; her efforts certainly pointed out the need for department heads and deans to be more exact in their annual evaluations.

Some faculty members had little interest in such issues as these tenure cases. They saw only problems that the administration should handle on an individual basis; they did not fall within the legitimate area of faculty concern. Such people had little or no interest in more faculty participation in university governance. Other members of the faculty were convinced that they should have a voice in the determination of policy. They claimed that the students had a better opportunity to present their views to the administration than did the faculty. A number of suggestions were made, and a plan for "a faculty advisory committee," presented by Faculty Regent Lowell Harrison, at last reached the president's desk, where it died. Downing insisted that the Academic Council served as an university-wide advisory group and that faculty concerns could be considered by its Faculty Affairs Committee. The Visiting Committee of the Southern Association "strongly suggested that the administration proceed immediately with the creation of the recently announced plans for a 'faculty advisory committee'—a committee which may advise the administration in matters of faculty affairs." The suggestion would have been made stronger had the committee known that the proposed advisory committee would not be formed.[38]

The AAUP chapter decided to push the issue by appointing an *ad hoc* committee to draft a constitution for a proposed senate. When a draft proposal was sent to President Downing in September 1975, the committee reported that of the 354 faculty who responded to a poll, 329 favored the creation of a senate, and 25 opposed it. In the meantime Downing appointed a sixteen-person committee (eleven faculty members and five administrators) to study "the ways and means through which faculty members can participate in the development and formation of academic policy recommendations." The AAUP committee turned its draft and background materials over to the president's committee, with which it promised full cooperation. But AAUP president Charles Hendrickson warned that if meaningful progress was not made in the next few weeks, "we have an obligation to resume deliberations and proceed with our original plans."[39]

Work progressed steadily, and by early 1976 the faculty was asked to respond to a draft constitution. Of the 312 who replied, 89.4 percent voted approval with a number of suggestions added. A regents committee made some changes, then the board approved the creation of the Faculty Senate on April 24, 1976. Most of Downing's administrative advisors recommended a positive reaction to it, and the president provided support for its early implementation. The first meeting was held on October 22, 1976, when Dr. Delbert Hayden, chair of the Faculty Affairs Committee of the Academic Council and co-chair of the drafting committee, called the meeting to order. President Downing suggested a number of areas in which work was needed and expressed his hope for mutual trust and cooperation. Phil Constans, Jr., (education) was elected president. The other officers were: Hugh Thomason (government), vice-president; James Sanders (academic services), secretary-treasurer; and Joan Krenzin (sociology), parliamentarian. On November 8 Constans notified Downing that the Senate was organized and gave him a list of the members of the standing committees.[40]

The Senate's birth after a lengthy period of gestation was viewed with mingled sentiments. Downing, a number of administrators, and some faculty viewed it with distrust and apprehension. President Downing pointedly referred to it as only an advisory body. But many of the faculty and some administrators saw in its formation the promise of a collegial relationship that might bring Western closer to the mainstream of university life in the last quarter of the twentieth century. Downing received little credit for the formation of the Senate and the adoption of policies and procedures that did much to strengthen the position of the faculty. Many faculty members perceived him as resisting all such changes until forced to accept them. Indeed, some faculty members saw an adversary relationship between the president and much of the faculty. The relationship between the president of the university and the first chair of the Senate confirmed that impression.

Phil Constans joined the Western faculty in 1969 after being active in teachers' unions in Florida; in the not distant past, that background would have disqualified him for membership on the Western faculty. Constans and Downing viewed many campus issues from such different perspectives that a clash was almost inevitable. Constans set the tone of his administration when he said at the first Senate meeting, "The administration may ignore us, but they will ignore us at their peril." He intended to secure for the faculty a more meaningful role in determining institutional policies and participating in their implementation. He reminded Downing that the official name of the new body was the Faculty Senate, not the Advisory Senate that Downing was using. "I would suggest," Constans concluded, "that you correct the correspondence and documents in which you have made this error." Downing believed that "a relatively strong executive authority is essential for the university to operate effectively," and he opposed efforts that seemed designed to usurp his authority. It was vital, he wrote J. David Cole, chairman of the Board of Regents, "that the Board supports the administration of the University and continues to rely on the President and members of the administrative structure to function in the decision-making role for which the University officials are responsible."[41]

One of the early clashes occurred over the Senate's effort to gain greater faculty participation in both the selection and retention of administrators. The Senate proposed that it conduct periodic evaluations of all administrators from department head to president to ascertain if the faculty favored retention. Downing presented the Senate proposals to the regents on April 30, 1977, but warned that they would alter "the basic philosophy about the respective roles of the Board, the President, other administrative officers, and the faculties and faculty bodies with respect to governance, authority, and accountability to which this institution has been committed throughout its history." Downing then presented a policy statement that emphasized the president's "ultimate authority and responsibility" for making personnel recommendations to the Board. His plan called for faculty participation on administrative search committees with the president receiving three names for his consideration. If none was acceptable to him, the search would be reopened. Faculty Regent Buckman remarked on the significant differences between the Senate and Downing proposals and moved that the regents create a committee to study the matter. After Buckman's motion failed 4-5, the president's statement was adopted with only Buckman dissenting.[42]

Enraged by this action, Constans on May 6 blasted Downing's tactics in a furious letter to the faculty. Downing had made no effort to reconcile the two plans, Constans charged, and "Although he had agreed to discuss in detail the Senate proposal with me, he did not do so." Some senators believed their chair had gone too far, and in the fall semester, 1977, motions were introduced to censure him and to require the chair to clear policy statements with the Executive Committee before issuing them. Both motions failed, but the internal dispute did little to enhance the reputation of the Senate. A *Herald* editorial said that the Faculty Senate had put itself "in the company of such notable bodies as the U.S. Senate, the Board of Regents and Associated Student Government. Like these groups, the Faculty Senate has spent a huge amount of time doing nothing."[43]

The personal relationship improved after Tom Jones of the English department was elected to head the Senate in 1977. Jones disagreed with Downing on many issues, but he respected him for his dedication to the institution and his hard work. Jones came to believe that some of the negative attitude was unfair. Many faculty members were paranoid in their opposition to Downing, Jones said; "In a lot of ways Dero was not really given a chance by faculty members." But Jones also blamed Downing for ignoring the advice of the Senate and getting his "hurriedly contrived" selection policy adopted by the regents.[44] Downing wrote Constans on May 11, 1977, that a policy had to be devised quickly because search had to begin at once for several important vacancies, but he added that specific guidelines could be developed and he would be available to discuss the matter with Constans and other interested parties. Support for the president came from Dean Sandefur and the unit administrators of the College of Education; they believed that his policy "makes all the necessary concessions for faculty involvement." And, they added, "It is our opinion that the leadership of the Faculty Senate does not represent the feelings of the majority of the faculty." Most administrators favored the presidential plan, but so did a considerable number of faculty members.[45]

Another controversial issue was the faculty evaluation of administrators, particularly the president. Impetus for such a process came from the students' evaluations of teaching faculty that had been conducted intermittently since 1969; if faculty were evaluated by both students and administrators, why should the administrators not be evaluated by the faculty? A number of faculty were also concerned over what they saw as an unwarranted growth of the administration. M.B. Lucas of the Department of History presented a report to the Senate in October 1978. Called, "The Way We Grow," it cited a 69.8 percent increase in principal administrative staff between 1967 and 1978 while the faculty grew by 55 percent and the undergraduate full-time equivalent increased by only 1.6 percent and the graduate enrollment grew by 31.6 percent. Downing and other administrators cited the demands for more personnel in such areas as student recruiting and retention, student financial aid, and improved library facilities as justification for growth, but some faculty members believed that administrative evaluations would reveal weak and over-staffed areas. And some participants may have seen in the evaluation process a way to get rid of administrators who were expected to receive low ratings. Tom Jones recalled that after the Senate voted to conduct the evaluation, President Downing told him that the evaluation's purpose was to remove him from the presidency. Jones disagreed at the time but later concluded that Downing was right in his analysis.[46]

The regents became involved in controversy over administrative evaluations in 1975. Downing and Regent Ronnie Clark protested when Buckman proposed that the administrator evaluations go directly to the board members, not to the president. That move, Downing asserted, would violate the relationship between the president and governing body. Clark, defending Downing's position, reported that he had read only the president's evaluation: "He received a damn good rating and I am proud of the rating he received. I wonder what type of rating we as Board members would receive?" McCormack then cited two unsigned faculty letters and some telephone calls that indicated a climate of fear and secrecy, possibly tyranny, on the Hill. Downing replied that there was no reason for anyone to feel under duress, that both the evaluation procedure and the use of the results could be improved. A regional newspaper reported that a vice-president, a dean, and one other administrator were particular targets of some of the regents.[47]

The AAUP chapter had been involved in earlier evaluations, but in the fall of 1976 its executive committee decided "to maintain a low profile" so the new Senate would have a chance to become the "Voice of the Faculty." (The low profile has not been raised since then and the chapter is inactive.) Thus it was the Senate that on November 10, 1977, voted to undertake a controversial administrative evaluation. Tom Jones effected a working relationship with J. David Cole, chairman of the board. Cole believed that a younger, vigorous president was needed, but he also respected and admired Downing, who had health problems, and he wanted to ensure an orderly transition at a time of Downing's choosing. Jones and Cole decided that Jones would conduct the evaluation on behalf of the Senate and that Cole, at an appropriate time, would ask that the results be given to the board.

Jones delivered the evaluations to Downing with enough copies for all the regents. After Downing completed his presentation at the April 1978 meeting of the board, Cole said that the members would like to see the results of the Senate's evaluation of administrators. He later changed that to ask only for Downing's evaluation; the possible use of the other evaluations was carried over to the next meeting. Downing maintained that the Senate's evaluation was unsanctioned by that body's constitution. The results were confidential until they were leaked to the *Courier-Journal*, which carried a front page story on June 8. The paper reported that just over 70 percent of the 520 eligible faculty had participated. Of that number, 48 percent gave the president a vote of confidence, 33 percent did not, and the rest (19 percent) abstained. The newspaper declared that the president failed "to get majority in faculty confidence vote," but it was also true that of the faculty who answered that question nearly 60 percent voted confidence in Downing. Both Cole and Jones firmly denied being responsible for the leak.[48]

The Senate's evaluation created considerable controversy, both within and without the university community, with President Downing receiving support from numerous critics of the Senate's evaluative process. He had been unanimously elected to another term in 1977, and presumably the regents had evaluated his performance then. A local resident in a letter to the editor of the *Daily News* was highly critical of the "dissidents" who used "surreptitious methods ... to imprudently and maliciously vent their spleen" in an effort to destroy "a good and honorable man and the good administration of W.K.U." At its July 1 meeting the board reaffirmed its policy that only the regents could officially evaluate the president and that he was primarily responsible for the evaluation of other university personnel.[49] Had a comprehensive vote of confidence been taken after this episode, President Downing would probably have had a clear majority with both the faculty and the regents. But this Senate evaluation did erode the president's position and it encouraged those who wanted a change in the presidency.

In addition to the controversies that involved the faculty, and particularly the Faculty Senate, President Downing experienced problems with two bodies that had not normally presented major concerns to his predecessors. One was Western's own Board of Regents; the other was the Council on Public Higher Education.

The role of the Board of Regents changed dramatically during the 1970s. The regents had rarely challenged the recommendations of a president on any matter of consequence. The typical regent was a graduate of Western, and presidents were usually successful in getting staunch supporters appointed to the board. Meetings were held quarterly with the Executive Committee available to deal with interim issues that demanded consideration. Regents were kept informed and consulted, and the outcome of a vote was known before a recommendation was made.

It was ironic that many of the differences revolved around Dr. W.R. McCormack, a Bowling Green physician who had served on the board in 1956-60 and was reappointed in 1968. McCormack had close ties with Western, including long service as team physician during the Diddle era. He had been Downing's family physician for many years, and he was one of Downing's chief supporters for the presidency. Both men were conservative in their attitudes, but McCormack was more doctrinaire; he would retain a position adamantly when Downing finally decided that some change was necessary. "I'm ultra-conservative, and if I had remained on the Board I would have remained conservative," McCormack told a reporter in 1976 when he left the Board of Regents. He hoped that the administration would stop "capitulating too much to a few students." Convinced that Downing was succumbing to campus forces that would destroy the principles that he saw as absolutely essential to the welfare of Western, McCormack became one of Downing's severest critics.

Some of his major allies were also members of the medical profession. Dr. W. Gerald Edds, a physician from Calhoun, served on the board in 1960-68 and in 1972-76. Dr. Chalmer P. Embry, an Owensboro dentist, served in 1966-70 and 1972-76. Dr. Coy E. Ball, a physician from Owensboro, was on the board in 1970-74. Another conservative member was Glasgow attorney Joe Lane Travis, 1970-74. Downing had staunch supporters on the board, but he had no one who was able or willing to curb McCormack. Unchecked, McCormack often made a shambles of both the agenda and parliamentary procedure to advance his views. Thus at both the September 29 and November 17, 1973, board meetings he ignored the prepared agenda to launch into what the secretary with admirable tact called "a comprehensive verbal statement" on drug usage and other topics about which he felt strongly. The conservative element had little understanding of either the faculty or the academic side of the institution. They saw the Western faculty as being almost identical with public school teachers and therefore entitled to the same salary level. In the early 1970s before the "Sunshine Law" ended most closed sessions, a proposal was made that except for the president a salary limit of $14,500 should be mandated for the rest of the campus personnel. By the same reasoning nurses' income should equal that of physicians.[50]

After his election as faculty regent in 1974, William Buckman was sometimes allied with members of the conservative group, an alliance that puzzled and bothered some of his constituents. Downing's conservative opponents at times adopted a liberal stance in order to forge an antiadministration majority. On the 5-3 vote to override the president and grant tenure to Dillingham and Padilla the majority consisted of McCormack, Edds, Embry, Buckman, and Stephen L. Henry, the student regent. This coalition was not permanent, but Downing was subjected to pressures and criticism that none of his predecessors had endured. McCormack's campus informants supplied him with information and misinformation that he cited frequently at meetings to contradict university administrators. He also intervened in budget matters to insist on individual salary increases without regard for salary scales and policies. The encounters touched upon numerous issues, but two points were especially important. First, what was the proper role of the board? Was it to determine policies and empower the president to carry them out, or should the board deal in more detail with campus issues? Secondly, should a halt be made to the permissiveness that some saw as pervading the campus? Among the many manifestations of this trend were the controversies over drug use, dorm visitations, the general relaxation of regulations, and black student protests. The conservative bloc sometimes badly misjudged public trends. In an effort to halt the dorm visitation program, they insisted upon ascertaining parents' attitudes, but of 3,380 parents who were polled in 1975, only 160 objected to the liberalized policy. President Downing was caught in a crossfire, condemned by many students and some faculty for being reactionary and unwilling to accept national trends but accused by others, including some regents, of being too liberal and permissive.[51]

Major changes occurred on the Board of Regents after the mid-1970s, one of them being in personnel. Travis's term expired in 1974, those of Edds, Embry, and McCormack in 1976, and none of them was reappointed. The most influential of the new members was Bowling Green attorney J. David Cole, appointed by Governor Julian Carroll in 1975, who was chairman from 1976 to 1981. Downing asked Cole not to seek the appointment so that W.S. Moss, Jr., one of Downing's strongest supporters, could be reappointed, but Cole refused to do so. Some of Downing's opponents believed that Cole's appointment would create an anti-Downing bloc that could remove him from office, but Cole voted for another four-year term. Cole was the first non-Westerner on the Board, and he encouraged Governor Carroll to appoint others without close contacts with the university. By 1977 only Hugh Poland, Ronnie Clark, and John Ramsey of the public members had served before 1975. An interesting appointment was made in 1978 when Michael M. Harreld, a Louisville banker, came on the board. He had the distinction as a Western undergraduate of having Dero Downing suggest that he might do well to go elsewhere.[52]

When Bill Bivin, the university attorney, pointed out that the board had no bylaws, he and Cole began to work on them. Cole considered their compilation to be "really the first step in Board independence." The minutes were carefully searched and the board decisions extracted and codified, a process that revealed several areas for which policies needed to be formulated. Another major step was the establishment of a committee system. The Executive Committee remained, but several others were created, with the Finance Committee perhaps being the most important. As a consequence of this organization, presidential recommendations came under more detailed and knowledgeable scrutiny than ever before. "One of our strengths is our ability to openly discuss controversial problems," Cole explained later, "to disagree, and then vote independently, yet remain united in support of Western. There was a point in time when ... to disagree was disloyal. We have matured and long since passed that circumstance."[53]

An obvious sign of change came at the February 4, 1978, meeting when by a vote of 9-1 the regents voted to abolish the "door ajar" rule for dormitory visitations.[54]

During the 1970s the president and other administrators had to devote an increasing amount of time to the state agency most responsible for higher education. The presidents of the state colleges and universities had lost their vote in 1966 when the legislature restructured the Council on Public Higher Education, but they continued to exert powerful influence. The council gradually became stronger and more active as demands increased that it provide more direction and coordination to the state schools. But each attempt to do so raised the spectre of domination by a central board and of possible unfairness in the treatment of the schools. President Downing was adamantly opposed to such centralization. Creation of another organization "can be and often is merely a gloss and a way of avoiding facing up to central difficult questions." He was sure that the working relationship that had evolved was the best means of continuing progress.[55]

The 1972 General Assembly gave the council increased powers, including approval of graduate programs and of all capital construction projects of over $100,000, and the new executive director, A.D. Albright, played a more active role than had his predecessor. At the council's October 1973 meeting he warned, "The development of a comprehensive plan for higher education in Kentucky is fundamental to the exercise of all other Council mandates." When the council authorized the development of a Comprehensive Plan for Higher Education in Kentucky Downing warned Albright in the spring of 1975, "We will resist through every avenue available to us any attempts which may be made to prevent Western from fulfilling the educational role and the mission of the University in the areas of teaching, research and service." Downing disagreed strongly with the implication that the state universities had done a poor job, and he expressed his concerns to a number of people, including Governor Julian Carroll, in an effort to halt the trend he saw developing. But the document, "Kentucky and Comprehensive Planning for Higher Education," that was produced by January 1976 contained many of the points Downing and the other presidents of the regional universities had feared.[56]

The selection of Harry Snyder as the council's executive director on October 13, 1976, added another dimension to the problem. A thirty-four-year-old lawyer, Snyder had been on the council's staff for three years before his appointment; prior to that tenure he had held administrative posts at Georgetown College and the University of Kentucky. Some council members and Governor Carroll were reported to have reservations about his age and experience. Snyder had an abrasive personality, and some who saw him operate felt that he was sometimes petty and a bully when he could get away with it. But he possessed the knack of survival, for he once told Tom Jones that three governors had wanted him fired. He and President Downing were of quite different temperaments and were not likely to establish a close relationship under ordinary circumstances; Snyder's moves to increase the powers of the council and to redefine the missions of the state universities made collisions inevitable.[57]

Governor Carroll increased the power of the council on April 15, 1977, when by executive order he changed the name to the Council on Higher Education. Effective July 1, 1977, it was given authority "to define and approve" all degree and certificate programs. Within the next few months the council's jurisdiction was extended to the sale or purchase of property worth over $25,000, renovation projects costing over $100,000, and computer purchases. Toward the end of the year, as it prepared for the 1978 legislative session, the council decided to recommend no state funding for capital construction and to review building proposals regardless of the method of financing. Most alarming was the council's move to redefine the role and mission statements. The plan's thesis was defined in the "System for Higher Education in Kentucky" that the council adopted in January 1977: "What is needed in Kentucky is a system of higher education designed to fill the needs of the Commonwealth as a whole, rather than relatively autonomous institutions pursuing their own best interests." To the regional schools that pronouncement seemed a code indication that they were to be subordinated to the council and the universities of Louisville and Kentucky.[58]

Downing was especially concerned about the role and mission statements, for they could go far toward determining Western's future. Mandated by the General Assembly and encouraged by the governor, a draft was adopted in principle by the council in April 1977. Hastily drafted, often with little detailed knowledge of the institutions concerned, the proposals were attacked by most of the presidents. Critics of Snyder asserted that the entire process showed his tendency "to shoot from the hip" without sufficient information or thought. The protests led to some adjustments as the presidents voiced their objections, but the revised statements were approved by the council on June 8, 1977. Western's statement then read:

Western Kentucky University shall serve the people of Kentucky in the areas of instruction, research and creative activity, and public service. As a center of higher education, the University shall provide a broad range of traditional, technological, and professional programs at the associate, baccalaureate and master's degree levels, shall provide specialist programs in education, and shall provide pre-professional preparation. Located in an agrarian area in which increasing economic activity and rapid industrial development are occurring, the University shall meet the growing needs for technological and traditional graduate, baccalaureate, and associate degree programs related to business and industry as well as continuing to meet the needs for programs related to agriculture and health. The University shall conduct basic and applied research to support instructional programs, to expand knowledge, and to address state, regional, and national needs. The University shall provide opportunities for adult and continuing education, cultural enrichment, and professional and technical assistance to communities, agencies and citizens of the Commonwealth.

From Western's viewpoint the final statement was less bad than the original draft, but it was a strait jacket that would restrict the university's future development.[59]

"Our efforts to reason with Harry have in most respects been futile," Downing wrote Regent Cole in July when an effort was underway to make Western discontinue graduate work in education in Jefferson County after 1980. "I get the feeling at times that Western is getting 'done in' by more and more of the decisions initiated by the Council on Higher Education." The Jefferson County proposal was tabled after Downing protested, but he was still incensed over the efforts to restrict off-campus teaching. There "appears to be a growing attitude emanating from the Council staff," he chided Snyder in August, "to the effect that you are rendering a great service if you can devise some means to place limitations and impose restrictions on educational services, particularly at the regional universities." Decisions were being made without regard for the needs of the people Western served and by people who knew little of the history of higher education in the state. After considerable debate at the August 22 council meeting, Western was allowed to continue teaching most of its scheduled off-campus courses. Downing believed that Western's "greatest single concern" was "the departure of the Council from a coordinating role to one of dominance and control."[60]

When Harry Snyder spoke at Western in the spring of 1978, he tried to dispel such doubts. Western was "as solid as a rock and as sound as a dollar," and he saw no need "for drastic changes on this campus." (For anyone aware of the declining value of the dollar and with prescience of the eruption of Mount St. Helens, these comparisons were alarming.) "Being a regional university," he assured listeners, "does not imply second class status." Downing and other presidents of the regional universities continued to fight the restrictions being placed on their institutions, but their autonomy was gradually reduced. As presidential power declined, the beleaguered administrators may well have resented the creation in 1979 of a student committee and a faculty body (Congress of Senate Faculty Leaders) to act as advisors to Executive Director Snyder. The COSFL was organized by Western's Tom Jones who headed it in 1980-82. The presidents would have been even more disturbed had they known that in 1980 Governor John Y. Brown, Jr., would end even their nonvoting membership on the council.[61]

Unless he read over his large volume of correspondence, President Downing was probably not aware that as the years passed, "frustration" appeared more frequently in his letters. When he responded in 1975 to some student questions about required housing he was asked if there was a simple answer. No, the president replied, "I find it hard to find simple answers to any of our issues these days."[62] That was more true of his administration than it had been for any of his predecessors. His problems with a more assertive student body and faculty, a more powerful state agency, more demanding state and federal regulations, and a more divided Board of Regents all contributed to the growing sense of frustration. Presidential power had been eroded by changing conditions. Cherry would never have tolerated the presence of some of the students and faculty with whom Downing had to deal. Imbued with the Western traditions of an earlier day, Downing sometimes found it difficult to adjust to the new people and the new conditions.

Raymond Cravens, who worked closely with Downing for years, was convinced that Downing accepted the presidency from a sense of duty. Downing believed that unless there was some compelling reason to do otherwise one accepted whatever task and whatever post one was asked to assume. He had done so several times before, and so he answered "Yes" when asked in 1969 if he would accept the presidency. Downing became president determined to preserve the excellence that he believed Western had already achieved. He was fond of citing the achievements of distinguished alumni as proof of the quality of the institution's products. University status had been achieved only recently, and he saw some needed reorganization. Some additional construction was required, and the improvement of faculty salaries and library facilities ranked high on his list of priorities. He hoped for improvement; he was determined that there would be no regression. And to that end, power must rest largely with the president. As he told a regent, "I believe in and am committed to a plan of University administration which recognizes the significant responsibilities of the administrative offices. ... [They] must have the delegated authority as well."[63]

"The thing that bothers me most," he wrote friends in 1972, "is the intense desire for Western to excel in every endeavor, and obviously there are some areas of the University which fall below our level of expectancy." Financial problems plagued the later years of his administration. Inflation, he warned in 1977, might force Western "to forego some of the things that we aspire to do." The growing frustrations and the strain of coping with the ceaseless demands upon him may have contributed to Downing's health problems. He was recovering from surgery for varicose veins and from postoperative problems caused by returning too soon to his office when he was elected president in 1969. In 1974 he was forced to spend some time in the hospital and at home by exceedingly painful sinusitis attacks. Treatment by Nashville and Kansas City specialists brought some relief but the debilitating condition remained with him.[64] His health placed restrictions upon what he could do, and his personal code would not allow him to do less than what he thought Western needed from her president.

In 1977 Downing was elected to his third four-year term, beginning September 12. A hint of dissent came from Faculty Regent Buckman who suggested that the board "take deliberate type action and have plenty of time to consider the alternatives before making a decision of this nature," but no one cast a negative vote. Although there was opposition to him, Downing had the support of a majority of the regents to the end of his tenure.

Then on September 9, 1978, President Downing told the regents that he wanted to resign as of January 8, 1979. Vice-President Minton was informed of the action only the day before the meeting, and few if any other members of the administration had longer warning. Downing explained that when he accepted election in 1977, Western was deeply involved in the Role and Scope Study of the Council on Higher Education and in the development of the 1978-80 budget, and he thought it best to continue work on them. The 1977-78 year had been on the whole a good one, and it was an opportune time to step down. There was no immediate problem, but he realized that his health would not improve if he continued in his position. Did the faculty evaluation influence his decision, a reporter asked. It had no bearing on his decision, Downing declared; he viewed the survey "as an expression of support on the part of a lot of faculty." He had no quarrel with those who had expressed a contrary view. Near the end of his prepared statement of resignation Downing asserted that Western has "a quality ... that is sought in vain by most institutions of higher education. Call it a spirit, an attitude, or whatever you will—Westerners know that it exists and have remained determined that it must be preserved, nourished, and sustained."

The *Courier-Journal*, often critical of Downing and Western, declared that "Dr. Downing thus leaves Western in a sound position. His school, with its strong alumni loyalties, has often been criticized, with some justice, as an inbred institution with a narrow perspective. Though Dr. Downing almost personifies the Hilltopper spirit, the revitalization during his administration has weakened the validity of that criticism. His successor will have a solid foundation on which to build." One of Downing's major accomplishments was guiding Western through a difficult transitional period that saw substantial changes on the campus. His successor's task was made easier by the adjustments of the Downing administration.[65]

Ten

New Departures
1979-1986

FINDING a successor to Downing, Chairman Cole told the other regents, is "the most important decision which we ... will make in the life of the board." Before the meeting adjourned on September 9, he appointed a committee to determine criteria and formulate plans for Western's first formal, national search for a president. Speculation about possible successors began almost the moment news of the resignation became known. The on-campus names often mentioned were these of Paul Cook, Raymond Cravens, James Davis, Rhea Lazarus, Marvin Russell, and J.T. Sandefur. Off-campus speculative possibilities included Governor Julian Carroll, State Superintendent of Public Instruction James Graham, and Harry Snyder. Differences of opinion developed over the presidential qualities that were most important and whether the person selected should have close ties with Western.

Downing requested and the regents granted a sabbatical during which he would organize his files and papers. He was eager to leave office on the date agreed to, but it soon became apparent that if a comprehensive national search was made, a successor would not be selected by January 8, 1979. Vice-President John Minton had indicated firmly that he was not interested in becoming president, and on December 9 the board appointed him interim president as of January 8 and endowed him with full powers of that office. Minton served from January 8 to July 31, 1979, and in recognition of his services the regents later made him the president for that time. Despite his intimate knowledge of the university, Minton admitted after he became president, "I really didn't conceive the magnitude of this office. It makes me have an even greater appreciation for the men that have preceded me." Minton remained neutral during the search process, but he wanted a selection as soon as possible: "There were too many important issues facing this university that could not be properly dealt with by a temporary president."[1]

The Board of Regents moved quickly to establish criteria for the presidential vacancy and to advertise the position nationally. The criteria were:

Demonstrated scholarly competence with weighed preference to persons holding the earned doctorate or equivalent;

Qualities of educational leadership and ability to maintain effective relationships with faculty, students, administrative staff, and others;

Successful experience in a college or university setting with preference given to experience in college or university classroom teaching;

Broad understanding of academic affairs as related to long-range planning and commitment to continued professional development;

An appreciation for and a willingness to work in an atmosphere of 'community of scholars';

Exceptional facility in human relations, including governmental relations; and

Demonstrated administrative competence.

Applications and nominations were due by November 20, 1978. A screening committee would narrow the applicants to twenty, then turn the selection process over to the entire board. The committee consisted of Chairman Cole, the student and faculty regents, two other regents, two faculty members, a student, an administrator, president of the Bowling Green Chamber of Commerce, and an alumnus. A few days later a second administrator and a second alumnus were added, bringing the membership to thirteen. After protests of inadequate minority representation, the board voted to add two minority members to the committee in any of the membership categories. The process took so long that the *Herald* asked, "If it is going to take forever to agree on the membership of the presidential screening committee, will we ever be able to agree on a president?"[2]

By January 11, 1979, 179 nominations and applications had been received. Many were easily eliminated, and before the end of January the screening committee gave the regents twenty unranked names. After a lengthy closed session on March 31, the regents voted to consider five candidates: Dr. S. Kern Alexander, Jr., University of Florida; Dr. Norman A. Baxter, California State University-Fresno; Dr. Todd H. Bullard, Rochester Institute of Technology; Dr. James E. Drinnan, Jr., University of Tennessee-Chattanooga; and Dr. Donald W. Zacharias, University of Texas-Austin. In addition to bringing the five candidates to campus for intensive two-day sessions with various groups, the regents sent small teams, usually two members, to each candidate's campus to get a feel for his performance there. Some doubt as to the value of the latter visit developed when the Western representatives failed to discover that Dr. Baxter was being ousted from the presidency of Fresno State.[3]

The campus candidates among the top twenty were eliminated before the top five names were released, but then snags developed. One regent alleged that supporters of Dr. Gene Farley, professor of school administration, promised a substantial political contribution if Farley was selected or at least included in the final cut. Student regent Steve Thornton reported threatening telephone calls and the disappearance of files from his office. All this created excitement on campus and unwanted publicity outside. Tom Jones, a member of the search committee, had a tag made that read, "THANK YOU FOR NOT ASKING ME ABOUT THE PRESIDENTIAL SEARCH."

The most sensational aspect of the search came in April when Dr. Alexander withdrew his candidacy the day before he was to arrive on campus. With closer ties to Western than any of the other finalists, he was considered to be the favorite candidate of the "Old Guard" faction. Alexander declared that he was upset by attacks upon him and his family that had come from Western's campus. He saw "a bitter control struggle within the university, which has overflowed beyond school boundaries" and which might make it difficult for a president to serve beyond one term. Efforts failed to get him to reconsider his decision or to reopen the selection process to include some candidates who had been dropped. Dr. Drinnan also withdrew after deciding to remain at UT-Chattanooga. On April 28, after a closed session of nearly three hours, the regents voted 8-2 to meet on Sunday, May 6, and select a president from among the remaining candidates, Baxter, Bullard, and Zacharias. Regents Emberton and Sheffer wanted more time before making a decision.[4]

The search appeared on the verge of collapsing, for Bullard also withdrew and Baxter's impending departure from Fresno State made him an improbable choice. Zacharias declared himself "stunned" by the board's decision to delay its decision another week while a committee consulted with Alexander in an effort to get him to change his withdrawal. "If I weren't fond of a lot of people on that campus I would probably have dropped out last week," Zacharias asserted; he would withdraw if a choice was not made the next Sunday. Regent Sheffer called the selection process "a fiasco and a failure," and at the May 13, 1979, meeting he and Emberton tried to postpone the decision. But a majority of the regents had been favorably impressed by Don Zacharias's credentials and campus appearances and they wanted to end the too-long process. After a closed session of over an hour, the regents voted 8-2 to offer Zacharias the presidency. Terms included faculty tenure, a three-year contract, a minimum salary of fifty-five thousand dollars with annual raises, payment of his Teachers Insurance and Annuity Association (TIAA) retirement annuity, and an official residence at no cost to him.

Ronnie Clark expressed disappointment "that the next president is not a Westerner," but he believed that additional delay would "further erode the credibility of the University." Therefore, he voted for Zacharias and called upon all Westerners to rally behind him. Sheffer and Emberton repeated their doubts, but they were outvoted. In his closing remarks Cole warned, "This is not a time to say the job is done. Rather, this is the first step in what I would perceive to be a new era." Cole called Zacharias during the closed session and told him the vote would be 8-2. Zacharias indicated that he would not accept if there was a split on the board, but Cole assured him that the two dissenters would become staunch supporters, and the Texas candidate accepted the offer when it was finally made.[5]

In retrospect it is clear that the search lasted far too long; the regents put too little trust in the screening committee. Instead of twenty names the list should have been less than half that number. The decision to send investigative teams to the campuses of the finalists did not appear productive to many critics. The process teetered on the brink of failure; had Zacharias withdrawn, the results would have been damaging to the institution.

President Minton and other members of the administration pledged their support to achieve a smooth transition, and Zacharias came to campus several times to become acquainted with Western and its people, although he did not officially become president until August 1, 1979. He told the regents at their July 14 meeting that he wanted to keep Minton, Davis, Largen, Cook, and Bivin in their key positions. Dr. Randall Capps, head of the communications and theatre department, became assistant to the president as Rhea Lazarus, who had served in that position for five years, left the university to concentrate on business interests.[6]

In May 1980 President and Mrs. Zacharias and their three children moved into the presidential home at 1700 Chestnut Street, a block east of the lower campus. The escalating costs of the house and its renovation led to some criticism of the purchase and an occasional suggestion that the president should be given a housing allowance and directed to the open market. The new grounds were cramped, and parking remained a problem for any sizable event held at the president's home.[7]

Donald W. Zacharias, Western's sixth president, was not formally installed until Saturday, April 26, 1980, nearly nine months after assuming office. The colorful academic ceremony, the first formal installation of a Western president, was moved indoors under the threat of rain. Cole told the audience, "The goal of this university—without exception, without compromise—is academic excellence, and this Board will accept nothing else." Zacharias called for full support from within and outside the campus community to achieve that goal. In an unusual vote of confidence, the regents replaced his three-year contract that would have expired on July 31, 1982, with a four-year one that ran to April 25, 1984, and increased his salary from $55,000 to $60,000. After a formal board evaluation in January 1983, the regents praised Zacharias and gave him a new four-year contract with a minimum salary of $70,000.[8]

By the day of the installation, the president and the university community had become better acquainted with each other. Zacharias was an energetic forty-three-year-old when he assumed office. Tall, balding, and articulate, he wore glasses and had a penchant for brown suits. A native of Salem, Indiana, he received the B.A. degree from Georgetown (Ky.) College in 1957. After a year as a high school teacher, he enrolled in the graduate school at Indiana University and earned his M.A. (1959) and Ph.D. (1963) degrees there. His terminal degree was in speech communications with specialties in communications and conflict management, communication and social change, and organizational communication; his minor area was American history. A graduate teaching assistant at Indiana University, Zacharias joined the faculty there in 1963. In 1969 he moved to the University of Texas at Austin as an associate professor, and in 1972 he was promoted to professor. He won teaching awards at both Indiana and Texas, but Zacharias became involved in University administration in 1974 when he became assistant to the president of the university of Texas at Austin. When selected as Western's president, he was executive assistant to the chancellor of the University of Texas system. One of the few suspect points in his excellent credentials was the fact that his administrative experience had been limited to staff positions; he had not held a post in which the final responsibility was his.[9]

Zacharias drew upon his communications skills and his stamina during his first few months in office as he sought to know Western, her people, and the state. In addition to formal meetings, he met informally with a large number of individuals and groups. It was a honeymoon period, and Zacharias received a good press, along with widespread campus support. A *Herald* overview of his presidency near the end of the 1980 spring semester concluded, "Zacharias has performed admirably in the past months." The author, Alan Judd, had only two questions: "... the demotion of Dr. Raymond Cravens from public service and international programs dean to a full-time government professor and the recent confusion over just how much of a salary increase the faculty would get this year." No explanation was given for the abrupt change in Cravens's status.[10]

Finances were one of Western's major problems in the first half of the 1980s. Among the causes were some over which the state had little or no control, such as the high rate of inflation and general economic distress. Kentucky had become a relatively poor state, and in some respects the tax base was inadequate. Raising taxes, always an unpopular move, would have required determined leadership from officials who could explain the need for more adequate funding; such leadership was seldom visible in either the legislative or executive branch of the government. It was easy for people who know little about the realities of, and the necessity for, higher education to charge the universities with being wasteful and encouraging duplication. The state universities had sometimes been guilty of spending money unwisely, and there was unneeded duplication, especially on the graduate and professional levels, but the college and university system in Kentucky had been enlarged with little consideration for the adverse effect such growth would have upon the existing institutions. In a state where the educational level was among the lowest in the nation, only a small constituency advocated the cause of higher education. As a consequence the proportion of state funds going to the universities declined, and the University of Kentucky and the University of Louisville with their powerful legislative support were able to influence the distribution of funds in their favor. An obvious inequity was the requirement until 1980 that faculty at the regional universities pay a higher percentage of salary toward their retirement programs than did the faculty at UK and UL.

Budget cuts had been required before, but only the reductions in the early 1930s exceeded those of fifty years later. In July 1980, Governor John Y. Brown, Jr.'s administration became aware of a sharp decrease in state revenues, caused in part by the hasty removal in 1979 of the sales tax on utilities and the imposition of a ceiling on property taxes. The universities' share of the mandated reductions was approximately $30 million, and Western was told to cut some $3,200,000 during the 1980-82 biennium, 8 percent of the budget. The problem was made worse because the edict came after the start of the new budget year; changes could have been made more easily before July 1. When Zacharias spoke to the Bowling Green Chamber of Commerce in January 1981, he let loose his frustrations. He charged the state leadership with "playing a deadly game of 'let's pretend.' Let's pretend that the universities are fat with resources and overfunded. Let's pretend that you can dismiss university personnel with fifteen to twenty years of experience, and they and their families won't feel it. Let's pretend that the public does not really like universities and would just as soon they were closed. Let's pretend that there is really only one university in the state, and that it is located in Lexington. Let's pretend that the people of the state's comprehensive universities (called regional universities by those who are fond of categories) are incapable of recognizing when they are being robbed of their resources." He had never seen higher education so underfunded. "If we were a business, Western would be filing bankruptcy papers or looking for a new partnership."[11] He was especially rankled because Western awarded 16.2 percent of the degrees granted in 1979-80 by the state universities but received only 8.7 percent of the appropriation for higher education. In the same year UK and UL awarded 43 percent of the degrees and received 62 percent of the available funds.

Faculty and staff salaries had been given top priority at Western, and as the budget was reworked salaries were untouched. A number of unfilled positions were left vacant, maintenance of buildings and grounds was reduced, some purchases of equipment were cancelled or postponed, departmental budgets were slashed, library hours were reduced, a college was eliminated, some departments were consolidated. Fees were imposed or increased for many services. Students and faculty were entitled to one free university catalog; additional copies cost two dollars each. And plans for a new 1981-82 catalog were dropped. The Western campus began to look somewhat dowdy as the effects of the fiscal pinch became noticeable.[12]

The cries of rage at least attracted attention in Frankfort. Cabinet Secretary James O. King, replying to Zacharias's comments, charged Western's president with "a glaring omission" by failing to consider the state's serious economic condition that had resulted in the revenue shortfall. Then on March 2 Governor Brown chided the universities for being the "biggest crybaby" in dealing with the state-wide budget cuts. "I feel that they are just all asking for money instead of addressing the issue," Brown declared as he predicted a budget shortfall of $183 million for fiscal 1981-82. He told universities to eliminate duplication of programs, "to specialize in two or three areas of expertise, instead of trying to be such broad colleges." Brown rebuked Edward F. Prichard, Jr., and ex-Governor Bert T. Combs, key members of a citizens' group called the Committee on Higher Education in Kentucky's Future which had proposed no more budget cuts for higher education and suggested a restoration of recent tax cuts. Prichard, one of the state's staunch battlers for education, replied, "If the governor would examine the prospective plight of higher education in Kentucky under additional budget cuts, even he might be moved to tears."[13]

At the March 11 meeting of the Council on Higher Education, Governor Brown announced that the universities must cut their 1981-82 budgets by just over $20 million. Although the governor admitted that he did not know much about higher education, he gave some illustrations of how waste could be eliminated. Ignoring much shorter distances between some schools in the eastern part of the state, he declared Western and Murray close enough that they did not need to duplicate services. Thus if one of them had the better agriculture program, it would handle that area but would turn over such work as English or German to the other school. Governor Brown was also unsure of just what college professors did; "I don't know why a professor would need two hours to prepare for one hour of class."[14]

Several of the university presidents expressed relief that the ordained cuts were not worse, but in July Brown, armed with a more dismal revenue forecast, called for a cut of 5 percent in the 1981-82 budget. Ironically, in August the Committee on Higher Education in Kentucky's

Future called for massive new funding for the state universities. Western's share of the mandated reduction was $1.2 million, and at its August meeting the regents approved President Zacharias's plan for implementing the order. Reductions in planned expenditures amounted to $937,500 with nearly $600,000 of that sum coming from unfilled positions, and the revenue increase was estimated at $294,000. Few internal budgets escaped the slashing, and reduced services across the campus showed the effects of the budget crisis. Less noticeable but even more important was the slump in faculty morale. Surveys showed that Western's salaries ran well behind the average at the benchmark institutions against which Western was measured, and the average faculty salaries at Western were lower than those at all the state universities except Kentucky State. When Zacharias presented the institutional budget requests for 1982-84 to the regents in September 1981, he pointed out that the cuts had totaled nearly $5 million. Western requested an increase of $8 million in state funds for 1982-83 and an additional $6.5 million for 1983-84, but not even Pollyanna would have expected it to be appropriated. Before Thanksgiving 1981 the faculty learned that 23.5 faculty positions and 88 nonfaculty positions had been lost.[15]

Another blow came in October 1981 when the council staff prescribed a plan for the reallocation of funds for higher education. Based on the mission statements adopted in 1977, the plan proposed to increase the shares going to the University of Kentucky and the University of Louisville. Promptly labeled "The Bluegrass Plan," it aroused strong protests from the other institutions. Western's administration and regents spent much of their time during the next several months opposing the scheme that, Zacharias charged, said Western "has insignificant value to the state in comparison with other institutions." An almost unprecedented joint meeting of the Murray and Western governing boards in November called for a fair and equitable distribution of funds. The council's proposal, they charged, "takes needed funds from the six universities and adds those funds to the two universities that already have a lion's share of state appropriations." On November 12 Zacharias told the council that the staff's proposed budget would cause major changes in Western's assigned mission. "This is not acceptable," he said, "and we don't intend to accept it unless some fundamental changes are made." Veterans of Kentucky's educational disputes compared the struggle with the one of 1966 when a lay council was the trade-off for university status for four colleges. Opponents of higher education were delighted by the public dispute.[16]

Presidents Otis A. Singletary (UK) and Donald C. Swain (UL) lobbied for the Bluegrass Plan and sought the governor's support. State Senator Robert R. Martin, president of Eastern Kentucky University from 1960 to 1976, told Brown at a legislative committee meeting that the plan was unfair to the regional schools, that he had been given false information about what had actually occurred in higher education. A three hour meeting of the presidents with the council staff on January 10, 1982, failed to produce a solution, but a few days later the staff recommended that each school get at least a 6 percent funding increase over its 1981-82 appropriations. That would shift some $1.1 million from UK and UL to the regional schools for 1982-83, but the appropriation for the next year would follow the Bluegrass formula.[17]

Governor Brown delayed making a recommendation when he presented a proposed budget on January 7. Opponents and proponents of the plan continued to lobby with him, but they also carried their case to the legislature where one veteran legislator predicted that the budget issue could become "a blood battle." The regional universities presented a compromise plan for consideration, and on February 5, 1982, Governor Brown released a budget for higher education that averted open warfare. Western received an extra $114,000 in the first year of the biennium and was promised an increase of 3 percent in each of the two years. The remainder of the new money would be allocated on the basis of the council's mission formula which sent just over 75 percent to UK, UL, and Northern. Zacharias expressed pleasure that additional funding had been provided for all the schools, but he warned that the formula must not discriminate against any institution. The legislature, hoping to avoid biennial replays of the 1982 fight, required the council to work with the presidents and other concerned parties to develop an acceptable formula. The consulting firm of Price Waterhouse was employed to make a study of higher education in Kentucky that might identify nonproductive and duplicative programs.[18]

A by-product of the mission-budget controversy was an unusual outpouring of support for Zacharias. Countless letters and lengthy petitions backing his requests went to state administrators and members of the General Assembly. "Higher Education IS Kentucky's Future" and "BACK ZACK" signs suddenly dotted the campus and community in a rare display of unity. Some community dissent developed over the release of sixteen nontenured faculty members with particular support for Vesvolod Lezhnev, a Russian refugee cello professor and chamber orchestra director. Supporters insisted that his departure would wreck the "low strings" program, both on campus and in the region, but the decision stood.[19]

The 1982 legislature reconstructed the Council on Higher Education by requiring the appointment of at least one member from each Congressional district and a representative from each regional university. Opposed by UK and Council Director Snyder, the proposal was designed to make the council more responsive to the views of all the state schools. Western's 1982-83 budget, aided by tuition and dormitory increases, provided for faculty and staff salary raises of 5.5 percent, and the administration voiced cautious optimism for the future. The fiscal situation improved to the point that internal dissent became possible, and Zacharias was criticized by some faculty and townspeople for allowing himself to be considered for the presidencies of North Texas State University and the University of Wyoming. A *Herald* editorial in March 1982 praised him for being an effective spokesman in troubled times but warned, "His support here could erode unless he recommits himself to being full-time president of Western—not a potential president for other schools." Zacharias soon announced that he would not allow his name to be considered at any other school.[20]

Western ended the 1981-82 fiscal year in better shape than had once seemed possible. Revenues exceeded the estimate by $208,000, and the surplus at the end of the fiscal year totalled $1,534,000. Contingency funds had almost disappeared, and $1.1 million was set aside for possible emergency use. Auditors were critical of the reserve fund that was only 2 percent of the budget; 7 percent would provide a safer cushion. The 1982 legislature allowed Western to handle locally some fiscal matters (such as writing checks) that had previously been done by state agencies. The council carried out its study of the appropriation formula, and when a hearing was held on Western's campus on July 21, 1982, Zacharias struck an optimistic note. He sensed "a new spirit on the part of the Council and Council staff that emphasizes what is right about higher education and what higher education with modest funding has accomplished in Kentucky."[21]

In April 1983 the Council on Higher Education approved a revised formula for determining appropriation requests. A major change for which Paul Cook had labored was the agreement to fund equally the programs offered in common. "The formula is not a perfect solution," Zacharias commented. "It is better than what we had, but there are still problems." No president was totally pleased with the formula, but all endorsed it for the sake of unity. They agreed with ex-Governor Burt T. Combs when he urged the council to lead the fight for more adequate funding: "Higher education is in danger unless the General Assembly is willing to make some sacrifice."[22]

Western's 1984-86 budget requests were based on the formula with supplementary funds sought for such areas as computer software and public service activities. The council denied the supplementary requests and recommended approximately $36 million for 1984-85 (a 10.2 percent increase) and $40 million for 1985-86 (an 11.7 percent increase). But Governor Martha Layne Collins's budget slashed Western's increase in state funds from $3.2 million to $1.2 million in 1984-85 and from $3.8 million to $1.8 million in 1985-86. Her budget plan fell into disarray when she had to withdraw proposals for substantial tax increases, and Western got a continuation budget with inadequate increases of $.63 million and $1.4 million for the biennium. The universities had usually received their appropriations in a lump sum that gave them some discretion in determining institution priorities, but for 1984-86 the line item approach was used. Of most immediate concern to the faculty were the limits of 2 percent and 3 percent growth in salaries for the next two years. They derived cold comfort from learning that faculty salaries nationally increased by 6.6 percent in 1984-85 with the increase exceeding the rate of inflation for the fourth consecutive year. Nationally, an increase of 18.9 percent would be required to bring faculty salaries back to their 1970-71 level in terms of real purchasing power; for Western's faculty even more would be needed.[23]

The fiscal problems at Western and the other Kentucky universities were complicated by other factors. In the 1980s when the state began another of its infrequent and belated periods of attention to the plight of education, the focus was on the precollege level. Given the much larger constituency of the public schools, the universities soon found their requests shoved into the background. A recurring "solution" for their financial woes was the admonition to cut duplication and waste. But most legislators shied away from any suggestion that the expensive professional schools of law, dentistry, and medicine were the obvious target, and the immediate solution of the 1984 General Assembly was to order a detailed scrutiny of the state's eight universities by October 31, 1985. "We may be inadequately funding what we have," said Senator Michael R. Moloney, a major sponsor of the study. "But then, the question is, do we need everything we have? That's the guts of the study."[24]

As Western sought to make do with a tighter budget and the threat of a stagnant future, a report prepared for the National Institute of Education asserted that Kentucky ranked sixth nationally in 1982-83 in its per-student expenditure and twelfth in the percentage of revenue allocated to higher education, although the state was only forty-sixth in tax revenue. The chief author of the report later acknowledged some erroneous conclusions, most of which came from a lack of standard reporting of statistics from state to state, and corrections were made. Kentucky's spokesmen for higher education obviously feared that opponents of higher education would use the study to deny the need for additional funding.[25]

"I am reminded of the untimely death of a gentleman who had just returned to Kentucky after a vacation in Florida where he had acquired a great tan," Zacharias wrote Harry Snyder. "At his open casket all his friends kept remarking about how healthy he looked." The misleading statistics, Zacharias suggested, were equivalent to the tan; "To determine the true condition on our campuses, you have to check our vital signs." One of the most disturbing of these signs was in the intangible but vital area of faculty and staff morale. "Morale is growing worse as good people leave administration or teaching; our career employees are feeling neglected and unappreciated.... They are asking for a sign that someone cares as much as they are asking for money."[26]

Many longtime faculty members agreed that morale was lower in 1984-85 than they had ever seen it on the Western campus. They probably agreed with the conclusion of a national survey of higher education: "There is a perception that things are bad and getting worse." The loss of valued personnel was an obvious problem; less evident was the danger that some faculty would decide to "Give them what they pay for." In the mid-1980s Western still had a relatively young faculty with many of its members tenured full professors with two or more decades to go before retirement. A limited program to encourage early retirements was initiated in 1985, but too little attention had been devoted to ways of providing career motivation in a bleak financial environment. Some faculty members were also alarmed over a sudden emphasis upon research and public service as essential elements in determining promotions, tenure, and merit salary increases. The latter was particularly alarming since half of the inadequate salary increase for 1985-86 was to be awarded on a merit basis and there were hints that only merit would be used thereafter. The faculty had obvious concerns about what constituted merit and who would evaluate it.[27] But when the Faculty Senate requested that across-the-board increases be given since the total was inadequate for significant merit awards, President Zacharias replied testily, "The Faculty Senate does not set salaries at Western Kentucky University." And, he declared, the vice-president for academic affairs was the voice of the faculty, not the Senate chair or individual teachers.[28]

As a result of faculty dissatisfaction with salaries and its concern with the general cause of higher education in Kentucky, a new faculty lobbying group called the Association of Western Faculty was formed in the spring of 1985. Dr. Harry Robe (psychology), then state president of the Congress of Faculty Senate Leaders, played a major role in the formation of the new group. Designed as a state-wide organization, its purpose was to present faculty views and concerns to the legislature and other bodies and to secure more faculty participation in matters of faculty concern on the campuses. Although the organization was not affiliated with any national group, its goal of seeking "recognition as the negotiating body of the faculty on matters of salary, benefits, faculty welfare and faculty status" clearly implied the possibility of unionization and national affiliation in the future.[29] Few events in recent years indicated more vividly than the start of this organization the extent to which Western had changed.

The 1984 General Assembly left Western in the position well described in Exodus 5:7: "Ye shall no more give the people straw to make brick, as heretofore; let them go and gather straw for themselves." Confronted with the financial exigencies of the 1980s, Western joined a host of universities and other organizations in trying to raise funds to supplement the bare-boned appropriations. The problem was compounded by the diminution of federal support. Clark Kerr, one of the nation's most knowledgeable authorities on higher education, warned in 1985 that for at least the next thirty years new public money would have to come from the states, not from Washington.[30] As a public institution, Western's efforts to find private support were handicapped by the frequent assertion, "Our taxes are already taking care of you." Yet some results were visible.

To cope with the fiscal restrictions of the 1980s, Western's administration used many of the measures employed fifty years earlier. Unit budgets were slashed or held to minimal increases, maintenance was delayed or left undone, some employees were let go, and some vacancies were not filled. The campus developed a slightly seedy appearance, and anyone familiar with maintenance techniques realized that the current neglect meant larger expenditures in the future. The venerable Home Economics-Industrial Education Annex that had been built from the stone of President Cabell's home was razed in 1983 and a parking lot replaced the quadrangle behind it. Renovation would have cost over six hundred thousand dollars, and that sum was not available. The Fine Arts Festival was discontinued for 1985-86, and its future was uncertain.[31]

Some reorganization of the early 1980s was attributed to efforts to save money, although some of the changes would probably have been made anyway. The most extensive was the dissolution of the College of Applied Arts and Health in 1981. The dean's position was eliminated, and the departments were scattered among the Education, Ogden, and Potter colleges. (Some of those cast adrift referred to themselves as the academic boat people.) Library science and instructional media became a part of the Department of Teacher Education, as did the communication disorders program; dental hygiene and the medical records program were combined, as were industrial education with engineering technology, and folk and intercultural studies with modern languages. The vice-president for administrative affairs became the vice-president for student affairs, and the scholastic development area was moved into his jurisdiction. President Zacharias told the regents that the anticipated savings would be $200,000 to $300,000 annually, but he added that the changes would strengthen the organizational structure and encourage high-level performance. Some of the regents and a larger number of faculty feared that the changes would result in neglect for the merged departments and programs. The president and Academic Vice-President Davis assured them that such was not the case, and the regents approved the changes that became effective July 1, 1981. In 1985 the names of the four undergraduate colleges were changed to reflect the reorganization that had occurred. They became the College of Arts, Humanities and Social Sciences; the College of Business Administration; the College of Education and Behavioral Sciences; and the College of Science, Technology and Health.[32]

In addition to curtailing expenditures, the university sought to increase revenue in many ways. The most obvious step was to raise student tuition and fees. The legislature gave this power to the Council on Higher Education with the individual governing boards simple endorsing its decision. By the fall of 1985 in-state tuition had risen to $477 a semester for full-time undergraduates and $521 for full-time graduate students. The comparable figures for out-of-state students was $1,362 and $1,494. Dormitory fees for double occupancy increased to $360-375 in 1985, and, allowing for considerable variation in appetite, meals were estimated to cost $550-775. Books were said to average $125 per semester. After the summer of 1985 students who wanted room telephones had to purchase their own, for the ones leased by the University were removed. Savings after the first year were estimated to be $71,000.[33]

A problem with the tuition, housing, and food service revenues was the continuing decline in enrollment. The fall 1982 headcount of 12,885 dropped to 12,666 the following year, in part because the out-of-state tuition waiver for four Indiana and two Tennessee counties was discontinued. (In an enlarged and modified form, it was reinstated in 1985.) Western began a selective admissions policy in 1983 which may have had some adverse effect on freshman enrollment. Enrollment in the fall of 1984 was 11,771, a drop of 7 percent from the preceding year. What was most significant was the 4.85 percent decline in the number of new freshman. The fall 1985 enrollment declined 4 percent to 11,259, but the number of entering freshmen remained stable and their average ACT score increased to 18.6. Dean Sutton projected a probable decline in the fall of 1986, stability at that level for two years, then another slow decline until 1991 when an increase may be expected. Demographic patterns and the state's poor record in the percentage of high school graduates who entered college made declines almost certain. The main questions concerned the extent and the duration of the slump.[34]

The College Heights Foundation played an important role in the effort to obtain additional funds. It had first sought funds for construction of the Kentucky Building and for small loans to students, and in the post World War II years it had not actively engaged in fund raising. That situation changed after the retirement of President Thompson who, following a year's sabbatical, turned his administrative abilities to a reorganization and enlargement of the foundation as its president.[35] He was aided, as he had been as president, by his efficient secretary and assistant, Georgia Bates, who became the foundation's executive secretary-treasurer. Results were soon evident. Between 1969 and 1978 the perpetual Memorial Fund grew from $193,650.78 to $2,450,199.74, and the foundation was able to expand its program again and again. Prior to the 1969-70 academic year, scholarships had totaled under $25,000 over a period of forty-six years; in 1969-78 just under $491,000 was donated to that purpose. The foundation supplied $173,280 for scholarships in 1979-80 and $205,147 in 1980-81. Disbursements from such special funds as the Rodes-Helm Lecture Series and the Margie Helm Library Fund also increased. Even greater future growth was hidden in wills and codicils which promised more foundation income in years to come. The loan program also continued as an important foundation function. During the nine years that Thompson headed the foundation, 7,953 loans totaled $1,228,077; during the preceding forty-six years the 22,614 loans had totaled $1,066,887. The foundation was proud of a loan loss of only 1.77 percent.

The foundation's operations also included the university bookstore and laundry; their assets were $630,709.41 in 1978. The revolving loan program was based on an investment of $137,500 and the perpetual Memorial Fund was $2,450,199.74, making total foundation assets of $3,218,409.15. Since safety was a prime concern, the rate of invested return in 1977-78 was 7.76 percent.

Hundreds of Western's friends contributed to the growth of the foundation, and there was an increasing number of benefactors each year. Especially generous were Charles Roy Martin, longtime financial consultant to the E.I. du Pont de Nemours group, and Dr. and Mrs. C. Ray Franklin, both former Western students, whose gifts enhanced the work of the foundation.[36]

In 1979 after President Downing's retirement, the College Heights Foundation Board voted him president of the foundation as of February 1, 1980, when Kelly Thompson became chairman of the board, a new position created for him. Mrs. Mary Sample, Downing's executive secretary, moved into that position at the foundation, and Miss Bates continued as treasurer until her retirement in 1980. The foundation maintained its rapid growth. At the beginning of 1985, the Memorial Fund had a market value of $5,064,784.43 although the amount given to scholarships had increased to $286,655.73 in 1984-85. The 1,057 loans (for $134,516) in 1984 was the largest number since 1980. Most of the loans were for emergencies with repayment expected within a few months. By 1983 state agencies were taking a greater interest in such university affiliated organizations as the College Heights Foundation. In February 1984 Western agreed to resolve some questions that had been raised at the state level by purchasing the bookstore and laundry, a move Downing called "timely and appropriate." Because of the university's shortage of funds, the purchase at a cost of some $1,100,000 would not be completed for five years.[37]

In 1974 President Thompson told the regents that the College Heights

Foundation was not an office of development, but he predicted that Western would some day establish such an office. Five years later President Zacharias gave priority to its creation. The regents established the position of Director of Development at their December 1, 1979, meeting, and in September 1980 John W. Sweeney from the University of Missouri-Columbia was appointed to the post. At the November board meeting, Zacharias presented "A Plan for Development of Western Kentucky University from Private Sources" that Sweeney had prepared. "No institution, in my opinion," Zacharias explained, "can face the 80s with anything in the way of a hope of accomplishing more than mediocrity without widespread individual support and corporate support for various programs." He predicted some dividends from the program within five years and substantial impact from it within twenty years. A steering committee coordinated this program with the work of the College Heights Foundation. In the following summer, Sweeney presented an ambitious plan for endowed chairs ($500,000) distinguished professorships ($250,000) and endowed scholarships ($30,000) that got few immediate results. One of the most visible efforts to raise outside money was the fall phonothon. During a three-week period, some seven hundred students called several thousand alumni and secured pledges of over $34,000, and the project became an annual event. The 1985 campaign set a new record with pledges of approximately $49,000.[38]

Western also accelerated its search for funding of athletics. Ted Hornback had been largely responsible for originating the Hundred Club in 1965, and it had proved invaluable in recruiting athletes. But a decade later the modest sums it raised were no longer adequate if Western teams were to compete successfully with schools that enjoyed greater resources. Western's fifth place finish in the 1978 OVC All-Sports championship—its lowest ever—pointed up the need for action. Gene Keady, the new basketball coach, was instrumental in organizing the Red Towel Club that added a new fiscal dimension to the athletic program. The administration and Board of Regents approved special parking and seating privileges for persons who contributed $750 annually to the program. Special roll-away, theater-type seats replaced the student-occupied, floor-level bleacher seats on one side of Diddle Arena; the program was so successful that soon the bleachers on the opposite side also fell victim to special seating. Chuck Witt, a recent basketball player at Western, spearheaded the early drive for members. Then in 1981 Gary West was employed as the full-time executive director of the Hilltopper Hundred Club, which, including the Red Towel component, had grown to approximate five hundred members. By December 1981 club members occupied 834 of the 3,888 chairback seats in the arena, and more seats were needed to meet the demand. In 1981-82 the club's operations cost 20 percent of the $104,000 budget with the remainder divided among the intercollegiate sports. Basketball (35 percent) and football (30 percent) were the major beneficiaries of the program.[39]

Although some of the fund raising programs were not likely to reveal their potential for several years, concrete results were soon evident. In the 1982-83 fiscal year, 4,018 people contributed $788,399.90 to the university. Of this sum, $315,986 went to the Development Program, $199,218 to the College Heights Foundation, $271,079 to the Hundred Club, and $2,115 to the Ogden College Foundation. A year later the total passed the million dollar mark for the first time ($1,092,271), thanks to a 40 percent increase in donations and a 25 percent increase in donors. By then a number of campus projects had benefitted from small grants from the unrestricted development fund.[40] Fund raising had become a permanent part of the fiscal scene.

The most significant development in Western's athletic program in many years was the decision to leave the Ohio Valley Conference and join the far-flung Sun Belt Conference. Such a move had been discussed frequently, for many Westerners believed that the reputation of the OVC hurt Western's chances for national recognition. The main value to the proposed move was seen to be in basketball; none of the Sun Belt schools even had a football team. At a special regents meeting on March 8, 1982, President Zacharias, with the unanimous agreement of the Athletic Committee, recommended that Western accept the proffered Sun Belt invitation. The initiation fee was $50,000, and a new member had to purchase a share of the annual conference budget. The main arguments advanced in favor of the move were more national visibility and greater possibilities for television revenue. Regent Cole declared that it was "a day of taking a rightful place in overall national athletics by virtue of what Western Kentucky University has accomplished in the past."[41]

The other Sun Belt members in 1982 were South Florida, Jacksonville, South Alabama, Alabama-Birmingham, North Carolina-Charlotte, and Virginia Commonwealth. Old Dominion was then added as the eighth team. Organized in 1976, the Sun Belt basketball teams had earned credibility with frequent appearances in postseason play. Western soon found that the calibre of play was well above OVC standards, although the men's cross country team won the conference championship in November 1982. Clem Haskins, one of Western's all-time basketball greats, had joined the staff as a part-time assistant coach in 1977. When Gene Keady resigned in 1980 to go to Purdue University, Haskins became Western's seventh head basketball coach. His 1980-81 season record of 21-8 won the OVC championship, but the Toppers lost in the first round of the NCAA tournament to Alabama-Birmingham of the Sun Belt Conference. The 19-10 season in 1981-82 earned a conference cochampionship, but Western lost its final OVC game in the tournament when Middle Tennessee won 54-52. Invited to the National Invitational Tournament, Western fell in the first round to Keady's Purdue team.

Then came the move to the Sun Belt and records of 12-16 in 1982-83, 12-17 in 1983-84, and 14-14 in 1984-85. Including conference tournament play, the Sun Belt record was a disappointing 15-31, a winning percentage of 32.6. The basketball program was reprimanded and censured by the NCAA in 1984 for recruiting violations the previous year. The violations were relatively minor, as the penalties indicated, and the players were not affected. Neither was Western's eligibility for television appearances or postseason play. Unfortunately, the latter issue did not arise in 1985. Western's selection to play seven games in Japan during August 1985 led to hopes that the additional practice and experience would result in a better 1985-86 record.[42]

The move to the Sun Belt was not acclaimed by those people devoted to the Western football program. When assistant coach Lawrence "Butch" Gilbert retired in 1985, he called that conference move the low point of his sixteen years on the Western staff. "They destroyed a good all round program, when they opted to leave the OVC," he explained. "They went from the best competition to no competition in the Sun Belt." Many people assumed that the change of conferences must lead to a downgrading of the football program if it were continued at all. The most expensive of the varsity sports, it was the major contributor to the escalating athletic budget. But in May 1982 the regents voted to continue the football program at the I-AA level for two years. If "special activities" failed to increase income and to shrink the deficit, "the Board will have to consider some major revisions in current policy."[43] The lack of conference affiliation meant that an almost perfect record would be required to gain a postseason invitation, and the rapid increase of the number of teams in I-AA made the competition much stronger than it had been. Feix later admitted, "It was tougher than I ever imagined to compete as an independent. I miscalculated the effects on the program." Drastic changes in the televising of games decreased the possibilities of obtaining revenue from that source, and costs had escalated to the point that ticket sales for a sold-out stadium could not finance the program. The Western football coach faced a difficult situation.

The head coach who confronted these problems in 1984 was Dave Roberts, who had been the backfield coach at Vanderbilt for several years. During his last seasons, Jimmy Feix's teams continued to post roller-coaster records. Following a mediocre 5-5 season in 1979, the 1980 squad won its first nine games and the OVC championship and appeared certain to go into postseason play. But it suffered an humiliating 49-0 defeat at Murray, and no bid came. The 1981 record was 6-5 and the 1982 one was 5-5. After the 1982 season the Board of Regents voted 5-3 to add another full-time coach to the staff, release assistant coaches from teaching responsibilities, increase grants-in-aid from 65 to 70, and reaffirm a commitment to Division I-AA football. The mandate for improvement was clear, but the 1983 season produced a disappointing 2-8-1 record. Toward the end of the season Feix told a reporter, "I really believe in my heart that I can turn it around," but before the end of November he asked to be relieved of coaching. As he ended sixteen years as head coach, the longest tenure in Western's football history, Feix cited "a lack of under-standing ... and the lack of support and the unfair treatment of the team" as reasons for his decision. He became associate director of alumni affairs and taught in physical education, then was promoted to director of alumni affairs in the summer of 1985 when Lee Robertson retired.[44]

Moving with unusual dispatch, a search committee had made its recommendation and Roberts had been announced as the new head coach before Christmas. Most of the assistant coaches departed, and the list of signees soon showed a much wider geographical distribution with fewer of the athletes coming from Kentucky. Roberts installed a passing offense in 1984, but the record for the rebuilding year was 2-9, although three games were lost by one point margins, and attendance showed little indication of increased interest. The 1985 record improved to 4-7 with a welcome victory over Murray in the final game. For the second year, the football staff resorted to a *Herald* classified advertisement when a desper-ate need developed for a center who could snap for punts and field goals.

The combination of pruned university budgets and continued athletic deficits led to increased criticism of Western's priorities. Why pour money into the football program when the school had so recently and so joyfully joined a nonfootball conference? A *Herald* commentator reported that after the 1983 season the football budget was increased from $632,354 to $738,345; "It seems that the worse a program gets, the more money gets shoveled into it." The Faculty Senate studied the issue at length during the 1984-85 academic year. The total athletic budget increased from $1,139,536 in 1979-80 to $1,940,004 in 1984-85 and the total revenue, including such nonticket sources as the Hundred Club, grew from $411,300 to $1,054,403 over the same period. The deficit of $728,236 in 1979-80 decreased to $486,737 in 1981-82 but then increased to an estimat-ed $885,601 for 1984-85. In his defense of the athletic program, President Zacharias pointed out that since 1979-80 the deficit had declined as a percentage of both the athletic and total university budgets. He did not stress the increase of the athletic budget from 2.31 percent of the total university budget in 1981-82 to 2.97 percent in 1984-85.[45]

At its October 1984 meeting, the Faculty Senate passed unanimously a resolution proposed by Professor Gene Evans that there be no further increases in the athletic budget. The Fiscal Affairs Committee, headed by Dr. David Lee, was charged to review the athletic budget. The Lee report, presented to the senate on February 14, 1985, recommended that "the university study the advisability of moving to Division III in football." Since Division III teams do not offer athletic grants-in-aid, the athletic deficit would be reduced sharply while intercollegiate football competition would still be available. The committee found little evidence that winning athletic programs had significant impact upon either fund raising or student enrollments. It discovered that the athletic deficits were even larger than reported, for in both 1982-83 and 1983-84 the budget overruns had exceeded 20 percent. "The resources available to higher education in Kentucky are steadily eroding," the report concluded. "We must choose between luxuries and necessities. Our ability to offer quality academic programs depends on our willingness to act boldly on this problem."[46]

Despite its restrained tone, such criticism was rare in Western's history, and the report let to considerable discussion and controversy. President Zacharias dismissed it by saying that he saw nothing new in it and that it "sensationalized" the amount spent on athletics. He suggested that the faculty focus its efforts on improving the quality of academics at Western. Senate Chair Tom Coohill retorted that the senate was attempting to do just that since the athletic deficit "affects the whole university." In a somewhat more conciliatory tone Zacharias admonished Coohill that the report had "put our football recruiting efforts in a very difficult situation" since the general public did not understand the senate's advisory role. He challenged the senate to make studies in nine areas; athletics was not one of them. This flareup soon subsided, but, as Lee said in an interview, "The issue won't go away."[47] If it did nothing else, the exchange indicated that the president's honeymoon period was over.

Action taken by the NCAA convention in January 1985 may be helpful. Effective September 1, 1986, Division I schools would be allowed to sponsor a minimum of six varsity sports for men and six for women instead of the eight for men and eight that were to be required for women by 1988. In 1984-85 Western sponsored ten sports for men (football, basketball, baseball, soccer, swimming, cross-country, indoor track, outdoor track, golf, and tennis) and seven for women (cross-country, volleyball, basketball, indoor track, outdoor track, golf, and tennis). The Sun Belt Conference required only six sports for men (basketball, cross-country, soccer, baseball, golf, and tennis) so that in 1986 it would be possible to meet both conference and NCAA requirement after dropping four of the men's sports. From the budget viewpoint, the important question would be the future of football.[48]

The move to the Sun Belt Conference required Western to add soccer as an intercollegiate sport. Given minimum support, including an inadequate playing field, graduate coach Neophytos Papaioannou compiled records of 6-7-2 and 9-8 before resigning in late 1983. His successor, David Holmes, received more institutional support, but the 1984 record was a disappointing 4-13-1. The 1985 season saw a sharp improvement to 12-7, although the Strikers lost their first match in the Sun Belt Tournament.[49]

One of the highlights in the athletic program in the early 1980s was the success of the Lady Toppers basketball team. When Eileen Canty resigned after the 1981-82 season, Paul Sanderford, a successful coach at Louisburg Junior College in North Carolina, was selected for the position. An excellent recruiter, he found much of his talent within Kentucky. The 1982-83 squad had a 22-7 season, finished second to Old Dominion in the Sun Belt's first tournament for women's basketball, and Sanderford was conference coach of the year. With only one senior on that squad, prospects looked good for the next season. But Lillie Mason, a 6'2" All-American from Russellville who had scored over one thousand points in her first two years, injured a knee in a preseason scrimmage and was lost for the year. The 1983-84 record was 21-11, and the Toppers lost again in the conference tournament to nationally ranked Old Dominion. Invited to the National Women's Invitational Tournament, the Toppers defeated California, then closed the season with losses to Vanderbilt and Clemson.[50]

Lillie Mason was back in 1984-85, and Clemette Haskins, Kentucky's Miss Basketball in 1983, and the other talented recruits had gained poise and experience. An early season highlight was an overtime 72-67 win over Georgia, then the third ranked team in the nation. Before the season's end the Toppers also appeared in the national ratings. The regular season record was 23-4, and a new single game scoring record was set in the final game when Cincinnati was smashed 122-72. Unfortunately, Old Dominion was still in the Sun Belt, and Western lost to them in the tournament final. The 25-5 record earned the Lady Toppers a spot in the NCAA Division I Basketball Tournament and the advantage of playing the regional games in Diddle Arena. Western outlasted Middle Tennessee of the OVC 90-83, then upset number one ranked Texas 92-90 before a crowd of 4,900. Two days later a record crowd of 6,500 saw Western defeat sixth-ranked Ole Miss 72-68. Haskins and Mason made the all-tournament team with Mason voted the most valuable player.[51]

Practically every sports writer who wrote about the Final Four called Western a Cinderella team. Midnight came too early for the Lady Toppers as Georgia avenged the early season loss with a 91-78 win. The best season in the history of women's basketball at Western closed with a record of 28-6, and Coach Sanderford and his assistants intensified their efforts to recruit the players who could maintain the program on that level. A preseason poll for 1985-86 ranked the Lady Toppers sixth in the nation.[52]

Another bright spot in the athletic program was swimming where Coach Powell continued to produce winning squads that regularly dominated the Midwestern Independent Intercollegiate Championship. A milestone was achieved in March 1985 when Steve Crocker, a senior from Franklin, Kentucky, won All-American honors by finishing fourth in the 50-yard freestyle finals of the NCAA national championship. For the first time, a Western swimmer had reached the national finals.[53]

The baseball team also continued to win in extended seasons that gave players almost as much experience in one year as they had once received during a varsity career. In his first six years (1980-85), Coach Murrie's teams averaged 56 games a season. During those years his teams won 217 games, lost 115, and tied three. The 1985 season ended at 43-20 when Old Dominion won the Sun Belt title with an 11-10 victory in eleven innings. Third baseman Rob Tomberlin was the first Western player ever named to the Converse All-American first team. (Catcher Ralph Antone, who was also a football quarterback, had been named to the second team in 1983.) Tomberlin's credentials included a .398 batting average and 27 home runs that set a school and Sun Belt Conference record. Both the men's and women's cross country teams won conference titles in the fall of 1985, the men for the fourth consecutive year. The women's meet was the first in conference history.[54]

Changes continued to occur across the campus as Western neared the midpoint of the decade of the 1980s. They included several important shifts in administrative personnel. Of the six college deans in 1980, only two (Sanderfur, education, and Gray, graduate) retained those position when the 1985-86 academic year opened. When Dean Mounce left Potter College in 1980 to become president of a private college, he was replaced by towering (203.2 centimeters) Ward Hellstrom from the University of Florida whose academic field was English. Dean Robert E. Nelson (business) returned to teaching in 1984 and was followed by Robert A. Hershbarger who came to Western from Cleveland State University. Marvin Russell, dean of Ogden College for fourteen years, went back to the classroom and laboratory in 1980, and Dr. William G. Lloyd, who had been on the chemistry faculty from 1967 to 1974, returned to the Hill as his successor. When Lloyd requested reassignment to a faculty position, he was succeeded in 1985 by Dr. Charles E. Kupchella, a biologist from Murray State University. Dean Hourigan's position was abolished when the College of Applied Arts and Health was dissolved. Dr. Henry Hardin, dean of Academic Services, moved to a part-time status in the summer of 1985, and Dr. Carl Chelf, dean of Public Service and Continuing Education, returned to the government as the units under his jurisdiction were assigned to other areas.[55]

As the fall semester opened in 1985, Vice-Presidents Minton and Largen still headed student affairs and business affairs. But Vice-President for Academic Affairs James L. Davis had resigned the previous year and returned to the Department of Geography and Geology. His successor was Dr Robert V. Haynes, an historian who had been deputy provost at the University of Houston. And Dr. Minton announced that he would retire in the summer of 1986.[56]

Personnel changes were also numerous among the department heads, directors, and other administrators. In the spring of 1985, for example, Ogden College was searching for four department heads as well as a dean. Some vacancies occurred when faculty and staff members sought relief from the Kentucky fiscal situation by accepting positions elsewhere. In other instances, campus speculation inevitably considered whether a person who left an administrative post had done so voluntarily or as the result of pressure. Both reasons help explain the considerable turnover in the 1980s. In many cases an administrator simply became tired of dealing with constant irritations and frustrations and sought relief in the haven of the classroom. Since Western did not experience a "Saturday night massacre," faculty and staff sometimes did not realize the extent of the changes. The numerous shifts were another indication of the adjustments being made in the institution as it sought to establish its identity under rapidly changing conditions.

If the mood of Western in the summer of 1985 had to be defined in one word, "uncertainty" would be a good choice. The academic community was both uncertain and apprehensive of what the future might bring from the state government and the Council on Higher Education. Would inadequate funding continue? Would Western lose still more of its autonomy? Would programs be curtailed or abolished by outside agencies? Would the state concentrate its commitment to higher education on a few institutions to the detriment of the rest? Uncertainty also shrouded on-campus decisions that would help determine Western's future. Would enrollment decline significantly in the next several years? What would be the fate of faculty in the areas that experienced sharp declines? What could be done with surplus facilities that often were not just what the school needed? How much stress would be placed on research and public service? Who would judge performance in the various areas of faculty responsibilities, and what criteria would be used? How could students be given at least an introduction to a liberal education when there were strong pressures both within and without the university to stress vocational programs? What were the institutional priorities? How would they be implemented?

The uncertainty was increased by the efforts of the Council on Higher Education to draft a "Strategic Plan for Higher Education in Kentucky." Mandated by the legislature and with an autumn deadline, a council draft was released in August 1985. It was so vague and ambiguous that institutional leaders could envision disastrous consequences if it was implemented in that form. Institutional responses and a series of public hearings across the state led to a number of changes. The universities of Louisville and Kentucky were so concerned over the possible loss or curtailment of professional schools that their advocates dominated much of the public hearing held at Western on August 19 with impassioned defenses of their schools, although hearings had already been held in both Lexington and Louisville. Many observers resented their intrusion and saw in it the arrogant attitude that the two institutions sometimes displayed toward the rest of the state universities. The council's draft of early October bore little relationship to the strong recommendations of the Prichard Committee, and the *Paducah Sun* charged that the council "caved in" to the universities that had professional schools. The report adopted on November 8, 1985, hardly justified the intensive studies that had been made, and even so the *Herald* predicted that the General Assembly would probably weaken the recommendations even more. By the late summer the Western faculty, hampered by frequent changes in format and emphasis, was also working on strategic planning for the departments, colleges, and the university, although no one could predict with certainty what effect outside decisions would have upon institutional plans and goals.[57]

The summer uncertainty was enhanced by the resignation of President Zacharias. Nominated for the presidency of Mississippi State University, in late July he informed the regents that he was one of the finalists for that position. Although the Mississippi school's enrollment was not much larger than Western's, it had both professional schools and doctoral programs, and its annual budget was nearly two and half times as large as Western's. Mississippi had already made a commitment to higher education that Kentucky was only beginning to consider in tentative terms. Zacharias visited the Starkville campus, then was elected unanimously by the governing board. At an August 19 meeting, Western's Board of Regents accepted with regret his resignation as of August 31. Dr. Paul Cook, for fifteen years a part of the president's office, was elected interim president. As budget director and with budget preparation and consideration expected to dominate much of the 1985-86 year, Cook was the logical choice for the position.[58]

The six years of the Zacharias presidency were near the average tenure of American university presidents in the late twentieth century. Excluding Dr. Minton's short term, each Western president has served a shorter term than his predecessor. If this trend continues, a permanent presidential search committee may become necessary.

No university president can please all of his many constituents, and after his honeymoon period ended Zacharias was faulted by some persons for such diverse sins as his defense of the football program and its deficit, his adamant opposition to faculty evaluation of the president, his interest in the presidency of other universities, and his unexpected sensitivity to what appeared to be personal criticism. In a farewell editorial the *Herald* complained, "He was an external president, not an internal president. Students backed him when he first came to Western but drifted away over the years as Zacharias reached toward his outside goals." But his overall evaluation was favorable. When he resigned Faculty Regent Mary Ellen Miller said, "We should be proud to have had him for six years and I can understand why someone else would want him." Board chairman Joe Iracane praised him as "an outstanding leader for higher education in Kentucky, and he has been an outstanding president for Western."[59] Zacharias fought stubbornly for the role and the resources that he believed Western should have, though he was often less parochial in his outlook and more positive in his leadership than were most of the other state university presidents, and he had become a leading spokesman for higher education in the state. A specialist in communication, Zacharias was an effective speaker who was comfortable with, and even enjoyed, his contacts with media people.

His years at Western were dominated by fiscal crises and budget constraints. He did not have a normal year in which to work, and many proposals had to be delayed, curtailed, or abandoned because of inadequate funds. A considerable amount of administrative reorganization occurred with inevitable dissatisfaction on the part of some who were affected, but the changes did not cause the turmoil that plagued some of the other state universities. Zacharias's success with the development program and the enlistment of more outside support for the institution cannot be measured until several years have passed.

At its August meeting the Board of Regents, after obvious advance consultation, appointed an advisory search committee of fifteen members. Senate Chair Eugene Evans was later added to the group. No regent served on the committee, but chairman Iracane attended all sessions as an observer and kept the other regents informed of the progress of the search. Bowling Green attorney Joe Bill Campbell, a former chairman of the Board of Regents, headed the committee. Retired Indiana University business professor Les Waters was employed as a consultant; he received high praise for his assistance and advice. University attorney William Bivin was in charge of the support staff. The committee held its first meeting on September 7.

Determined to avoid the pitfalls of the last presidential search, the committee worked behind an effective curtain of secrecy, with Campbell making all announcements. Except for interim president Paul Cook who announced his candidacy on October 9, the campus community had few clues to the identity of candidates. Campbell announced on October 22 that 170 nominations and applications had been received; ten of the nominees had refused consideration. The candidates were overwhelmingly off-campus white males; women, minority, and on-campus candidates were few. By November 5 the searchers had narrowed the list to "between ten and thirteen," and Campbell announced that the committee hoped to submit five names to the regents in December.[60]

During marathon sessions in Nashville's Opryland Hotel on November 23-24, the committee interviewed the ten top candidates and cut the list in half. The five names submitted to the Board of Regents were released to the public on December 6, and the basic work of the search committee was completed.

The most surprising name on the short list was that of Dr. Samuel Kern Alexander, professor of education at the University of Florida and director of Florida's Institute for Educational Finance. A finalist in 1979, he had withdrawn because of what he called political interference with the selection process. Dr. Paul Cook, the interim president, was the only on-campus candidate on the short list. Dr. Thomas A. Bond, president of Clarion State University, Pennsylvania, and Dr. Edward B. Jakubaukas, president of the State University of New York at Genesco, were the only finalists with presidential experience. Dr. Raphael O. Nystrand, professor of education and dean of the School of Education at the University of Louisville, had experience with Kentucky state administration. Both Alexander and Cook had ties to Western, and, unlike the situation in 1979, this was seen as an advantage.[61]

By the time the public announcement was made, the regents, organized in two teams of four members each, had started visiting the candidates on their home campuses. A "visit" was also made to Dr. Cook on the Western campus. Although there were a few complaints about the paucity of information released by the search committee, the search had been conducted in an exemplary manner. But at a series of informal reports to various campus constituencies on December 6, Iracane announced that the regents would meet in continuous session on Monday through Wednesday, December 9-11. Each of the finalists would visit the campus for half a day; in 1979 each finalist had spent the better part of two days on campus. The abbreviated visits allowed only quarter-hour sessions with most campus groups and effectively eliminated the question and answer sessions that had been a valuable part of the campus appearances. Nor were the candidates' resumés made available to the campus community. In letters to the *Herald* Gary E. Dillard (biology) called the process insulting and Richard D. Weigel (history) asserted that the accelerated format "cast serious doubt upon the integrity of the entire process." In a later issue W. Henry Baughman (health and safety) endorsed their criticism. The *Herald* predicted that the 1985 search "may be remembered for its last-minute announcement of the finalists and the board's apparent decision to virtually ignore the students and faculty who will be directly affected by their decision."

The decision to move so rapidly was based upon the belief that a prolonged process would increase the possibilities of political interference. Also, the fall semester was near its end, and visits that were not completed before the Christmas vacation began would have to be postponed until the beginning of the spring semester in January. Asked their preference, all candidates opted for a quick decision. From the university's viewpoint, there were obvious advantages to having a president as soon as possible, particularly because the General Assembly would meet in early January.[62]

The finalists galloped through their hurried sessions and completed their visits by noon on December 11, and the regents met in closed session that afternoon. No vote was taken, but by the time they adjourned Alexander and Cook were clearly the front runners. No announcement was made, but campus speculation, correct for once, also had them as the top choices. A majority of the faculty favored Cook, who was liked, respected, and a known quantity. The regents did not meet again until December 14 when they held a closed meeting of less than twenty minutes. Then in the open session Mrs. Patsy Judd nominated Dr. Alexander and Student Regent Mitchell McKinney seconded the nomination. On December 11 the regents had discussed the value of having a unanimous decision, and on December 14 that vote was cast when Alexander emerged as the majority's choice as Western's seventh president.

Alexander was given a three-year contract that started at $75,000 per year, plus the usual perquisites of the position. Because of his Florida commitments, his tenure would not officially begin until May 15, but he had arranged with the University of Florida to spend most of the spring semester at Western with the University of Florida being compensated by Western for that portion of his services. This vague and confused agreement was clarified at the regents meeting on January 25, 1986, when Alexander was confirmed as president as of that date but was promised enough released time to complete his Florida obligations.[63]

The forty-six-year-old Alexander was born in Marrowbone, Kentucky, in 1939. He attended elementary and junior high schools in Bowling Green, then graduated from Jefferson County's Valley High School. His parents, two sisters, and a brother all earned bachelor and master degrees at Western. Kern Alexander did his undergraduate work at Centre College, where he majored in English. Then he joined the family tradition by taking a Master of Education degree at Western in 1962 with a minor in history. He received a doctorate in education at Indiana University in 1965, then did postdoctoral work at Oxford University. His professional career began with two years of high school teaching, after which he accepted positions during the 1960s with the Kentucky Department of Education and then the U.S. Department of Education. In 1968 he joined the faculty of the College of Education, University of Florida, as an associate professor; two years later he was promoted to full professor.

From 1972 to 1981, and again in 1985-86, he was director of the Institute for Educational Finance at the University of Florida, and in 1982-84 he also served as education policy coordinator in the governor's office. A prolific author and editor with school finance and school law as his major areas of interest, Alexander compiled an impressive list of book and article publications. He served frequently on state, regional, and national educational bodies, and he delivered numerous professional papers. Several of his studies dealt with aspects of Kentucky's educational system. He made an excellent impression during his interviews and campus visit.

Iracane said in the announcement of Alexander's election that he was selected because of "his vision for Western." During his campus visit, Alexander emphasized his opposition to the designation of Western as a regional university. "The boundaries should be drawn in educational programs," he asserted, "and not by something as simple as geographic boundaries." Rejecting the assumption that "we're in an era of limits," he called for better student recruitment and retention, an expanded curriculum that would attract more students, and adequate funding for Western's myriad needs. With the General Assembly meeting in January 1986 for a session that was vital to the future of higher education in the state, Alexander said that he would lobby for appropriations that would help Western meet its pressing needs in such areas as salaries and maintenance. A welcoming editorial in the *Courier-Journal* commented that "part of his task will be to convince Kentuckians of something their neighbors already seemed to have learned—that quality education is an investment that's costly to make, but far more costly to ignore."

At a press conference on December 17, Dr. Alexander announced that at the regents meeting on January 25 he would recommend that Cook be appointed executive vice-president for administrative affairs. Cook would continue with his budget and planning functions; the scope of his other responsibilities would be determined later. Chairman Iracane was enthusiastic as he praised the best "1-2 combination" in the state. Observers of the transitional period soon saw that Alexander and Cook had established the foundations for a good working relationship.[64]

Interviewed a few weeks before he became academic vice-president in 1984, Dr. Haynes remarked, "One of the great problems facing higher education today is how to do more with less, how we can build quality with fewer resources, and that's a tough challenge. But it's a challenge we all have to face."[65] As Western nears the start of her ninth decade, the institution faces some of the most difficult decisions in its history. They present particular concern because, to a large degree, they are different from those of the past. Except for the aberrations of the Great Depression and World War II, both of which were expected to be of limited duration, most of Western's problems have dealt with aspects of a booming future—

288 / Western Kentucky University

how to feed, house, and educate an ever increasing student body. Such problems were usually confronted with the optimistic expectation that they could and would be resolved in some reasonably satisfactory way. And if bigger was not always better, many people believed that it was.

Few Westerners in the mid-1980s would predict a return to such conditions. Surging enrollments and expanding facilities will not resume in the foreseeable future, if ever, and a boom campus will no longer obscure problems that were once shrugged off as being relatively unimportant in a era of growth. Hard decisions will have to be made as Western seeks to ascertain what her role will be in the last years of the twentieth century and beyond.

Board of Regents
(to January 1986)

Until 1972 the State Superintendent of Public Instruction was Chairman Ex-Officio, as indicated by an asterisk. Faculty regents are designated by (F); student regents by (S).

James H. Fuqua*	1906-7
H.C. Miller	1906-8
E.H. Mark	1906-11
J. Whit Potter	1906-22
H.K. Cole	1906-18
Dr. J.G. Crabbe*	1907-9
Judge Conn Linn	1909-10
Ellsworth Regenstein*	1909-11
C.W. Richards	1910-11
Barksdale Hamlett*	1911-15
Judge John H. Haswell	1912-24
W.J. Gooch	1915-19
V.O. Gilbert*	1915-19
John A. Dean	1919-20
George W. Colvin*	1919-23
Mrs. John Gilmour	1920-24
Sterrett Cuthbertson	1922-35
Mrs. J.W. James	1924-28
H.H. Denhardt	1924-28
Dr. McHenry Rhoads*	1923-27
Col. Henry J. Stites	1926-29
W.C. Bell*	1927-31
Judge Max B. Harlin	1928-32
Col. E.B. Bassett	1928-32
M.O. Hughes	1929-36
Dr. J.H. Richmond*	1931-35
Judge Henry B. Hines	1932-36
Charles G. Franklin	1932-36
Clarence H. Bartlett	1935-36; 1940-55
Harry W. Peters*	1935-39
Judge Fielding Pentecost	1936-40

Huston B. Quinn	1936-38
Mrs. W.P. Drake	1936-40
B.J. Borrone	1936-47
Judge Charles I. Dawson	1938-48
John W. Booker*	1939-43
J.P. Masters	1940-44; 1948-55
John Fred Williams*	1943-47
Judge John B. Rodes	1944-48
Boswell Hodgkin*	1947-51
John E. Richardson	1947-55
Vernon L. Shallcross	1948-55
Wendell Butler*	1951-55; 1959-63; 1967-70
Bemis Lawrence	1955-66
Sheridan Barnes	1955-58
W.R. Patterson	1955-56
Don Campbell	1955-56
Robert R. Martin*	1955-59
Dr. W.R. McCormack	1956-60; 1968-76
Robert M. Spragens	1956-60
Sam Ezell	1957-59
Hugh R. Poland	1957-81
Douglas Keen	1958-70
Owen C. Hammons	1959-63
Maxey B. Harlin	1960-68
Dr. W. Gerald Edds	1960-68; 1972-76
Dr. J.T. Gilbert	1963-71
Dr. Harry M. Sparks*	1963-67
Dr. Chalmer P. Embry	1966-70; 1972-76
Albert G. Ross	1968-76
William E. Menser (S)	1968
Dr. Herbert Shadowen (F)	1968-71
Paul E. Gerard, III (S)	1968-70
Dr. Coy E. Ball	1970-74
Joe Lane Travis	1970-74
John R. Lyne (S)	1970-71
W.S. Moss, Jr.	1971-74
Dr. Lowell H. Harrison (F)	1971-74
Linda E. Jones (S)	1971-72
Dr. Lyman Ginger*	1972
Michael A. Fiorella (S)	1972-73
Steven D. Yater (S)	1973-74
Ronald D. Clark	1974-
John L. Ramsey	1974-78
Gregory Lee McKinney (S)	1974-75
Dr. William G. Buckman (F)	1974-83
Stephen L. Henry (S)	1975-76
John David Cole	1975-83
William M. Kuegel	1976-80

Ronald G. Sheffer   1976-84
Christy K. Vogt (S)   1976-77
Thomas D. Emberton   1976-80
Carroll F. Knicely   1976-80
Robert Earl Moore (S)   1977-78
Steven Owen Thornton (S)   1978-79
Michael M. Harreld   1978-82
James Earl Hargrove (S)   1979-80
Joe Bill Campbell   1980-84
Steven J. Fuller (S)   1980-81
Joseph Iracane   1980-
Sandra K. Norfleet (S)   1982
Patsy Judd   1980-
James A. Page   1982-
Julius E. Price, Sr.   1981-83
Margaret Ragan (S)   1982-83
Hughlyne P. Wilson   1983-
Mary Ellen Miller (F)   1983-
Jack D. Smith (S)   1983-84
Joseph A. Cook   1983-
Judge John S. Palmore   1984-
Danny Butler   1984
Mitchell S. McKinney (S)   1985-86

University Faculty
Distinguished Service Awards

Excellence in Productive Teaching

1968-69	H.L. Stephens (biology)
1969-70	Elmer Gray (agriculture)
1970-71	Jack W. Thacker (history)
1971-72	Francis Thompson (history)
1972-73	Fuad G. Baali (sociology)
1973-74	John Scarborough (secondary education)
1974-75	J. Julius Scott (philosophy and religion)
1975-76	Faye Carroll (government)
1976-77	William E. McMahon (English)
1977-78	Delbert Hayden (home economics and family living)
1978-79	Kathleen Kalab (sociology, anthropology, and social work)
1979-80	Jimmie O. Price (health and safety)
1980-81	Donald R. Tuck (philosophy and religion)
1981-82	John W. Reasoner (chemistry)
1982-83	Linda S. Pulsinelli (mathematics)
1983-84	Carroll G. Wells (mathematics)
1984-85	Curtis C. Wilkins (chemistry)

Distinguished Contributions in Research or Creativity

1968-69	Mary Washington Clarke (English and folklore)
1969-70	George Masannat (government)
1970-71	Lowell Harrison (history)
	William G. Lloyd (chemistry)
1971-72	Hart Nelsen (sociology)
1972-73	William G. Buckman (physics)
1973-74	Thomas Madron (government)
1974-75	Donald R. Rowe (environmental engineering technology)
1975-76	Thomas Coohill (biophysics)
	Jim Wayne Miller (foreign languages)
1976-77	Carlton Jackson (history)

1977-78	Randall Capps (communication and theatre)
	Gary Dillard (biology)
1978-79	Norman Holy (chemistry)
1979-80	James T. Baker (history)
1980-81	Ronald Nash (philosophy)
1981-82	Laurence J. Boucher (chemistry)
1982-83	W. Lynwood Montell (modern languages and intercultural studies)
1983-84	William L. Lane (philosophy and religion)
1984-85	Nicholas C. Crawford (geography and geology)

Distinguished Contributions in Public Service

1978-79	Willard Cockrill (geography and geology)
1979-80	Billy M. Adams (agriculture)
1980-81	W. Henry Baughman (health and safety)
1981-82	Jim Wayne Miller (modern languages and intercultural studies)
1982-83	Joseph P. Cangemi (psychology)
1983-84	Evelyn Thurman (library services)
1984-85	James S. Flynn (English)

College Faculty Excellence Awards

1979-80	Jimmie O. Price (College of Applied Arts and Health)
	Richard P. Cantrell (College of Business Administration)
	Thaddeus R. Crews (College of Education)
	John H. Crenshaw (Ogden College of Science and Technology)
	Mania Ritter (Potter College of Arts and Humanities)
1980-81	Martha Jenkins (College of Applied Arts and Health)
	J. Michael Morgan (College of Business Administration)
	Jo Ann Verner (College of Education)
	Thomas P. Coohill (Ogden College of Science, Technology and Health)
	David D. Lee (Potter College of Arts and Humanities)
1981-82	Jack O. Hall, Jr. (College of Business Administration)
	Reta Hicks (College of Education)
	James P. Worthington (Ogden College of Science, Technology and Health)
	Donald R. Tuck (Potter College of Arts and Humanities)
1982-83	Charles M. Ray (College of Business Administration)
	H. Philip Constans, Jr. (College of Education)
	David Coffey (Ogden College of Science, Technology and Health)
	Dale Wicklander (Potter College of Arts and Humanities)
1983-84	Jerry E. Boles (College of Business Administration)
	Leroy Metze (College of Education)
	Doral Glen Conner (Ogden College of Science, Technology and Health)

Thomas P. Baldwin (Potter College of Arts and Humanities)

1984-85   Robert W. Pulsinelli (College of Business Administration)
Daniel L. Roenker (College of Education)
Larry C. Byrd (Ogden College of Science, Technology and Health)
Richard V. Salisbury (Potter College of Arts and Humanities)

Major Buildings

The date indicates when the building was completed or occupied. A second date indicates a major addition.

Academic-Athletic Building No. 1, 1963 (Diddle Arena)
Academic-Athletic Building No. 2, 1968 (L.T. Smith Stadium)
Academic Complex, 1969
Agriculture Exposition Center, 1979
Barnes-Campbell Hall, 1966
Barracks, 1918. Razed 1924
Bates-Runner Hall, 1959 (Regents Hall)
Bemis Lawrence Hall, 1966
Cabell Hall, 1889. Razed 1926
Central Hall, 1962
Cherry Hall, 1937
Craig Alumni Center, 1931 (president's home to 1960)
Cravens Graduate Center & Library, 1971
Diddle Dorm, 1900 (private home to 1923, then music building, girl's dorm, men's
    dorm, basketball dorm)
Douglas Keen Hall, 1968
Downing University Center, 1970
East Hall, 1955
Education Complex, 1970
Environmental Sciences & Technology, 1975
Faculty House, 1921 (Cedar House)
Florence Schneider Hall, 1929 (White Hall, Whitestone Hall, West Hall)
Garrett Conference Center, 1951, 1965 (Garrett Student Center)
Gilbert Hall, 1963 (Terrace Hall)
Gordon Wilson Hall, 1927 (Library to 1965)
Grise Hall, 1966
Hardin Planetarium, 1967
Health and Physical Education Building, 1931 (Helm Library, 1965)
Heating Plant, 1927, 1963
Helm Library, 1931, 1965 (Health and Physical Education Building to 1964)
Hugh Poland Hall, 1969
Industrial Education, 1929

Industrial Education Annex, 1927 (Home Economics to 1968). Razed 1982
Ivan Wilson Center For Fine Arts, 1973
Jones-Jaggers Lab School, 1969
Kentucky Building, 1936, 1977
McCormack Hall, 1961 (State Hall to 1969)
McLean Hall, 1947
Music Hall, 1937. Razed 1975
North Hall, 1955
Ogden Hall, 1870(?). Razed 1966
Parking Structure, 1970
Pearce-Ford Tower, 1971
Physical Plant Building, 1958, 1962, 1970
Potter Hall, 1920
President's Home (on campus [Craig Alumni Center], 1931; 1536 State St., acquired, 1964; 1700 Chestnut St., acquired, 1979)
Recitation Hall, 1889. Razed 1936
Rodes-Harlin Hall, 1966
Rural School, 1924. Razed 1955
Science & Technology Hall, 1925 (Training School to 1970)
Snell Hall, 1926
South Hall, 1959
Services Supply Building, 1970
Thompson Science Complex, Central Wing, 1967
Thompson Science Complex, North Wing, 1960
Van Meter, 1911, 1957
West Hall, 1960
Wetherby Administration Building, 1967

Unless the first citation indicates otherwise, manuscript collections are in the Western Kentucky University Archives and the oral interviews are in the Oral History Project, Department of History, WKU.

Abbreviations and short forms used in the notes:

Courier-Journal	Louisville *Courier-Journal*
Daily News	Bowling Green *Park City Daily News*
EKU	Eastern Kentucky University
GC	General Correspondence
Herald	*College Heights Herald*
OVC	Ohio Valley Conference
PC	Personal Correspondence
SC	Special Correspondence
UK	University of Kentucky
UL	University of Louisville
WKSTC	Western Kentucky State Teachers College
WKU	Western Kentucky University

1. In the Beginning

1. Jonathan Messerli, *Horace Mann: A Biography* (New York, 1972), 298-301, 437; Robert Bingham Downs, *Horace Mann: Champion of Public Schools* (New York, 1974), 48-57; E.I.F. Williams, *Horace Mann, Educational Statesman* (New York, 1937), 191-204; E. Alder Dunham, *Colleges of the Forgotten Americans: A Profile of State Colleges and Regional Universities* (New York, 1969), 27-29, 33.

2. Moses Edward Ligon, *A History of Public Education in Kentucky*, Bulletin of the Bureau of School Service, College of Education, University of Kentucky, 14, no. 4 (Lexington, 1942), 287-90; Carl P. Chelf, "A Selective View of the Politics of Higher Education in Kentucky and the Role of H.H. Cherry, Educator-Politician" (Ph.D. diss., University of Nebraska, 1968), 44-46; James P. Cornette, *A History of the Western Kentucky State Teachers College* (Bowling Green, 1938), 2-4.

3. Speech of J.R. Alexander, 1931, in Henry Hardin Cherry Papers, box 57: Cherry and Faculty.

4. *Acts of the General Assembly, 1876*, 2:266.

5. Cornette, *History of WKSTC*, 23-48, discusses the Glasgow Normal School in considerable detail.

6. Ibid., 43.

7. Alvin Fayette Lewis, *History of Higher Education in Kentucky* (Washington, 1899), 295-96; *Acts of the General Assembly, 1885-1886*, 1:1087-88; Cornette, *History of WKSTC*, 48-50.

8. *Teachers College Heights* 13 (Jan. 1932):39.

9. Cornette, *History of WKSTC*, 57.

10. *Herald*, July 2, 1948; Cordell Hull, *The Memoirs of Cordell Hull*, 2 vols. (New York, 1948), 1:18-19.

11. H.H. Cherry Scrapbook for 1902-4 contains many of the school's letterheads and brochures. See also *Teachers College Heights* 20 (April 1943):5.

12. Interview of J.R. Alexander, by James P. Cornette, April 8, 1938, in Cornette, *History of WKSTC*, 60-61; Lewis, *Higher Education in Kentucky*, 296; J. Lewie Harman, Sr., *Brief Historical Sketch of the Bowling Green Business University* (Bowling Green, 1948), 6.

13. Ligon, *History of Public Education, passim*; Thomas D. Clark, *A History of Kentucky* (Lexington, 1960), 212-24, 353-64; Henry Hardin Cherry, 1931 speech, in Charles William Dabney, *Universal Education in the South*, 2 vols. (Chapel Hill, 1956), 2:365; Carl W. Kreisler, "Henry Hardin Cherry" (Ed.D. diss., Indiana University, 1964), 5-11; Ellis Ford Hartford, *The Little White Schoolhouse* (Lexington, 1977), *passim*.

14. H.V. McChesney, *Biennial Report of the Superintendent of Public Instruction of Kentucky, 1899-1901* (Louisville, 1901), 8-14, 345, 364-67, 406-9, 428-31, 434-35, 440-41, 457, 501.

15. *Twelfth Census: 1900: Population* (Washington, D.C., 1902), part 2, xcv, xcvii, c.

16. McChesney, *Biennial Report*, 345, 440-41, 444-45, 446-49, 454-55.

17. James H. Fuqua, *Biennial Report of the Superintendent of Public Instruction of Kentucky, 1905-1907* (Louisville, 1907), 22.

18. Cornette, *History of WKSTC*, 63.

19. Ibid., 63-65; Cherry Scrapbooks.

20. Cornette, *History of WKSTC*, 64-65.

21. Harman, *Brief Historical Sketch*, 6; *Southern Educator* (May 1905), 1; Cornette, *History of WKSTC*, 76-77.

22. Harman, *Brief Historical Sketch*, 9.

23. *Teachers College Heights* 13 (Nov. 1931), 13. They were printed often in Cherry's promotional literature.

24. "It's what's above the rim that counts" did not deal with rebounding on the basketball court, contrary to some beliefs.

25. H.H. Cherry speech manuscript, "Some of the Past and Present," in Cherry Papers, box 85: folder 4. It was probably given about 1931.

26. Cornette, *History of WKSTC*, 89-90.

27. Ibid., 89-92; *Southern Educator* (July 1889):2-8.

28. Cherry speech, "Some of the Past and Present"; Cornette, *History of WKSTC*, 81-85.

29. Cornette, *History of WKSTC*, 86-87; *Southern Educator* (Aug. 1906):3, (Nov. 1907):8.

30. Cornette, *History of WKSTC*, 87, 93; *Southern Educator* (July 1899):2-3.

31. Cornette interview with T.C. Cherry, March 31, 1938, in Cornette, *History of WKSTC*, 96.

32. *Southern Educator* (Jan. 1899):8; Lewis, *History of Higher Education*, 297.

33. Cornette, *History of WKSTC*, 70-72, 91-93. The tuition rates are listed in most of Cherry's promotional literature.

34. Cornette interview with J.R. Alexander, April 1, 1938, in Cornette, *History of WKSTC*, 92.

35. Bowling Green *Times-Journal*, May 12, 1901; *Daily News*, May 12, 1901.

36. Kelly Thompson, "Athletics at Western" (M.A. thesis, WKSTC, 1943), 3-4; *Herald*, March 6, 1953.

37. *Teachers College Heights* (Dec. 1938):33: Cherry to John R. Kirk, Kirksville, Mo., Feb. 14, 1931, Cherry Papers, box 18, GC 1931.

38. Harman, *Brief Historical Sketch*, 9; Bowling Green *Times-Journal*, June 7, 1901.

39. Harman, *Brief Historical Sketch*, 10. The 341-page volume was published in Bowling

Green by the Southern Educational Publishing Co., which was apparently Cherry's own imprint.

40. Silas Bent, "His Memorial Is Western State," *Courier-Journal Magazine* (Sept. 12, 1937):3; Sarah Thompson to author [mid-1982].

41. J. Lewie Harman, "Now and Then," *Elevator* 6 (Jan. 1915):135-36; H.L. Donovan, commencement address, Aug. 1, 1956, in H.L. and Nell S. Donovan Papers, Special Collections, Margaret I. King Library (University of Kentucky), Box 4.

42. Ligon, *History of Public Education*, 292; Cornette, *History of WKSTC*, 17-19.

43. Nicholas C. Burckel, "J.C.W. Beckham (1869-1940)", in Lowell H. Harrison, ed., *Kentucky's Governors* (Lexington, 1985), 115-18.

44. *Report of the Superintendent of Public Instruction, 1908-1909* (Frankfort, 1909), 335-36; Barksdale Hamlett, *History of Education in Kentucky* (Frankfort, 1914), 283.

45. Cornette, *History of WKSTC*, 19-20; Cherry's account of the founding, Cherry Papers: Box 85, folder 4, probably written about 1931.

46. Ligon, *History of Public Education*, 292-93. The Cherry Scrapbook for 1906-13 has a map on page 57 showing the original line. It was to be adjusted after census counts.

47. Cherry's account of the founding; *Teachers College Heights* (Nov. 1931):23.

48. Cornette, *History of WKSTC*, 107-8.

49. *State Normal Bulletin* (Feb. 1907):5-6; A.L. Crabb, "Founder's Day Address," Nov. 16, 1942, in A.L. Crabb Papers (Manuscript Division, Kentucky Library); J.R. Alexander, "Sketch of A.J. Kinnaman," *Teachers College Heights* (March 1934):29-30.

50. In 1918 the Board of Regents finally reimbursed Cherry for these advertising expenses. Cornette, *History of WKSTC*, 110.

51. Ligon, *History of Public Education*, 293; Harman, *Brief Historical Sketch*, 13-14; Cherry's account of the founding; *Teachers College Heights* (Nov. 1931):24.

2. The Normal Years

1. H.L. Donovan, "Autobiography," Donovan Papers (Special Collections, University of Kentucky), 1-5, 9, 26; H.L. Donovan to Kelly Thompson, June 17, 1958, Thompson Papers: box 16, D-GC. All references to the Donovan "Autobiography" are to volume 1.

2. Listed in Cornette, *History of WKSTC*, 111.

3. Oct. 9, 1966, Gordon Wilson Diaries, 1905-19, Gordon Wilson Collection (Manuscript Division, Kentucky Library); *Herald*, Oct. 27, 1944; Cornette, *History of WKSTC*, 91, 111; A.L. Crabb, "Founder's Day Address, Nov. 16, 1942."

4. *Herald*, April 7, 1944, Oct. 2, 1953; *Elevator* 5 (March 1914):249-50. He died on February 18, 1959.

5. Gordon Wilson Diary, Oct. 14, 1968; *Courier-Journal*, Aug. 5, 1954; A.M. Stickles, "Autobiography," in A.M. Stickles Collection (Manuscript Division, Kentucky Library); unidentified, undated transcript of interview with A.M. Stickles, probably early 1960s, Oral History Archives; Parker Liles to author, April 19, 1979.

6. James P. Cornette, *John Henry Clagett* ([n.p.], 1938), *passim*; A.L. Crabb, "Founders' Day Address, 1942," 9-10; Willson Wood, "Founders' Day Address," Nov. 14, 1975, in *Western Alumnus* 45 (Winter 1975-76):10; *Herald*, April 2, 1937.

7. Gordon Wilson Diary, June 4, 1963, March 9, 1964; A.M. Stickles, "Sketch of M.A. Leiper," *Teachers College Heights* (March 1935):26; Gordon Wilson, "Professor Leiper as a Teacher," in ibid., 26-27; A.L. Crabb, "Founders' Day Address, 1942," 10-11; Liles to author, April 19, 1979; John R. Cooper to author, May 19, 1979. Dr. Leiper died in Bowling Green on June 17, 1936.

8. A.L. Crabb, "Founders' Day Address, 1942," 12-13; A.L. Crabb, editorial, *Herald*, Oct. 21, 1949; *Daily News*, Aug. 10, 25, 1949. She died in Bowling Green on August 9, 1949.

9. *Teachers College Heights* 7 (Aug. 1924):10; Cornette *History of WKSTC*, 90.

10. Arthur Carlton White, Jr., "Professor Franz Joseph Strahm," April 26, 1982, in Alumni Papers: box 36J; Paul L. Garrett, "Strahm Memorial", Paul L. Garrett Papers: box 11; A.M. Stickles, "Tribute to Strahm, 1942," in Cherry Papers: box 60; Liles to author, April 19, 1979.

11. Algie Kinslow Pace, "Early Home Economics at Western," speech given at Iva Scott Club banquet in May 1957; *Herald*, March 1928; *Normal Heights* (July 1921)):2.

12. *Daily News*, Jan. 6, 1965; *Herald*, Oct. 11, 1935, Oct. 5, 1967.

13. *Herald*, Feb. 25, 1926, Nov. 7, 1947, Oct. 17, 1952.

14. Burton to Cherry, Nov. 23, 1911, Cherry Papers: box 1, GC 1911.

15. Burton W. Gorman, *Wit and Wisdom of Alonza Carroll Burton* ([n.p.], 1934), 11-19; Kelly Thompson interview, by Carlton Jackson, Oct. 26, 1977, Oral History Archives; H.H. Cherry to Superintendent J.R. Meador, Hardinsburg, Dec. 9, 1924, Cherry Papers: box 8, GC 1924; R.L. Robertson to author, April 11, 1979.

16. *Courier-Journal*, April 13, 1970; *Herald*, April 17, 1970; *Western Alumnus* 44 (Spring 1975):25; Marie Nunley, *Nashville: Beloved Hearth Stone: A Biography of Alford Leland Crabb* (privately printed, 1974), 130-31. A decade after his retirement Wilson wrote, "No other ten years have been any more active, any more enjoyable, any more filled with recognition by friends, and more productive of what I wanted to do." Miscellaneous item, Gordon Wilson Collection: box 3.

17. R.C. Roberts, "Life of Marion Commer Ford," Research in Education paper, summer 1941, George Peabody College, copy in Box 36I; M.C. Ford file, Cherry Papers: box 57.

18. Regents minutes, May 7, 1959; *Normal Heights* (Oct. 1922):1; Grise to H.H. Cherry, Aug. 25, 1924, Cherry Papers: box 7, GC, 1923-24; Gordon Wilson Diaries, Sept. 30, 1968. Dr. Grise died in October, 1973.

19. *Herald*, Oct. 2, 1942, Jan. 16, 1953. She died in early January 1953.

20. *Western Alumnus* 38 (Summer 1970):17; Gayle Carver interview, by Sara Tyler, [n.d.], early 1972, Oral History Archives.

21. *Daily News*, Jan. 7, 1983.

22. *Elevator* 7 (June 1916):287-91; *Teachers College Heights* (Oct. 1927):4; *Daily News*, Oct. 3, 1979. Dr. Crabb died at age 96 on Oct. 1, 1979.

23. *Herald Magazine*, Nov. 6, 1980:4-5. Mr. Page died in Bowling Green on March 5, 1985.

24. Cherry to President D.B. Waldo, Kalamazoo, Michigan, Jan. 8, 1917, Cherry Papers: box 26, SC-W; Cherry to Lucie Holeman, April 6, 1922, Cherry Papers: box 4, GC 1922; Strahm to Cherry, July 30, 1910, Cherry Papers: box 1, GC 1910; Stickles to R.E. Parker, Sept. 22, 1942, Cherry Papers: box 60, A.M. Stickles. Miss Holeman, who had taught in the Training School 1911-14, did not return in the 1920s.

25. Stickles chapel speech, Jan. 20, 1933, in *Herald*, Feb. 17, 1933.

26. Guilliams autobiographical sketch, in Cherry Papers: box 21, folder 6, 1934.

27. Cherry to Editor, Louisville *Evening Post*, Feb. 27, 1922, Cherry Papers: box 4, GC 1922; Cherry to Guilliams, Jasper, Florida, June 2, 1916, Cherry Papers: box 3, GC 1916.

28. Cherry, Financial Report to Regents, 1908-9, Cherry Papers: box 74, Report to Regents; Cherry to Nat B. Sewell, State Inspector and Examiner, April 6, 1916, Cherry Papers: box 2, GC 1916.

29. Cherry to Robertson, May 28, 1925, Cherry Papers: box 9, GC 1925; Cherry to Taylor, June 18, 1925: box 10, GC 1925; Cherry to Jewell T. Alexander, May 6, 1930, Cherry Papers: box 15, GC 1930.

30. Gordon Wilson, "Autobiography: My Educational Career," Gordon Wilson Collection: box 2, 112-13.

31. Strahm to Cherry, July 9, 1911, Cherry Papers: box 2, GC 1911.

32. Cornette, *History of WKSTC*, 122, 125-26; *Teachers College Heights* (April 1924):1.

33. Cornette, *History of WKSTC*, 121-24.

34. Donovan "Autobiography," 5-6; Donovan to Kelly Thompson, June 17, 1958, Kelly Thompson Papers, box 16: D-General.

35. Gordon Wilson Diary, May 30, 1959; Gordon Wilson speech, 1970 awards banquet, Gordon Wilson Collection: box 17.

36. Cornette, *History of WKSTC*, 112-13, 116-19.

37. *State Normal Bulletin, 1915*:17-18.

38. Regents minutes, Dec. 18, 1907; Cornette, *History of WKSTC*, 118-19. She taught in the Training School 1907-12.

39. Donovan, "Autobiography," 1-3; Cornette, *History of WKSTC*, 118-19.

40. Faculty minutes, Jan. 11, 24, Nov. 4, 1907.

41. *State Normal Bulletin, 1915*:20-41.

42. Burton to Cherry, Aug. 20, 1910, Cherry Papers: box 1, GC 1910; Kirk to Cherry, Nov. 11, 1907, Cherry Papers: box 1, GC 1907.

43. Gordon Wilson Diary, Jan. 19, 20, 1908.

44. Leiper to Cherry, Aug. 31, 1911, Cherry Papers: box 2, GC 1911.

45. H.L. Donovan, "Autobiography," 37-42.

46. Cherry's account of the founding of the school, 1931(?), Cherry Papers: box 85, folder 4. A longtime resident of Bowling Green and member of the Western faculty, Ward Sumpter had heard that the hill was named after an old woman, Betsy Vinegarhill, who had lived in a little cabin on the west slope in the nineteenth century. Ward Sumpter interview, by James D. Bennett, Dec. 15, 1976.

47. Lewis, *History of Higher Education*, 257-59; *Golden Rod*, 1908, the Potter College yearbook; *Potter College Catalog, 1908-1909*; *Herald*, April 1929; Catlettsburg (Ky.) *Central Methodist*, March 2, 1889, typescript in Kentucky Education Collections: box 22, Special Collections (University of Kentucky); *Lexington Leader*, Jan. 26, May 20, 1909. President Cabell died in September 1909. Western did not receive the Potter College records, which apparently just disappeared. Cherry to Ninna Gayle Palfrey, Oct. 13, 1913, Cherry Papers: box 2, GC 1913.

48. Cherry's account of the founding of the school, 1931(?), Cherry Papers: box 85, folder 4; *Acts of the General Assembly, 1912*, 148-50; Regents minutes, Sept. 9, 1912, Nov. 11, 1913; *House Journal* (March 2, 1912):1615, 1620; *Senate Journal* (Jan. 28, 1916):501, (March 14, 1916):3004; Lexington *Herald*, April 6, 1916.

49. Regents minutes, Aug. 25, 1909; Davis to Cherry, July 22, 1909, Cherry Papers: box 1, GC 1909; Ann Brown, " 'Those Good Old Days at Western' Recalled By Two Couples There," Madisonville *Messenger*, April 19, 1979; Jean Howerton Coady, "Brinton B. Davis: A Kentucky Name Written in Stone," *Courier-Journal*, Jan. 14, 1980. Davis died in 1952, age 90.

50. *Teachers College Heights* (Dec. 1936):20; Wright to Cherry, March 27, June 19, 1909, Cherry Papers: box 2, GC 1909. Wright worked closely with Western until his death in 1936.

51. Gordon Wilson Diary, Feb. 3, 1911; Gordon Wilson, "Diary to Kelly [Thompson]," May 21, 1965, Gordon Wilson Collection; *Elevator* 2 (March 1911):89; *State Normal Bulletin* (May 1911):1, 12. From May 14, 1959, to January 7, 1970, Wilson sent occasional "Notes about Western and its problems" to President Thompson whom he greatly admired. Wilson called the notes "Diary to Kelly."

52. *State Normal Bulletin* (May 1911):1; Sumpter interview, Dec. 15, 1976.

53. *State Normal Bulletin* (May 1911):1.

54. *Elevator* 2 (March 1911):89-90; account of moving day, Cherry Papers: Box 73, Moving Day, 1911. The formal dedication was on May 5. An annex for business offices was added in 1957. The main administration offices moved to Wetherby Administration Building in 1967.

55. Gordon Wilson, "Diary to Kelly," Dec. 14, 1967; Regents minutes, Sept. 11, 1918, March 21, 1919; *Normal Heights* (Aug. 1918):3 (Dec. 1918):1-2: Cherry to O.L. Cunningham, Hdq. SATC, Camp Grant, Ill., Nov. 2, 1918, Cherry Papers: box 3, GC 1918; Gordon Wilson Diary, Nov. 28, 1918.

56. L.Y. Lancaster interview, by Sara Tyler, April 11, 1973; Regents minutes, March 21, 1919, Sept. 27, 1924; materials on the barracks, Cherry Papers: box 85, folder 5; Gordon Wilson, "Diary to Kelly," June 21, 1962.

57. Potter Dormitory: Cherry Papers: box 3, GC 1920; Cherry to John H.C. Fritz, July 27, 1923, Cherry Papers: box 6, GC, 1923: Report to Regents on the dormitory, Nov. 18, 1920, Cherry Papers: box 74, Report to Regents; *Normal Heights* (Jan. 1921):1; *Herald*, July 16, 1925.

58. Faculty minutes, Jan. 30, 1921.

59. Cherry to George W. Cherry, June 8, 1922, Cherry Papers: box 76, PC, 1920-22; *Teachers College Heights* (June 1925):6; *Herald*, May 1928, May 23, 1941; Mattie McLean to Earl M. Bruce, Nov. 17, 1928, Cherry Papers: box 12, GC 1928; Report to the Regents, April 2, 1926, Cherry Papers: box 74; Building Report to the Council on Public Higher Education, 1957, Thompson Papers: box 15; *Daily News*, April 11, 1928, Aug. 12, 1976.

60. *Acts of the General Assembly*, 1920, 190-91.

61. Regents minutes, Nov. 19, 1920; Cherry to Roemer Bros. Lumber Co., Jan. 24, 1920, Cherry Papers: box 26, Ro; L.Y. Lancaster interview, by J. Crawford Crowe and Helen Crocker, Dec. 6, 1976.

62. Regents minutes, Nov. 19, 1920; Cherry to C.L. Clement, June 20, 1922, Cherry Papers: box 4, GC 1922; *Herald*, April 1928.

63. Cherry to G.F. Barnes, Feb. 17, 1922, Cherry Papers: box 3, GC 1920.

64. *Herald*, Dec. 1926, Jan. 1927, Jan. 1929; Minutes of Senior Class, July 9, 1920, Aug. 9, 1921, in Marjorie Clagett Collection (Manuscript Division, Kentucky Library), box 13; *Normal Heights* (Nov. 1921):2; Regents minutes, Dec. 30, 1919, Nov. 19, 1920; faculty minutes, Sept. 22, 1919.

65. Donovan, "Autobiography," 36-37.

66. Gordon Wilson, "Diary to Kelly," Dec. 15, 1967.

67. *Elevator* 2 (Oct. 1911)):256-57; Cornette, *History of WKSTC*, 131-35; *State Normal Bulletin* (November 1913):4-5; faculty minutes, Nov. 20, 1922.

68. *Elevator* 4 (April 1913):193-95; 5 (May 1914):332-36. Cherry's volume was used as a textbook for years in the public schools.

69. Cherry biography, Cherry Papers: box 77; *State Normal Bulletin* (Aug. 1908):29; Sumpter interview, Dec. 15, 1979; Tom Ellis interview, by James D. Bennett, July 11, 1978.

70. Cherry to John W. Cherry, Oct. 20, 1911, Cherry Papers: box 76, PC 1909-12; Cherry to T.B. Logan, March 8, 1918, Cherry Papers: box 3, GC 1918; Cherry to Ball State Teachers College, Muncie, Indiana, March 27, 1925, Cherry Papers: box 9, GC 1925; J.W. Compton to Cherry, May 17, 1926, Cherry Papers: box 10, GC 1926; H.L. Donovan, "Autobiography," 21; Robertson to author, April 11, 1979.

71. Faculty minutes, Dec. 2, 1918; Cherry to J.R. Alexander, July 2, 1918, Cherry Papers: box 3, GC 1918; Gordon Wilson Diaries, March 14, 1917; *State Normal Bulletin* (Feb. 1913):46

72. *Elevator* 2 (Dec. 1910):32; Gordon Wilson Diaries, Nov. 7, 1911, March 18, 1912.

73. A.M. Stickles eulogy, Cherry Papers: box 60, A.M. Stickles, 1942.

74. *State Normal Bulletin* (Aug. 1912):12; *Elevator* 5 (Feb. 1914):186.

75. A.L. Crabb, "Founders' Day Address, 1942," 12-13; *State Normal Bulletin* (Aug. 1907):28, (May 1911):21; Margie Helm and others, "History of the Libraries, 1907-1967," 1-5; Cornette, *History of WKSTC*, 160; Florence Ragland to Andrew Carnegie, Jan. 26, 1912, Cherry Papers: box 2, GC 1912.

76. Faculty minutes, Sept. 10, 1919, April 6, 1923. Miss Ragland resigned as head librarian in 1923 because of ill health, then taught in the English department until retirement in 1930. Miss Margie Helm succeeded her as head librarian. Helm, "History of the Libraries," 5.

77. Nancy Disher Baird, Carol Crowe-Carraco, and Michael L. Morse, *Bowling Green: A Pictorial History* (Norfolk, Va., 1983), 73; H.L. Donovan, "Autobiography," 6-7, 18-20; Nels P. Sorensen to author, April 20, 1979.

78. *Elevator* 3 (Oct. 1912):259-62.
79. *State Normal Bulletin* (Aug. 1908):29.
80. Faculty minutes, Feb. 3, 24, 1913, Jan. 4, 1915.
81. Mrs. J.A. Harding to Mrs. R.P. Green, [n.d.], 1913; George F. Roser to R.P. Green, June 12, 1913; Green to Roser, June 23, 1913; Cherry to Roser, June 3, 1913, all in Cherry Papers: box 2, GC 1913.
82. Cherry to J.J. Squire, Jan. 16, 1913, Cherry Papers: box 2, GC 1913; H.H. Lilly to Cherry, Nov. 25, Dec. 1, 1907, Cherry Papers: box 1, GC 1907.
83. *State Normal Bulletin* (Nov. 1913):23; Cherry to John W. Cherry, Feb. 12, 20, 1912, Cherry Papers: box 76, PC 1913-14. Nephew John dropped out of school.
84. Gordon Wilson, "Diary to Kelly," Dec. 16, 1967.
85. Sumpter interview, Dec. 15, 1976.
86. Gordon Wilson Diaries, Oct. 27, 1911.
87. Ibid., May 7, 1909. See also *Elevator* 5 (June 1914):380-82, and *Herald*, July 30, 1925.
88. Gordon Wilson Diaries, March 24, 1911.
89. Cornette, *History of WKSTC*, 134-36.
90. *Elevator* 1 (Nov. 1909):7; *State Normal Bulletin* (Aug. 1910):11; Cornette, *History of WKSTC*, 138, 140; Cherry to Edwin D. Thompson, Aug. 16, 1916, Cherry Papers: box 3, GC 1917. Copies of the *Vista* are in the university archives.
91. Faculty minutes, Feb. 21, 1910.
92. *Elevator* 1 (May 1910):4-5, (July 1910)):24. Greer's first name was not given.
93. *Elevator* 2 (June 1911):179, 3 (May 1912):137; G.H. Reams to E.M. Murphy, March 26, 1912, Athletic Committee papers, 1931-55. Murphy, apparently the coach at Bethel College in Russellville, wanted to schedule a game. Reams, at Western only a short time, had played baseball at the State University. In 1913 student Victor Strahm was coach. *Elevator* 4 (April 1913):242.
94. Mutchler to Barker, March 17, 1913, Cherry Papers: box 2, GC 1912; Cherry to Marvin Allen, March 3, 1916, Cherry Papers: box 3, GC 1916.
95. *State Normal Bulletin* (Catalog number, 1915):3; *Elevator* 7 (June 1916):305-6.
96. *Elevator* 7 (Dec. 1915):99.
97. *State Normal Bulletin* (Nov. 1913):8; *Elevator* 6 (Feb. 1915):218.
98. Cherry to Herbert Woodruff, Jan. 31, 1920, Cherry Papers: box 26, SC Wo; *Normal Heights* (April 1922):6.
99. *Elevator* 6 (March 1915):269-70, (June 1915):403-4; faculty minutes, June 24, 1913.
100. *Elevator* 6 (March 1915):269-70, (June 1915):396; faculty minutes, Dec. 4, 1916; Mary T. Moore, "Girls' Basketball at Western," radio program notes for Feb. 20, 1953, Mary T. Moore Collection (Manuscript Division, Kentucky Library), item 35; *Herald*, March 6, 1953.
101. *State Normal Bulletin* ([n.d.] 1915):22; O.G. Byrn to Ben H. Bernard, Eastern State Normal, Jan. 22, 1917, Business Office Records: Athletic Records: 1909-55; Cherry to J. Coates, March 5, 1920 Cherry Papers: box 3; *Acts of the General Assembly, 1920*, 190-91.
102. M.A. Leiper to E.E. Bratcher, Nov. 8, 1920, Cherry Papers: box 5, GC 1923; faculty minutes, Dec. 12, 1921.
103. Mary C. Roark to Cherry, April 23, 1909, Cherry Papers: box 1, GC 1909; Ward C. Sumpter interview, by O.J. Wilson, March 8, 1967.
104. Cherry to W.M. Pearce, Oct. 7, 1913, Cherry Papers: box 2, GC 1913; Sumpter interview, March 8, 1967; faculty minutes, Dec. 7, 1925; Kinnaman to Virgil Chapman, March 3, 1916, Dean of the Faculties: Kinnaman Correspondence.
105. E.A. Diddle, quoted in Kreisler, "Henry Hardin Cherry," 29; Cherry to Fred W. Chunn, Nov. 29, 1911, Cherry Papers: box 1, GC 1911; Cherry to Mrs. H.H. Cherry, Daytona Beach, Florida, Feb. 25, 1918, Cherry Papers: box 76, PC 1917-21; Cherry to George W. Cherry, March 7, 1917, in ibid.
106. Cherry to Josephine Cherry, May 17, 1919, Cherry Papers: box 76, PC 1917-21;

Cherry to St. Louis Sash and Door Works, Dec. 8, 1919, in ibid.; Cornette, *History of WKSTC*, 168, 170. The 1931 contract for the president's house was $26,050.00

107. Sketch of H.H. Cherry by W.J. Craig, [1931?], Cherry Papers: box 77, Biography; Harman, *Brief History of BGBU*, 26; Cherry to A.S. McKenzie, Oct. 11, 1919, Cherry Papers: box 3, GC 1919; Cherry to George W. Cherry, Jan. 8, 1922, Cherry Papers: box 76, PC 1920-22; A.L. Crabb, "Founders' Day Address, 1942"; *Normal Heights* (Aug. 1919):1; James H. Poteet interview, by Lowell H. Harrison, Aug. 20, 1981.

108. Cherry to J.M. Guilliams, July 2, 1914, Cherry Papers: box 2, GC 1914; Cherry to Lucas Brodhead, Jan. 5, 1914, in ibid.; Regent H.K. Cole to Cherry, May 10, 1913, in ibid., GC 1913; Cherry to Mrs. J.W. Cherry, Aug. 3, 1910, Cherry Papers: box 85, Addresses and Chapel Talks, 4.

109. Faculty minutes, July 24, 1934; Roberts, "Life of Ford," 15-16, 26-29.

110. Cherry to L.C. Guffey, June 22, 1925, Cherry Papers: box 9, GC 1925; Copy Letters, Cherry Papers: box 77.

111. *State Normal Bulletin* (Nov. 1913):26. The Cherry Papers contain a considerable mass of correspondence concerning this program. See especially boxes 2, 78, 85.

112. *Teachers College Heights* (April 1927):6; Bowling Green *Times-Journal*, June 20, 1929; *Herald*, June 1930.

113. Gordon Wilson Diaries, Feb. 16-23, 1917; *Normal Heights* (April 1917):22, 34; *Teacher College Heights* (July 1937):24.

114. *Elevator* 3 (Dec. 1911):36-37; Baird, Crowe-Carraco, Morse, *Bowling Green*, 82.

115. Kelly Thompson interview, by Carlton Jackson, Oct. 26, 1976; J.L. Harman, "The Founder: Dr. Henry Hardin Cherry," Harman Papers; Cherry to Leslie Brown, May 3, 1918, Cherry Papers: box 3, GC 1918; Cherry to George P. Potter, Oct. 27, 1917, in ibid., GC 1917; Cherry to C.A. Singer, April 30, 1923, in ibid.; box 7, GC 1923-24.

116. Harman, "Founder," 7; Poteet interview, May 26, 1976.

117. *Herald*, April 28, 1965; H.P. Endsley to Cherry, Nov. 11, 1927, Cherry Papers: box 10, GC 1926; W.C. Dickey to Cherry, May 7, 1932, Cherry Papers: box 19, GC 1932; Cherry to Mrs. Adelia Cherry Ward, Jan. 20, 1931, Cherry Papers: box 18, GC 1931. The Cherry Papers contain numerous examples of articles lost and bills paid late.

118. Cherry to S. Walton Forgy, Dec. 2, 1911, Cherry Papers: box 1, GC 1911; Cherry to Mrs. Pearl Hindman Harris, Sept. 8, 1914, in ibid.: box 2, GC 1914; Cherry to Rev. J.T. Cherry, March 11, 1914, in ibid.: box 76, PC 1913-14; *Daily News*, March 31, 1914.

119. *Elevator* 6 (Feb. 1915):202-3; Louisville *Evening Post*, April 5, 1915; Regents minutes, January 12, 19, 1915.

120. Regents minutes, May 19, 1915; Chelf, "Politics of Higher Education," 179-92; Cherry to Tom T. McBreath, June 23, 1915, Cherry Papers: box 2, GC 1915.

121. Cherry to Laura Frazee, Nov. 9, 1915, Cherry Papers: box 3, GC 1915; Cherry to G.C. Woodson, Oct. 16, 1918, in ibid.: box 26, SC Wo; Carl P. Chelf, "H.H. Cherry: The Educator Politician," typescript, Cherry Papers: box 77, 21-30; *Daily News*, April 8, 1919; *Courier-Journal*, April 8, 1919.

122. James F. Hopkins, *The University of Kentucky: Origins and Early Years* (Lexington, 1951), 211-16, 248-60; Cherry to J.W. Cherry, March 13, 1912, Cherry Papers: box 76, PC 1913-14; Cherry to A.W. Mell, March 22, 1912, in ibid.: box 2, GC.

123. Barker to Cherry, May 24, Oct. 18, 1911, Cherry Papers: box 77; Cornette, *History of WKSTC*, 157; Gordon Wilson, "Diary to Kelly," June 9, 1963.

124. Numerous examples of Crabb's concerns are in the Cherry Papers: box 2, GC 1914-15. See also, Cherry to Coates, Sept. 7, 1916: Cherry Papers: box 3, GC 1916; *Herald*, Oct. 1928.

125. Cherry to Diddle, May 13, 1936; Diddle to Cherry [n.d.]; Cherry to Ford, May 4, 1936; Ford to Cherry, May 4, 1936, all in A.L. Crabb Collection: box 9. Craig pointed out that he was a member of the Bowling Green University of Kentucky Alumni Club.

126. Harman, "Founder," 6; Donovan, "Autobiography," 20; J. Lewie Harman, Sr.,

Speech at Dedication of Cherry Statue, Harman Papers: Speeches; Cherry to J.A. Oaks, March 9, 1920, Cherry Papers: box 4, GC 1920.

3. ... And Teachers College

1. Normal Executive Council Minutes, May 22, 1926; *Christian Science Monitor*, undated clipping, 1922; Ligon, *Public Education*, 216-23.

2. Cherry to Haswell, Nov. 10, 11, 1921, Cherry Papers: box 4, GC 1921; Regents minutes, Nov. 19, 1921; Cherry to White, Dec. 20, 1921, Cherry Papers: box 26, SC, Wh.

3. Cherry to E.M. Highsmith, July 3, 1922, Cherry Papers: box 4, GC 1922; Cherry to A.W. Mell, Oct. 10, 1922, Cherry Papers: box 5, GC 1922; Chelf, "Politics of Higher Education," 204; Cora M. Morehead to Cherry, May 31, 1924, Cherry Papers: box 8, GC 1924; *Acts of the General Assembly, 1922*, 51-52, 97; A.M. Wilson to Cherry, July 20, 1925, Cherry Papers: box 10, GC 1925.

4. Faculty minutes, April 17, 1922; Cherry to D.W. Boitnott, March 23, 1922, Cherry Papers: box 4, GC 1922; Cherry to D.W.C. Bagley, June 12, 1922, in ibid.

5. *Teachers College Heights* (March 1934):29-30; *Herald*, Jan. 28, 1926; Cherry to Mattie L. Hatcher, Jan. 7, 1926, Cherry Papers: box 10, GC 1926.

6. *Normal Heights* (Aug. 1922):1; (Oct. 1922):4; Regents minutes, June 4, 1925; *Teachers College Heights* (June 1925):8; Cherry to Josephine Cherry, Oct. 12, 1922, Cherry Papers: box 76, PC 1920-23; Cherry to Gamble, Nov. 6, 1933, Cherry Papers: box 20, GC 1933.

7. Cherry to A.L. Crabb, June 17, 1925, Cherry Papers: box 9, GC 1925.

8. *Teachers College Heights* (Oct. 1927):4; Cherry to Crabb, July 30, 1924, Cherry Papers: box 7, GC 1923-24; *Herald*, June 1927.

9. *Western Alumnus* 43 (Winter 1973-74):40: Gordon Wilson, "Diary to Kelly," Sept. 30, 1968; James H. Poteet to author, Aug. 20, 1981; Grise to Sybil Stonecipher, Jan. 30, 1934, F.C. Grice Correspondence; Paul Cook interview, by Lowell H. Harrison, Aug. 2, 1985.

10. Cherry to Canon, May 2, 1925, Office of the Registrar Papers; Dero G. Downing interview, by James D. Bennett, March 22, 1978; Murray *Ledger & Times*, Oct. 13, 1977; A.L. Crabb, "An Ode to a Half Century" speech, Thompson Papers: box 14, C-General.

11. *Herald*, Oct. 19, 1956, Feb. 3, 1959; Georgia Bates interview, by James D. Bennett, Dec. 1, 1977.

12. Cornette, *History of WKSTC*, 174-76; Cherry to A.W. Mell, Oct. 10, 1922, Cherry Papers: box 5, GC 1922.

13. Cherry to Henry James, Jan. 20, 1921, Cherry Papers: box 6, GC 1923.

14. Cherry to J.W. Guilliams, July 24, 1921, Cherry Papers: box 26, SC 1922-31; Cherry to H.W. Lay, June 27, 1922, in ibid.: box 5, GC 1922; Cherry to J. Brown, July 18, 1923, in ibid., GC 1923.

15. Cornette, *History of WKSTC*, 179; Cherry to J.R. Coleman, Aug. 18, 1924, Cherry Papers: box 7, GC 1923-24; Cherry to L.P. Jones, Feb. 20, 1928, in ibid., box 13, GC 1928. Cherry was upset by a rumor that Murray was cutting rates.

16. *Acts of the General Assembly, 1924*, 109-20; *1926*, 297-301; Ligon, *History of Public Education*, 228-29.

17. Some required courses and minor exceptions have been omitted. A foreign language was not required for agriculture and home economics majors. The certificates and degree requirements are in the *Teachers College Heights, Catalog Number, 1930-1931* (Aug. 1930):61-80.

18. Board of Regents minutes, Feb. 23, 1930; faculty minutes, Feb. 16, 1931; C.P. McNally to Cherry, Dec. 2, 1930, Cherry Papers: box 18, GC 1931; Neal Calhoun to Charles W. Sisk, March 5, 1975, L.Y. Lancaster Papers; Richard F. Grise tribute, *Western Alumnus* 45 (Winter 1975-76):3; *Herald*, Feb. 1931, March 6, 1936; Tim Lee Carter interview, by Carl P. Chelf, Oct. 21, 1981.

19. Cornette, *History of WKSTC*, 154-56, 158; *Catalog, 1920-1921*, 14-16, 18; *Acts of the General Assembly, 1918*, 12-15; Faculty minutes, Oct. 11, 1920; Cherry to George N. Crowell, Oct. 2, 1922, Cherry Papers: box 4, GC 1922.

20. Quoted in Chelf, "Politics in Education," 206.

21. Cherry to George W. Cherry, June 8, 1922, Cherry Papers: box 76, PC 1920-22; Cherry to Henry Wright, June 2, 1922, ibid.: box 5, GC 1922.

22. Cherry to McHenry Rhoads, Jan. 15, 1923, Cherry Papers: box 7, GC 1923; Cherry to R.E. Williams, Jan. 26, 1924, in ibid: box 8, GC 1924; Cherry to A.L. Crabb, Feb. 20, 1924, in ibid.: box 7, GC 1923-24; Cherry to J.B. Walters, in ibid.: box 8, GC 1924; Cherry to Mrs. A.T. Hert, May 24, 1924, in ibid.: box 7, GC 1923-24; Cherry. "Some of the Past and Present," in ibid.: box 85, folder 4; Cherry to F.L. Whitney, Nov. 12, 1924, in ibid.: box 8, GC 1924.

23. Cherry to James A. Barnes, April 7, 1926, Cherry Papers: box 10, GC 1926; Cornette, *History of WKSTC*, 163-66. See especially tables 19 and 20 in Cornette.

24. *Talisman, 1924*, 122; *Daily News*, Jan. 23, 1923, Nov. 11, 1924; *Pioneer*, Dec. 1922; Cherry Papers: box 6, Federal BD BOYS folder.

25. *Teachers College Heights, Catalog Number 1930-31*, 58; Lancaster interview, Dec. 6, 1976; Regents minutes, Nov. 18, 1920, April 3, 1923.

26. Cornette, *History of WKSTC*, 166, 167.

27. Cherry to Bowling Green Board of Education, June 7, 1918, Training School Miscellany; Regents minutes, Nov. 19, 1920; Cherry to H.P Jarrett, Nov. 22, 1924, Cherry Papers: box 8, GC 1924-25; *Daily News*, Oct. 30, 1925, March 27, 1926.

28. *Normal Heights* (Feb. 1920):1-2; Bowling Green *News-Democrat-Messenger*, Feb. 15, 1924; Kelly Thompson to Mae Wilson Pedigo, Aug. 2, 1975, Thompson Papers: Box 24, Rural School; Mae Wilson Pedigo, "The Rural Training School," in Rural Training School, Box 3.

29. *Normal Heights* (Dec. 1918):8; Faculty minutes, Sept. 10, 1919; Regents minutes, Nov. 19, 1920; *Herald*, May 7, 1925.

30. Helm, "History of the Libraries," 1-3; *Normal Heights* (April 1923):1, 3; Regents minutes, April 2, 1926.

31. *Herald*, July 1, 1926, Jan. 1928; Jan. 31, 1939; *Daily News*, June 12, 1926, Feb. 4, 1928; Arndt M. Stickles, "A Confederate Fort and Historical Marker on the Western Kentucky State College Campus," *Filson Club History Quarterly* 39 (Oct. 1965):326-30.

32. *Teachers College Heights* (Oct. 1924):1; *Daily News*, Jan. 3, May 11, 1928; *Herald*, July 1928.

33. *Daily News*, March 29, 1927; *Herald*, March 1927; *Teachers College Heights* (July 1927):1, (Sept. 1926):3.

34. *Daily News*, March 27, 1926, April 4, Sept. 28, 1927; Regents minutes, April 2, 1926, April 29, 1927; *Teachers College Heights* (July 1926):1,6; *Herald*, Oct. 1927, March 27, 1939.

35. *Daily News*, Sept. 28, 1927.

36. Regents minutes, June 3, 1926; *Daily News*, Aug. 23, 1926; *Herald*, Jan. 31, Feb. 10, 1939; *Talisman, 1949*, 8.

37. *Herald*, May 1928; *Teachers College Heights* (Jan. 1929):2, 3.

38. Regents minutes, April 14, May 9, 1930; Cherry to Henry Clay Anderson, March 25, April 11, 1930, Cherry Papers: box 15, GC 1930; *Herald*, Feb. 1931.

39. *Herald*, July, Nov. 1928, Nov. 1930; *Daily News*, Oct. 15, 1928; Regents minutes, June 3, July 7, 1931; *Teachers College Heights* (Nov. 1931):33.

40. Minutes of 25th Anniversary Committee, July 25, 1931, Cherry Papers: box 83A; *Teachers College Heights* (April 1937), 32.

41. *Elevator* 1 (April 1910):9; *Normal Heights* (Oct. 1922):2; Cherry, "Report to Regents," April 16, 1924, Cherry Papers: box 74; *Daily News*, Jan. 27, 31, Sept. 18, 1927; *Herald*, Jan. 1927; Business Office, Farm Reports, 1920-28, Bursar Papers: box 25D.

42. Regents minutes, Nov. 16, 1929; Griffenhagen Report, 1933, 94; *Herald*, Jan. 16, 1948.

43. Jesse B. Johnson and Lowell H. Harrison, "Ogden College: A Brief History," *Register of the Kentucky Historical Society* 68 (July 1970):189-220; Don Armstrong, "Ogden College: A Report," *Western Alumnus* 47 (Winter 1976-77):6-7. The University Archives contains extensive materials on Ogden College. The Ogden farm, on part of which the Fairview Shopping Center is located, was sold in 1945 for fifty thousand dollars. Regents minutes, Aug. 25, 1945.

44. Griffenhagen Report, 1933, 89; Cherry to Cuthbertson, Sept. 20, 1933, Cherry Papers: box 20, GC 1933; Cherry to H.L. Donovan, Sept. 25, 1933, in ibid.

45. Wilson, "Diary to Kelly," Nov. 19, 1968; Carver interview, typescript, 34-37; Carver, "The Kentucky Library and Museum, 1950." Many of her collecting letters are in the Cherry Papers: box 59, G. Robertson.

46. Donovan, "Autobiography," 14-16; Pamphlet, *Information Concerning the College Heights Foundation, 1923-1925*, 10; Cherry to Lalla R. Boone, Sept. 19, 1922, Cherry Papers: box 4, GC 1922.

47. *Teachers College Heights* (Aug. 1923):2-4, 22-34, (Aug. 1924):8; *Daily News*, April 3, 1923; Regents minutes, April 6, 1923, Jan. 12, 1924; Cherry to Thomas Logan, June 6, 1924, Cherry Papers: box 8, GC 1924; Cherry to Mary McGimsey, June 26, 1925, in ibid.: box 9, GC 1925; Cherry to J.F. Lippard, March 5, 1928, in ibid.: box 71, Kentucky Building Campaign.

48. *Daily News*, Oct. 6, 1925; *Teachers College Heights* (Sept. 1926):2-3; College Heights Foundation, Treasurer's Annual Report, Oct. 3, 1938, 14.

49. Regents minutes, April 2, 1926; *Teachers College Heights* (Aug. 1928):2-5 (June 1929):11; *Daily News*, Oct. 26, 1928; W.B. Hill to Cherry, March 25, 1929, Cherry Papers: box 14, GC 1929.

50. Cherry to Mrs. H.H. Cherry, March 8, 13, 1930, Cherry Papers: box 76, PC 1923-30; Cherry to Henry Clay Anderson, Sept. 29, 1930, in ibid.: box 15, GC 1930; *Herald*, July 1930; Regents minutes, April 16, 1931; Laib & Co. to R.H. Seward, Nov. 4, 1931, College Heights Foundation Miscellaneous Records, 1924-49; Seward to Logan & Co., Dec. 23, 1931, in ibid.; Gene Ferrell to Cherry, April 18, 1931, in ibid.; Barrett to WKSTC, April 22, 1931, in ibid.; Grainger and Co. to Captain Brinton B. Davis, April 22, 1931, in ibid.

51. Cherry to Henry Clay Anderson, July 27, 1931, Cherry Papers: box 17, GC 1931; *Herald*, Jan. 28, 1933; *Teachers College Heights* (Dec. 1934):18.

52. Cornette, *History of WKSTC*, 177; Cherry to Helm, Jan. 14, 1928, Cherry Papers: box 12, GC 1928. There is no all time student equivalent figure available for 1922-23.

53. *Herald*, Dec. 1926, March, April, 1930; Helm, "History of the Libraries," 3-4.

54. Vera Grinstead and Imogene Simpson, "Library Service at Western Kentucky University," Libraries: History, 1909-72.

55. Cornette, *History of WKSTC*, 189-95.

56. Cherry to Mrs. R.E. Overton, Oct. 12, 1922; Mrs. Overton to Cherry, Oct. 19, 1922, Cherry Papers: box 5, GC 1922; Sumpter interview, Dec. 15, 1976.

57. Ted Hornback interview, by J. Crawford Crowe and Lowell H. Harrison, Nov. 4, 1976; Dean Grise memos, after conversations with President Cherry, Oct. 23, Nov. 9, 1929, Grise Correspondence; Cherry to Col. Guilliams, June 12, 1922, Cherry Papers: box 4, GC 1922.

58. *Teachers College Heights* (Nov. 1931):63; Wilson, "Diary to Kelly," Dec. 9, 1967.

59. Cornette, *History of WKSTC*, 197-99; *Teachers College Heights* (July 1936):4 ff.; Faculty minutes, Feb. 17, 1925, Jan. 10, 1934; Congress Debating Club minutes, introduction, 1-2.

60. *Teachers College Heights* (Dec. 1938):33; Grise to Cherry, Nov. 10, 19300, Grise Correspondence, A-Co; Cherry to John R. Kirk, Feb. 14, 1931, Cherry Papers: box 18, GC 1931.

61. University Events: Homecoming 1927; *Herald*, Nov. 1927; *Teachers College Heights* (Nov. 1932):11.

62. Frances Richards interview, by James D. Bennett and Lowell H. Harrison, Dec. 14, 1977; *Teachers College Heights* (June 1925):6, (Nov. 1926):2, (July 1932):9; *Herald*, March 11, 1926, March 1930; *Daily News*, May 24, 1927.

63. *Teachers College Heights* (Aug. 1924):5; *Daily News*, April 17, 1926, Jan. 28, 1927; *Herald*, Aug. 1927.

64. Faculty minutes, Dec. 2, 1918, April 14, 1919; Regents minutes, Feb. 22, 1919, March 20, 1937; *Normal Heights* (Dec. 1919):3, (June 1920):2; *Teachers College Heights* (Sept. 1933):11.

65. *Herald*, Oct. 11, 1974; *Daily News*, Sept. 3, 1976.

66. Cherry to "Dittle," May 26, June 6, 1922, Cherry Papers: box 4, GC 1922; Smith to Diddle, June 6, 1922, in ibid.; Ellis interview, July 11, 1978; Ted Hornback interview, Nov. 4, 1976; Dero G. Downing interview, by James D. Bennett, April 3, 1978. The statistics were compiled from the results kept by the Sports Information Office.

67. Unidentified clipping, Cherry Scrapbooks, General 1924-29; *Talisman, 1927*; *Herald*, Nov. 1927, Oct. 1929; Cherry Scrapbooks, Athletics, 1929-30; *Hilltopper Football: 1983*, Press Guide, 27.

68. *Herald*, Oct. 1929; *Daily News*, Dec. 5, 1930; Bowling Green *Times-Journal*, Dec. 6, 1930.

69. Cherry, Report to Regents, June 30, 1929, Cherry Papers: box 74; *Herald*, Oct. 1927, March 1929, May 1930, May 24, 1935.

70. *Normal Heights* (Jan. 1922):3, (April 1922):5; *Talisman, 1924-1931*.

71. Faculty minutes, Jan. 20, 1925; *Herald*, Jan. 1927, Jan. 1931.

72. F.E. Cooper to Cherry, Jan. 17, 1927, Cherry Papers: box 12, GC 1927; Cherry to Cooper, Jan. 26, 1927, in ibid.; Cherry to A.L. Crabb, Sept. 30, 1935, in ibid.: box 23, GC 1935.

73. *Herald*, March 12, 1925, Nov. 2, 1978; Don Armstrong, "Where the Spirit Originates," *Western Alumnus* 44 (Winter 1974-75):12, 18-19: *Talisman, 1956*, 50; *Teachers College Heights* (Feb. 1930):1. The school colors were changed to red and white in 1956. Regents minutes, Dec. 19, 1956.

4. End of an Era

1. Based on *Catalog, 1930-31* and *1937-1938, 1938-1939* (combined in one).

2. Cornette, *History of WKSTC*, 180-81.

3. *Catalog, 1935-1936*; *Catalog, 1937-1938, 1938-1939*, 73-98.

4. Donovan's speech to registrars, April 5, 1929, Donovan Collection: box 8; Donovan to Cherry, May 3, 1931, Cherry Papers: box 18, GC 1931.

5. Regents minutes, April 16, June 3, 1931; faculty minutes, April 20, May 12, 1931; *Teachers College Heights* (July 1931):2-3; William H. Vaughn to Grise, Dec. 23, 1931, Grise Correspondence, General, 1931; Cherry Papers: box 73, Graduate Work folder.

6. *Catalog, 1931-1932*, 85-91; *Catalog, 1933-1934, 1934-1935*, 90-96; "A Brief Resumé of Graduate Work," Grise Correspondence, 1931-36, F-KEA, 4, 7.

7. Griffenhagen & Associates, "Report on Kentucky's Education, 1933," 48-52; Secretary M.C. Huntley to Cherry, Dec. 22, 1933, Grise Correspondence, 1931-36, KEA's; Cherry to Huntley, Oct. 3, 1934, in ibid.

8. Charles H. White, "The Kentucky Council on Public Higher Education: An Analysis of a Change in Structure" (Ph.D. diss., Ohio State University, 1967), 67-70; Frank Steve Barkovich, "The Kentucky Council on Public Higher Education" (M.A. thesis, University of Louisville, 1970), 17-18; Normal Executive Council minutes, March 25, 1927; McVey memo, undated, 1933-34(?), McVey Papers: box 37, folder 12. The McVey memo outlined the provisions for the act much as they appeared in its final form.

9. Adron Doran, "The Work of the Council on Public Higher Education in Kentucky"

(Ed.D. diss., University of Kentucky, 1950), 54-65, 77-78, 80-84, 86, 89, 92-96, 123-25, 146, 152; White, "Council on Public Higher Education," 70-71.

10. Cherry to Lida Lee Tall, [n.d., 1932], Cherry Papers: box 19, GC 1932; Cherry to Raimey T. Wells, Jan. 2, 17, 27, 30, Feb. 6, 1933, in ibid.: box 20, GC 1933; Donovan to Cherry, May 14, 1935; Cherry to Donovan, [n.d., May, 1935], in ibid.: box 23, GC 1935.

11. Minutes of Council of Public Higher Education, March 24, Nov. 24, 1936; Dean Grise to Governor Chandler, April 9, 1936, Chandler Papers: box 86 (Special Collections, University of Kentucky); Pentecost to Cherry, June 17, 1936, Cherry Papers: box 24, GC 1936.

12. Cherry to J.C. Howard, Dec. 30, 1936, Cherry Papers: box 24, GC 1936; Cherry to Guilliams, June 27, 1936, in ibid.; Cherry to Grise, July 10, 1937, in ibid.: box 25, GC 1937.

13. Table 19 in Cornette, *History of WKSTC*, 194.

14. H.L. Donovan, "I Remember Eastern," Donovan Papers: box 1, 56-59.

15. Cherry to O.L. Shutz, Jan. 18, 1932, Cherry Papers: box 19, GC 1932; faculty minutes, April 11, 1892; Regents minutes, April 14, 1932; Cherry to George W. Cherry, April 28, 1932, Cherry Papers: box 76, PC 1931-33.

16. Cherry's report, Regents minutes, July 1, 1933; Cherry to E.H. Canon, July 28, 1933, Cherry Papers: box 20, GC 1933; Day to Cherry, April 28, 1932, in ibid.: box 19, GC 1932; Stickles to John A. Coffin, Jan. 18, 1932, in ibid.: box 59, A.M. Stickles 1931-36; Sewell's report to Governor Ruby Laffoon, in Bowling Green *Times-Journal*, April 29, 1933; Cherry to W.H. Fraysure, Jan. 8, 1932, Cherry Papers: box 19, GC 1932; Faculty minutes, April 30, 1934.

17. Salary list, 1934-35, Cherry Papers: box 73, Salaries List, 1935-36; Paul L. Garrett to President William H. Vaughn, Morehead, July 6, 1943, Garrett Papers: box 4, 1941-46,V; Gordon Wilson, "Diaries to Kelly," May 21, 1969; Cornette to author, Feb. 24, 1984.

18. Cherry to Estell Fakes, Oct. 28, 1932, Cherry Papers: box 19, GC 1932; *Teachers College Heights* (Feb. 1927):4; Griffenhagen Report, 1933, 43; Cherry to State Auditor J. Dan Talbot, Dec. 17, 1935, Cherry Papers: box 24, GC 1935; Cherry to Ida Cozart, March 30, 1933, in ibid.: box 20, GC 1933; Cherry's report to Regents, May 25, 1936.

19. Breckinridge County Superintendent Marshall Norton to Cherry, Jan. 18, 1932, Cherry Papers: box 19, GC 1932; Davis to Cherry, Nov. 17, 1930, in ibid.: box 15, GC 1930; Marie Adams interview, Dec. 14, 1976; A.B. Clayton to Cherry, Jan. 2, 1933, Applications: History; Governor Sampson to Cherry, July 7, Aug. 31, 1930, Cherry Papers: box 16, GC 1930; Max B. Harlin to Cherry, Feb. 7, 1931, in ibid.: box 18, GC 1931.

20. Depression Supper pamphlet, University Publications: Brochures, 1906-30; Social Science Club Banquet, April 15, 1933, Student Organizations.

21. *Teachers College Heights* (Nov. 1931):61, (Nov. 1932):7; A.L. Crabb to Cherry, Feb. 28, 1933, Cherry Papers: box 20, GC 1933; Cherry, report to Regents, May 25, 1936, Cherry Papers: box 74; *Herald*, March 8, 1935; Cornette, *History of WKSTC*, 190.

22. *Teachers College Heights* (Dec. 1934):30; table 24 in Cornette, *History of WKSTC*, 189; *Herald*, April 7, 1939; A.B. Clayton, Principal, Boston High School, to Garrett, March 14, 1939, Garrett Papers: box 1, 1937-40, Ci-Cz.

23. Cherry to R.E. Cooper, Jan. 31, 1935, Cherry Papers: box 22, GC 1935; Mattie McLean (?) to Viola O'Bryan, Dec. 14, 1929, in ibid.: box 14, GC 1929.

24. Treasurer's annual report, Oct. 3, 1938, College Heights Foundation papers.

25. *Herald*, Sept. 28, 1934, Jan. 25, 1935; Mattie McLean to C.R. Depp, Sept. 6, 1934, Cherry Papers: box 21, GC 1934; Cherry to Mrs. H.H. Cherry, Sept. 19, 1934, in ibid.: box 36I, Miscellaneous letters.

26. Cherry to Ruth L. Brown, Sept. 26, 1935, Cherry Papers: box 21, GC 1935; *Herald*, June 19, 1936; L.T. Smith to Paul Lyon, July 23, 1936, Cherry Papers: box 59. L.T. Smith 1931-36; *Herald*, Oct. 2, 1942.

27. Hornback interview, Nov. 4, 1976; *Herald*, March 22, 1940, Oct. 23, 1979; "Recommended Policies and Procedures Governing the Establishment of the Fraternity System at Western," for President Thompson, Jan. 25, 1962, Dero G. Downing Papers: box 51, Fraternities, 1970

28. *Herald*, Jan. 28, 1933, Jan. 24, 1936, Nov. 4, 1972; Hornback interview, Nov. 4, 1976.

29. Mrs. Gertrude Allbritton to Cherry, April 27, 1936, Cherry to Mrs. Allbritton, April 29, 1936, Cherry Papers: box 58, SC. The daughter's letter of April 3, 1936, to her mother was sent to Cherry.

30. Undated [1933?] Grise Correspondence, A-Co.

31. Statistics compiled from the team records in the annual football press guides; *Herald*, Jan. 12, 1934, Sept. 27, 1935, March 20, April 3, 1936.

32. Statistics compiled from the team records in the annual football press guides; *Herald*, Nov. 16, 1967, Dec. 2, 1932, March 27, 1939.

33. *Herald*, March 30, 1934; *Talisman, 1930-1937*.

34. Cherry to W.C. Bell, July 8, 1931, Cherry Papers: box 17: GC 1931; Regents minutes, July 7, 1931; *Herald*, May 26, 1933.

35. Report of Dean Grise, 1933, Grise Correspondence, A-Co.

36. Regents minutes, Oct. 4, 24, 1933, Jan. 25, 1936; *Acts of the General Assembly, 1934*, 370-77; Cherry, Report to Regents, May 25, 1936, Cherry Papers: box 74; Cherry's chapel speech, Oct. 10, 1935, in ibid.: box 85, folder 5; PWA file, in ibid.: box 29.

37. *Herald*, Jan. 10, Feb. 7, 1936, Oct. 7, 1938; Regents minutes, May 17, 1937.

38. Regents minutes, June 18, 1935, April 25, May 17, July 10, 1936; *Teachers College Heights* (Dec. 1936):37, (April 1937):32; *Herald*, Oct. 27, 1936, Nov. 16, 1937.

39. *Herald*, Aug. 1927, Oct. 1929; Cherry to Dr. C.W. Dowden, Jan. 9, 1933, Cherry Papers: box 20, GC 1933; Cherry to Mrs. H.H. Cherry, Feb. 27, 1937, in ibid.: box 29, SC, C; Cherry to Dr. J.W. Manning, Aug. 28, 1936, in ibid.: box 24, GC 1936.

40. Cherry to M.B. Adams, Feb. 19, 1935, Cherry Papers: box 23, GC 1935; Crabb to Cherry, Aug. 29, 1936, in ibid.: box 24, GC 1936; Study of the Administration of the College, by A.L. Crabb's class, 1936, A.L. Crabb Collection, box 9.

41. Cherry to Matt Williams, July 31, 1925, Cherry Papers: box 10, GC 1925; Cherry's address to the faculty, Jan. 19, 1937, in ibid.: box 85, folder 5 (1935-37); Henry W. Bradley to Cherry, Aug. 25, 1931, in ibid.: box 17, GC 1931; *Herald*, July 1, 1926.

42. Cherry to A.E. Shide, Nov. 21, 1930, Cherry Papers: box 16, GC 1930; Cherry to L.P. McCuistion, Nov. 9, 1931, in ibid.: box 18, GC 1931; *Teachers College Heights* (Jan. 1932):7.

43. Regents minutes, Nov. 2, 1934, April 12, 1935; Cherry to H.L. Donovan, Dec. 26, 1934, Cherry Papers: box 21, GC 1934.

44. Cherry to Lela Wright, Dec. 20, 1927, Cherry Papers: box 12, GC 1927; Cherry to Perry Snell, Dec. 29, 1925, in ibid.: box 10, GC 1925; Cherry to Louis P. Robare, Feb. 8, 1937, in ibid.: box 29, SC 1937; Cherry to W.G. Bush & Co., Nashville, Aug. 27, 1936, in ibid.: box 24, GC 1936; Cherry to Mrs. H.H. Cherry, March 11, 1937, in ibid.: box 29, SC, C.

45. Walter Nalbach interview, by Lowell H. Harrison, Dec. 7, 1976.

46. Louisville *Herald-Post*, Feb. 19, 20, 26, 1931; *Louisville Times*, Feb. 19, 20, 26, 1931; Louisville *Courier-Journal*, Feb. 20, 26, 1931; H.E. Sanders to Cherry, Feb. 19, 1931, Cherry Papers: box 19, GC 1931; Donovan to Cherry, Feb. 26, 1931, in ibid.; Guilliams to Cherry, Jan. 28, 1932, in ibid.

47. March 9, 1931, Cherry Papers: box 76, PC 1931-33.

48. *Courier-Journal*, Aug. 1, 2, 1937; Bowling Green *Times-Journal*, Aug. 2, 1936; M.C. Ford to D.R. Theophilus, Sept. 16, 1937, Cherry Papers: box 57, M.C. Ford 1937-40. A persistent account of the accident holds that Cherry, while in a drunken state, fell as he was trying to crawl through a window. Attorney Charles Bell who was with Cherry the night of the accident denied the story. Quoted in Stickles interview.

49. Stickles, "Autobiography," 107; Ford to Garrett P. Hayes, Aug. 18, 1937, Cherry Papers: box 57, M.C. Ford 1937-40; McLean to Crabb, Sept. 5, 1937, in ibid.: box 25, GC 1937; Mrs. Cherry to the Student Body, Aug. 12, 1937, in ibid.

50. J.R. Whitmer, "Story of the Statue," *Teachers College Heights* (Dec. 1937):12-20.

5. An Interlude

1. *Courier-Journal*, Aug. 3, 1937; Bowling Green *Times-Journal*, Aug. 4, 1937; Roberts, "Life of Ford," 14-15, 26.

2. Owensboro "Former Student of Western" letter to editor, *Courier-Journal*, Aug. 3, 1937; J.H. Poteet interview, by Lowell H. Harrison, Jan. 28, 1982; Faculty minutes, Aug. 3, 5, 1937.

3. Regents minutes, Sept. 1, 1937; Glasgow *News*, Sept. 2, 1937; O.J. Wilson interviews with Chandler, March 11, 1967, with Mrs. W.P. Drake, April 3, 1967, with H.W. Peters, March 14, 1967, O.J. Wilson interviews extracts; Pentecost to Chandler, Aug. 30, 1937, Sneed to Chandler, Aug. 24, 1937, Chandler to Sneed, Aug. 26, 1937, Chandler Papers, box 86; *Lexington Leader*, Sept. 6, 1937.

4. Bradley to Chandler, Sept. 8, 1937, Chandler Papers. Regent Quinn refused to sign Garrett's contract and resigned from the Board. Attorney General Hubert Meredith to Lt. Gov. Keen Johnson, Sept. 14, 1937, Chandler Papers.

5. *Daily News*, Sept. 1, 1937; *Courier-Journal*, Sept. 17, 1950; *Herald*, Oct. 1, 1937, March 11, 1955.

6. Bob Wallace, "Western's 3 Presidents Build College Spirit," *Herald*, July 13, 1956, 3; Kelly Thompson interview, by Carlton Jackson, June 27, 1977; Frances Richards interview, by James D. Bennett and Lowell H. Harrison, Dec. 14, 1977; Wendell Butler interview, by Carlton Jackson, Nov. 22, 1979; Poteet interview, Jan. 28, 1982; Hornback interview, by J. Crawford Crowe and Lowell H. Harrison, Nov. 4, 1976; Owen Lawson interview, by James D. Bennett and Lowell H. Harrison, Feb. 13, 1986.

7. Kelly Thompson interview, June 27, 1977; Walter Nalbach interview, by Lowell H. Harrison, Dec. 7, 1976; Stickles to Virginia McCalister, Oct. 1, 1937, Cherry Papers: box 59, A.M. Stickles, 1937-40; L.Y. Lancaster interview, by J. Crawford Crowe and Helen Crocker, Dec. 6, 1976; J.H. Poteet interview, by Carlton Jackson, May 26, 1976; Gordon Wilson, "Diaries for Kelly," Dec. 13, 1964; Sibyl Stonecipher interview, by James D. Bennett, Jan. 5, 1978.

8. Garrett to Edwin R. Ward, Nov. 3, 1938, Paul L. Garrett Papers: box 2B, 1937-40, Wa-Wh; Garrett to Mrs. Roger E. White, July 27, 1946, in ibid.: box 4, 1941-46,W-Wid.

9. Regents minutes, July 11, Sept. 29, Dec. 23, 1938, Jan. 15, Sept. 16, 1939; *Teachers College Heights* (Jan. 1940):2-18; *Herald*, Nov. 21, 1939.

10. Regents minutes, March 20, 1937; *Herald*, April 30, 1937; *Teachers College Heights* (Jan. 1940):25.

11. Gayle Carver, "Report on the Kentucky Museum, 1939-1940," to President Garrett, Gayle Carver Papers; *Herald*, April 17, 1947.

12. *Daily News*, April 23, 1937, Jan. 31, 1940; Bowling Green *Times-Journal*, July 30, 1937.

13. Statistics were compiled from the Annual Reports of the Registrar.

14. Ibid.; *Talisman, 1937-1943*; Simpson Diary, Feb. 12, 1949; Joan Soete to author, Sept. 20, 1980.

15. Grise, "Suggestions for Improvement of Chapel," 1932(?), Grise Correspondence—Chapel; *Herald*, March 8, 1940, May 7, 1943; *Teachers College Heights* 18 (Sept. 1941):46; Sara Tyler to Garrett, Nov. 19, 1944, Garrett Papers: box 4, 1941-46, T.

16. "Study of the Administration of the College," 1936(?), A.L. Crabb Collection: Box 9; *Herald*, Nov. 4, 1938; *Teachers College Heights* (Dec. 1938):33.

17. Griffenhagen and Associates, "Report No. 10: Western Kentucky State Teachers College," April 25, 1947, 81; Garrett's response to Griffenhagen report, Garrett Papers: box 11.

18. *Herald*, March 13, 27, April 10, 1942; Hornback interview, Nov. 4, 1976.

19. *Herald*, Nov. 27, 1942, Jan. 15, 29, 1943.

20. *Herald*, Oct. 8, Dec. 3, 1943; Jan. 28, Feb. 25, March 10, 1944.

21. *Herald*, Oct. 7, 1938; Garrett to Carmichael, Nov. 4, 1938, Garrett Papers: box 1, 1937-40, Aa-Ch; Regents minutes, Sept. 7, 1938; Garrett to Donovan, Sept. 16, 1939, Donovan to Garrett, Sept. 18, 1939, Garrett Papers, box 1, Dj-Dz; *Herald*, Oct. 21, 1938.

22. *Herald*, Oct. 3, 1941, Oct. 2, Nov. 27, 1942; *Talisman, 1943*, 93; *Herald*, Oct. 26, 1945.

23. *Herald*, Dec. 14, 1934, Feb. 21, May 10, 1935, March 27, 1939; "Track and Field at Western, 1915-1965," Thompson Papers: box 17, Spring Sports; *Talisman, 1939*, 86, *1940*, 135; *Herald*, Feb. 23, 1940; Garrett to President J.D. Williams, Marshall College, April 6, 1944, Garrett Papers: box 4, 1941-46.

24. Winkenhofer to Everett Horton, Feb. 27, 1940, Garrett Papers: box 1, Hj-Hz; Donovan to Garrett, Aug. 1, 1939; Garrett to Donovan, Aug. 12, 1939, Garrett Papers: box 1, Dj-Dz.

25. O'Donnell to Garrett, April 5, 1944, Garrett Papers: box 3, 1941-46, O.

26. Garrett to James O. Knauss, Feb. 28, 1944, Garrett Papers: box 10, Insurance, 1939-46; *Herald*, March 24, 1938.

27. *Herald*, March 22, 1940; Stickles's remarks at Ford's funeral, Cherry Papers: box 60, A.M. Stickles, 1940; *Herald*, June 21, 1940, Oct. 3, 1941; Garrett, "Strahm Memorial," Garrett Papers: box 11; John Vincent to C.E. Lutton, June 21, 1941, Cherry Papers: box 61, SC, J. Vincent, 1941.

28. Southern Association Reports, 1936-46, Garrett Papers: box 6, Southern Association; Johnson to Garrett, Sept. 19, Oct. 12, 1940, Garrett to Johnson, Oct. 1, 9, 23, 1940, Garrett Papers: box 1, 1937-40, J.

29. Faculty minutes, Jan. 17, 1938; Garrett to Mrs. Edna Renfrow, Nov. 6, 1940, Garrett Papers: box 1, 1937-70, Ra-Rh.

30. Page 23; *Herald*, April 9, 1937.

31. *Herald*, Jan. 16, 1942; Garrett to H.W. Trimble, June 29, 1943, Garrett Papers: box 4, 1941-46, T; Oshira to Garrett, Dec. 30, 1941, Jan. 20, 1944, Garrett Papers: box 3, 1941-46, O.

32. Garrett's chapel talk, Dec. 12, 1941, Garrett Papers: box 10, Talks, 1937-40; Margie Helm, "The War and the Library," *Kentucky School Journal* 23 (Feb. 1945):22-23; Gordon Wilson, "Autobiography: My Educational Career," 143.

33. Karen Owen, "World War II left Western with few men," *Herald*, Oct. 25, 1979; Garrett to T.W. DeZena, Southeastern Greyhound Lines, Nov. 12, 1942, Garrett Papers: Box 5, Defense; E.E. Unger, Weather Bureau, to Mary C. Marks, March 11, 1944, Garrett Papers: box 3, 1941-46, Ma-Mc; J. Reid Sterrett to Lt. Cavanaugh, Camp Campbell, Feb. 12, 1943, Cherry Papers: box 59, SC, J. Reid Sterrett, 1940; John N. Vincent to R.W. Hamilton, July 22, 1942, in ibid.: box 61, SC, J. Vincent 1942.

34. Garrett to Chandler, Sept. 24, 1942, Chandler to Garrett, Feb. 11, 1941, Garrett Papers: box 3, 1941-46, Ca-Ch; Garrett to Vaughn, Nov. 5, 1942, Vaughn to Garrett, Aug. 15, 1942, in ibid.: box 2B, 1937-40, V; Thompson interview, June 27, 1977.

35. Gordon Wilson, "Diary to Kelly," March 29, 1968; *College Training Detachment Unit History* (1944):1-3, 21; James P. Cornette, "No Magic Formula," *Peabody Journal of Education* 22 (Sept. 1944):72-76; Army Air Corps papers, Garrett Papers: box 5.

36. Garrett to McNutt, Nov. 29, 1943, in ibid.; Bert J. Borrone to Dorthie Hall, April 19, 1943, Dorthie Hall Collection (Manuscript Division, Kentucky Library), Borrone folder.

37. Annual Reports of the Registrar, 1933-54; Garrett to President H.T. Hunter, Western Carolina Teacher College, April 20, 1944, Garrett Papers: box 3, 1941-46, He-Hz; salary lists, 1930-52, Garrett Papers: box 9; Regents minutes, July 31, 1948; Garrett to William H. Vaughn, May 26, 1945, Garrett Papers: box 4, 1941-46, V.

38. Garrett to Col. Gordon R. Catts, Dec. 29, 1945, Garrett Papers: box 3, 1941-46, Bu-By; *Herald*, March 16, 1945, Feb. 15, March 1, 1946, Jan. 24, 1947.

39. William James Higginbotham, Jr. "Veteran Impact on the Four Regional State Universities of Kentucky" (Ed.D diss., Indiana University, 1969), 7-9, 12-15, 35, 59.

40. *Herald*, March 15, Oct. 11, 1946; Garrett to Ann McDaniel, April 17, 1946, Garrett Papers: box 3, 1941-46, Ma-Mc.

41. *Herald*, Nov. 8, 1946, Jan. 24, Feb. 7, April 17, 1947.

42. *Herald*, Nov. 8, 1957, April 17, 1970; Owen Lawson to Hubert Griffin, March 11, 1965, Thompson Papers: box 19, Housing; Griffin to Dero G. Downing, July 29, 1970, Downing Papers: box 28, Veterans Village; Lawson interview, Feb. 13, 1986.

43. Garrett to Ray Pearce, April 6, 1945, Garrett Papers: box 3, 1941-46 P; Regents minutes, Sept. 28, 1946; *Herald*, Feb. 27, 1959.

44. Garrett Papers: box 5, Dormitory, 1946; *Herald*, Nov. 22, 1946, Dec. 10, 1948, Oct. 7, 1949, Dec. 10, 1954, Jan. 21, Nov. 18, Dec. 9, 1955, Jan. 18, Feb. 22, 1957.

45. *Herald*, March 2, 1945.

46. Garrett to Governor Lawrence Wetherby, Jan. 23, 1951, Garrett Papers: box 7, Finance: Budget; Garrett to A.Y. Lloyd, Nov. 29, 1951, in ibid.: box 8, Lloyd; Garrett to W.T. Judy, March 16, 1954, in ibid.: box 26, State Property and Building Commission; Cravens interview, Nov. 20, 1984.

47. Garrett to H.P. Smith, Nov. 24, 1943, Garrett Papers: box 3, 1941-46 S; Garrett to Clements, Dec. 27, 1947, in ibid.: box 7, Finance: Budget; Regents minutes, March 25, 1950; *Herald*, April 24, June 26, 1953.

48. *Herald*, March 12, April 23, 1948, March 21, 1947.

49. *Herald*, March 19, 1954. The team records and statistics discussed in this section are taken from the records maintained in the office of the Director of Sports Information.

50. Ed Given, "The Origin and History of the Ohio Valley Conference," *Ohio Valley Conference Press Guide, 1975-1976*, 5-8; W.F. O'Donnell to Garrett, Oct. 20, Garrett to O'Donnell, Oct. 22, 1949, W.F. O'Donnell Papers (University Archives, Eastern Kentucky University), box 66; Regents minutes, June 6, 1953; Garrett to R.J. Cambre, June 16, 1953, Garrett Papers: box 9, SIAA; minutes of UL Board of Trustees, Dec. 9, 1949 (UL Archives).

51. Jack S. Smith, President Bowling Green Ministerial Association, to Garrett, Dec. 2, 1952, March 4, 1953; Garrett to Smith, March 15, 1953, Garrett Papers: box 8, M.

52. *Herald*, Oct. 26, 1945, May 24, Oct. 25, 1946, March 26, 1948; Clayton to Garrett, Sept. 6, 1954, Garrett Papers: box 7, Athletics; athletic papers, in ibid.: *Herald*, Jan. 18, 1957.

53. *Herald*, March 21, May 30, 1947.

54. Griffenhagen and Associates, *Report No. 10: Western Kentucky State Teachers College* (April 25, 1947); 78-80.

55. Annual Financial Statements, 1953-54, Garrett Papers: box 7; Garrett to Charles R. Spain, March 5, 1954, Garrett Papers: box 9, S-1950.

56. *Herald*, Oct. 11, 1935, Oct. 3, 1941, Nov. 5, 1943, Oct. 29, 1981, Jan. 13, 1983.

57. Donovan to Garrett, May 18, Aug. 31, 1940, Garrett Papers: box 1, 1937-40, Dj-Dz; "What Is Happening to Teachers Colleges?" and Report from Special Committee, Sept. 27, 1940, in ibid.: box 5, Graduate Work, 1934-44.

58. *Herald*, Oct. 11, 1940; "Inspection of Graduate Work of Western Kentucky State Teachers College at Bowling Green, Dec. 11, 1942," Garrett Papers: box 7, Accreditation, 1955; Garrett to Superintendent E.F. Blackburn, Princeton, May 19, 1942; in ibid.: box 3, 1941-46, Bu-Bz.

59. Data compiled from the Annual Reports of the Registrar, 1941-54.

60. Contract of agreement for sale of the Bowling Green Business University, April 10, 1907, The University: History, box 1H.

61. For examples, see Cherry to Fannie B. Harrington, Feb. 8, 1936, Cherry Papers: box 24, 6C 1936; Garrett to L.B. Jones, Sept. 9, 1941, Garrett Papers: box 3, 1941-46 J; Ashburn to Garrett, Jan. 10, 1952, Garrett Papers: box 7, Faculty, and attached note, Ashburn to Garrett.

62. *Fall Schedule, 1953*, 31, 57-58; Grise to Garrett, Sept. 25, 1953, Garrett Papers: box 7, Dean.

63. *Herald*, Feb. 9, 1940; John Fred Williams to Garrett, March 29, 1944, Garrett Papers: box 4, 1941-46, W-Wil; Garrett to H.P. Smith, Jan. 17, 1952, in ibid.: box 9, S-1950.

64. Regents minutes, August 28, 1953; *Herald*, Dec. 11, 1953, May 7, 1954; Garrett to John C. West, Jan. 20, 1954, Garrett Papers: box 9, W 1950.

65. *Herald*, May 7, 1954; Garrett to John C. West, June 26, 1954, Garrett Papers: box 9,

W 1950; Garrett to Regent Clarence Bartlett, Sept. 15, 1954, in ibid.: box 8, Regents; Richardson to Clarence Bartlett and Vernon Shallcross, Nov. 23, 1954, in ibid.: box 7, Regents; Thompson to H.L. Donovan, Jan. 24, 1955, Donovan Papers: box 6; *Herald*, March 11, 1955.

6. More Stately Mansions

1. Garrett to John C. West, June 26, 1954, Garrett Papers: box 9, W 1950; Regents minutes, March 26, 1955.

2. Kelly Thompson interviews, Oct. 26, 1976, June 27, 1977; Thompson to Miss McLean, June 19, 1929, Cherry Papers: box 15: GC 1929.

3. Miss McLean to Thompson, July 25, 1929, Cherry Papers: box 15, GC 1929; Cherry to R.E. Taylor, March 11, 1931, in ibid.: box 18, GC 1931; Thompson, "The Most Unforgettable Person I Have Ever Known," Founders' Day Address, 1972, Thompson Papers: box 53.

4. *Teachers College Heights* (March 1934):25; *Herald*, Dec. 3, 1937.

5. Thompson to Garrett, Oct. 31, 1945, Garrett to Thompson, Nov. 7, 1945, Garrett Papers: box 10, Thompson; Regents minutes, May 25, 1946; W.F. O'Donnell to Garrett, Jan. 6, 1954, Garrett Papers: box 8, O.

6. Lowman to Bartlett, Dec. 20, 1954, Thompson Papers: box 3, Election in 1955; interview with ex-Governor Wetherby, *Courier-Journal*, Jan. 4, 1970.

7. Wendell Butler interview, by Carlton Jackson, Nov. 22, 1977; Joe Creason, "Kelly Thompson, Home-Grown Educator," *Courier-Journal*, Oct. 23, 1955; Thompson interview, June 27, 1977; Bartlett to John Richardson, copies to other regents, March 10, 1955, Bartlett to Stickles, March 10, 1955, A.M. Stickles Collection, box 17; Raymond L. Cravens interview, by James D. Bennett and Lowell H. Harrison, Feb. 8, 1985.

8. *Herald*, Nov. 2, 1978; Thompson interview, June 27, 1977; Butler interview, Nov. 22, 1977.

9. *Courier-Journal*, July 12, 14, Aug. 11, 1955; *Lexington Leader*, July 3, 8, 1955.

10. Regents minutes, Oct. 3, 17, 1955; *Courier-Journal*, Oct. 18, 19, 1955; Louisville *Times*, Oct. 17, 1955; *Daily News*, Oct. 17, 1955; *Herald*, Oct. 21, 1955; Bartlett to Thompson, Oct. 19, 1955, A.M. Stickles Collection: box 17.

11. Table 2, Council on Public Higher Education minutes, April 21, 1962; Kelly Thompson, *A Decade in Review, 1955-1965*, 7; Regents minutes Nov. 30, 1940; memorandum, Dero G. Downing to Thompson, July 1, 1965, Thompson Papers: box 51, Trade School.

12. John L. Miller, executive secretary, Council on Public Higher Education, to Thompson, Dec. 30, 1957, Thompson Papers: box 15, Council on Public Higher Education; memorandum, Cravens to Thompson, Oct. 13, 1961, Thompson Papers: box 16, Dean; *Herald*, Sept. 30, 1965; Lawson interview, Feb. 13, 1986; James Russell Harris to author, Nov. 23, 1982.

13. Governor A.O. Stanley to Cherry, Sept. 16, 1916, Cherry Papers: box 77, Governor's Correspondence; Cherry to L.N. Taylor, May 6, 1927, in ibid.: box 12, GC 1927; Nickols to Cherry, Nov. 17, 1926, in ibid.: box 11, GC 1926.

14. Garrett to Donovan, Nov. 3, 1938, Garrett Papers: box 1, 1937-40 Dj-Dz; Negro Education in Kentucky folders, in ibid.: box 10; Atwood to Garrett, Jan. 12, 1940, in ibid.: box 10, Survey folder; Cherry to D.E. Carmon, Nov. 23, 1926, Cherry Papers: box 12, GC 1927; Garrett to Mrs. Lorenzo Dow Terry, Sept. 12, 1950, Garrett Papers: box 8, Regents; Thompson to Irene Boyd, Sept. 11, 1955, Thompson Papers: box 19, Integration.

15. Garrett to Wendell P. Butler, May 22, 1954, Garrett Papers: box 8, Regents; Council on Public Higher Education minutes, Nov. 23, 1955, Thompson Papers: box 15, Council P.H.E.

16. J.E. Jones interview, *Herald*, April 8, 1977; Donovan to Thompson, July 24, 1956, Donovan Papers: box 6; Thompson interview, June 27, 1977; Gordon Wilson to A.L. Crabb, June 24, 1956, Crabb collection, box 8, Correspondence of Bowling Green Persons.

17. *Herald*, Oct. 2, 1963; W.B. Owen to Thompson, Feb. 6, 1963, Thompson to Owen, Feb. 9, 1963, Thompson Papers: box 21, O general.

18. Thompson, *A Decade in Review*, 16; Lawson interview, Feb. 13, 1986.

19. *Herald*, May 6, 1949, Feb. 19, 1960; *Institutional Self-Study Report, 1962*, 103-6, 113.

20. Regents minutes, Dec. 13, 1960; *Herald*, Dec. 7, 1963, special edition.

21. Memorandum, Downing to Thompson, July 31, 1933, Thompson Papers: box 12, Dean of Admissions; *Herald*, Dec. 7, 1963, Sept. 30, 1965; Downing to Norman Kahn, Oct. 18, 1965, Thompson Papers: box 20, K; Cravens interview, Feb. 8, 1985.

22. *Herald*, Oct. 10, 1958, April 10, 1963, Dec. 16, 1964, March 10, 1965; *Daily News*, Oct. 10, 1961; *Western Alumnus* 43 (Winter 1973-74):40; Regents minutes, Dec. 7, 1963.

23. Downing to Felix Joyner, Jan. 23, 1964, Thompson Papers: box 14, City-College Cooperative School; *Herald*, Jan. 16, 1963.

24. Regents minutes, Oct. 20, 1964, March 22, 1965, Jan. 22, 1966; Thompson, *A Decade in Review*, 33-34; Lawson interview, Feb. 13, 1986.

25. Thompson, *A Decade in Review*, 15, 24-25; *Catalog, 1955-1957*, 52, *1965-1967*, 14; Council on Public Higher Education minutes, April 20, 1962, Thompson Papers: box 15.

26. Memorandum, Harry K. Largen to Downing, March 3, 1972, Downing Papers: box 21, Housing; Regents minutes, July 21, 1964; Downing to Regents, Oct. 9, 1975, Downing Papers: box 23, Master Plan; Thompson to James L. Miller, Jr., July 27, 1963, Thompson Papers: box 21, M.

27. *College Catalog, 1955-1957*, 16-17; Regents minutes, Sept. 26, 1958, May 7, 1959.

28. Regents minutes, May 7, 1959; *Herald*, May 22, 1959; James L. Davis interview, by Lowell H. Harrison, June 13, 1984; Dero G. Downing interview, by James D. Bennett, April 15, 1985; Raymond L. Cravens interview, by J. D. Bennett and L. H. Harrison, Nov. 20, 1984.

29. Garrett to Governor Wetherby, Nov. 2, 1954, Garrett Papers: box 7, Board of Regents; *Courier-Journal*, Nov. 17, 1954; *Herald*, Jan. 13, 1950, July 13, Oct. 19, 1956, July 19, 1957; Thompson, *A Decade in Review*, 26-27; Lawson interview, Feb. 13, 1986. When Miss Schneider retired in 1958 she had been at Western for forty-eight years, the longest service in the school's history.

30. Thompson, *A Decade in Review*, 28-29; Downing interview, April 3, 1978.

31. *Courier-Journal*, Dec. 14, 1960; W.L. Matthews to Thompson, July 20, 1961, Thompson Papers: box 13, Bowling Green College of Commerce; *Daily News*, April 24, 1963; *Herald*, May 15, 1963; list of personnel, Thompson Papers: box 8, College of Commerce, 1963; Cravens interview, Feb. 8, 1985; William M. Jenkins interview, by Lowell H. Harrison, Feb. 11, 13, 1986.

32. Cravens to Thompson, Dec. 11, 1964, Thompson Papers: box 24, Reorganization; Regents minutes, March 22, 1965; *Herald*, March 24, July 1, 1965; "Program Accomplishments and Advances ... 1964-66 and 1966-68," Downing Papers: box 46, Budget, 1968-70, file 2; Regents minutes, Aug. 4, 1966; Cravens interview, Feb. 8, 1985; Jenkins interview, Feb. 11, 13, 1986.

33. Thompson, *A Decade in Review*, 10-11; *Herald*, Oct. 7, 1960, April 6, 1971; memorandum, Downing to Thompson, Jan. 31, 1969, Thompson Papers: box 37, Budget, Instructional; Thompson to Crabb, Sept. 28, 1960, Thompson Papers: box 14, C; Thompson to J. Douglas Groce, Feb. 27, 1969, in ibid.: box 11, Faculty Applications; *Institutional Self-Study Report 1962*, 125-27.

34. Toby Hightower to Sara Tyler, Oct. 3, 1972, Downing Papers: box 44, GC, He-Hi; Robert K. White to Thompson, July 25, 1961, Thompson to White, July 29, 1961, Thompson Papers: box 8, New Faculty, 1961-62; Thompson to William Loy, July 30, 1958, in ibid.: New Faculty 1958-59; *Institutional Self-Study Report, 1962*, 118; memorandum, Cravens to Thompson, Dec. 21, 1964, Thompson Papers: box 13, Budget; James F. Matthews to Thompson, April 13, 19964, in ibid.: box 16, Biology; Allan G. and Lucia Anderson to Thompson, March 13, 1965, in ibid.: box 27, Mathematics; First Follow-Up Report to Southern Association, 1965, 6.

35. Thompson to Randolph Richards, July 30, 1956, Thompson Papers: box 8, Faculty,

New, 1957-58, and Salary Appointment Acceptances, 1964; Regents minutes, May 25, 1963; memoranda, Cravens to Thompson, March 7, 1964, April 27, 1966, Thompson Papers: box 49, Rank, Faculty Committee.

36. Regents minutes, Jan. 14, 1949, May 25, 1963; Garrett to Judson C. Gray, Feb. 5, 1953, Garrett Papers: box 7, G.

37. Thompson, *A Decade in Review*; memorandum, E.H. Canon to faculty, July 8, 1956, Thompson Papers: box 3, James L. Miller.

38. Garrett to Col. Noel Gaines, July 19, 1951, Garrett Papers: box 7, G; W.L. Matthews, Jr. to Thompson, Feb. 20, 1956, Thompson Papers: box 12, AAUP; *Herald*, March 10, 1965; AAUP, 1967-70, Downing Papers: box 43; Thompson interview, Oct. 20, 1977; Gordon Wilson "Diaries to Kelly," July 22, 1968; Burch E. Oglesby to William P. Fidler, Dec. 10, 1965, Thompson Papers: box 35, AAUP.

39. Terrell to S. Reza Ahsan, Dec. 28, 1961, Thompson Papers: box 17, Geography and Geology; memorandum, Oct. 7, 1961, in ibid.: box 16, Dean; *Institutional Self-Study Report, 1962,* 181-82.

40. Thompson to Research Committee, Feb. 7, 1962, Thompson Papers: 43, Faculty Research Committee; Faculty Research Committee *Bulletin, 1966*; memorandum, Cravens to Thompson, May 6, 1966, Thompson Papers: box 41, Dean of the Faculties; William R. Hourigan to faculty, [n.d.], 1968, in ibid.: box 43, Faculty Research Committee.

41. Garrett to Mrs. Flora B. Cherry, Dec. 14, 1944, Garrett Papers: box 3, 1941-46, Ca-Ch; Garrett to Mrs. B. Johnson Todd, Sept. 30, 1953, in ibid.: box 9, T-1950; Sara Tyler to Margery L. Settle, Nov. 14, 1963, Thompson Papers: box 12, AAUW; Thompson to women graduates, Dec. 13, 1963, in ibid.

42. *Courier-Journal*, May 5, 1962; memoranda, Cravens to Thompson, Aug. 13, 1962, Thompson to Cravens, Aug. 17, 1962, Thompson Papers: box 8, New Faculty, 1960-61.

43. Questionnaire results, "Handbook for Executive Board Members, 1967," and minutes of the meetings are in Faculty Wives Club Collection; minutes of faculty meeting, Nov. 2, 1960, Thompson Papers: box 18, Faculty Meetings.

44. Nimocks to Thompson, Oct. 5, 1964, Thompson Papers: box 17, History.

45. Regents minutes, May 18, 1960; memorandum, Cravens to Thompson, Dec. 5, 1960, Thompson Papers: box 24, Reorganization; John D. Minton interview, by James D. Bennett, March 10, 1980.

46. Report of the UK committee, in Thompson Papers: box 18, Graduate Degree Programs; Paducah *Sun-Democrat*, June 9, 1963; *Courier-Journal*, June 9, 1963.

47. Memorandum, Cochran to Thompson, Sept. 26, 1963, Public Affairs and Public Relations: President Thompson; Regents minutes, April 14, 1966.

48. *Herald*, Feb. 29, 1968.

49. Wilson to Thompson, April 4, 1955, Thompson Papers: box 3, Campus Improvements 1955; Keown's report to Thompson, Aug. 3, 1961, in ibid.: box 18, Fraternities and Sororities; Regents minutes, Aug. 23, 1961; *Herald* March 17, Oct. 10, 1962, April 22, 1964.

50. Keown to Maynard H. Coe, May 31, 1965, Fraternities; Keown to Thompson, March 23, 1966, Thompson Papers: box 50, Dean of Student Affairs.

51. *Herald*, Oct. 23, 1959; *Catalog, 1965-1966,* 20.

52. Gordon Wilson interview by O.J. Wilson, March 1, 1967; *Institutional Self-Study Report, 1962,* 159; *Herald*, March 3, 1961, Feb. 28, 1962.

53. Materials in Thompson Papers: box 26, Student Problem Cases; *Kentucky Kernel (UK)*, March 26, 1985; *Daily News*, Feb. 24, March 5, 1965; Thompson to Regents, April 2, 1965, Thompson Papers: box 50, Harry M. Sparks; Bob Adams, "Hilltopics," *Herald*, Feb. 24, 1965.

54. Memoranda, Lazarus to Keown, Jan. 25, 1965, Keown to Thompson, Feb. 17, 25, 1965, Thompson Papers: box 26, Student Government; *Daily News*, April 22, 1965; *Herald*, May 13, 1965, April 7, 28, May 5, 1966.

55. *Herald*, March, 1930, Oct. 11, 1940, May 20, 1965; Garrett to O'Donnell, April 28, 1942, O'Donnell Papers, EKU, box 66.

56. Garrett to A.C. Russell, April 26, 1945, Garrett Papers: box 6, Publicity, 1951-55; *Herald*, Oct. 7, 1949; *Kentucky Kernel*, March 26, 1965.

57. *Herald*, Dec. 10, 16, 1965, Jan. 13, 1966; Regents minutes, Dec. 18, 1965, Jan. 8, Feb. 26, 1966; *Daily News*, Jan. 9, 1966; KCLU and AAUP reports in John W. Oswald Papers (Special Collections, University of Kentucky); *Courier-Journal*, March 26, 1966; Jenkins interview, Feb. 11, 1986.

58. *Catalog, 1965*, 23; problem cases, Thompson Papers: box 3, Students, 1955-56; memorandum, Keown to Thompson, Nov. 8, 1965, in ibid.: box 26, Dean of Students; *Daily News*, Feb. 8, 1968.

59. *Student Handbook, 1964-1965*, 12, 28-30.

60. *Student Handbook, 1964-1965*, 28, *1967-1968*, 25, 45, *1968-1969*, 25; Edwards, "Guest Editorial," *Herald*, May 5, 1966; Mary E. Heltsley to O.J. Wilson, Aug. 5, 1966, Thompson to Heltsley, Aug. 15, 1966, Thompson Papers: box 44, H-General 1968-70.

61. Memorandum, Keown and Owen Lawson to Thompson, May 10, 1962, Thompson Papers: box 48, Parking and Traffic; Council on Public Higher Education minutes, July 9, 1962, Downing Papers: box 35, Council; *Louisville Times*, July 11, 1962; Regents minutes, Aug. 16, 1972.

62. It must be confessed that the heading for that section of the survey was "Enrollment Analysis By." Thompson Papers: box 49, Questionnaires.

63. *Daily News*, March 15, 1962, April 22, 1964; *Herald*, March 21, 1962; *Courier-Journal*, April 23, 1964; *Nashville Banner*, April 22, 1964.

64. George H. Riggs to Thompson, Nov. 20, 1958, Thompson Papers: box 24, R; Gale M. Stiles and Herbert D. Cobb to Thompson, March 12, 1960, in ibid.: box 25, S-General; *Herald*, March 22, 1960.

65. *Herald*, July 1, 1964; Fred Russell, "Winningest Basketball Coach," *Saturday Evening Post* 229 (Jan. 19, 1957):78; records in the Sports Information Office; *Herald*, Feb. 19, 1959, Feb. 13, March 6, 1963.

66. Hartford *Ohio County Times*, Feb. 23, 1967; *Daily News*, March 24, 1964.

67. *Herald*, March 17, Dec. 8, 1966; records in the Sports Information Office.

68. *Herald*, Jan. 18, 1957; *Daily News*, Feb. 3, 1957; *Courier-Journal*, April 9, Nov. 30, 1975; Athletic Committee minutes, Feb. 1, 1957.

69. Records in the Sports Information Office; *Courier-Journal*, Nov. 21, 1967; *Herald*, April 20, 1971.

70. Thompson to L. Felix Joyner, Jan. 4, 1965, Thompson Papers: box 29, Academic-Athletic Building 2; *Herald*, Sept. 26, Oct. 26, 1968.

71. Thompson to Dave Whitaker, Sept. 3, 1958, Thompson Papers: box 28, W.

72. Records in the Sports Information Office; *Herald*, April 18, Dec. 5, 1962, March 11, May 19, 1964, March 3, 1966; Ecker to Connan Smith, June 10, 1965, Glenn E. Presnell to Ecker, June 21, 1965, Ecker to Presnell, June 29, 1965, Thompson Papers: box 17, Spring Sports; OVC minutes, March 1963, Eastern Kentucky University Archives.

7. Forming the University

1. Thompson, *Decade in Review*, 29; memorandum, Cravens to Thompson, Dec. 14, 1965, Thompson Papers: box 52, University Status; Thompson notes on the "Principal Recommendations of the Survey Team," Thompson Papers: box 14, Commission on Higher Education; Cravens interview, Feb. 8, 1985.

2. Thompson to James P. Cornette, Feb. 2, 1966, Thompson Papers: box 52, University Status, Louisville *Times*, Jan. 4, 1966; Chelf, "Politics of Higher Education," 4-5, 9.

3. Regents minutes, Feb. 26, 1966; *Daily News*, Feb. 27, 1966; *Herald*, March 3, 1966; Craven's speech, *Alumni Bulletin* 33 (Sept. 1966):5.

4. *Report of the University Institutional Self-Study Program for the Commission on Colleges, Southern Association of Colleges and Schools, 1971-1973*, 789-93 (cited hereafter as *Southern*

Association Self-Study, 1972); *Western Alumnus* 41 (Fall 1972):6-7; Regents minutes, Feb. 23, 1967, May 17, 23, 1981.

5. *Daily News*, Oct. 2, 1963; Regents minutes, May 7, 1957, Dec. 13, 1960, Dec. 7, 1963; Thompson interview, Oct. 20, 1977; *Herald*, March 18, 1964. A great deal of detailed information is in the Thompson Papers: box 13, City of Bowling Green; box 39, Condemnation of Property; box 46, Land Purchases; and box 52, Urban Renewal.

6. *Herald*, Sept. 14, 1967.

7. Thompson Papers, box 52, Western Towers; Downing Papers: box 28, Western Towers; *Herald*, Sept. 23, 1969, March 10, 1970, Jan. 29, 1971; Denny Brand to author, April [n.d.], 1979.

8. *Teachers College Heights* (Jan. 1929):1; Regents minutes, April 18, 1929; *Herald*, May 1, 1963; Report of Steering Committee to Thompson, Oct. 3, 1963, Downing Papers: box 38, Report on 20 Story Building; Thompson Papers, box 31: New Classroom Building; Downing interview, April 13, 1978; Carl D. Johnson to Downing, Sept. 14, 1971, Downing Papers: box 28, Water Tank; Cravens interview, Feb. 8, 1985.

9. Regents minutes, Oct. 30, 1964; Thompson Papers: box 30, Bid Opening, President's Home; memorandum, Thompson to Harry Largen, Aug. 1, 1966, Thompson Papers: box 37, Business Office, 1966-67; *Herald*, Oct. 6, 1966, Feb. 14, 1980; *A Day of Commemoration and Dedication* brochure, 1967.

10. Regents minutes, Sept. 21, 1968; *Herald*, Sept. 21, Oct. 10, 1968; *Lexington Herald*, Sept. 24, 1968; Paducah *Sun-Democrat*, Sept. 25, 1968; Louisville *Times*, Sept. 24, 1968; memorandum, Downing to Thompson, Sept. 27, 1968, Thompson Papers: box 45, Kentucky Southern College; Thompson interview, Oct. 20, 1977; Cravens interview, Feb. 8, 1985.

11. Regents minutes, Oct. 9, 1968; *Courier-Journal*, Oct. 8, 1968; memorandum, Downing to Thompson, Oct. 8, 1968: Thompson Papers: box 45, Kentucky Southern College; *Daily News*, Oct. 28, 1968; Kris W. Kindelsperger, "A Study of the Factors Leading to the Entrance of the University of Louisville into the State System of Higher Education in Kentucky (M.A. thesis, University of Louisville, 1976), 81; Cravens interview, Feb. 8, 1985.

12. Campbell to Thompson, Feb. 3, 1956, Thompson Papers: box 13, Don Campbell, Regent; Thompson to Chandler, March 1, 1956, Feb. 25, 1958, Chandler Papers: box 427 (Special Collections, University of Kentucky); Thompson to Governor Bert Combs, March 22, 1962, Thompson Papers: box 14, Governor Combs; memorandum, Downing to Thompson, June 30, 1962, in ibid.: box 12, Dean of Admissions; transcript of Bemis Lawrence address Oct. 15, 1961, in ibid.: Box 16, Dedication—Science Hall; Bates interview, Dec. 1, 1977.

13. *Southern Association Self-Study, 1972*, 15-18; *Herald*, April 26, 1957, April 4, May 16, 1968.

14. Memorandum, Cravens to Thompson, Jan. 17, 1962, Thompson Papers: box 16, Dean Cravens; Regents minutes, Jan. 18, 1962, May 21, July 8, 1969; *Herald*, May 22, 1969; Cravens to Harry L. Keith, Aug. 3, 1965, Thompson Papers: box 14, Commission on Higher Education.

15. University catalogs for these years.

16. *Herald*, April 28, 1965; Nov. 10, 1966; Oct. 6, 1970.

17. University catalogs for these years.

18. Ibid.; Willson E. Wood, "A Brief History of the English Department, Western Kentucky University, 1907-72"; *Southern Association Self-Study, 1972*, 454-56; Thompson Papers: box 48, Joint Doctoral Programs; Downing Papers: box 28, Joint Doctoral Program; *Courier-Journal*, March 21, 1972; Regents minutes, April 26, 1972; Mary and Kenneth Clarke to author, Jan. 10, 1984.

19. *Herald*, Nov. 20, 1963; *Daily News*, April 25, 1974; Regents minutes, April 27, 1974.

20. *Southern Association Self-Study, 1972*, 489, 495-96, 592-6; Debbie Dickey, "Western's Graduate College Is On Its Way," *Western Alumnus* 40 (Fall 1971):1-3; *Herald*, Jan. 22, 1971.

21. *Southern Association Self-Study, 1972*, 464-65; memorandum, Cravens to

Thompson, March 20, 1969, Thompson Papers: box 44, Graduate Extension; Regents minutes, May 21, 1969; Academic Affairs Papers: Owensboro.

22. Thompson to Dean J.J. Oppenheimer, Sept. 15, 1955, Thompson Papers: box 28, White House Conference; memorandum, Thompson to Downing and Largen, Nov. 20, 1967, Thompson Papers: box 50, Harry M. Sparks; Largen to Downing, Oct. 10, 1967, Downing Papers: box 17, Funds Available.

23. Griffenhagen Report, 1947, 82-84; L. Felix Joyner, Deputy Commissioner of Finance, to Garrett, Aug. 24, 1954, Thompson Papers: box 4, Budget 1954-55; James L. Miller, Jr. to Thompson, June 21, 1956, in ibid.; budget, 1956-57; *Daily News*, Feb. 9, 1964.

24. Miller, "The 'College Budget Formula' As A Method of Determining State Appropriations to Colleges and Universities," (1959), 4, 8, 17-20, Thompson Papers: box 15, Council on Public Higher Education; Miller to Executive Committee, Aug. 25, 1958, in ibid.; Report of the Advisory Committee on Financial Studies to the Council, April 20, 1963, Thompson Papers: box 21, Minimum Foundation; *Courier-Journal*, April 21, 1963.

25. Thompson to Harry M. Sparks, chairman, Council on Public Higher Education, Dec. 4, 1965, Thompson Papers: box 37, Budget, State, 1966-70; memorandum, Downing to Thompson, Nov. 18, 1965, in ibid.; Henderson *Gleaner-Journal*, Dec. 7, 1965.

26. *Catalog, 1970-1971*, 16; Notes on 1969-70 Budget, Thompson Papers: box 37, Budget, 1968-69, 1969-70; Thompson, *A Report to the Board ... 1955-1969*, 38-40.

27. *Southern Association Self-Study, 1972*, 176-92, 202-16; Thompson, *A Report to the Board ... 1955-1969*, 10-22; Wood, "Brief History of the English Department," 22-24; Report to Council on Public Higher Education: Full-time Faculty, Nov. 12, 1968, Downing Papers: box 35.

28. Memorandum, Keown to Thompson, July 1, 1964, Thompson Papers: box 14, Chapel Assembly; Thompson interview, Oct. 26, 1976; John A. Scarbrough to author, May 1, 1979.

29. James Russell Harris to author, Nov. 23, 1982; Thompson to William Lawton, March 12, 1957, Thompson Papers: box 16, Department of Economics; Cravens to Thompson, Oct. 27, 1964, Oct. 10, 1968, Nov. 26, 1968, April 22, 1969, May 5, 1969, Thompson Papers: box 49, Sabbatical Leave Program; Regents minutes, Feb. 15, 1969; *Southern Association Self-Study, 1972*, 196.

30. Minton interview, March 10, 1980; Clark to Minton, April 24, 1967, Minton to Clark, April 26, 1967, Clark to Thompson, June 5, 1968, John D. Minton Papers: UPK; minutes of the Editorial Board, March 15, 1969, in ibid.; Lowell H. Harrison, "Dedicated to the Preservation of Knowledge," *Western Alumnus* 42 (Summer 1973):44.

31. *Western Alumnus* 37 (Summer 1969):24-25; 41 (Fall 1972):14-15.

32. Regents minutes, Aug. 4, 1966; *Herald*, Nov. 11, 14, 1969, Jan. 13, March 20, 1970, Aug. 22, 1972; Composition of Academic Council, with Regents minutes, Jan. 25, 1973.

33. *Daily News*, Oct. 28, 1965; *Herald*, March 31, 1966, March 16, 1967, April 4, 1968; Dec. 4, 1969; Mrs. Stanley Lambert to Thompson, Feb. 6, 1968, Thompson Papers: box 46, L General.

34. Letters on the "Dixie" issue are in the *Herald*, March 17, 24, 1966. *Herald*, Oct. 31, 1969; minutes of Athletic Committee, Nov. 6, Dec. 4, 1967, Feb. 2, 1968.

35. *Herald*, Oct. 3, 1968.

36. *Herald*, Nov. 17, 1966, Sept. 18, 1969.

37. *Herald*, Nov. 20, 1963; Concerts, 1967-68, Downing Papers: box 43, ASG 1968-69; Regents minutes, Aug. 25, 1961; *Herald*, Sept. 27, 1961; program, Romulo Address, University Programs: Misc., box 2; Cravens to O.J. Wilson, June 13, 1967, Thompson Papers: box 52, University Lecture Series; William G. Lloyd to Editor, *Herald*, March 13, 1969.

38. *Herald*, Jan. 16, 1963, Feb. 1, 1972; *Catalog, 1969-1970*, 30.

39. *Herald*, Dec. 19, 1968, March 27, 1970.

40. *Football Press Guide, 1983*; 7; *Basketball Press Guide, 1981-82*, 6-7; *Herald*, Feb. 16, March 2, 16, 1967.

41. *Football Press Guide, 1983*; memorandum, Downing to Thompson, Dec. 2, 1968, Thompson Papers: box 41, Football, 1966-69; *Herald*, Sept. 18, Oct. 28, Dec. 4, 1969.

42. Ed Givin, "A Week's Work = 150 miles—on Foot!" *Western Alumnus* 41 (Summer 1972):14-17; *Talisman, 1970*, 338; Sports Information Office records; *Herald*, May 22, Sept. 18, 1969, May 19, 1970.

43. *Herald*, May 15, 1963, April 11, 1968; Hornback interview, Aug. 1, 1984.

44. *Football Press Book, 1983*, 103; memorandum, Hubert Hardaway to Downing, Oct. 11, 1968, Thompson Papers: box 41, Director of Athletics; Thompson interview, June 27, 1977.

45. Thompson, *A Report to the Board ... 1955-1969*, 1, 4; *Herald*, Oct. 27, 1977, Nov. 2, 1978; memorandum, Thompson to Cochran, Jan. 21, 1968, Thompson Papers: box 48, Public Affairs & Public Relations; Thompson's resignation statement, Regents minutes, May 21, 1969; Hornback interview, Nov. 4, 1976; Nalbach interview, Dec. 7, 1976; *Herald*, May 2, 1975.

46. Thompson to Donovan, April 16, 1946, Donovan Papers: box 6; Thompson to S.C. Van Curon, Sept. 24, 1962, Dickey Papers: box 26, folder 282; Thompson to Judge Pat Turner, April 6, 1968, Thompson Papers: box 51, T General; Thompson to Harry Lee Waterfield, Feb. 1, 1961, in ibid.: Box 14, C General.

47. Regents minutes, April 13, 1967; Thompson to Noble W. Abrahms, Sept. 11, 1962, Thompson Papers: box 12, A General; Thompson to M. Howard Bryant, Nov. 2, 1965, in ibid.: box 28, U.S. Dept. of HEW; Thompson to Russell E. Helmick, Jan. 27, 1966, in ibid.: box 44, H General; Thompson to C.W. Theleen, April 16, 1967, in ibid.: box 51, T General; Thompson to John H. Horton, Oct. 10, 1967, in ibid.: box 46, Lindsey Wilson College; Thompson to John W. Oswald, Feb. 14, 1968, President's Office: Oswald: box 7, folder 239 (Special Collections, UK).

48. Regents minutes, May 21, June 11, 1969; *Herald*, May 22, July 11, Aug. 7, 1969; Tom Jones interview, by Lowell H. Harrison, Oct. 26, 1983; *Daily News*, Oct. 22, 1975; Thompson interview, Oct. 20, 1977; Cravens interview, Feb. 8, 1985; Dero G. Downing interview, by James D. Bennett, Oct. 23, 1984.

49. Wilson, "Diaries to Kelly," May 22, 1969.

8. Leveling Off

1. *Herald*, May 22, July 11, 1969; Regents minutes, Aug. 22, 1969; memorandum, Regents' Faculty Advisory Committee to Faculty, July 3, 1969 (author's file); *Courier-Journal*, Aug. 23, 1969; *Daily News*, Aug. 23, 1969; Downing interview, by James D. Bennett, Oct. 23, 1984; Cravens interview, Feb. 8, 1985; Shadowen interview, Aug. 21, 1984.

2. "Remember When? The Downing Years," *Western Alumnus* 50 (Winter 1978-79):4-7; Downing interviews, by James D. Bennett, March 22, April 3, 1978; Paige Jones, "Dear Ol' Downing," *Herald Magazine*, Oct. 31, 1985, 10-12.

3. Downing interview, April 3, 1978; Ed Ryan, "Dero Downing: Gentle, but Strong," *Courier-Journal*, Aug. 24, 1969, Jan. 6, 1979; memorandum, Downing to Thompson, Jan. 29, 1968, Thompson Papers: box 51, Teaching Loads; Jones interview, Oct. 26, 1983; *Talisman, 1976*, 193; Thompson interview, Oct. 20, 1977; Cravens interview, Feb. 22, 1985; Buckman interview, Oct. 5, 1984; Cook interview, Aug. 6, 1985; H. Phillip Constans interview, by Lowell H. Harrison, Jan. 8, 1986; Jenkins interview, Feb. 11, 13, 1986; Lawson interview, Feb. 13, 1986.

4. Downing to Dr. William A. Webb, April 2, 1968, Thompson Papers: box 39, Council on Public Higher Education; *Self-Study Report, 1971-1973*, 102; *Self-Study Report, 1982-1984*: Standard II, Organization and Administration, 15.

5. Pritchard to William A. Abell, Jan. 23, 1970, Downing Papers: box 13, UL; Downing to Dr. David Drutz, Aug. 5, 1971, Downing Papers: box 55, Legislative Interim Study Commission.

6. Memorandum, Downing to deans, Feb. 8, 1973, Downing Papers: box 49, Enrollment, Spring 1973; *Herald*, Oct. 29, 1974; enrollment report, 1972-73, Downing Papers: box 49; memorandum, Downing to Cravens, Feb. 19, 1975, Downing Papers: box 49A, Faculty Positions, 1973-75.

7. *Herald*, Dec. 16, 1975; Graduate College *Annual Reports 1972-1982.*

8. *Herald*, April 5, 1977, Sept. 20, 1979; Faculty Senate Institutional Goals and Planning Committee, "Enrollment Projections," 3, 10.

9. Memorandum, Largen to Downing, Feb. 20, 1973; Presidents: Council on Public Higher Education: box 2, Off-Campus Offerings; Regents minutes, May 23, 1981.

10. Downing Papers: box 14, Eagle University folders; Regents minutes, July 17, 1972; "Eagle University," *Western Alumnus* 42 (Winter 1972-73):14-15; *Daily News*, Nov. 29, 1977; *Herald*, Dec. 1, 1977, Aug. 1, 1978, Sept. 27, 1979; Cravens interview, Feb. 22, 1985.

11. Memoranda, Cravens to Thompson, March 20, Aug. 14, 1969, Thompson Papers: box 44, Graduate Extension Consortium; Regents minutes, May 21, 1969; Cravens interview, Feb. 22, 1985.

12. Taylor to Cravens, Feb. 5, 1971; Downing to Governor Ford, Dec. 7, 1971; Mayor Taylor to Governor Ford, Dec. 9, 1971, March 28, 1973, Academic Affairs Records: Owensboro Graduate Consortium; Owensboro *Messenger-Inquirer*, July 25, 1974.

13. Curris to the three presidents, Dec. 12, 1973; Downing to Curris, Dec. 19, 1973, Academic Affairs Records: Owensboro Graduate Consortium; memoranda, Cravens to Downing, June 12, 1974; Cook to Downing, June 17, 1974; Downing to Curris, Oct. 23, 1975, Downing Papers: box 57, Owensboro Consortium, 1972-75; *Daily News*, July 23, 1974.

14. Both reports are in Academic Affairs: Owensboro Graduate Consortium; memorandum, Chelf, Gray, and Taylor to Downing, Oct. 6, 1976, Downing Papers: box 57, Owensboro Consortium, 1972-75.

15. Regents minutes, April 14, 1979; *Herald*, April 12, 1979; Cravens interview, Feb. 22, 1985; Donald Zacharias to Constantine W. Curris, Aug. 27, 1980; Curris to Zacharias, Sept. 15, 1980; Harry M. Snyder to Curris, Aug. 4, 1980, Donald Zacharias Papers.

16. Southern Association, *Self-Study Report, 1980-1982*; Notes on 1969-70 Budget, Thompson Papers: box 37, Budgets, 1968-69, 1969-70; *Herald*, April 15, Dec. 6, 1977.

17. Memorandum, Downing to Vice Presidents, Aug. 29, 1970, Downing Papers: box 46, Budget Reduction 1970-71; memorandum, Largen to Downing, Sept. 19, 1973, Downing Papers: box 17, Funds Available; Regents minutes, Jan. 12, 1976; *Daily News*, Jan. 13, 1974.

18. Largen to Downing, May 17, 1973, Downing Papers: box 46, Budget, 1972-74; *Catalog, 1974-75*, 23; *Catalog, 1979*, 24; *Chronicle of Higher Education*, Oct. 10, 1978, 15; *Herald*, Oct. 20, 1977.

19. Regents minutes, April 10, 1973 (with Downing to McCormack, April 16, 1973), April 26, Sept. 20, 1975; *Daily News*, April 27, 1975; Downing to Ramsey and Clark, Jan. 23, 1975, with Regents minutes, Jan. 25, 1975.

20. Southern Association, *Self-Study Report, 1971-1973*, 119; *Herald*, Feb. 13, Sept. 17, 1979; Downing to Regents, Jan. 10, 1975, Downing Papers: Regents 1975.

21. James Russell Harris to author, Nov. 23, 1982; List of Campus Buildings, University Archives.

22. Nat H. Love, L & M Book Co., to Jack Van Meter, State Highway Department, June 27, 1974, Downing Papers: box 20, Highway Department, 1973-74; *Herald*, Sept. 30, 1975, Feb. 3, 1976.

23. Regents minutes, May 1, 1970, Jan. 9, July 9, 1971; *Herald*, Sept. 18, 1970, Feb. 12, July 13, 1971, Oct. 2, 1973, April 30, 1976, Feb. 22, 1977, May 1, 1979, Feb. 28, 1984.

24. Regents minutes, Aug. 6, 1970, May 14, Oct. 29, 1977; *Daily News*, Oct. 30, 1977; Cravens interview, Nov. 20, 1984; Jenkins interview, Feb. 11, 1986.

25. *Herald*, Jan. 22, 1971, Feb. 6, 1973; *Daily News*, Oct. 5, 1973, *Western Alumnus* 38 (Summer 1970):29; Regents minutes, Nov. 1, 1977.

26. Memorandum, Sara Tyler to Members of Academic Community, May 15, 1970,

Thompson Papers: box 42, Margie Helm Library, 1966-69; *Western Alumnus* 39 (Summer 1971):20-21; *Herald*, Feb. 7, 1978, Dec. 7, 1971; John Manning Sr., to editor, *Herald*, Nov. 9, 1971; Faculty Senate Newsletter, Oct. 26, 1979; Earl Eugene Wassom, *Annual Report, 1983-1984*, 2-3, 9.

27. Memorandum, Cravens to Downing, Oct. 8, 24, 1969, Downing Papers: box 53, Helm Library, 1968-69; Academic Council minutes, Dec. 17, 1969; Engel to "Dear Colleagues," Aug. 30, 1971, Downing Papers: box 22, Helm Library, 1971-1973; Libraries Annual Report, 1979, 21; *Institutional Self-Study, 1982-1984*, 235-37; WKU Program Status Report, 1981-82, 28; Wassom, *Annual Report 1983-1984*, 11; Downing interview, April 15, 1985; Library Program Status Report, Jan. 1, 1985-Dec. 31, 1985.

28. Cherry to Leiper, Nov. 13, 1931, Cherry Papers: box 18, GC, 1931; Sara Muhs Scott, "The Development of Western Kentucky University Archives," paper for Library Science 409G, Dec. 1974; Downing Papers: box 7, Archives—University; Libraries Correspondence, 1961-72; Regents minutes, July 26, 1975; *Herald*, Sept. 6, 1984, Feb. 5, 1985.

29. *Herald*, Feb. 4, 1938, Oct. 11, 1940, June 30, 1961, Sept. 18, 1969, Jan. 29, 1973, May 2, 1975; memoranda, Paul Cook to Whitaker, Aug. 30, 1978, Whitaker to Downing, Davis, Cook, Mounce, Sept. 4, 1978, Downing Papers: box 22, Dept. of Journalism; Regents minutes, Oct. 30, 1976, April 28, 1979; *Herald*, April 5, Aug. 28, 1984.

30. *Herald*, Oct. 30, 1984.

31. *Western Alumnus* 42 (Winter 1972-73):1-2; *Herald*, Oct. 1, 1974, Oct. 17, 1975; *Western Alumnus* 51 (Summer 1979):24; *Herald*, May 6, Oct. 7, 30, 1980; Regents minutes, May 23, 1981.

32. Garrett to H.L. Donovan, March 18, 1938, Garrett Papers: box 1, 1937-40, Di-Dz; Moore to Garrett, June 30, 1939, Cherry Papers: box 58, SC, Earl Moore, 1937-40; Garrett to Robert L. Kennett, WHAS, May 24, 1939, Garrett Papers: box 1, 1937-40, Dj-Dz; *Herald*, Nov. 23, 1945; Downing to Hugh Thomason, AAUP president, Dec. 11, 1969, Downing Papers: box 43, AAUP 1967-70.

33. Regents minutes, Oct. 20, 26, 1974, Feb. 4, 1978, June 26, 1982; *Fourth Estate*, Nov. 1, 1975; *Courier-Journal*, Nov. 2, 1980; *Talisman, 1981*, 134; *Herald*, Sept. 25, 1979.

34. Thompson to George H. Brown, Jr., Bowling Green, April 22, 1957; Thompson to Robert Leman, Bloomington, Indiana, May 2, 1957; Thompson to Vernon Bronson, Director, National Association of Educational Broadcasters, Aug. 11, 1962, Thompson Papers: box 27, Television-Educational; Downing to Goodman, Aug. 30, 1966, in ibid., box 37, Dean of Business Affairs; *Herald*, Feb. 6, 1970, Feb. 18, 1982, Feb. 7, 1984; Regents minutes, Aug. 20, 1983.

35. *Herald*, March 10, 1970; *Hilltopper Basketball, 1981-1982*.

36. *Hilltopper Basketball, 1981-1982*; *Herald*, March 2, 1971.

37. *Daily News*, March 14, 1971.

38. *Daily News*, March 19, 1951; *Courier-Journal*, Jan. 9, 1972; Bert Nelli, *The Winning Tradition: A History of Kentucky Wildcat Basketball* (Lexington, 1984), 85, 90.

39. *Courier-Journal*, March 21, 28, 1970; *Daily News*, March 19, 26, April 6, 1971.

40. *Daily News*, April 9, 1971; *Courier-Journal*, April 24, June 11, 1971; Downing interview, April 15, 1985.

41. *Hilltopper Basketball, 1981-1982*, 45, 55-57; *Herald*, Sept. 3, 1971; *Courier-Journal*, Feb. 23, 1976.

42. *Herald*, Jan. 29, 1971, Feb. 18, March 7, 1972; *Daily News*, Jan. 24, 25, March 31, 1970; Athletic Committee minutes, Jan. 27, 1971; Byars to Downing, Feb. 16, Downing to Byars, Feb. 19, 1971, Downing Papers: box 23, Jim McDaniels; *Courier-Journal*, Feb. 12, March 7, 1972; Downing interview, April 15, 1985.

43. Athletic Committee minutes, June 7, July 19, Sept. 11, Dec. 4, 6, 1972, Jan. 10, 1973; *Nashville Tennessean*, Jan. 11, 1973; *Louisville Times*, March 23, 1973; *Courier-Journal*, June 22, 23, 27, Aug. 27, Nov. 23, 1974: *Daily News*, June 27, 1974; Athletic Committee minutes, July 17, Sept. 4, Nov. 26, 1974; Regents minutes, executive committee, May 18, 1974.

44. *Herald,* Sept. 6, 1974, Feb. 22, March 1, April 1, 1976; *Daily News,* Feb. 29, 1976; *Courier-Journal,* March 14, 1976; *Hilltopper Basketball, 1981-1982,* 48.

45. *Daily News,* Aug. 30, Oct. 17, Nov. 23, 1977, Jan. 20, 22, 1978; *Courier-Journal,* Jan. 22, March 12, 17, 1978; Ed Givin, "Coach and Gentleman," *Western Alumnus* 48 (Spring 1978):10-11; *Herald,* March 7, 23, 1978; Richards to Oldham, Jan. 18, 1978, Downing Papers: box 8, Coach Richards; Cole interview, Feb. 4, 1984; *Western Alumnus* 49 (Summer 1978):10-11.

46. *Herald,* Oct. 10, 30, Dec. 11, 18, 1970; Ray Henderson, "A Piece of the Rock," *Western Alumnus* 46 (Spring 1976):8-9; *Herald,* Dec. 2, 9, 16, 1975.

47. *Herald,* Nov. 22, 1977, Nov. 28, 1978; *Western Alumnus* 50 (Spring 1979):24; Regents minutes, Feb. 4, 1978.

48. Clark Hanes column, *Daily News,* Nov. 19, 1979; *Herald,* Oct. 25, Nov. 20, 1979.

49. Hornback interview, Nov. 4, 1976; *Daily News,* April 29, 1975, April 20, 1976, Sept. 1, 1981.

50. *Courier-Journal,* May 15, 1976; *Daily News,* Sept. 3, 1976, June 7, 1979; *Herald,* Aug. 28, 1979.

51. Athletic Committee minutes, March 16, 1970; *Herald,* Sept. 18, 1969, Feb. 23, 1971, March 23, 1973, Feb. 21, 1978, Feb. 20, 1979; *Talisman, 1979,* 241.

52. *Daily News,* Nov. 25, 1974, May 11, 12, 1976; *Herald,* April 27, 1973, Jan. 11, Aug. 27, 1974, Nov. 25, 1975, Nov. 16, 1976; *Talisman, 1979,* 245.

53. *Herald,* June 27, 1978, Oct. 29, 1981, *Magazine; Hilltopper Basketball, 1981-82,* 84.

54. Regents minutes, July 26, 1975; *Herald,* Aug. 30, 1975.

55. *Herald,* Oct. 17, 1972; Athletic Committee minutes, Sept. 29, Oct. 2, Nov. 6, 1972, April 2, Nov. 7, 1973, Sept. 14, 1974, Feb. 3, March 3, 1975.

56. Sheila Conway, "Women's Athletics Arrives," *Western Alumnus* 43 (Spring 1974):12-13; *Courier-Journal,* Jan. 3, 1974; Ed Given, "Whither the Women?" *Western Alumnus* 44 (Winter 1975-76):18-19; *Chronicle of Higher Education,* Jan. 18, 1984.

57. *Herald,* Feb. 5, Nov. 22, 1974; *Lady Topper Basketball, 1983-84,* 40-41.

58. *Herald,* Nov. 16, 1978, April 1, 1982, March 1, 1983; Beth Taylor, "A-FILLIE-ated: life in the fast lane," *Herald Magazine,* Feb. 6, 1979, 6-7.

59. *Herald,* March 6, April 24, 1973, April 9, 1974; Regents minutes, Aug. 22, 1981.

60. Cole to Downing, Feb. 16, 1977, Downing Papers, box 9, Board of Regents—Cole.

9. Troubled Times

1. Downing interview, Oct. 23, 1984.

2. *Herald,* April 9, 1971; memorandum, Dean Keown to Vice President Minton, July 29, 1975, Downing to Student Officers, Nov. 25, 1975, Downing Papers: box 7, ASG 1975.

3. Causey to Editor, *Daily News,* May 24, 1970; *Herald,* Oct. 7, 10, 21, 28, Nov. 11, 18, 1969; Moratorium Committee to faculty, Oct. 10, 1969; Downing interview, Oct. 23, 1984.

4. Katherine Stewart Van Warner to author, Feb. 3, 1984; *Herald,* May 8, 12, 1970.

5. *Herald,* May 12, 1970; Bill Weaver to author, Aug. 10, 1979; Regents minutes, Oct. 14, 1970; Harris to author, Nov. 23, 1982; Downing interview, April 15, 1985.

6. *Herald,* May 15, 19, 1970; *Courier-Journal,* May 20, 1970; Katherine Stuart Van Warner to author, Feb. 3, 1984; Downing interview, April 3, 1978; copies of Restraining Order, Injunction, Volunteers' appeals in author's file; *Daily News,* May 24, 1970.

7. *Courier-Journal,* March 2, 1975, Feb. 27, 1977: *Herald,* Oct. 31, 1969; Downing to President Robert Martin, EKU, Aug. 5, 1970, Kenneth T. Stanley to Downing, July 21, 1970, Martin Papers: box 169, folder WKU 1969-70 (EKU archives); *Daily News,* Oct. 2, 1970.

8. Ford to Downing, March 28, 1971, Downing to Ford, April 12, 1971, Downing Papers: box 9, Black Students; *Herald,* Dec. 8, 1970; *Daily News,* Sept. 10, 12, 1972; Downing interviews, Oct. 23, 1984, April 15, 1985.

9. Turner letter, *Herald*, March 22, 1974; *Herald*, March 2, 30, 1971.

10. Livers's letter, *Herald*, April 2, 1974; *Herald*, Feb. 8, 11, 1977, Oct. 17, 1978; Christy Vogt Mollozzi to author, Oct. 4, 1984.

11. *Herald*, Dec. 7, 1982, had a special in-depth study called "Equal But Separate."

12. Mollozzi to author, Oct. 4, 1984; James C. Ladd interview, by James D. Bennett, May 21, 1981; *Herald*, Sept. 22, 1970, March 2, 1971, Feb. 8, 1972, April 24, 1973, Jan. 15, Aug. 27, 1974, Nov. 2, 1978; Southern Association, *Self-Study Report, 1982-1984*, 31-32; Downing interview, April 15, 1985; Craig Dezern, "Gender Bender," *Herald*, Aug. 27, 1985.

13. *Herald*, March 2, 1971.

14. *Courier-Journal*, Oct. 3, 8, 1969; *Daily News*, Oct. 3, 7, 19, 1969.

15. Jim Snodgrass, "The Hub of the Hill," *Western Alumnus* 47 (Fall 1976):8-10; *Herald*, April 15, 1977, Feb. 7, 9, April 15, June 27, 1978, Sept. 15, 1981; Downing Papers: box 6, Alcoholic Beverage License, contains most of the correspondence; *Daily News*, Sept. 9, 1978, Feb. 27, 1979; Regents minutes, Sept. 9, 1978.

16. *Herald*, Jan. 19, 1973.

17. Regents minutes, Sept. 29, 1973; *Courier-Journal*, Sept. 30, 1973; *Herald*, Oct. 2, 5, 12, 1973; Downing interview, April 15, 1985. Downing Papers: box 48, Drug Problems Committee, and Box 14, Drug Abuse Advisory Council, contain a great deal of information on the subject.

18. Charles A. Keown interview, by Lowell H. Harrison, July 24-25, 1984; Downing interview, April 3, 1978; *Herald*, Feb. 4, 11, 1972.

19. *Herald*, Feb. 29, March 24, 28, April 25, 1972, Oct. 12, 1973; Keown interview, July 24-25, 1984.

20. *Courier-Journal*, June 17, 1970; *Herald*, Jan. 23, Sept. 18, 1973, Jan. 22, 1974.

21. *Daily News*, Feb. 12, 1970; *Expatriate*, [n.d.], Sept. 3, 30, Oct. 28, 1970.

22. *Daily News*, Nov. 18, 1971; *Courier-Journal*, Nov. 19, 1971; *Spread Eagle*, Nov. 1971.

23. *Daily News*, March 7, 8, 21, 1974; *Herald*, March 5, 22, April 2, 1974; Regents minutes, March 20, 1974.

24. *Herald*, April 28, 1950, Oct. 31, 1985; Coy Hibbard statement, 1936, Cherry Papers: box 24, GC 1936; Jenkins interview, Feb. 13, 1986; Lawson interview, Feb. 13, 1986.

25. Memorandum, Downing to Regents executive committee, Feb. 6, 1974; Regents minutes, March 20, 1974; *Herald*, March 22, 1974, Oct. 13, 1977.

26. Major General F.H. Britton to Thompson, April 29, 1965, Thompson Papers: box 17, Dept. of Military Science; memorandum, PMS Major Normal E. Orr to Thompson, Jan. 16, 1967, Thompson Papers: box 42, MS 1966-67; *Herald*, Jan. 28, 1972, Sept. 21, 1973, Sept. 15, 1977; memorandum, PMS Lt. Colonel Gary A. Riggs to Dean Hourigan, Oct. 28, 1976, Downing Papers: box 53, MS 1976.

27. Herbert E. Shadowen interview, by Lowell H. Harrison, Aug. 21, 1984; William G. Buckman interview, by Lowell H. Harrison, Oct. 5, 1984.

28. *Southern Association Fifth Year Report, 1978*, 60; Program Status Report, Jan. 1-July 31, 1978, 8; Council of Academic Deans, Jan. 24, 1979.

29. Memorandum, Cravens to Thompson, Dec. 21, 1964, Thompson Papers: box 13, Budget; Southern Association *First Follow-up Report, 1965*, 6; Willson E. Wood to Cravens, Nov. 5, 1970, Downing Papers: box 50, Faculty Teaching Load, 1970; Vice President James L. Davis to Downing, June 26, 1978, Downing Papers: box 5, Vice President for Academic Affairs, 1970; Regents minutes, April 28, 1979; *Southern Association Fifth Year Report, 1978*, 63.

30. *Southern Association Fifth Year Report, 1978*, 63; Faculty Research Grants, Downing Papers: box 9, Board of Regents, Cole.

31. Memorandum, Cravens to Thompson, Oct. 27, 1964, Thompson Papers: box 49, Sabbatical Leave Program; Regents minutes, Feb. 15, 1969; Downing to Regent Cole, March 7, 1977, Downing Papers: box 9, Board of Regents, Cole; memorandum, Downing to Davis, Dec. 23, 1977, Downing Papers: box 26, Sabbaticals 1977.

32. Memorandum, Thompson to Faculty and Staff, June 10, 1970, Thompson Papers: box 18, Faculty House; numerous papers in Downing Papers: box 16, Faculty Recreation

Association; *Western Alumnus* 37 (Summer 1969):24; Regents minutes, Feb. 15, 1969, Sept. 19, 1978; *Southern Association Self Study, 1971-1973*, 161; *Herald*, Aug. 22, 1972.

33. Memorandum, Paul Cook to Downing, Feb. 17, 1971, Downing Papers: Box 3, Faculty Regents-Election; *Herald*, Feb. 6, 1970, Jan. 25, 1983; Regents minutes, Sept. 23, 1972; Buckman interview, Oct. 5, 1984.

34. Regents minutes, May 25, 1963, Oct. 25, Dec. 20, 1975; material in Downing Papers: box 49A, Faculty Tenure Committee; *Courier-Journal*, Dec. 21, 1975; *Daily News*, Oct. 26, 1975; Buckman interview, Oct. 5, 1984; *Herald*, Dec. 7, 1976, Jan. 21, 1977.

35. Regents minutes, May 31, July 26, Sept. 20, Oct. 25, 1975; *Herald*, Aug. 26, Sept. 19, 23, 30, Oct. 10, 28, 1975; Buckman interview, Oct. 5, 1984; Cole interview, Feb. 4, 1984; Downing interview, April 15, 1985; Cravens interview, Feb. 22, 1985.

36. Regents minutes, Jan. 31, April 24, 1976; *Daily News*, Nov. 4, 1975; *Herald*, Dec. 7, 1976, Jan. 21, 1977.

37. Regents minutes, April 21, 1971, May 18, 1974, Jan. 25, Aug. 26, 1975; Jim Tomes to Harry Largen, June 18, 1971, Downing Papers: box 15, Faculty Life Insurance; *Herald*, Nov. 19, 1974; Downing interview, April 15, 1985; Jenkins interview, Feb. 13, 1986.

38. Notes of AAUP members interview with Downing, Oct. 8, 1973, Downing Papers: box 7, AAUP 1972 +; Report of the Visiting Committee, Downing Papers: box 21, Institution Self-Study; Jones interview, Oct. 26, 1983.

39. *Ad hoc* Committee on a Faculty Senate to Downing, Sept. 17, 1975, Faculty Senate: box 36/1; *Herald*, Sept. 30, 1975; Eugene Evans interview, by Lowell H. Harrison, Jan. 9, 1986.

40. Committee on Faculty Participation to Downing, Jan. 27, 1976, Faculty Senate: box 1; President's Informational Notes, May 3, 1976; administrators responses to Downing, Jan. 1976, Downing Papers: Box 16, Faculty Senate, 1976-77; Senate minutes, Oct. 22, 1976; *Herald*, Oct. 26, 1976; memorandum, Constans to Downing, Nov. 8, 1976, Downing Papers: box 16, Faculty Senate, 1976-77.

41. Buckman interview, Oct. 5, 1984; Jones interview, Oct. 26, 1983; Constans to Downing, May 2, 1977, Downing to Constans, May 6, 1977, Downing to Cole, Feb. 7, 1977, Downing Papers: box 16, Faculty Senate, 1976-77; Constans interview, Jan. 8, 1986.

42. Regents minutes, April 30, 1977.

43. Constans to Faculty, May 6, 1977, Faculty Senate: box 1, Administrator Selection Policy; Senate minutes, Sept. 8, 1977; *Herald*, Sept. 13, Oct. 20, 1977.

44. Jones interview, Oct. 26, 1983; Senate minutes, April 13, 1978; Constans interview, Jan. 8, 1986.

45. Downing to Constans, May 11, 1977; Sandefur to Downing, May 12, 1977; James L. Davis to Downing, June 6, 1977, Downing Papers: box 5, Recommended Policy Statement for Selection and Retention of Administrators.

46. Memorandum, ASG President Larry Zielke to Faculty, [Sept.?] 1970, Downing Papers: box 43, Associated Students, 1970; *Herald*, April 27, 1971, Feb. 25, 1972, Dec. 4, 1973; Senate minutes, Nov. 9, 1978; Lucas report, Senate minutes, October 1978; Downing to Faculty Regent Buckman, May 29, 1975; Jones interview, Oct. 26, 1983.

47. Regents minutes, July 26, Sept. 20, Oct. 25, Dec. 20, 1975, Feb. 28, 1976; *Herald*, Dec. 5, 9, 1975; Russellville *Logan Leader*, March 1, 1976.

48. Senate minutes, Nov. 10, 1977; Jones interview, Oct. 26, 1983; J. David Cole interview, by Tom Jones, Feb. 4, 1984; *Daily News*, May 30, 1978; *Courier-Journal*, June 8, 1978.

49. James R. Hines to Editor, *Daily News*, June 13, 1978; *Daily News*, July 2, 1978; *Courier-Journal*, June 13, 1978; Jones interview, Oct. 26, 1983; *Herald*, Aug. 22, 1978: Downing interview, Oct. 23, 1984.

50. Downing interview, Oct. 23, 1984; *Daily News*, April 5, 1976; Regents minutes, Sept. 29, Nov. 17, 1973; Cravens interview, Feb. 8, 1985; Jones interview, Oct. 26, 1983; Thompson interview, Sept. 27, 1979; Cook interview, Aug. 6, 1985.

51. *Herald*, Aug. 26, 1975, April 6, 1976; *Daily News*, April 2, 5, 1976; *Talisman, 1974*, 182; Jones interview, Oct. 26, 1983; Cravens interview, Feb. 8, 1985; Keown interview, July 24-25, 1984.

52. Regents minutes, Oct. 26, 1974; Christy Vogt Mollozzi to author, Oct. 4, 1984; Jones interview, Oct. 26, 1983; Cole interview, Feb. 4, 1984; Zacharias to Governor Collins, June 11, 1984, Zacharias Papers: Collins folder.

53. Cole interview, Feb. 4, 1984; Jones interview, Oct. 26, 1983; Buckman interview, Oct. 5, 1984; *Herald*, Oct. 29, 1981, April 28, 1983.

54. Regents minutes, Feb. 4, 1978.

55. Barkovich, "Council on Public Higher Education," 27, 30-39; *Courier-Journal*, Aug. 3, 1966; Downing statement, copy to President Martin, (n.d. [Dec. 1969?]), Martin Papers, EKU Archives, box 169, folder WKU, 1969-70; Downing to State Senator Roy B. White, Jan. 14, 1970, Downing Papers: box 44, GC Wh-Wz. The Council's role is examined in Cathy Lynn Cole, "A Historical Perspective of the Kentucky Council on Higher Education" (Ph.D diss., Southern Illinois University, 1983).

56. Council minutes, Oct. 3, 1973, Downing Papers: box 36; Downing to Albright, May 30, Dec. 3, 1975, Presidents' Council on Public Higher Education: box 1; Downing to Governor Carroll, Jan. 27, 1975, Carroll to Downing, Feb. 17, 1975, Downing Papers: box 18, Governor's Office, 1975.

57. *Courier-Journal*, Oct. 14, 1976; Jones interview, Oct. 26, 1983; Buckman interview, Oct. 5, 1984; Davis interview, June 13, 1984; Cravens interview, Feb. 22, 1985.

58. Council minutes, June 8, 1977; *Courier-Journal*, April 20, May 10, June 5, Nov. 17, 1977; report in Council minutes, Jan. 19, 1977; Cole, "Council on Higher Education," 237, 252.

59. Special memorandum, Downing to Faculty and Administrative Staff, March 31, 1977, Presidents of the University: Council on Public Higher Education; *For Your Information*, April 25, 1977; *Courier-Journal*, June 5, 1977; Regents minutes, April 30, 1977; Southern Association *Institutional Self-Study, 1982-1984*, 38; Cook interview, Aug. 6, 1985.

60. Downing to Cole, July 13, 1977, Presidents: Council on Public Higher Education, 2; *Courier-Journal*, July 17, 1977; Downing to Snyder, Aug. 17, 1977, Downing Papers: Regents, 1977; Regents minutes, Aug. 24, 1977; Downing to Robert R. Martin, Nov. 4, 1977, Downing Papers: box 9, Ma-Mi.

61. *Herald*, April 25, 1978, April 17, 1979, Aug. 26, 1980; Jones interview, Oct. 26, 1983; *Daily News*, Jan. 1, 1979, Dec. 6, 1978.

62. Downing to Jon Thad Humpert, Nov. 26, 1975, Downing Papers: box 20, Housing, Required.

63. Cravens interview, Feb. 22, 1985; Downing interview, Oct. 23, 1984; Downing to J. David Cole, Feb. 7, 1977, Downing Papers: box 9, Board of Regents, Cole; Cole interview, Feb. 4, 1984.

64. Downing to Mr. and Mrs. L.A. "Sonny" Allen, Feb. 7, 1972, Downing Papers: box 44, GC, A; *Herald*, Oct. 27, 1977; Downing to Don C. Bale, Nov. 18, 1974, Downing Papers: box 29, BAs; Downing to Thomas Frist, Sr., July 12, 1976, Downing Papers: box 29, Fr-Fu; Downing to Lawrence E. Forgy, Jr., July 19, 1977, Downing Papers: box 28, Wilson; Thompson interview, Sept. 27, 1979; Downing interview, April 15, 1985.

65. Cole interview, Feb. 4, 1984; Regents minutes, Jan. 29, 1977; *Western Alumnus*, 47 (Spring 1977):23; John D. Minton interview, by James D. Bennett, March 10, 1980; *Herald*, Sept. 12, 1978; Alan Judd, "Bidding Farewell," *Herald*, Jan. 1, 1979, 9-12; *Courier-Journal*, Sept. 16, 1978, Jan. 6, 1979; Cook interview, Aug. 6, 1985.

10. New Departures

1. Regents minutes, Sept. 9, Dec. 9, 1978; *Herald*, Sept. 12, 1978; Minton interview, March 10, 1980; *Western Alumnus* 50 (Spring 1979):3-4; Downing to Regents, Nov. 17, 1978, Downing Papers: box 3, Regents, 1978.

2. *Herald*, Sept. 11, Oct. 17, 24, 31, 1978; Regents minutes, Sept. 24, Oct. 21, 1978; Cole

interview, Feb. 4, 1984; Chad Carlton, "Secrecy, Threats Mark Last Search," *Herald*, Oct. 31, 1985, 1-2A

3. *Herald*, March 29, April 5, 10, 1979; Buckman interview, Oct. 5, 1984; Cole interview, Feb. 4, 1984.

4. Alan Judd, "Threats, offers hamper selection," *Herald*, April 24, 1979; Regents minutes, April 29, 1979; Cole interview, Feb. 4, 1984; Jones's tag, Faculty Senate: box 1, Presidential Search; Jones interview, Oct. 26, 1983; Buckman interview, Oct. 5, 1984.

5. *Courier-Journal*, May 7, 14, 1979; *Daily News*, May 7, 10, 1979; Regents minutes, May 6, 13, 1979; Cole interview, Feb. 4, 1984; *Herald*, Aug. 28, 1979.

6. Minton interview, March 10, 1980; Cole to Search Committee, May 17, 1979, John D. Minton Papers: Presidential Search Folder; Regents minutes, July 14, 1979; *Herald*, Aug. 28, 1979.

7. Material in Downing Papers: box 40, Construction, President's Home; Regents minutes, Feb. 12, March 1, 1979; *Herald*, Feb. 20, 27, March 6, 1979, Feb. 14, May 9, 1980; *Daily News*, March 2, 1979.

8. Inauguration folder, Zacharias Papers; *Courier-Journal*, April 27, 1980; *Talisman, 1980*, 136; *Daily News*, April 27, 1980; *Herald*, Jan. 25; Feb. 1, 1983; Regents minutes, Jan. 29, 1983.

9. *News from Western* press releases, May 13, Oct. 8, 1979; Jim Highland, "Western Selects a Sixth President," *Western Alumnus* 51 (Summer 1979):1-5; Buckman interview, Oct. 5, 1984.

10. *Herald*, Aug. 28, 1979. April 24, 1980; Cravens interview, Nov. 20, 1984; Zacharias to Ronald G. Sheffer, March 18, 1981, Zacharias Papers: Board of Regents, Sheffer folder.

11. *Daily News*, July 18, Aug. 1, 1980, Jan. 9, 1981; Zacharias speech, Jan. 8, 1981, Student Affairs: Student Rallies, 1981; *Courier-Journal*, Feb. 26, 1981.

12. *Herald*, April 26, 1983; *This Week at WKU*, March 2-22, 1981; Lawson interview, Feb. 13, 1986.

13. *Courier-Journal*, Jan. 27, March 3, 4, 1981; King to Zacharias, Jan. 21, 1981, Zacharias to Governor Brown, Jan. 22, 1981, Zacharias Papers: Back Zack folder.

14. *Daily News*, March 11, 1981; *Herald*, March 19, April 16, 1981.

15. *Courier-Journal*, July 29, Aug. 2, 23, 1980; *Daily News*, July 24, 29, 1980; Zacharias to Vice-Presidents, Jan. 5, 1981, Zacharias Papers: Board of Regents correspondence, 1981 folder; *Herald*, Aug. 22, Sept. 17, 1981; Regents minutes, Executive Committee, Sept. 4, 1981; Faculty Senate minutes, Nov. 12, 1981.

16. Regents minutes, Oct. 19, 31, Nov. 21, 1981; *Courier-Journal*, Oct. 2, 30, Nov. 13, Dec. 14, 1981; *Daily News*, Oct. 18, 1981; Cole interview, Feb. 4, 1984.

17. *Courier-Journal*, Dec. 17, 1981, Jan. 11, 15, 1982.

18. *Courier-Journal*, Jan. 8, 25, Feb. 7, 1982; *Daily News*, Feb. 7, July 20, 1982; Cole to William H. McCann, March 26, 1982, Zacharias Papers: Regents, Cole folder; Zacharias to Brown, Feb. 8, 1982, Zacharias Papers: Brown folder.

19. *Daily News*, Oct. 7, 15, 18, 1980; *Courier-Journal*, Nov. 3, 1981; *Herald*, Oct. 20, 1981.

20. *Daily News*, April 25, June 1, 1982; *Herald*, Feb. 2, March 4, 25, April 20, 1982.

21. Regents minutes, Nov. 13, 1982, Jan. 29, 1983; *Daily News*, Nov. 9, 1982; Zacharias statement, "Western Kentucky University and Formula Funding," July 21, 1982, Zacharias papers.

22. *Herald*, April 19, 1983; Zacharias to Lt. Gov. Martha Layne Collins, May 25, 1983, Zacharias Papers: Collins folder; Cook interview, Aug. 13, 1985.

23. *Herald*, Nov. 17, 1983, Jan. 31, March 22, 1984, April 30, 1985; *Update*, Aug. 26, 1983; Financial Resources, Southern Association, *Self Study, 1982-84*, 4:1-7; Regents minutes, April 27, 1985; *Chronicle of Higher Education* 30 (April 3, 1985):1.

24. Brown to Zacharias, March 23, 1982, Zacharias Papers: Brown folder; *Courier-Journal*, Sept. 24, 25, 1984.

25. *Courier-Journal*, June 13, Sept. 18, 1984, May 22, 1985.

26. Zacharias to Snyder, Feb. 12, 1985 (circulated by David Lee, Senate).

27. Regents minutes, Jan. 26, 1985; *Herald*, Feb. 21, 1985; *Courier-Journal*, Feb. 28, 1985; Ernest L. Boyer, "How Professors See Their Future," *Sunday New York Times: Education, Summer Survey* (Aug. 18, 1985), 361; Faculty Senate Institutional Goals and Planning Committee report to President Zacharias, Dec. 9, 1982, Senate Committee Reports.

28. *Herald*, Feb. 26, 1985.

29. *Herald*, Feb. 21, 28, March 7, 28, 1985; *Daily News*, March 7, 1985.

30. *Chronicle of Higher Education* 30 (April 3, 1985):1.

31. *Herald*, Oct. 21, 1982, April 9, 1985; Regents minutes, June 26, 1982; Buckman interview, Oct. 5, 1984; Senate Newsletter, May 2, 1985.

32. *Herald*, April 7, 1981; *Informational Notes*, April 28, 1981; Regents minutes, April 24, 1981, Jan. 26, 1985.

33. *Western Kentucky University Catalog, 1985-1987*, 20; *Herald*, April 25, 1985.

34. *Herald*, Oct. 6, 1983, Jan. 24, Dec. 11, 1984, Feb. 2, Oct. 24, 1985; *Update*, Oct. 12, 1983; *Daily News*, Jan. 14, 1985; Paul R. Wozniak, "Updated and Revised Projections of Western Kentucky Full-Time Undergraduate Enrollments by Class, Fall, 1983 to Fall, 1988," Faculty Senate Document; *Courier-Journal*, Oct. 24, 1985.

35. Regents minutes, June 11, 1969.

36. Thompson to Downing, Oct. 1, 1978, in *Western Alumnus* 50 (Special issue 1978):1-2, charts, 15, 16; Kelly Thompson, "Charles Roy Martin," *Western Alumnus* 50 (Special issue 1978):12-14; *Daily News*, Dec. 4, 1974.

37. *Western Alumnus* 50 (Fall 1979):18; *Daily News*, March 15, Aug. 14, 1979; Regents minutes, May 23, 1979, Feb. 4, 1984; *Herald*, Feb. 3, Aug. 23, 1983, Feb. 7, 1984, April 30, 1985; Mary Sample, executive secretary-treasurer, College Heights Foundation, to author, May 31, Aug. 15, 1985.

38. Regents minutes, July 27, 1974, Dec. 1, 1979, Nov. 1, 1980, Aug. 22, 1981; *Daily News*, Aug. 4, 1980; *Herald*, Nov. 6, 1980.

39. *Herald*, Oct. 10, 12, 17, 1978, Dec. 8, 1981; Cole interview, Feb. 4, 1984.

40. Regents minutes, June 26, 1982, Aug. 20, 1983; *Daily News*, Aug. 22, 1984; *Herald*, Sept. 11, 1984.

41. Regents minutes, March 8, 1982; *Daily News*, March 8, 1982; Buckman interview, Oct. 5, 1984.

42. *Herald*, March 4, 1977; Regents minutes, April 26, 1980; *Courier-Journal*, April 26, 1984; *Daily News*, June 2, 1985.

43. *Herald*, April 30, 1985; Regents minutes, April 24, 1982.

44. *Red Towel*, Dec. 2, 1983; *Hilltopper Football, 1984*, 12-13, 98; *Herald*, Dec. 1, 1983, Sept. 13, 1984, April 30, 1985; Regents minutes, Jan. 29, 1983; *Daily News*, Sept. 9, 1985; Cook interview, Aug. 13, 1985.

45. *Herald*, Dec. 13, 1984; Zacharias, "Athletics at Western Kentucky University," Senate meeting, Oct. 11, 1984.

46. *Herald*, Oct. 16, Nov. 8, 1984; Lee Committee Report, Feb. 1985; *Courier-Journal*, Feb. 16, 1985.

47. *Daily News*, Feb. 20, 1985; Zacharias to Coohill, Feb. 27, 1985, Faculty Senate; *Daily News*, March 6, 1985; *Herald*, Feb. 19, 1985; Eugene Evans interview, by Lowell H. Harrison, Jan. 9, 1986.

48. *Herald*, Jan. 17, 1985; Vice President Minton in Faculty Senate Newsletter, Dec. 20, 1984.

49. *Herald*, Aug. 26, 1982, Sept. 20, 1983, Jan. 12, Aug. 28, Oct. 30, 1984.

50. *Lady Toppers Press Guide, 1984-1985*.

51. *Herald*, Dec. 13, 1984, Feb. 28, March 26, 1985; *Courier-Journal*, March 23, 1985.

52. *Daily News*, March 31, 1985; *Herald*, April 2, 1985; *Courier-Journal*, Nov. 12, 1985.

53. *Herald*, March 21, 1985; *Daily News*, March 29, 1985.

54. *'85 Hilltopper Baseball*, 35; *Daily News*, May 15, June 2, July 2, 1985; *Herald*, Nov. 5, 1985.

55. *Daily News*, Aug. 19, 1980, Aug. 15, 1981, Feb. 27, Aug. 30, Sept. 27, 1984, July 11, 1985; *On Campus*, May 6, 1985.

56. *Daily News*, Nov. 29, 1985; *Courier-Journal*, May 13, 1984.

57. *Courier-Journal*, July 26, Aug. 6, Oct. 9, 10, Nov. 9, 1985; *Daily News*, July 31, Aug. 19, 1985; *Herald*, Oct. 15, 1985; Paducah *Sun*, quoted in Lexington *Herald-Leader*, Oct. 28, 1985; Council on Higher Education, "Strategic Planning" draft, Oct. 8, 1985.

58. *Daily News*, July 26, 30, Aug. 11, 30, 1985; *Courier-Journal*, Aug. 11, 13, 1985; Regents minutes, Aug. 19, 1985.

59. Zacharias to Senate Chair Richard Weigel, Sept. 6, 1983, Senate Papers: Weigel; *Daily News*, Aug. 11, 1985; *Herald*, Aug. 29, 1985; Lawson interview, Feb. 13, 1986; Mary Ellen Miller interview, by Lowell H. Harrison, Jan. 8, 1986. The Board of Regents stated its official policy on evaluation at its meetings of April 30 and Oct. 28, 1983.

60. *Daily News*, Sept. 8, Oct. 22, 23, 27, Nov. 5, 1985; *Herald*, Sept. 10, Oct. 22, 31, Nov. 5, 1985; Regents minutes, Sept. 7, 1985; Evans interview, Jan. 9, 1986; Miller interview, Jan. 8, 1986.

61. *Daily News*, Dec. 6, 1985; *Courier-Journal*, Dec. 7, 1985; Joe Bill Campbell, oral report to faculty, Dec. 6, 1985; Evans interview, Jan. 9, 1986; Miller interview, Jan. 8, 1986; Regents minutes, Dec. 9, 1985.

62. Campbell, report to faculty, Dec. 6, 1985; *Courier-Journal* Dec. 7, 1985; *Herald*, Dec. 10, 1985, Jan. 14, 1986; Miller interview, Jan. 8, 1986; Evans interview, Jan. 9, 1986.

63. *Daily News*, Dec. 11, 15, 1985, Jan. 26, 1986; *Courier-Journal*, Dec. 15, 1985; Miller interview, Jan. 8, 1986; *Herald*, Jan. 14, 1986; Regents minutes, Dec. 14, 1985, Jan. 25, 1986.

64. *Herald*, special edition, Dec. 17, 1985; *Daily News*, Dec. 17, 22, 1985, Jan. 26, 1986; *Courier-Journal*, Dec. 18, 27, 1985; Evans interview, Jan. 9, 1986; Miller interview, Jan. 8, 1986; Regents minutes, Jan. 25, 1986.

65. *Daily News*, June 14, 1984.

This study is based upon extensive research conducted over a period of several years. The endnotes are the best indicator of the materials used, but they represent only a fraction of the sources examined.

Manuscripts

Much of the research was done in the Western Kentucky University Archives. Although the Archives were not established until 1972, Miss Sara Tyler and her successors discovered extensive caches of material in odd spots across the campus. In addition to many printed sources, photographs, tapes, and films, the Archives contain over one thousand linear feet of manuscript materials, and the collection grows almost daily. Most of the university's administrative units and a number of individuals are represented in the collection. A major gap is the lack of papers that would document the academic lives of individual students and faculty members. The presidential collections of Cherry (eighty-seven boxes), Garrett (twenty-four boxes), Thompson (fifty-six boxes), and Downing (sixty-three boxes) are supplemented by presidential scrapbooks except for Garrett. The Cherry papers contain much general school correspondence since for many years the only typewriters on campus were in the president's office. Most of Minton's papers remained in the president's office, and in early 1986 only a few of the Zacharias papers had reached the Archives. Others were used from the files in the president's office.

The shortage of individual student and faculty materials was overcome to some degree by an appeal for "your memories of Western" which elicited some manuscripts, a number of photographs, and a few artifacts, all of which have been deposited in the University Archives. James P. Cornette provided excellent background information from his detailed knowledge of Western, and George B. Simpson supplied extensive extracts from the diary he kept during 1949-51. A number of contributors are cited in the endnotes.

The Manuscript Division of the Kentucky Library, in existence much earlier than the University Archives, has a considerable body of university-related papers, including those of several early faculty members. The Faculty Senate records are located in the Senate Office in the Faculty House.

The most useful off-campus manuscripts were the presidential papers in the Eastern Kentucky University Archives and those in Special Collections, Margaret I. King Library (University of Kentucky). The Herman L. Donovan autobiography in the latter was of particular interest. The A.B. Chandler Collection at the University of Kentucky was disappointing in view of Chandler's close relationship with Garrett. Use of the telephone has reduced substantially the volume of correspondence that once might have reached an archives.

Interviews

Taped interviews also helped fill some of the gaps in the manuscript collections. Unfortunately, systematic interviewing did not begin until 1976 when Dr. James D. Bennett of the Department of History started the Oral History Project which is located in that department. Inadequate funding has restricted the scope of the undertaking and has resulted in a large backlog of untranscribed tapes. Among the most helpful interviews were those with Presidents Thompson, Downing, Minton, and Zacharias, Regents J. David Cole, Herbert E. Shadowen, William G. Buckman, and Mary Ellen Miller, and administrators Paul B. Cook, Raymond L. Cravens, James L. Davis, and Charles E. Keown. As is the case with manuscripts, the interviews do not reveal much about the day-to-day activities of students and faculty members.

Newspapers

Much of the history of Western is contained in the *College Heights Herald* which began publication in 1925. An almost complete file is in the university archives. During its early years the *Herald* appeared monthly or biweekly, and it usually ignored controversial issues. The *Herald* moved to weekly publication in 1961 and to twice a week issues in 1969. By the late 1960s the *Herald* had achieved greater editorial independence, and stories were often critical of university policies, practices, and personnel. The *Herald* index in the University Archives is an invaluable research aid, but all extant issues were examined. The *Elevator* (November 1909-July 1916), the *Herald*'s predecessor, was as much a literary magazine as a newspaper.

As the notes indicate, the Bowling Green *Park City Daily News* and the Louisville *Courier-Journal* were used extensively. Many Westerners are convinced that the latter harbors a negative attitude toward the Hill. Other state papers were used frequently to sample opinions from different parts of the Commonwealth.

The *Chronicle of Higher Education* is the best national guide to contemporary issues relating to higher education, although the *New York Times* also frequently publishes thoughtful articles on the topic.

Institutional Publications

The school and its units have issued a bewildering variety of publications with the number increasing in recent years. Although they seldom make exciting reading, the school catalogs are indispensable for a comprehensive study of the institution. They have usually been issued annually, although occasionally an emergency (usually financial) has resulted in the omission of an issue. The graduate catalogs provide essential information about work on that level. Especially helpful in tracing the recent developments in graduate work are the annual *Graduate College Reports* (1973–).

Cherry had considerable success promoting the private school with the *Southern Educator*, and when the state normal was started he continued with the *State Normal Bulletin* (1906-15). It became *Western Normal Letter* (1915-16) and then a more comprehensive *Normal Heights* (1916-23). It continued as *Teachers College Heights* (1923-48) after Western was elevated to that status. This publication then became the vehicle for listing class schedules and announcing registration data.

The Southern Association of Colleges and Schools requires extensive institutional self-studies at ten-year intervals with five-year interim reports. Although institutions tend to become better at each editorial stage in the preparation of the reports, the final documents and the voluminous committee reports on which they are based do contain an enormous amount of information about the institution. The two most recent studies, 1971-73 and 1982-84, were especially detailed. Considerable data from earlier years are contained in the state studies of higher education conducted by Griffenhagen and Associates in 1933 and 1947.

Until 1964 the *College Heights Herald* was the main channel of communication to the alumni. The *Herald* was relieved of that function by the *Alumni Bulletin* (1964-66), the *Alumni Magazine* (1966-67), and the *Western Alumnus* (1967–). These publications have contained numerous articles about Western activities and personalities. The *Vista* was published in 1915, but the real beginning of the yearbook came with the appearance of the *Talisman* in 1924. In recent years it has contained descriptive and interpretative articles on college life that were rare in earlier issues.

Government Publications

Legislation that affected Western can be found in the *Acts of the General Assembly*, and their progress through the legislature can be followed in the *Journals* of the two houses. Since the Kentucky legislature does not report its debates and discussions as does the U.S. Congress in the *Congressional Record*, incomplete newspaper accounts are the best source for what was said on the floors. The annual *Report of the Superintendent of Public Instruction* was helpful for the years when Western's primary function was the training of teachers. Reports of other state agencies are also sometimes useful. In recent years this had been especially true of the reports and minutes of the Council on Higher Education.

Theses and Dissertations

A considerable amount of information about Western and higher education in Kentucky is concealed in theses and dissertations which are seldom readily available. Two current Western faculty members wrote about the school's first president: Carl W. Kreisler, "Henry Hardin Cherry" (Ph.D. diss., Indiana University, 1964), and Carl P. Chelf, "A Selective View of the Politics of Higher Education in Kentucky and the Role of H.H. Cherry, Educator-Politican" (Ph.D. diss., University of Nebraska, 1968). Chelf published "H.H. Cherry: The Educator Politican" in the *Western Kentucky University Faculty Research Bulletin* 8 (1983-84), 80-90.

The Kentucky Council on Higher Education has been examined in: Adron Doran, "The Work of the Council on Public Higher Education in Kentucky" (Ph.D. diss., University of Kentucky, 1950); Charles H. White, "The Kentucky Council on Public Higher Education: Analysis of a Change in Structure" (Ph.D. diss., Ohio State University, 1967); Frank Steve Barkovich, "The Kentucky Council on Public Higher Education" (M.A. thesis, University of Louisville, 1970); and Cathy Lynn Cole, "A Historical Perspective of the Kentucky Council on Higher Education" (Ph.D. diss., Southern Illinois University, 1983). Two other important and somewhat related aspects of higher education were examined in William James Higginbotham, Jr., "Veteran Impact on the Four Regional State Universities of Kentucky" (Ed.D. diss., Indiana University, 1969), and Jerry Gordon Alston, "The Role of The State Legislature in Public Higher Education in Kentucky, 1950-1968" (Ph.D. diss., Southern Illinois University, 1970).

A modern study is urgently needed to replace Alvin Fayette Lewis, *History of Higher Education in Kentucky* (Washington, D.C., 1899), and all of the state universities need comprehensive histories. Until these goals are achieved, some theses and dissertations help meet the need. Janet Gaynor Hibbard, "Eastern Kentucky University 1906-1960: Administrative Problems" (Ed.D. diss., Indiana University, 1973) provides information about Western's sister institution, and Harry Eugene Rose discusses "The Historical Development of a State College: Morehead Kentucky State College, 1887-1964" (Ed.D. diss., University of Cincinnati, 1965). Dwayne Cox, "A History of the University of Louisville" (Ph.D. diss., University of Kentucky, 1984) provides a comprehensive view of an institution with which Western has had many contacts. Kris W. Kindelsperger, "A Study of Factors Leading to the Entrance of the University of Louisville into the State System of Higher Education in Kentucky" (M.A. thesis, University of Louisville, 1976) examines a move that had a pronounced effect on the state's system of higher education.

Books and Pamphlets

As indicated in the preface, James P. Cornette, *A History of the Western Kentucky State Teachers College* (Bowling Green, 1938) was an invaluable source for the period ending with President Cherry's death in 1937. Two brochures, *A Decade in Review, 1955-1965* (Bowling Green, 1965) and *A Report to the Board of Regents* (Bowling Green, 1969), issued by President Thompson were very helpful for the developments during his administration.

Morton F. Stahl, *In His Image: The Family of John Stahl* (privately printed, 1980) contains information about the Cherry family. H.H. Cherry published a text called *Our Civic Image and Our Governments* (Bowling Green, 1904) and a collection of speeches titled *The Basis of Democracy* (Boston, 1926). His wife, Bess Fayne Cherry, wrote *Parlance of Kentucky Backwoods* (Louisville, 1933).

A few of the early faculty members have been memorialized in published works. Burton W. Gorman, *Wit and Wisdom of Alonza Carroll Burton* (privately printed, 1934) reveals something of "Daddy" Burton's sense of humor, although only a videotape could do justice to his rendition of "Bingen on the Rhine." James P. Cornette, *John Henry Clagett* (privately printed, 1938) captures the spirit of that Shakespearean scholar. C. Harvey Gardiner, *Coach Diddle: Mister Diddle: Motivator of Men* (Nashville, 1984) stresses the influence of the man. Marie Nunley, *Nashville:*

Beloved Hearthstone-A Biography of Alfred Leland Crabb (privately printed, 1974) tells the story of one of Western's early students who retained a lifelong interest in the school. The University Archives contain a number of biographical sketches that were given as speeches or written as class projects.

Although secondary works were not the major source for this study, some were essential for background information. Moses Edward Ligon, *A History of Public Education in Kentucky* (Lexington, 1942) and Barksdale Hamlett, *History of Education in Kentucky* (Frankfort, 1914) are standard works on this subject. They should be supplemented by Ellis Ford Hartford, *The Little White Schoolhouse* (Lexington, 1977). The Prichard Committee for Academic Excellence has done much in recent years to focus public attention on the plight and possible future of Kentucky's public schools. Its findings are summarized in *In Pursuit of Excellence* (Frankfort, 1981) and *The Path to a Larger Life: Creating Kentucky's Educational Future* (Frankfort, 1985).

The bibliography on American higher education is large and constantly growing. Frederick Rudolph, *The American College and University* (New York, 1962) remains one of the best surveys of the period it covers. Also useful was E. Alden Dunham, *Colleges of the Forgotten Americans: A Profile of State Colleges and Regional Universities* (New York, 1969), although many of the institutions he profiled would challenge his classification of them. Other useful general works were: Raymond C. Gibson, *The Challenge of Leadership in Higher Education* (Dubuque, Iowa, 1964); John S. Brubacher and Willis Reedy, *Higher Education in Transition*, 3d ed., rev. (New York, 1976); and Martha Boaz, *Issues in Higher Education and the Professions in the 1980s* (Littleton, Colorado, 1981).

The published histories of Kentucky's other state universities have been useful, although in some instances little attention has been paid to interinstitutional relationships. James F. Hopkins, *The University of Kentucky: Origins and Early Years* (Lexington, 1951) and Charles Gano Talbert, *The University of Kentucky: The Maturing Years* (Lexington, 1965) provide excellent coverage of their institution. Ralph H. Woods, *Fifty Years of Progress: A History of Murray State University, 1922-1972* (Murray, 1973) is organized by topics and administrative units and does not give a narrative history. J. Lewis Harmon, Sr., *Brief Historical Sketch of the Bowling Green Business University* (Bowling Green, 1948) presents an introduction to a school closely associated with Western.

Several books were helpful on specific topics. Nancy Disher Baird, Carol Crowe-Carraco, and Michael L. Morse, *Bowling Green: A Pictorial History* (Norfolk, 1983) is the best work on the city; *Beautiful Bowling Green* (Bowling Green, 1907?) depicts the city soon after Western became a state school. John Garry Clifford, *The Citizen Soldiers* (Lexington, 1972) describes the Student Army Training Corps of World War I, and Porter Hopkins, *K.E.A.: The First Hundred Years* (Louisville, 1957) relates the story of the organization to which all Western faculty members belonged for many years.

Articles

Campus publications have used innumerable articles that depict Western and her people, and many other articles have appeared in off-campus periodicals. Only a few can be mentioned here. Mrs. Frank P. Moore, "Western Kentucky State

College—Past and Present," *FCHQ* 28 (Oct. 1954):328-40, gave a brief history of Western from the beginning into the post-World War II era. Joe Creason, "He Told the World about Western," *Courier-Journal Magazine* (Feb. 27, 1949)):38-40, explained how Kelly Thompson had publicized the school, particularly the basketball program. Coach Diddle was a colorful personality who received national recognition in such articles as Robert Andrews, "Calamity from Kentucky," *Colliers* 113 (Feb. 26, 1944):24-27, and Fred Russell, "Winningest Basketball Coach," *Saturday Evening Post* 229 (Jan. 19, 1957):36, 74-78. His successor was profiled in Dave Kindred, "Oldham of Western," *Courier-Journal Magazine* (March 5, 1967):13-17. Miss Mattie McLean was the subject in Gordon Wilson, "Honor to Whom," *Peabody Journal of Education* 24 (Sept. 1946):107. A.M. Stickles and "Gabie" Robertson were lauded in Lowell H. Harrison, "Two Kentucky Historians: A Personal Appreciation," *Register* 69 (Jan. 1971):30-36.

Arndt M. Stickles related the story of one of Western's unique landmarks in "A Confederate Fort and Historical Marker on the Western Kentucky State College Campus," *FCHQ* 39 (Oct. 1965):326-30. An account of Ogden College was related in Jesse B. Johnson and Lowell H. Harrison, "Ogden College: A Brief History," *Register* 68 (July 1970):189-220. The impact of the World War II air force trainees was described in James P. Cornette, "No Magic Formula," *Peabody Journal of Education* 22 (Sept. 1944):72-76. Martin J. Robards, "Snowball Special to the Rescue," *L & N Magazine* (April 1960):4-7, 31, told of the stranding of hundreds of Western basketball fans in the sudden severe snowstorm of March 1960. An interesting view of Western as the boom era ended was presented in John Egerton, "Western Kentucky University: Facing the No-Growth Era," *Change* 6 (Sept. 1984):36-42. Eastern Kentucky State College president W.F. O'Donnell recalled the early roles of Eastern and Western in "Five Decades of Teacher Education in Kentucky," *FCHQ* 30 (April 1956):115-24.

Countless articles have considered the multiple aspects of higher education. Such publications as *Change*, the *Chronicle of Higher Education*, and the *New York Times* attempt to keep abreast of contemporary trends and issues. Interesting comments on two vital campus groups were made in Jean Evangelauf, "Freshmen Found 'More Materialistic and Less Altruistic' than Predecessors," *Chronicle of Higher Education* (Feb. 1, 1984):12-14 and Ernest L. Boyer, "How Professors See Their Future," *New York Times: Education, Summer Survey* (Aug. 18, 1985):36-37.

Index